Great Motorhome Tours of Northern France

by

Alan Russell

Copyright © 2018 by Alan Russell

All rights reserved. No part of this book may be reproduced or used in any manner without written permission of the copyright owner except for the use of quotations in a book review.

Great Motorhome Tours of Northern France

	Page
Foreword	1
Types of Service Point	2
Staying at an Aire de Service	4

THE TOURS

ALSACE

Tour		Page
1)	7 Day Tour – Strasbourg & Southern Alsace	10
2)	5 Day Tour – Strasbourg & Northern Alsace	19
3)	6 Day Tour – The Vosges Mountains	26
4)	5 Day Tour – Maginot Line & Northern Vosges	33

BRITTANY

5)	5 Day Tour – Mont St Michel to Gulf of Morbihan	41
6)	6 Day Tour – Rennes to Pink Granite Coast	47
7)	4 Day Tour – Nantes to Carnac & Quimper	54
8)	8 Day Tour – Most Beautiful Towns & Villages	59

BURGUNDY

9)	4 Day Tour – Cathedrals & Churches of North Burgundy	68
10)	5 Day Tour – Chateaux around Auxerre	75
11)	2 Day Tour – Potteries of North Burgundy	82
12)	3 Day Tour – Abbeys around Auxerre	87
13)	2 Day Tour – Burgundy Vineyards	95
14)	3 Day Tour – Crypts, Caves & Tunnels	101
15)	3 Day Tour – Apothecaries & Old Hospitals	106
16)	5 Day Tour – Chateaux of South Burgundy	113
17)	3 Day Tour – Wines of the Cote d'Or	120
18)	4 Day Tour – Dijon & surroundings	125

CENTRE

19)	5 Day Tour – Towns & Chateaux around Tours	131
20)	4 Day Tour – Chartres & surroundings	137
21)	3 Day Tour – Vendome & the Loir	143
22)	4 Day Tour – Nancay to Bourges	149
23)	6 Day Tour – Montargis to Beaugency	155
24)	4 Day Tour – Blois to Chambord	162
25)	5 Day Tour – Richelieu to Amboise	168

26)	7 Day Tour – Azay le Rideau to Montlouis sur Loire	175
27)	3 Day Tour – Grand Pressigny to Eguzon	186
28)	5 Day Tour – Joan of Arc sites along the Loire	191

CHAMPAGNE-ARDENNES

29)	4 Day Tour – Fortresses of the Ardennes	199
30)	3 Day Tour – Abbeys of the Ardennes Forests	207
31)	2 Day Tour – Fortified Churches Tour	212
32)	3 Day Tour – Reims & surroundings	217
33)	5 Day Tour – Reims & the Champagne Vineyards	222
34)	3 Day Tour – Cistercian Abbeys of Haute-Marne	231

FRANCHE-COMTE

35)	6 Day Tour – Most Beautiful Towns & Villages	237

NORMANDY

36)	4 Day Tour – The Impressionists Tour	245
37)	5 Day Tour – Chateaux, Parks & Gardens	253
38)	5 Day Tour – Cathedrals & Abbeys	261
39)	4 Day Tour – Operation Overlord Tour	269
40)	3 Day Tour – Omaha Beach Tour	275
41)	3 Day Tour – Utah Beach to Cherbourg	282

NORD-PAS-DE-CALAIS

42)	3 Day Tour – Fortified Towns around Calais	287
43)	4 Day Tour – Fortified Towns around Lille	294

PAYS DE LA LOIRE

44)	5 Day Tour – Nantes to St Nazaire	302
45)	5 Day Tour – Most Beautiful Towns & Villages	309
46)	4 Day Tour – Vendee Coast & L'Ile d'Yeu	318

PICARDY

47)	1 Day Tour – The "Chemin des Dames" Tour	326
48)	4 Day Tour – Laon to Soissons	332
49)	2 Day Tour – Fortified Churches Tour	339
50)	2 Day Tour – Somme Remembrance Tour	345

About the Author	352

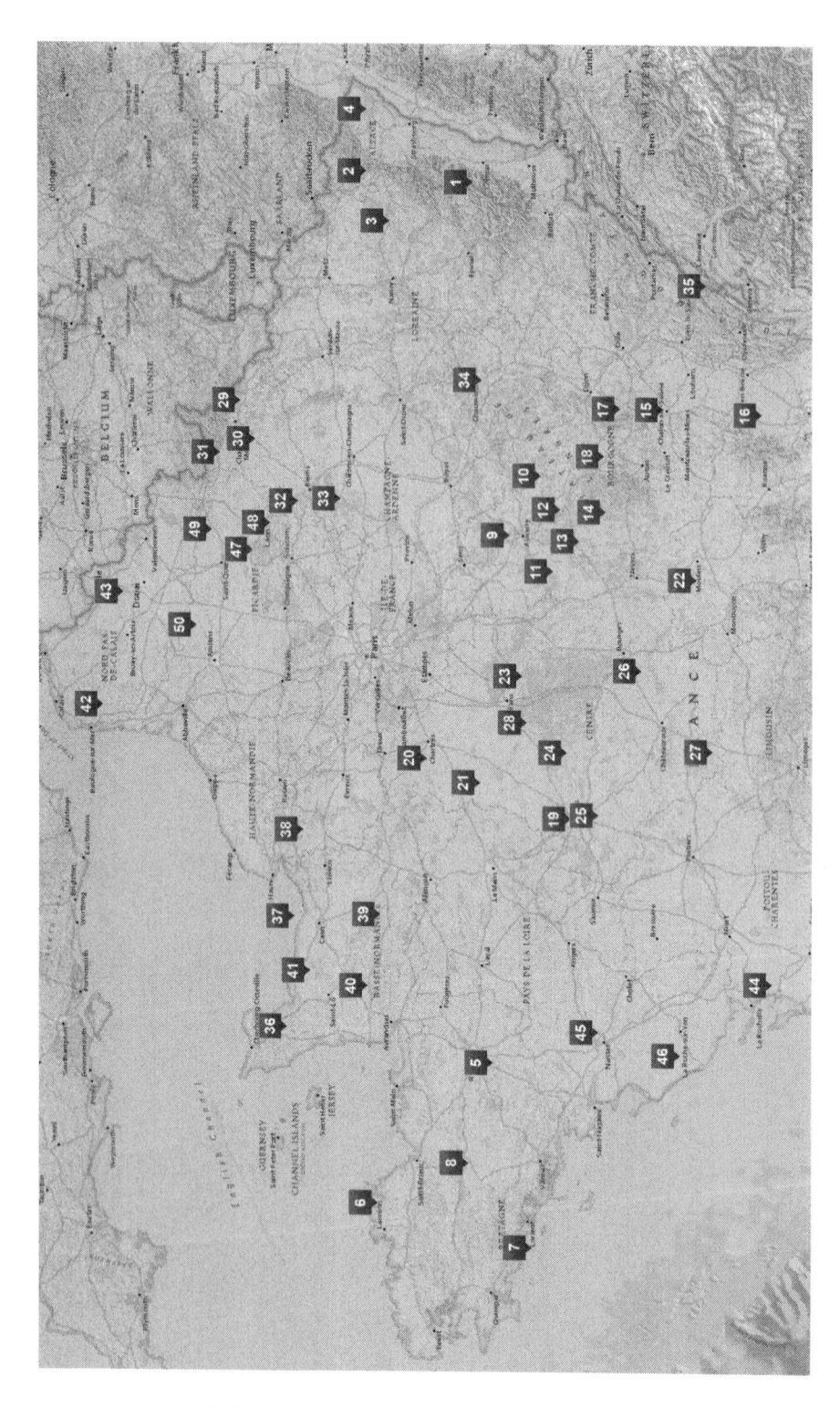

LOCATION MAP OF THE 50 TOURS

FOREWORD

France is the perfect country to visit in a motorhome, RV or campervan (but rather than use all three terms each time, I will simply refer to your vehicle as a motorhome). The roads are often traffic free, there are almost 10,000 campsites and over 4,000 aires, the car parks are mainly free and, unlike in the UK, overnight parking in a motorhome is subject to few restrictions. In addition to the above, France is the most visited tourist destination in the world, with many historic towns and villages, great beaches, picturesque mountain scenery and much more.

The 50 Great Tours in Northern France guide covers the 10 regions of Alsace, Brittany, Burgundy, Centre, Champagne-Ardennes, Franche-Comte, Normandy, Nord-Pas-de-Calais, Pays-de-la-Loire and Picardy. This is roughly the area north of a line drawn from La Rochelle in the west to Lons-le-Saunier in the east. A second book covers tours below this line, in the regions of Southern France.

The tours have been researched and planned for a motorhome, visiting locations that I hope you will find interesting and picturesque. Unfortunately the majority of campsites in France tend to open only during the summer months, with some of the Municipal campsites only opening in July and August. This would tend to restrict the timing of these tours, so they have primarily been planned using all-year-round aires as stopover places – with alternative campsites suggested, if preferred (and if they are open). As some 'motorhomers' may never have stayed at an Aire de Services, there is a chapter explaining their facilities and how to use them.

NOTE: The brief directions given are only suggested routes; please check individual roads for any width/ weight restrictions that may apply to your vehicle. Also bear in mind that these directions are by no means compulsory and variations to the routes can be taken. GPS coordinates (in Decimal Degrees) are given for the aires as these are quite often difficult to find due to the lack of signage in many locations. Campsites tend to be better signposted.

Abbreviations/ words used in the guide:

AireServices: Type of service point
Artisanal: Custom made service point
Autoroute: French motorway
Borne: Service point for water/ electric/ drainage
Ehu: Electric hook up
Euro-Relais: Type of service point
C: Century
Flot Bleu: Type of service point
ha: Hectare
km: Kilometre
Jeton: Token used at a service point
Mairie: Town hall
m: metre
OT: Office de Tourisme

TYPES OF SERVICE POINT FOUND AT AIRES

Above: An Euro Relais service

Left: AireServices service point

Right: Flot Bleu service point

Above: A well designed Artisanal service point

STAYING AT THE AIRES DE SERVICES

What are they?
There are two main types of aire – Aire de Services and Aire de Stationnement. An Aire de Stationnement is basically a parking area with no services (water, drainage or electricity) but overnight parking is usually allowed here. An Aire de Services is a stopping place for motorhomes that can offer a few options – ranging from just being able to fill up with fresh water or empty wastewater, to stopping for a few days, filling/emptying your various tanks, access to toilets and possibly hooking up to an electricity supply (and maybe even a wifi connection). Aires de Services generally fall into the following categories:

- Municipal Aire – Run by the town/village commune and usually provided as an encouragement to visitors to stop in the area and spend some money on local goods/ services (something it is wise not to forget when making use of these facilities). Although these stops are often free, a charge may sometimes be made - for parking, for using an electrical hook-up, or for refilling the fresh water tank. Emptying of the grey tank or chemical toilet is usually free. The permitted length of stay typically varies from 1 to 3 days, although this is seldom policed. Payment (if required) is often at the Mairie (town hall) or the Office de Tourisme (OT), or at a nearby ticket machine – it is useful to keep a supply of euro coins for this purpose.
- Private Aire - Privately owned, these may be provided by a local business, such as a supermarket or garage, and are often just a service point (although parking for a night may be allowed on the car park). Others are sometimes run by an individual, often along the lines of a small campsite, with a charge made for the parking and/ or the services.
- Aire de Services on a Campsite - Run by campsites but often located outside, these allow you to stay overnight but obviously for less than the cost of a night's stay on a site pitch. You would be able to able to use the various emptying/filling facilities, and possibly the campsite showers/ toilets. Many campsites run a scheme called Stop-Accueil Camping Car, allowing you to stay inside the site on a pitch for a reduced

price, so long as you arrive after 18.00pm and leave before 10.00am.
- Autoroute Aire - These often have the same facilities as private aires but are located in the motorway service areas. Whilst these may be useful for either refilling or emptying, and for a short break, they are not to be recommended for an overnight stay due to the various security problems (not to mention the noise) that have often occurred at these aires in the past – especially those in the South of France.
- Aires on Farms/vineyards – These are similar to CL's in the UK, but availability of services can vary from just a place to stay to having those similar to that of a good private aire. The France Passion scheme allows motorhomes to stay on French farms and vineyards overnight, for a one-off annual fee of 30 euros, at more than 2,000 stopover places in France. The disadvantages are that there may be no facilities provided, apart from a pitch for overnight parking, and it's not possible to book these pitches in advance (on average these are limited to 2 to 5 places per farm) - you just have to turn up and ask if there is a space. If you intend to use these farm stopovers, it's advisable to make your motorhome self-sufficient due to this possible lack of facilities. Advantages include; the low price, usually a nice rural location, the possibility of purchasing fresh farm produce, and often many of these locations can offer some basic services.
- Sani Station – These are just a space - often in garages or supermarket car parks - where you can refill/ empty your tanks and possibly recharge your battery, but they do not normally allow you to park overnight.

Aires can vary in what they present to the traveller, from a fairly unpleasant car park stopover to a beautiful location next to the Mediterranean, or tranquillity in the heart of a medieval walled town. They can also vary from offering just a couple of parking places to possibly having over 100 or more spaces.

Facilities available

Once again these vary but are usually either a couple, or possibly all, of the following:

- **Drinking Water** – a tap with a supply of drinking water (eau potable or eau propre) for refilling your fresh water tank – there may be a charge involved.
- **Waste Water** – either a drive over gully/ drainage platform, or just a grid where you can empty the waste water (eau vidange or usee) out of your motorhome's grey tank; this is usually a free service. The process may involve using a hose if there is no gully or if you cannot get close enough.
- **Chemical Toilet** – A compartment or covered grid with a flushing arrangement in which to empty the contents of your cassette (WC Chimique), again this is usually a free service.
- **Electricity** – An electrical connection (often at a low 3A amperage) for recharging your battery for an hour or so, a service that is usually charged for but is occasionally free. The socket is normally the standard European socket but may occasionally be a French socket.
- **Public Toilets** – Availability and standards vary depending on the location, often these are only available in service areas or town car parks.
- **Rubbish disposal** – Provision of recycling bins or waste bins (poubelles) for your waste, once again it is normally free.
- **Wifi** is becoming increasingly available, especially on campsites and private aires, and many Offices de Tourisme offer this facility as well.

The first four of the above services are often contained within a post arrangement or 'borne' which usually consists of 4 main types:

Euro-Relais or Raclet – This is a factory made service point built into a stainless steel or white triangular/square shaped unit, with separate taps for refilling water and rinsing, an integral drain for black waste and usually a separate grid or drainage platform for grey waste. There may also be electricity hook up sockets for recharging the leisure battery – these types of bornes are often operated by tokens (jetons), coins or credit card.

Flot Bleu – Another purpose built service point, usually blue in colour, with similar facilities as the Euro-Relais but often without a separate grey drain – the integral grey drainage point often requires a hose to use it. These are once again usually controlled by jetons or coins, although an increasing number are operated by credit cards.

AireServices or UrbaFlux – variations of the above, either oval shaped or a post arrangement.

Artisanal: These are custom made service points and can vary greatly in both quality and ease of use; they mainly consist of 1 or 2 fresh water taps, grey and black drainage points of some form and possibly an electric socket. Often the artisanal service point may only have a single tap for drinking and rinsing - care should obviously be taken with these with regard to hygiene. These 'bornes' are often free or are operated by coins or jetons.

Payment

As stated before, if you are lucky, all of the above may in some instances be free but there may be a charge (2 to 3 €) for the electricity and possibly the water, although the drainage facilities are usually free (gratuit). Don't forget your euro coins: if a payment is due for any of the previous services (and also possibly for the overnight stay), they are generally paid for by a ticket (billet) issued at a machine (horodateur) on site, or at the town hall or the tourist information office. Alternatively, it's possible that someone will call round to collect a fee. Frequently, it is required to buy a token for the service point, with instructions usually found on a sign nearby as to where you can buy them – usually from the OT (Office de Tourisme), Town Hall (Mairie) or the local shops. In many cases now, payment is only possible by credit card (Carte Bancaire or CB) and the machines generally accept UK cards without any problem. If for some reason your card isn't accepted, the only alternative I have found is to ask a friendly Frenchman if they will pay using their card and reimburse them in cash – they'll often oblige! Once again don't forget how much you would pay in the UK for these facilities (if you could get them) and be sure to spend some euros locally as a thank you.

Finding Aires

If you are lucky, you may come across a blue motorhome sign, which would indicate the exact location of an aire. However the easiest way to find them is either to consult the various aires sites online or buy a guide that lists Aires de Services. The most complete guidebook to Aires in France, the book 'LE GUIDE NATIONAL DES AIRES DE SERVICES CAMPING-CARS,' is published annually and lists around 4,000 various aires in France. This is available from www.amazon.fr or in decent bookshops/ supermarkets in France. They are however on a limited print run and often sell out well before the end of the summer, so make sure you get your copy soon after the March issue date. This book is, of course, in French – it is however fairly easy to translate and since most of the listings tend to have similar facilities, it is fairly easy to follow. The guide also comes with a map section showing the location of the aires. The main problem with the guide is that the directions to the aires are pretty minimal, and given that the aires tend not to be signposted until you are within close proximity (making them difficult to find at times) the GPS coordinates given are often essential.

Staying at an Aire

There are few differences in the practicalities between staying at a campsite or at an aire. The main difference will probably be regarding the spacing (if it is busy) – vans stopped at an aire will be closer together, whereas on a campsite you still have all of the pitch to yourself. Putting up your awning at an aire is usually frowned upon by other camping-caristes (French motorhomers), as it limits the available spaces, unless the aire is quite empty. If you require electricity you could find that a longer hook-up cable is required, as you may not be able to get as close to the connection as you would like. You may also need a hose for the wastewater tank, due to the arrangement of the emptying facility – it is sometimes built into the servicing post. Hose connectors may also be required for the freshwater connection – as these may vary from aire to aire. The length of your stay at an aire is obviously determined by the regulations on the site; this is commonly a maximum of 3-nights (although this is often not enforced), whereas there is usually no limit at a campsite.

Winter Use

In winter you may often find that the service point at an aire is unavailable, as the water has been turned off as a precaution against freezing, and you may have to visit several aires before you find one with the water connected (failing that you may have to find a campsite that is open).

In conclusion, I think that the biggest noticeable difference between aires and campsites will be the cost!

THE TOURS

ALSACE TOUR 1
STRASBOURG & SOUTHERN ALSACE - 7 DAYS

This 7-Day Tour starts in the Alsace capital of Strasbourg before travelling south to the mountain of St Odile and the popular Chateau Haut-Koenigsbourg. The picturesque villages of Ribeauville, Riquewihr and Kaysersberg are visited as well as the wine town of Colmar, before moving on to the historic town of Mulhouse and the open-air museum at Ungersheim. The sixth day of the tour follows the "Peak Route" to the mountain of Hohneck and a stay in the cheese town of Munster. The final day is spent in the Ballons des Vosges Nature Park.

Top: Colmar Photo by Gryffindor   Bottom: Ungersheim

KEY TO MAP (Right):
1) Strasbourg   2) Mont-Sainte Odile   3) Chatenois
4) Ribeauvillé 5) Riquewihr   6) Kaysersberg
7) Colmar   8) Mulhouse   **9) Ungersheim**
10) Hohneck   11) Munster

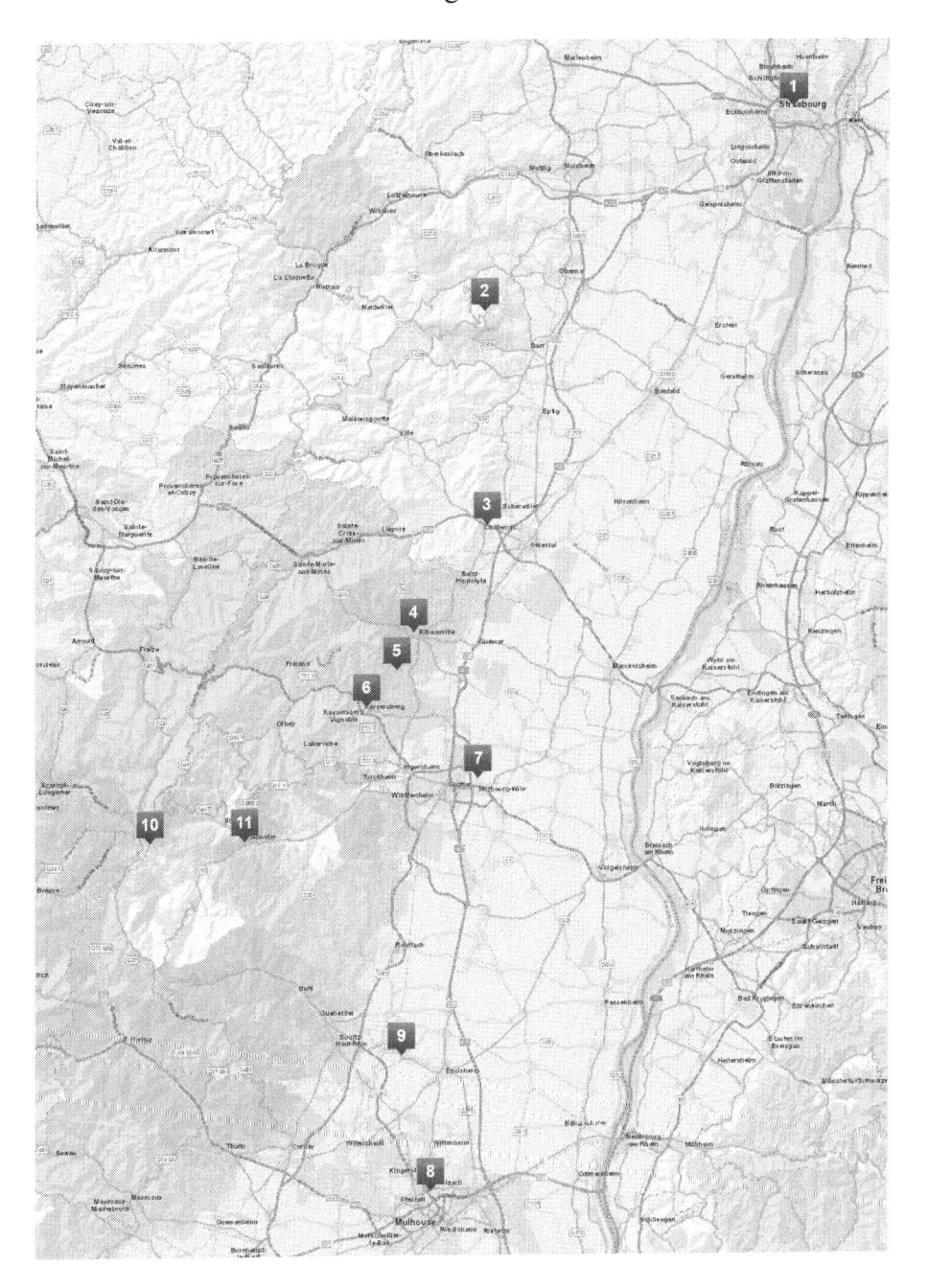

STRASBOURG & SOUTHERN ALSACE MAP

DAY 1
Strasbourg
STAY AT: the private aire in **Strasbourg**, outside the Indigo campsite on the Western side of Strasbourg, located in a medium-sized parking area off **Route de Schirmeck (D392).** The aire is close to shops and services, and about 1km from the city centre. The parking is shaded by trees in places and lit at night. Flot Bleu service point with drainage platform. Parking is also allowed in the city centre car parks, subject to height restrictions and car park charges. The campsite is also open all year and is probably a better location for not much more expense. Buses run into the city centre from outside the campsite.
Facilities: Water•Grey Drain•Black Drain•Toilets
No. of spaces: 12
Parking: 15-25€/24hrs
Services: Incl.
Opening times: All year
GPS Coordinates: N48.34278   E07.43469
Alternative: Indigo Campsite, Rue Auberge Jeunesse, 67000 Strasbourg Open: all year
Strasbourg: presents a wonderful mix: half-timbered houses, canals, the towering spire of its red sandstone gothic Cathedral, the encircling River Ill and Palais Rohan. Not to be missed is the central "island" encircled by the two arms of the river. Extending from the cathedral to the "Petite France" district, this is the city's well preserved historic area, with Renaissance houses, old-fashioned shops, three "Ponts-Couverts" (covered bridges) and various other river crossing points. The city is home to several museums, three of which are in the Rohan Palace, as well as the impressive "BarrageVauban" with its panoramic roof terrace. The Vauban Dam is a thirteen-arch defensive weir, constructed in 1686 to enable the city to use the river waters to flood land to the South of the city, thus rendering it impassable to the enemy. The dam was last used in 1870, when the city was besieged by Prussian forces. Outside of this central "island" can be found the botanic gardens and the Orangerie, a lovely park housing a rare bird reserve.
STAY AT: *The private aire in* ***Strasbourg****, off* ***Route de Schirmeck (D392)*** *or Indigo Campsite, Rue Auberge Jeunesse, 67000 Strasbourg*
DAY 2
TAKE A35 SOUTH TO Jn 12 & D1422/ D42 WEST TO:

Mont-Sainte Odile: Dedicated to Alsace's patron saint, the Mont is a site visited both by pilgrims, who come here to pay their respects, and by tourists attracted by the panoramic view offered from its peak, at an altitude of 763 m. Most of the buildings here date from the 17th C, and a number of chapels are older, as are the tombs cut into the rock. You can also see the remains of the pagan wall, the unbeatable view over the Alsatian plains, the Mont-Sainte Odile monastery and the marked out tourist trails, with an audioguide in English available.
GPS: N48.43649 E 07.40264
CONTINUE SOUTH ON D35/ D1422 TO SELESTAT & N59 WEST TO:
Chateau Haut-Koenigsbourg is one of France's most widely visited monuments, attracting 600,000 visitors per year. When it was built, back in the 12th C, the chateau occupied a strategic position with the aim of protecting the wine and wheat routes to the north, and the silver and salt routes running from west to east. It was reduced to rubble by the Swedes during the Thirty Years War and abandoned, but in 1899, Kaiser Wilhelm II decided to have the chateau fully rebuilt with the aim of making this a museum and a symbol of Alsace's return to Germany. As well as the impressive architecture of the chateau to admire, there is an amazing view over the Ballons des Vosges and the Alsatian plains. **GPS:** N48.24917 E07.34333
TAKE D159 & D35 NORTH TO:
Chatenois
STAY AT: *the Municipal aire in nearby* **Chatenois**, *located in* **Allee des Bains**, *close to the centre of this large village, provides level spaces on grass and tarmac - some shaded by mature trees - close to a children's play area with toilets adjacent, and is lit at night. Well designed artisanal service point with a large drainage platform. Parking is close to the small selection of shops - chemist, grocer, restaurant and garage.*
Facilities: *Water •Grey Drain •Black Drain •Toilets*
No. of spaces: *8*
Parking: *Free*
Services: *2€ Water*
Opening times: *All year*
GPS Coordinates: *N48.27472 E07.39899*
Alternative: *Municipal Campsite, Rue de la DFL, 67600 Selestat Open: 01/04 – 15/10*

DAY 3
TAKE D35 SOUTH TO:
Ribeauvillé: Nestling between the vineyards and the mountains, Ribeauvillé is a charming little town of just 5000 inhabitants which has successfully preserved its historical heritage. The village is typical of those to be found along the Wine Route, with its attractive old houses, charming narrow streets and its wealth of local wine producers. Miraculously spared during the last war, the village's most distinctive features are its 13th C Clock Tower, which once separated the upper town from the lower town, the remains of 3 chateaux, and the town hall housing a famous collection of 16th C silver vessels.

TAKE D18 SOUTH TO:
Riquewihr: With its fortified perimeter wall, narrow cobbled streets, quaint architecture and half-timbered houses, the medieval village offers visitors a lovely setting. The wealth of treasures to be discovered include a former prison, impressive stone buildings and flower-decked wells and fountains. There is an historic way-marked walk around the town – details from the Office de Tourisme.

TAKE D18 SOUTH TO:
Kaysersberg: A former imperial town, Kaysersberg has succeeded in retaining all of its mediaeval splendour. The village boasts an impressive range of architectural heritage sites with its ancient houses, chateau ruins, fortified bridge and church. The picturesque village of Kaysersberg was voted "France's Favourite Village" in 2017.

STAY AT: *the Municipal aire in* **Kaysersberg** *at* **Parking de l'Erlendab**. *This is a popular aire in a large tarmac car park on the edge of town, backing onto vineyards and with fine views of the surrounding countryside. It is 200m from the centre of town, where there is a good range of shops and eating-places. Service point is basic, but easy to use, with a large platform drain.*

Facilities: Water•Grey Drain•Black Drain•Toilets
No. of spaces: 50
Parking: 8€
Services: Incl.
Opening times: *All year, except for Xmas market*
GPS Coordinates: *N48.13593   E07.26231*
Alternative: *Municipal Campsite, Rue des Acacias, 68240 Kaysersberg Open: 01/04 – 30/09*

DAY 4

TAKE D415 SOUTH TO:
Colmar: As the capital of the Alsatian wine producing area, Colmar is a medium-sized town with many modern buildings built following the destruction of the two World Wars. In the old town, however, visitors will step into a picture postcard village. It is a maze of narrow streets, with colourful, well preserved half-timbered houses and traditional cafes/restaurants to be found on every street corner. The most charming area is the "Petite Venise" district (Little Venice) named after the many winding canals and Renaissance houses. Museums include the Unterlinden and the Bartholdi Museum in the old town on Rue des Marchands. Impressive 16th C. buildings include the Maison des Têtes, the Maison Pfister and others on the Grand'Rue. If time permits, a visit to Vaubans' fortified town at nearby Neuf-Brisach is certainly worthwhile.

*STAY AT: the Municipal aire in **Colmar**, about 400m from the centre of the town, on **Rue du Canal**, on the eastern side of the town, next to the canal but close to the D418 road. The aire has 30 spaces on tarmac or grass in a fenced/gated enclosure, bordered by grass. Trees provide shade in places, there is lighting at night, and picnic tables are available. Artisanal service point with grid, toilets adjacent, ehu's and wifi.*

Facilities: *Water•Grey Drain•Black Drain•Toilets•Electric•Wifi*
No. of spaces: *30*
Parking: *11-15€/24hrs*
Services: *Incl.*
Opening times: *All year*
GPS Coordinates: *N48.08051   E07.37395*
Alternative: *Camping de l'Ill, Allee du Camping, 68180 Colmar Open: 29/03 – 31/12*

DAY 5
TAKE A35 OR D83 SOUTH TO:
Mulhouse is a town with a rich industrial past and its charms are somewhat subtler than those of the neighbouring towns. However, Mulhouse's old town offers a number of attractive walks where visitors can soak up the cosmopolitan atmosphere of the town while discovering its historical monuments, including the Town Hall or the protestant church of Saint-Étienne. The "new" district, created at the time of the Industrial Revolution, is home to the "Square de la Bourse", the Roman baths, the Tour de l'Europe and numerous

attractive properties once belonging to local captains of industry. Finally, the leafy district of Rebberg, with its attractive and architecturally fascinating large private buildings, is certainly worth discovering before or after a visit to the remarkable zoological and botanical gardens which are also located in this area.If you have time, visit the Cité du train, the Cité de l'automobile, or the medieval quarter, including the Place de la Réunion and the Hôtel de Ville.

TAKE D430 NORTH TO:

Ungersheim: The open air museum has over seventy traditional buildings, ranging from farmhouses to artisans' workshops, that were disassembled piece by piece at their original sites and re-erected within the tree lined boundaries of the EcoMuseum. In almost 25 ha of park, there are Alsatian fields, a forest where charcoal burners work and fishing rivers, all combining to reproduce a bygone era.

STAY AT: *the aire in* ***Ungersheim*** *on* ***Chemin du Grosswald****. This is a private aire in the grounds of the* ***EcoMusee*** *(Open Air Museum), a nice location with grass pitches shaded by mature trees, accessed by a tarmac track. A restaurant and boulangerie can be found in the museum. Parking is guarded at night. Service point is basic but quite functional.*

Facilities: *Water•Grey Drain•Black Drain*
No. of spaces: *25*
Parking: *6€/24hrs*
Services: *Incl.*
Opening times: *All year*
GPS Coordinates: *N47.85175   E07.28579*
Alternative: *Camping Le Florival, Route de Soultz, 68500 Issenheim Open: 01/05 – 30/09*

DAY 6

TAKE D44 WEST TO: The "**Peak Route**"

Hartmannswillerkopf (which was renamed "Viel-Armand" by French troops during the First World War) is located in the Ballons des Vosges Regional Nature Park. At an altitude of 956 m, this heavily wooded rocky spur offers outstanding views over the Cernay area, the Alsatian plain, the Black Forest, the Jura range, the Swiss Alps and part of the Vosges. Its fertile subsoil contains the mineral water sources tapped at Wattwiller, near the town of Cernay.

The Grand Ballon: Also known as the Ballon de Guebwiller, the "Grand Ballon" is the high point of the Vosges mountain range. At an altitude of 1,424 m, its peak offers a truly unique view over the Alsatian plain, the Black Forest and even over Austria, Liechtenstein and Mont Blanc. Easily accessible on foot from the Route des Crêtes (the "Peak Route"), it is also possible to make an extended hike around this high point. Here, visitors can discover attractive forested slopes with fir and beech trees, in addition to a lake.

Hohneck: Situated at an altitude of 1,364m, the Hohneck overlooks the valley and its lakes, providing a wonderful opportunity to admire the Hautes Vosges from the Donon to the Ballon d'Alsace, in addition to the Alsatian plain, the Black Forest and, further still, the Alps. The area is raked by strong winds, which provide a constant reminder of nature's supremacy.

TAKE D417 EAST TO:
Munster
STAY AT: the municipal aire in **Munster**, located in **Rue du Dr Heid**, in a large tarmac parking area at the southern side of the town, 300m from the centre, where there are shops and services. The aire offers spaces on hard standing accessed by a tarmac road, it is lit at night, and is shaded by trees on the southern side. AireServices service point with ehu's, pressure washer, drainage platform and modern toilets adjacent.
Facilities: Water •Grey Drain •Black Drain •Toilets •Electric •Wifi
No. of spaces: 49
Parking: 8€/24hrs
Services: 3€ Electric or Water
Opening times: All year
GPS Coordinates: N48.03779   E07.13258
Alternative: Parc de la Fecht, Route de Gunsbach, 68140 Munster
Open: 21/04 – 02/09

DAY 7
Munster is a town famous for its cheese. Originally a fortified town, it was heavily shelled during WWI and lost most of its older buildings apart from the 16th C Town Hall, some of the Benedictine Abbey buidings and the market hall. There are some elegant 19th C houses in the town as well as a large public park.

TAKE D10 SOUTH TO:
Ballons des Vosges Nature Park: The combination of geological features and climatic differences have together created a surprising natural environment here. A number of (occasionally very steep) cliffs

and rock faces stand in contrast to the rounded peaks of the hills. These rarely exceed a height of 1300 m, but include all the features you would expect of a high mountain environment with its rich plant life and streams. Occasionally, the snowy peaks can even be admired through to the summertime.

STAY AT: *the municipal aire in* **Munster***, located in* **Rue du Dr Heid** *or Parc de la Fecht, Route de Gunsbach, 68140 Munster*

Top:Kaysersberg by Florival   Bottom: Riquewihr by Jpkrebs

ALSACE TOUR 2
STRASBOURG & NORTHERN ALSACE – 5 DAYS

This 5-Day Tour wends its way through the Kochersberg, the region of Hanau, the Regional Nature Park of the Northern Vosges and Alsace Bossue, where you will discover imposing, traditional farmhouses, mansions and stone churches by the wayside, together with the vast forested lands of the Northern Vosges and a landscape and architecture typical of Lorraine. Furthermore there are a number of sites located on this route, many of them open to visitors, which belong to both the Alsatian Jewish heritage and the brewing tradition.

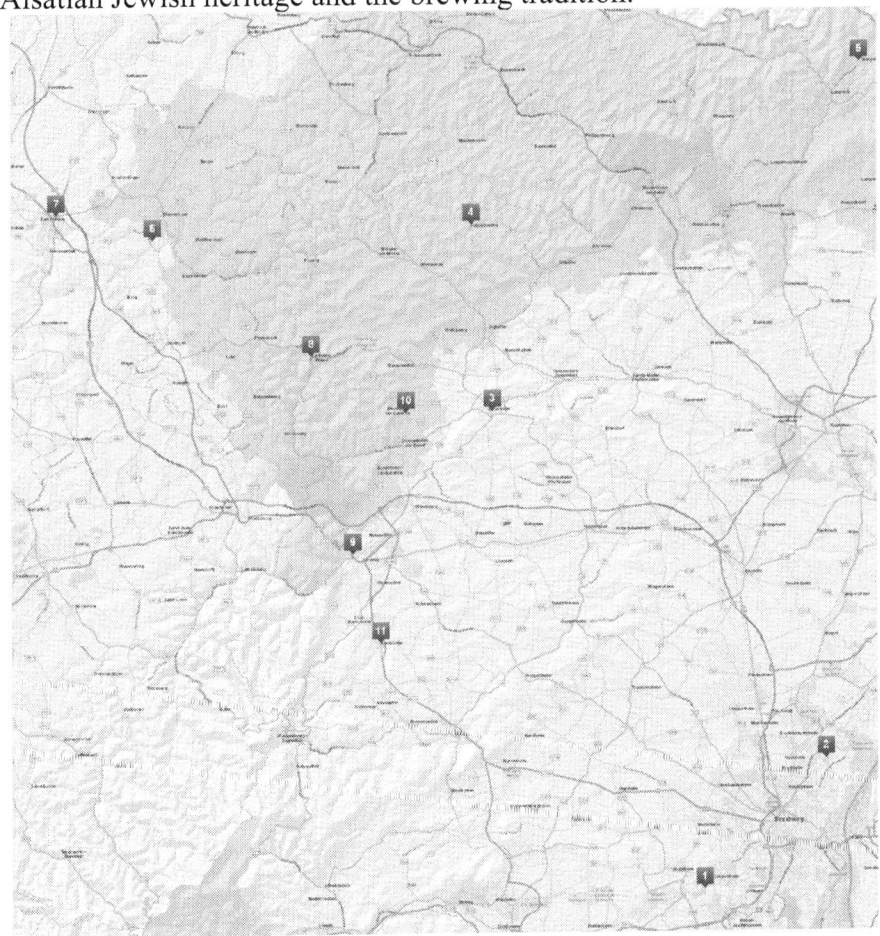

STRASBOURG & NORTHERN ALSACE MAP

KEY:
1) Strasbourg
2) Schiltigheim
3) Bouxwiller
4) Reipertswiller
5) Wingen
6) Mackwiller
7) Sarre Union
8) La Petite Pierre
9) Saverne
10) Neuwiller
11) Marmoutier

DAY 1
Strasbourg

<u>**STAY AT:**</u> *the private aire in* **Strasbourg***, outside the Indigo campsite on the Western side of Strasbourg, located in a medium-sized parking area off* **Route de Schirmeck (D392)***. The aire is close to shops and services, but is about 1km from the city centre. The parking is shaded by trees in places and lit at night. Flot Bleu service point with drainage platform. Parking is also allowed in the city centre car parks, subject to height restrictions and car park charges. The campsite is also open all year and is probably a better location for not much more expense. Buses run into the city centre from outside the campsite.*
Facilities: *Water•Grey Drain•Black Drain•Toilets*
No. of spaces: *12*
Parking: *15-25€/24hrs*
Services: *Incl.*
Opening times: *All year*
GPS Coordinates: *N48.34278   E07.43469*
Alternative: Indigo Campsite, Rue Auberge Jeunesse, 67000 Strasbourg Open: all year

Strasbourg presents a wonderful mix: half-timbered houses, canals, the towering spire of its red sandstone gothic Cathedral, the encircling River Ill and Palais Rohan. Not to be missed is the central "island" encircled by the two arms of the river. Extending from the cathedral to the "Petite France" district, this is the city's well preserved historic area, with Renaissance houses, old-fashioned shops, three "Ponts-Couverts" (covered bridges) and various other river crossing points. The city is home to several museums, three of which are in the Rohan Palace, as well as the impressive "BarrageVauban" with its panoramic roof terrace. The Vauban Dam is a thirteen-arch defensive weir, constructed in 1686 to enable the city to use the river waters to flood land to the South of the city, thus rendering it impassable to the enemy. The dam was last used in 1870, when the city was besieged by Prussian forces. Outside of this central "island" can be found the botanic gardens and the Orangerie, a lovely park housing a rare bird reserve.
<u>**STAY AT:**</u> *the private aire in* **Strasbourg***, off* **Route de Schirmeck (D392)** *or Indigo Campsite, Rue Auberge Jeunesse, 67000 Strasbourg*

DAY 2
TAKE D468 NORTH TO:
Schiltigheim: The capital of Alsatian brewing, housing 3 breweries as well as a rose garden. Markets are held weekly, on Thursday mornings and Saturday mornings. Beer festival on 1st weekend in August.

TAKE D263 NORTH TO BRUMATH & D419 NORTH TO:
Pfaffenhoffen has a museum of popular images such as glass painting, personal messages carved by penknife and commemorative plates. There is an entirely restored 18th C synagogue. A weekly market is held on Saturday mornings.

TAKE D919/ D24 WEST TO:
Bouxwiller is the former residence of the Hanau-Lichtenberg family. The town has a Renaissance town-hall with ramparts, magnificent Alsatian houses, and the Bouxwiller and Hanau regional museum as well as a Jewish-Alsatian museum in a former synagogue. There is a Geological trail at nearby **Bastberg**.

TAKE D7/D157 NORTH TO:
Lichtenberg (alt. 414 m) is a chateau built on a rock. Converted for the use of guns in the 16th C and extended in the 17th C, it is a good example of the history of military architecture. Two semi-circular towers flank the keep, which is open to visitors; there is a late gothic chapel with epitaphs of the previous owners, and remains of the barracks. High walls and a fortified moat surround the whole chateau.

TAKE D257/D157 NORTH TO:
Reipertswiller
STAY AT: *the nearby Municipal aire in **Reipertswiller**, in **Rue des Ecoles** on the northern outskirts of this small rural village. The aire is a gravelled parking area without shade or lighting, with a grass area and fishing lake adjacent. The aire is just 200m from the village centre with its boulangerie and a restaurant, and there are walks nearby. Artisanal service point with drainage platform.*
Facilities: *Water•Grey Drain•Black Drain•Rubbish*
No. of spaces: *6*
Parking: *Free*
Services: *5€ Water*
Opening times: *All year*
GPS Coordinates: *N 48.93375 E 07.46339*
Alternative: *Municipal Campsite, Rue de Zittersheim, 67290 Wingen sur Moder Open: 01/05 – 30/09*

DAY 3
TAKE D157/ D919 WEST TO:
Wingen-sur-Moder then take the route north to **Bitche** (D256), and passing the Stone of the 12 Apostles, you come to the crystal works of Lember in St Louis-les-Bitche, and the glass and crystal museum in **Meisenthal**. Return to **Wingen**, where you can visit the Lalique Museum just west of Wingen on the D919. The museum displays include not only exceptional pieces of jewellery, drawings, perfume bottles, tableware and chandeliers, but also photos, videos and the 1900 World Fair display stand.

CONTINUE ON D919 WEST TO;
Mackwiller: Remains of Gallo-Roman villa & thermal baths.

CONTINUE ON D919 & D8 WEST TO:
Sarre-Union is an old fortified town, with narrow and winding streets boasting a number of houses dating from the 16th C, a gothic church dating from the 15th C, and the regional museum of Alsace Bossue. Markets take place on the 2nd and 4th Wednesdays of the month.

RETURN TO MACKWILLER & TAKE D9 SOUTH TO:
La Petite Pierre: A mountain resort, with old houses from the 17th C and a chateau dating from the 13th C (alt. 340 m). It is also the centre of the Regional Nature Park of the Northern Vosges and has remains of the fortified walls built by Louis XIV on a rocky spur. There is a museum of Alsatian seals in the 17th C St Louis Chapel and a museum of popular arts and traditions. Animal park and a Botanical/forest trail at **Loosthal**.

TAKE D178 & D122 SOUTH TO:
Saverne

STAY AT: the nearby private aire in **Saverne,** on **Rue du Zornhoff**. The aire is located on the northern side of the town, in a large, level gravel parking area shaded by trees on one side, close to the yacht marina and the chateau. Entry is by an automatic barrier which is payable by credit card, as are the services. Mini Flot Bleu service point with drain, free wifi is also available here.

Facilities: Water•Grey Drain•Black Drain•Electric•Wifi
No. of spaces: 39
Parking: 7€/ 24hrs
Services: 2€ Water or Electric
Opening times: All year
GPS Coordinates: N48.74299   E07.36737

Alternative: Camping Portes d'Alsace, Rue Pere Libermann, 67700 Saverne Open: 30/03 – 04/11

DAY 4

Saverne is a Brewing town with an 18th C neo-classical château, a 17th C Jewish cemetery, an Archaeological museum, a Museum of Art and History, and a Rose Garden. There is also a 14th C Cloister, and a Church dating from 12th C. Other attractions are a woodland trail at Haut-Barr, 3 signposted mountain-bike trails, 4 signposted cycling routes, and a weekly market on Thursday mornings. Nearby, towards the Col de Saverne, is a botanical garden, and in the Zorn valley there are ruins of the 12th C chateau of Haut-Barr (alt. 457 m). Built on three sheer rock faces, two of which are connected by "the devil's bridge", it has remains of dwelling places and bastions, a Renaissance door and a pretty Romanesque chapel. You can also visit the ruins of petit and grand Geroldseck (12th C), belonging to Marmoutier Abbey, as well as the ruins of the 13th C chateau of Griffon, with two keeps, one of which is open to visitors.

TAKE D1004/ D115 NORTH TO:
Saint-Jean-Saverne has a Romanesque abbey church and St Michael's chapel (both 12th C).
Nearby are the ruins of the 12th C chateau of Daubenschlagfelsen at Warthenberg (alt. 400 m), one of the largest in Alsace, with remains of the keep and cisterns.

TAKE D219/ D14 NORTH TO:
Neuwiller-les-Saverne: St Peter and St Paul's Abbey church, dating from 12th C, with the tomb of St Adelphe and tapestries illustrating her life. There are inscriptions in Hebrew on the medieval town walls. Nearby are the ruins of Herrenstein chateau (alt. 401 m)

RETURN TO: **Saverne**
STAY AT: *the private aire in* **Saverne**, *on* **Rue du Zornhoff** *or Camping Portes d'Alsace, Rue Pere Libermann, 67700 Saverne*

DAY 5

TAKE D1004(N4) SOUTH TO:
Marmoutier: The Abbey here is one of the oldest in Alsace, with remains in the crypt of an 8th C church, tombs & a sarcophagus. It also houses the European Organ Centre, with a Silbermann organ dating from 1710. There is a Jewish museum in the town, situated in a beautiful old town house. Nearby, to the west, are the ruins of the 12th C chateau of Ochsenstein (alt. 584 m) - three separate chateaux on

steep rocks linked up to each other and accessible via stairways carved out of the rock. The Chappe telegraph tower is 15 km away, whilst there is the Arzviller boat lift on the Marne-to-Rhine canal.
RETURN TO: **Saverne**
STAY AT: *the private aire in* **Saverne**, *on* **Rue du Zornhoff** *or Camping Portes d'Alsace, Rue Pere Libermann, 67700 Saverne*

Top: Saverne by Manassas

Bottom: Aire at Saverne

Top: Strasbourg by Rabich

Middle: Marmoutier Church by Palauenc

Bottom: La Petite Pierre by © Ralph Hammann

ALSACE TOUR 3
THE VOSGES MOUNTAINS - 6 DAYS

A 6-Day Tour of the 1,100m high Vosges mountains. They are easy to access, with a full road network leading you up through mountain passes and on to mountain meadows or woodlands, and then back down into deep valleys. In addition to the more traditional sites, this region is famous for its vast open spaces and offers a range of sporting activities, such as walks and hikes, mountain-bike trails, downhill skiing and cross-country skiing.

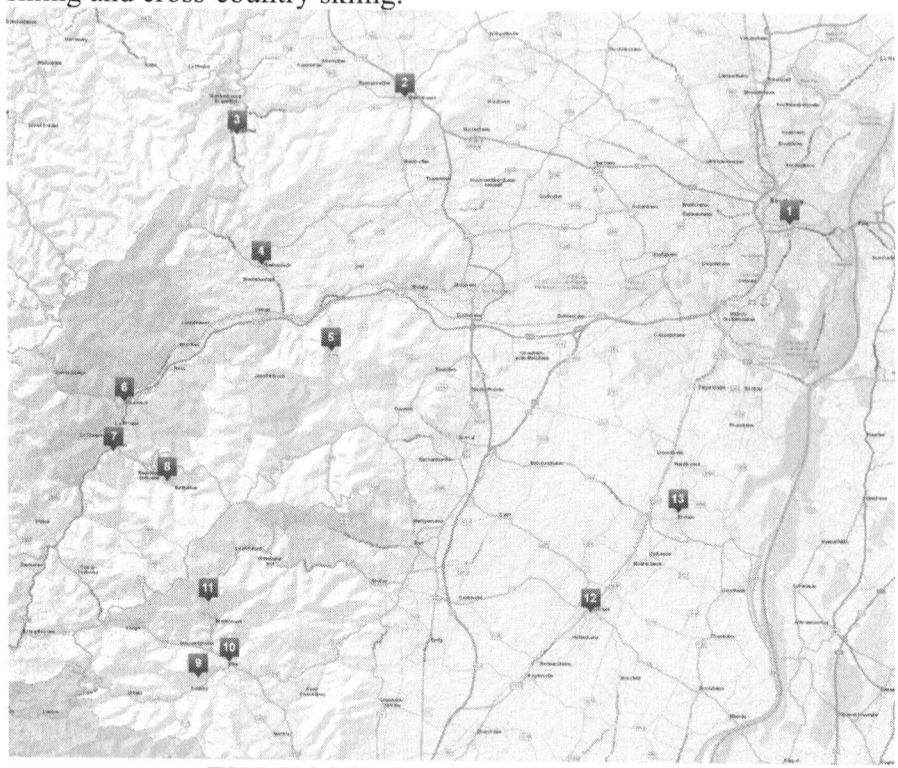

THE VOSGES MOUNTAINS MAP

KEY:

1) Strasbourg
2) Wasselonne
3) Wangenbourg
4) Oberhaslach
5) Mollkirch
6) Schirmeck
7) Rothau
8) Natzwiller
9) Bassemberg
10) Ville
11) Breitenbach
12) Benfeld
13) Erstein

Top Left: Strasbourg Cathedral by Taxiarchos228 Top Right: Urbeis

DAY 1
Strasbourg
STAY AT: *the private aire in* **Strasbourg***, outside the Indigo campsite on the western side of Strasbourg, located in a medium-sized parking area off* **Route de Schirmeck (D392)***. The aire is close to shops and services, and about 1km from the city centre. The parking is shaded by trees in places and lit at night. Flot Bleu service point with drainage platform. Parking is also allowed in the city centre car parks, subject to height restrictions and car park charges. The campsite is also open all year and is probably a better location for not much more expense. Buses run into the city centre from outside the campsite.*
Facilities: *Water•Grey Drain•Black Drain•Toilets*
No. of spaces: *12*
Parking: *15-25€/24hrs*
Services: *Incl.*
Opening times: *All year*
GPS Coordinates: *N48.34278   E07.43469*
Alternative: *Indigo Campsite, Rue Auberge Jeunesse, 67000 Strasbourg Open: all year*

Strasbourg presents a wonderful mix: half-timbered houses, canals, the towering spire of its red sandstone gothic Cathedral, the encircling River Ill and Palais Rohan. Not to be missed is the central "island" encircled by the two arms of the river. Extending from the cathedral to the "Petite France" district, this is the city's well preserved historic

area, with Renaissance houses, old-fashioned shops, three "Ponts-Couverts" (covered bridges) and various other river crossing points. The city is home to several museums, three of which are in the Rohan Palace, as well as the impressive "BarrageVauban" with its panoramic roof terrace. The Vauban Dam is a thirteen-arch defensive weir, constructed in 1686 to enable the city to use the river waters to flood land to the South of the city, rendering it impassable to the enemy. The dam was last used in 1870, when the city was besieged by Prussian forces. Outside of this central "island" can be found the botanic gardens and the Orangerie, a lovely park housing a rare bird reserve.
STAY AT: *the private aire in* **Strasbourg***, off* **Route de Schirmeck (D392)** *or Indigo Campsite, Rue Auberge Jeunesse, 67000 Strabourg*
DAY 2
TAKE A351 & D1004 WEST TO:
Wasselonne: A small town at the gateway to the Mossig valley, with chateau ruins and traditional houses from the 17th C decorated with the signs of various trades. Weekly market held on Monday mornings.
TAKE D224 WEST TO:
Freudeneck with the ruins of Freudeneck chateau (alt. 350 m).
& D224/ D218 ON TO:
Wangenbourg: A Mountain resort with five signposted mountain-bike trails, cross-country skiing and the ruins of the 13th C chateau of Wangenbourg (alt. 480 m). Irregular in design, its surrounding walls still stand, as do a Renaissance fireplace on the wall of the dwelling area and the keep, which is open to visitors. Nearby in Obersteigen there is a beautiful 13th C church, the former chapel of an Augustine convent.
TAKE D218 SOUTH TO:
Oberhaslach: In the **Hasel Valley** are a waterfall and the ruins of the 13th C chateau of Nideck (alt. 573 m), which is located on two rocks, one of which carries an imposing keep (open to visitors). The other, higher rock has the remains of the dwelling area. Nearby are the ruins of the 12th C chateau of Ringelstein (alt. 645 m) with its surrounding wall and two towers.
STAY AT: *the large riverside parking area in* **Oberhaslach,** *next to the village hall on* **Rue du Klintz** *on the western side of the village. This provides quiet parking, but no services, and it's a short walk to the shops and eating places in the village.*
Facilities: *None*

No. of spaces: 10
Parking: Free
Opening times: All year
GPS Coordinates: N48.54985   E07.32329
Alternative: Camping Amis de Nature, Rue du Chateau, 68140 Luttenbach Open: 21/03 – 13/11

DAY 3
TAKE D218 SOUTH THEN D392 EAST & D704 SOUTH TO:
Mollkirch: The "Stone Ladies" educational and archaeological trail, with menhirs and dolmens to discover. Nearby at Verloreneck, there is a second educational trail with more menhirs and dolmens, as well as the ruins of the 13th C chateau Guirbaden. This is the largest chateau in the Vosges, of which part of the keep and the surrounding walls remain, together with beautiful Romanesque windows and a chapel to St Valentine.

TAKE D204 WEST TO:
Grendelbruch: A mountain resort with beautiful mountain meadows.

CONTINUE WEST ON D204 TO:
Schirmeck: Here you will find the Alsace-Moselle Memorial and ruins of the 13th C chateau of Schirmeck (alt. 460 m), with the town museum being located in its tower. A weekly market is held on Wednesday mornings.

TAKE D392 WEST TO:
Grandefontaine: The Framont iron mine here was worked from as early as the 12th C and there is also a museum of Citroen 2CV cars. Nearby, at the Col du Donon (alt. 718 m), is an archaeological and historical discovery trail, whilst at the summit of the sacred Donon mountain (alt. 1,009 m), there is a small temple dating back to the 2nd C.

RETURN EAST TO SCHIRMECK & TAKE D1420 TO:
Rothau
STAY AT: the Municipal campsite, or on the Municipal aire in **Rothau**, off **Grande Rue (D1420)**. This is a modern aire, situated outside the Municipal campsite on the western outskirts of the town. Parking is on well-defined gravel spaces with a grass area and picnic tables adjacent. There are enjoyable country walks close to the aire, and a 600m walk to the town centre/shops. Flot Bleu service point with small drain. The town has a weekly market on Saturday mornings.

Facilities: *Water•Grey Drain•Black Drain•Toilets•Rubbish•Electric*
No. of spaces: *8*
Parking: *6.5€/24hrs*
Services: *2.5€ Water or Electric*
Opening times: *All year*
GPS Coordinates: *N 48.45245   E 07.19879*
Alternative: *Municipal Campsite, Rue de la DFL, 67600 Selestat Open: 01/04 – 15/10*

DAY 4

Nearby in **Neuviller-la-Roche** is a Heritage museum and the Serva waterfall. Also Salm, to the west of Rothau, has a Mennonite cemetery and ruins of the 12th C chateau of Salm (alt. 809 m), which has remains of the walls, a tower and a cistern.

TAKE D130 EAST TO:
Natzwiller: (alt. 718 m) A former Nazi concentration camp with a memorial to the people deported.

TAKE D130 EAST & D214 SOUTH TO:
Champ du Feu: alt. 1,100 m. This is the highest peak in the middle Vosges and is a winter sports centre for downhill and cross-country skiing.

TAKE D414 WEST TO:
Bellefosse/Belmont: with the ruins of the 12th C Chateau de la Roche (alt. 574 m), where there are remains of a door and lower staircase carved out of the rock.

CONTINUE WEST ON D57 & THEN TAKE D1420 SOUTH TO BOURG-BRUCHE & THEN D50/ D214 EAST TO:
Col d'Urbeis: (alt. 602 m) A woodland trail runs up the Le Climont mountain, which is crowned with an observation tower at an altitude of 966 m.

CONTINUE EAST ON D39 TO:
Urbeis: 16th C Théophile mine, and ruins of the pink sandstone Bilstein chateau (alt. 599 m) built by the Dukes of Lorraine on the salt road from Lorraine, with wonderful views over the valley.

CONTINUE EAST ON D39 TO:
Bassemberg

<u>**STAY AT:**</u> *the Parking outside the Sports Complex in* **Bassemberg,** *off Route de Ville. There are half a dozen level spaces here on tarmac next to the campsite, on the east side of the village, in a quiet shaded location that is lit at night. A pleasant little residential village, there*

are no services here, but shops and eating-places can be found in Luttenbach, 1km to the East.
Facilities: *None*
No. of spaces: *6*
Parking: *Free*
Services: *None*
Opening times: *All year*
GPS Coordinates: *N 48.33705   E 07.28869*
Alternative: *Camping Le Giessen on Route de Ville, 67220 Bassemberg Open: 30/03 – 30/09*

DAY 5
CONTINUE NORTH-EAST ON D39 TO:
Ville: A major town in Val de Villé, renowned for its brandies. There are 6 sign-posted mountain-bike trails and a weekly market is held on Wednesday mornings. Nearby, encircled by a prehistoric wall called the "Pagan Wall", are the ruins of the 12th C chateau Frankenbourg (alt. 714 m), which still boasts the remains of its keep and elliptical castle walls.

TAKE D424/D425 NORTH TO:
Breitenbach: Museum of rural traditions in an 18th C house, as well as the Alsace Adventure Park.

CONTINUE NORTH ON D425 PAST the Col du Kreuzweg (alt. 768 m) & ON TO:
Le Hohwald: A mountain resort with a waterfall, an arboretum, two sign-posted mountain-bike trails plus downhill and cross-country skiing pistes in winter.

TAKE D425 EAST TO EICHOFFEN & THEN D5 EAST TO:
Benfeld is an important tobacco-growing centre with a town hall dating from 1531, which has a clock with figurine. A weekly market is held on Monday mornings.

STAY AT: *the Private aire in* **Benfeld,** *which is located outside the showrooms of the motorhome sales depot of* **CLC-Alsace**, *next to the* **D1083**. *Parking is in a medium-sized tarmac parking area with no shade, supermarket nearby. Euro-Relais service point with drainage grid.*
Facilities: *Water•Grey Drain•Black Drain• Rubbish•Electric*
No. of spaces: *2*
Parking: *Free/24hrs*
Services: *Free*

Opening times: *All year*
GPS Coordinates: *N48.37759   E07.59770*
Alternative: *Camping Le Reid, Rue du Camping, 67860 Boofzheim*
Open: 21/04 – 16/09
DAY 6
TAKE D829 & D288 NORTH TO:
Osthouse: 16th C Manor house and the remains of a 19th C synagogue destroyed by the Nazis.
CONTINUE NORTH ON D288 TO:
Erstein: This picturesque village has beautiful rural houses, three way marked walks, the Erstein water park and the Erstein forest nature reserve. A weekly market is held on Thursday mornings.
TAKE D1083 NORTH BACK TO:
Strasbourg
STAY AT: *the private aire in* **Strasbourg***, off* **Route de Schirmeck (D392)** *or Indigo Campsite, Rue Auberge Jeunesse, 67000 Strasbourg.*

Top Left: Grandefontaine by Guillo Top Right:: Erstein by © Ralph Hammann

Aire at Rothau

ALSACE TOUR 4
THE MAGINOT LINE & NORTHERN VOSGES - 5 DAYS

This 5-Day Tour goes beyond the forest of Haguenau to the Northern Alsace. Bordered by the Rhine to the east and encroaching on the Regional Park of the Northern Vosges to the west, this is a land of hills, valleys and woodlands. The major tourist attractions lie in the picturesque villages, potters' villages, spa towns, chateaux and the Maginot Line.

DAY 1
Strasbourg

STAY AT: the private aire in **Strasbourg**, outside the Indigo campsite on the Western side of Strasbourg, located in a medium-sized parking area off **Route de Schirmeck (D392)**. The aire is close to shops and services, and about 1km from the city centre. The parking is shaded by trees in places and lit at night. Flot Bleu service point with drainage platform. Parking is also allowed in the city centre car parks, subject to height restrictions and car park charges. The campsite is also open all year and is probably a better location for not much more expense. Buses run into the city centre from outside the campsite.

Facilities: Water •Grey Drain •Black Drain •Toilets
No. of spaces: 12
Parking: 15-25€/24hrs
Services: Incl.
Opening times: All year
GPS Coordinates: N48.34278   E07.43469

Strasbourg: presents a wonderful mix: half-timbered houses, canals, the towering spire of its red sandstone gothic Cathedral, the encircling River Ill and Palais Rohan. Not to be missed is the central "island" encircled by the two arms of the river. Extending from the cathedral to the "Petite France" district, this is the city's well preserved historic area, with Renaissance houses, old-fashioned shops, three "Ponts-Couverts" (covered bridges) and various other river crossing points. The city is home to several museums, three of which are in the Rohan Palace, as well as the impressive "BarrageVauban" with its panoramic roof terrace. The Vauban Dam is a thirteen-arch defensive weir, constructed in 1686 to enable the city to use the river waters to flood land to the South of the city, rendering it impassable to the enemy. The dam was last used in 1870, when the city was besieged by Prussian forces. Outside of this central "island" can be found the botanic gardens and the Orangerie, a lovely park housing a rare bird reserve.

STAY AT: *the private aire in* **Strasbourg**, *off Route de Schirmeck (D392) or Indigo Campsite, Rue Auberge Jeunesse, 67000 Strasbourg*

DAY 2

TAKE A4/ A35 NORTH TO JCN 53 TO:

Bischwiller: A small town renowned for its textile industry, with a textile museum and an art museum. For organ enthusiasts, there is a Silbermann organ dating from 1724 in the Protestant church. A weekly market is held on Saturday mornings.

TAKE D37 NORTH & D28 WEST TO:

Hatten: The Maginot Line Museum presents a reconstruction of a barracks in the defensive line, as well as an outdoor display of armoured vehicles on a 4-acre site. Nearby in **Oberroedern** are the remains of a Rieffel bunker, also part of the Maginot Line.

TAKE D28 & D243 WEST TO:

Betschdorf: A town of sandstone buildings and pottery workshops, with a pottery museum. A pottery festival is held in September.

STAY AT: *the* **Municipal aire in Betschdorf** *off* **Rue de la Gare**, *located next to a minor road between the villages of Betschdorf and Niederbetschdorf. This is in a slightly remote spot and provides a few parking spaces on tarmac in a lay-by, with some shade provided by trees. Euro-Relais service point with drainage grid. The Intermarche supermarket is within a short walk and the village centre is about 800m away. Swimming pool and tennis courts adjacent, with more parking.*

Facilities: *Water•Grey Drain•Black Drain*
No. of spaces: *4*
Parking: *Free*
Services: *Free*
Opening times: *All year*
GPS Coordinates: *N48.89498   E07.91076*
Alternative: *Camping Les Pins, Rue de la Piscine, 67500 Haguenau Open: 21/04 – 31/10*

KEY:
1) Strasbourg   2) Bischwiller   3) Hatten
4) Betschdorf   5) Hunspach   6) Wissembourg
7) Lembac   8) Niedersteinbach   9) Windstein
10) Niederbronn   11) Reichshoffen   12) Woerth
13) Haguenau   14) Brumath

Page 35

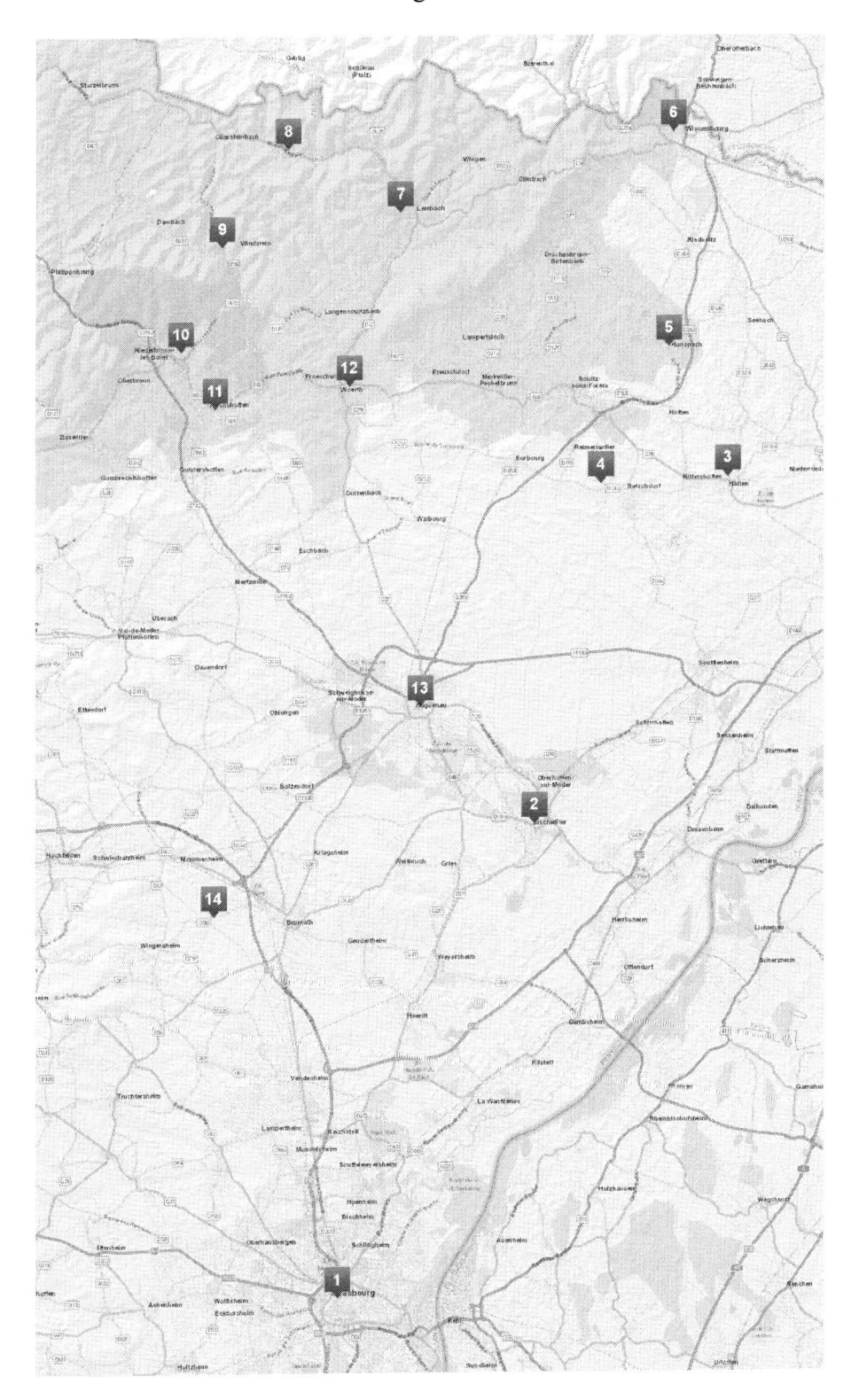

THE MAGINOT LINE & NORTHERN VOSGES MAP
DAY 3
TAKE D243 & D263 NORTH TO:
Hunspach is labelled as one of the "Most beautiful villages in France" and holds a traditional festival on the Sunday before the first day of Summer. Nearby is the Schoenenbourg Fort on the Maginot Line.
CONTINUE NORTH ON D249 TO:
Seebach: A picturesque village having traditional houses with timber frames and canopies.
CONTINUE NORTH ON D34 TO:
Wissembourg: Former town of the Décapole alliance of 1354, Wissembourg was originally founded on the banks of the river Lauter in the 7th C St Peter and Paul's church, the largest gothic building in Alsace after Strasbourg Cathedral, has exceptional stained glass windows, whilst also in the town are ramparts, a Salt House and the Westercamp Museum in the historic quarter. A weekly market is held on Saturday mornings.
Nearby in **Altenstadt** is a Romanesque church from the 11th C, and in **Weiler** is a pilgrimage chapel with a botanical/forest trail.
TAKE D3 SOUTH TO: **Col du Pigeonnier** (alt. 432 m) *& ON TO:*
Lembach, where nearby you can find the ruins of the 12th C troglodyte-style Chateau of Fleckenstein (alt. 363 m), which is the largest in the Northern Vosges, built on an imposing rock measuring 40 m high, 50 m long and 10 m wide. Also nearby is the Four-à-Chaux fort on the Maginot Line, which has a museum and 2 sign-posted cycling routes.
Nearby on a narrow peak are the ruins of the 13th C Chateau Hohenbourg (alt. 551 m), a picturesque site with remains of the keep, dwelling area and beautiful Renaissance sculptures. There are also ruins of the 13th C Chateau Loewenstein (alt. 520 m) having remains of the walls, a turret stairway and door frames.
CONTINUE NORTH ON D3 TO:
Niedersteinbach: nearby are the ruins of the 13th C Chateau Froensbourg (alt. 310 m), remains of two towers, a cistern, well and a dwelling carved into the rock.
STAY AT: *the municipal aire in* **Niedersteinbach***, located opposite the hotel "Cheval Blanc" on the north side of this small rural village. Parking is on tarmac in the circular hotel car park. The aire is located about 100m to the north of the village centre in a quiet location, with*

woods and farmland to the west. There is an artisanal service point with drainage grid. This is a small village with no facilities apart from two hotel/restaurants.
Facilities: *Water •Grey Drain •Black Drain •Electric*
No. of spaces: *2*
Parking: *Free*
Services: *2€ Water or Electric*
Opening times: *All year*
GPS Coordinates: *N49.03155   E07.71017*
Alternative: *Camping Fleckenstein, Route de Bitche, 67510 Lembach Open: 24/03 – 02/10*

DAY 4
CONTINUE WEST ON D3 TO:
Obersteinbach has a landscaped trail crossing the border in to Germany. The ruins of the Petit Arnsbourg Chateau, with remains of a tower and the dwelling area: the stairs, doors, rooms, moat, and corridors are carved out of the rock. Nearby are ruins of the 13th C Chateau Wasigenstein (alt. 340 m), two buildings separated by a deep ditch, and the remains of Wittschloessel Chateau and Lutzelhardt Chateau (alt. 351 m), the latter located on a rock 60 m long and 20 m high.

CONTINUE WEST ON D3 & D53 SOUTH TO:
Windstein: Built on two steep rocks are the ruins of the 13th C Chateau of Vieux Windstein (alt. 340 m), that has remains of chambers and stairways carved from the rock. The remains of Nouveau Windstein Chateau (alt. 376 m), built on two levels, boasts beautiful Gothic windows on the upper sections.

Nearby at **Dambach-Neunhoffen** is the Maginot Line fort of Neunhoffen, and the Maginot discovery trail in the Schwarzbach valley. A Blueberry festival is held on the 3rd weekend in July. There are three sign-posted mountain-bike trails, whilst also in the area are the ruins of three 13th C chateaux:

Chateau Hohenfels, with dwelling remains and cisterns hollowed out of the sandstone; Chateau Schoeneck, on two rocks separated by a moat and having significant remains of the dwelling areas and the towers; and Chateau Wineck, (alt. 368 m), with a surrounding wall and pentagonal keep.

TAKE D53 & D653 SOUTH TO:

Niederbronn-les-Bains is a mineral spa town, with a Casino, a Museum of Archaeology of the Northern Vosges, and a sign-posted historical trail around the town. Nearby are the Herrenberg botanical trail, three sign-posted mountain-bike trails and the ruins of the 13th C Chateau of Wasenbourg (alt. 433 m). Built near a Roman outpost, this chateau has an interesting facade on the dwelling area still visible and a facade of nine windows carved out of a single block of sandstone. Grand Wintersberg observation tower is the highest point in the Northern Vosges (alt. 581 m). A weekly market is held on Friday mornings.

*STAY AT: the Parking in **Niederbronn-les-Bains**, located on **Avenue Foch**, near the centre of this large rural village. Parking is on tarmac in a medium-sized parking area, located about 100m from the village centre in a quiet location. Shops, eating places and services nearby.*
Facilities: None
No. of spaces: 6
Parking: Free
Services: Toilets, water available at campsite when open
Opening times: All year
GPS Coordinates: N48.94855 E07.64647
Alternative: Camping l'Oasis, Rue de Frohret, 67110 Oberbronn
Open: All year

DAY 5

Nearby, **Oberbronn**: has traditional houses, recalling the fact that the village used to produce wine. There is a sign-posted historical trail around the village, whilst nearby is Wasenkoepfel observation tower (alt. 526 m).

TAKE D662 SOUTH TO:

Reichshoffen has an Iron museum and there is a Nature trail in Neuwald, with bird-watching on Reichshoffen lake. The weekly market is held on Thursday mornings and there is a Beer festival on 2nd Sunday in September.

TAKE D28 EAST TO:

Woerth: An 1870 battlefield with a hiking trail around it and a museum of the Battle. Nearby is a 12th C chateau, and at **Langensoultzbach** is a Gallo-Roman exhibition.

TAKE D27 SOUTH TO:

Haguenau is another former town of the Décapole alliance of 1354, founded in the 11th C. It has two old churches, 12th C St George's church and 14th C St Nicholas' church, as well as a neo-classical style synagogue. There are two museums to visit, an Alsace Life museum and a local history museum, as well as the Nautiland water park. Historical trails are signposted around the town, and weekly markets are held on Tuesday and Friday mornings.

TAKE D263 SOUTH TO:
Brumath has an Archaeological museum in the chateau and a Parc d'Aventures for the children. The weekly market is held on Wednesday mornings.

TAKE A4 SOUTH TO:
Strasbourg
<u>**STAY AT:**</u> *the private aire in* **Strasbourg, off Route de Schirmeck (D392)** *or Indigo Campsite, Rue Auberge Jeunesse, 67000 Strasbourg.*

Top: Strasbourg by Martz
Below: Maginot Line Fort by Richieman

Top : Wissembourg by Stako   Middle: Haguenau by Geak

Above: Aire at Niedersteinbach

Page 41

BRITTANY TOUR 5
MONT-ST-MICHEL TO THE GULF OF MORBIHAN – 5 DAYS

This 5-Day Tour starting in Mont St Michel travels west along the coast to Cancale, St Malo and Dinard before moving south to Dinan, Rennes and Josselin. The tour then heads west again to the Gulf of Morbihan and the town of Vannes before finishing in Carnac.

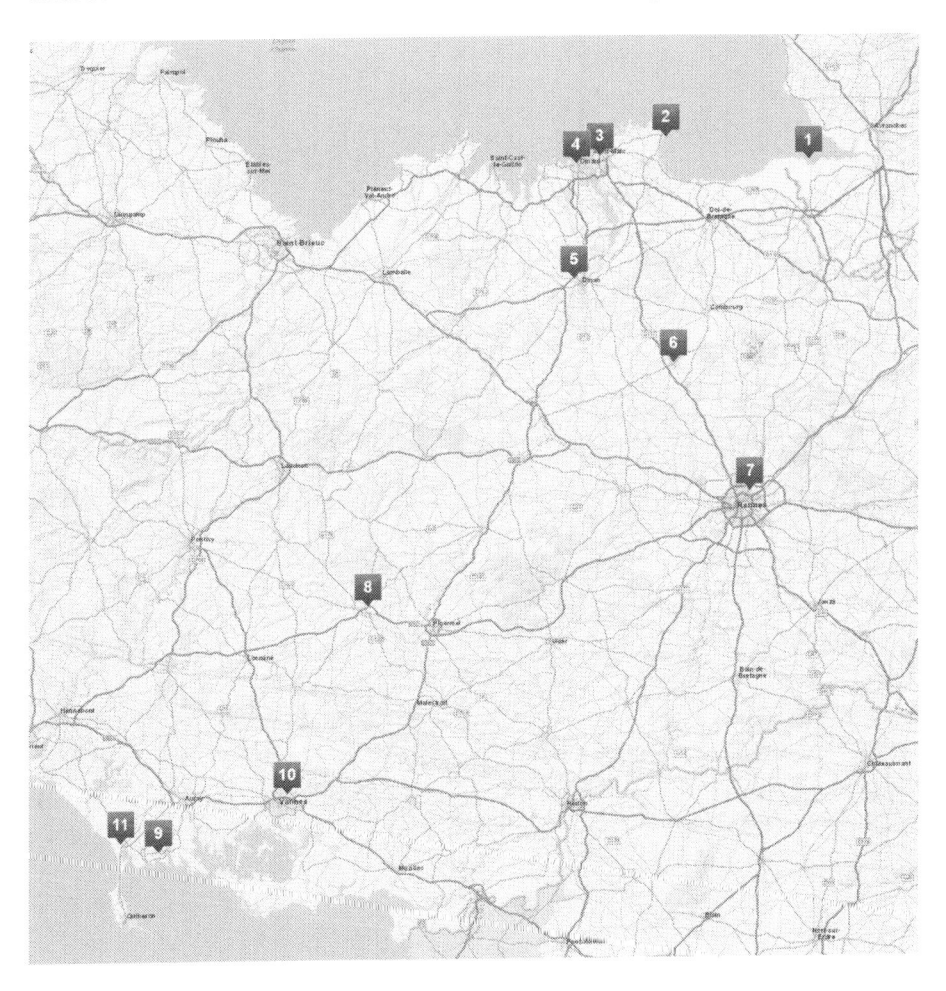

MONT-ST-MICHEL TO THE GULF OF MORBIHAN MAP

KEY: 1) Mont St Michel   2) Cancale   3) St Malo
      4) Dinard   5) Dinan   6) Tinteniac
      7) Rennes   8) Josselin   9) Carnac
      10) Vannes   11) Plouharnel

DAY 1
Mont St Michel

STAY AT: *the large purpose-built private aire on **Route Mont St Michel** in **Mont St Michel**, with 190 level spaces (each is 100 sq m, all with 10A hook ups and free wifi) on tarmac. The rows of spaces are separated by grass strips (no shade) and the area is lit at night. The aire is about 2kms from the departure point of the shuttle buses for Mont St Michel (so about 4kms from the Mont). There is a restaurant and a boulangerie adjacent, with shops in the village as well as a cycle hire depot. AireServices borne with a drainage platform.*

Facilities: Water•Grey Drain•Black Drain•Electric
No. of spaces: *190*
Parking: *13-18€/24hrs*
Services: *Incl.*
Opening times: *All year*
GPS Coordinates: *N48.61383 W01.50142*
Alternative: *Camping Mont St Michel, La Caserne, Mont St Michel Open: 30/03 – 01/11*

Mont-St-Michel, classified as a World Heritage Area by UNESCO, is a medieval fortified town standing proudly in the middle of the vast mud flats of the bay of Mont-Saint-Michel, which boasts the strongest tides in Europe. The town has many fine old buildings, three museums, tourist shops, restaurants, an Abbey - "The Wonder of the Western World" - where there is a small 13th C cloister garden with herbaceous plants and lovely views, as well as a light display show. Allow around 2-3 hours for a visit to the town and Abbey.

STAY AT: *the large purpose-built private aire on **Route Mont St Michel** in **Mont St Michel** or Camping Mont St Michel, La Caserne, Mont St Michel*

DAY 2
TAKE D797 & D155 WEST ALONG THE COAST TO:

Cancale is a traditional small fishing harbour, and a large oyster-farming centre which produces thousands of tons of Portuguese and European flat oysters. Visit the port of La Houle, where the direct sale of oysters takes place on the harbour, and possibly visit the Marine Farm, a family-run oyster farm.

TAKE D355 WEST TO:

St Malo is a very nice town with good shops, a Cathedral, an old fort, a museum and ramparts. It achieved world renown from the 16th C onwards for its town walls, built by Vauban, adding yet more charm to this beautiful town. Trips are available to Saint Malo bay along the river Rance (a large selection of excursions and departure times available from Saint Malo O.T.) and there is also an aquarium.

STAY AT: the Municipal aire in **Rue Paul Feval, St Malo**. *Located in a very large tarmac car park on the western edge of town, it has little shade and is about 2km from the old town but benefits from a free shuttle bus (runs every 15 mins) from the parking area. The aire is next to the large "Stade Marville" hippodrome (racecourse) and can best be found by following signs "Parking+Navette". It has a well designed AireServices borne with two large drainage platforms either side of it.*

Facilities: *Water•Grey Drain•Black Drain*
No. of spaces: *60*
Parking: *7.5€/24hrs*
Services: *Incl.*
Opening times: *All year*
GPS Coordinates: *N48.64271   W01.99482*
Alternative: *Camping Alet, Allee Gaston Buy, St Servain, 35400 St Malo   Open: 01/07 – 14/09*

DAY 3
CROSS THE RANCE RIVER ON D168 & D266 TO:
Dinard: A charming family seaside resort with its very beautiful 19th C British-style villas. There are guided boat trips of the valley of the Rance (wooden boat with viewing deck), where you can enjoy a meal at the bar, bring along a picnic, or select from one of the gourmet menus.

TAKE D266 & N176 SOUTH TO:
Dinan with its ramparts towering over the Rance valley, is one of the oldest medieval towns in Brittany, with the port area and buildings along Jerzual Street being particularly attractive.

TAKE D794 & D137 SOUTH TO:
Tinteniac
STAY AT: the Municipal aire on **Quai de la Donac** in **Tinteniac**, *which is located on the northern outskirts of this small town on the banks of the canal, next to the Musee de l'Outil. Parking consists of 8 level spaces on gravel, bordered by grass and with little shade. The*

aire is about 400m from the town centre and its shops. AireServices service point with drainage platform. A Tool museum is adjacent, but open in summer only, and there are nice walks along the canal towpath as well as a 25km cycle path.
Facilities: Water•Grey Drain•Black Drain•Rubbish
No. of spaces: 8
Parking: 6€/24hrs
Services: Incl.
Opening times: All year
GPS Coordinates: N48.33171   W01.83198
Alternative: Camping Les Peupliers, La Besnelais, 35190 Tinteniac Open: 01/04 – 30/09

DAY 4
TAKE D137 SOUTH TO:
Rennes: Visit the medieval cobbled streets, lined with timber-framed houses that contrast with 18th C buildings, and two royal squares (Place du Parlement and the l'Hôtel de Ville). There are many theme-based tours around the town, as well as the Brittany museum, the museum of Fine Arts and the Cathedral to visit.

TAKE N24 WEST TO:
Josselin is an historic town (Petit Cite de Caractere) sitting alongside the Oust canal, with many 16th C half-timbered buildings and a Basilique with beautiful 15th C stained glass windows. Its chateau offers a surprising contrast between its exterior, which is a remainder of the former medieval fortress, and its interior with its Renaissance-style sculpted granite. The museum, in the former stables of the castle, houses the family collection of dolls.

STAY AT: *the Municipal aire in* **Josselin***, located in* **Place St Martin** *in a very large tarmac parking area within a short walk of the town centre (150m). The parking has some shade around the sides and adjacent grass areas. There is an AireServices service point with drainage grid and toilets nearby. There is a weekly market on Saturdays, with shops, cafes and two supermarkets (Carrefour and Super U) in the town.*
Facilities: Water•Grey Drain•Black Drain•Toilets
No. of spaces: 50
Parking: Free
Services: 2€ Water
Opening times: All year

GPS Coordinates: N47.95611   W02.54958
Alternative: Domaine de Kerelly, Bas de la Lande, 56120 Josselin
Open: 30/03 – 28/09

DAY 5
TAKE N24 WEST & D768 SOUTH TO:
Carnac: An enjoyable visit for its five sandy beaches sheltered from the wind, the traditional rural architecture of its small village, and especially for the famous 6,000 year old megaliths, one of the most extensive Neolithic standing stone collections in the world.

TAKE D768 & N165 EAST TO:
Vannes on the Gulf of Morbihan area is a very old town, its rampart encircling one of the most beautiful examples of perfectly preserved and richly decorated architecture in Brittany, including a 16th C Renaissance cathedral. Boat trips can be enjoyed on the adjacent Gulf of Morbihan - a vast inland sea covering more than 12 000 hectares, sheltered from the Atlantic winds and containing over 350 islands.

TAKE D768 SOUTH TO:
Plouharnel

STAY AT: *The Municipal aire in* **Plouharnel** *on* **Route de Quiberon** *is next to the entrance to the campsite, Les Sables Blancs, where there are about 40 level spaces on grass overlooking the sea. There is little shade here but it is a quiet spot with walks and cycle tracks adjacent. About 20 spaces have hook ups available. The aire is accessed via an automatic barrier entered with a credit card. Artisanal service point and drainage grid.*

Facilities: Water•Grey Drain•Black Drain•Electric
No. of spaces: 40
Parking: 10€/24Hrs
Services: 4€ Electric
Opening times: All year
GPS Coordinates:
N47.57178   W03.12625
Alternative: Camping des Sables Blancs, Route de Quiberon, 56340 Plouharnel
Open: 01/04 – 30/09

Carnac by Myrabella

Mont St Michel by Uwe Brodrecht

Dinan by Alec

Rennes Cathedral by Man vyi

Aire at Tinteniac

BRITTANY TOUR 6
RENNES TO THE PINK GRANITE COAST – 6 DAYS

A 6-Day Tour starting from the medieval city of Rennes, visiting the magnificent Abbey town of Mont-Saint-Michel and continuing along the "Emerald Coast" to St Malo, stopping at the quaint fishing village of Binic and on to the Pink Granite coast at Tregastel.

Top: St Malo by Pline   Bottom: Cancale by chisloup

DAY 1
Rennes
<u>**STAY AT:**</u> *the municipal aire on* **Route de la Valette,** *located on the eastern outskirts of* **Cesson-Sevigne***, which is on the eastern side of* **Rennes***. The aire is in a small tarmac parking area next to the road/ roundabout, offering half a dozen level spaces with some shade on the northern side and lighting at night. AireServices service point with drainage grid. Near to a Carrefour supermarket and a stop for buses into Rennes.*
Facilities: *Water•Grey Drain•Black Drain*
No. of spaces: *6*
Parking: *Free*
Services: *2.5€ Water*
Opening times: *All year*
GPS Coordinates: *N48.11799   W01.59098*
Alternative: *Camping Mont St Michel, La Caserne, Mont St Michel*
Open: 30/03 – 01/11
Rennes: Visit the medieval cobbled streets, lined with timber-framed houses contrasting with the 18th C buildings, and two royal squares (Place du Parlement and the l'Hôtel de Ville). There are many theme-based tours around the town, as well as the Brittany museum, the museum of Fine Arts and the Cathedral to visit.

DAY 2
TAKE A84 NORTH & D275 WEST TO:
Mont-St-Michel is classified as a World Heritage Area by UNESCO, and is a medieval fortified town standing proudly in the middle of the vast mud flats of the bay of Mont-Saint-Michel, which boasts the strongest tides in Europe. The town has many fine old buildings, 3 museums, tourist shops, restaurants, an Abbey - "The Wonder of the Western World" - which has a cloister garden as well as a light display show. Allow around 2-3 hours for a visit to the town and Abbey.
<u>**STAY AT:**</u> *the large purpose-built private aire on* **Route Mont St Michel** *in* **Mont St Michel***, with 190 level spaces (each is 100 sq m, all with 10A hook ups and free wifi) on tarmac. The rows are separated by grass strips (but no shade) and the area is lit at night. The aire is about 2kms from the departure point of the shuttle buses for Mont St Michel (so about 4kms from the Mont). There is a restaurant and a boulangerie adjacent, with shops in the village as well as a cycle hire depot. AireServices borne with drainage platform.*

Facilities: Water •Grey Drain •Black Drain •Electric
No. of spaces: 190
Parking: 13-18€/24hrs
Services: Incl.
Opening times: All year
GPS Coordinates: N48.61383   W01.50142
Alternative: Camping Mont St Michel, La Caserne, Mont St Michel
Open: 30/03 – 01/11

DAY 3
TAKE D797 & D155 WEST ALONG THE COAST TO:
Cancale: Traditional small fishing harbour, and a large oyster farming centre which produces thousands of tons of Portuguese and European flat oysters. Visit the port of La Houle where there is the direct sale of the oysters on the harbour, and possibly visit the Marine Farm, a family-run oyster farm.
<u>**STAY AT:**</u> the Municipal Aire in **Cancale** in **Rue Ville Ballet**. Sited in large gravel parking area with additional spaces on grass, but not much shade. Parking is close (½ km) to the old port with its shops, etc. The Aire has 2 x AireServices bornes, platform drainage and lighting at night. This is a nice, well-managed location sited above the Old Port, with good walks and a footpath down through to the port, its shops and restaurants.
Facilities: Water •Grey Drain •Black Drain
No. of spaces: 80
Parking: 10€/24Hrs (Free in winter)
Services: 3.5€ Water
Opening times: All year
GPS Coordinates: N48.67017   W01.86591
Alternative: Camping Grouin, Ave Cote d'Emeraude, 35260 Cancale
Open: 05/03 – 19/10

DAY 4
TAKE D355 WEST TO:
St Malo is a very nice town with good shops, a cathedral, an old fort, a museum and ramparts. It achieved world renown from the 16th C onwards for its town walls, built by Vauban, adding yet more charm to this beautiful town. Trips are available to Saint Malo bay along the river Rance (a large selection of excursions and departure times available from Saint Malo OT) and there is also an aquarium.

STAY AT: *the Municipal aire in* **Rue Paul Feval, St Malo.** *Located in a very large tarmac car park on the western edge of town, it has little shade and is about 2km from the old town but benefits from a free shuttle bus (runs every 15 mins) from the parking area. The aire is next to the large "Stade Marville" hippodrome (racecourse) and can best be found by following signs "Parking+Navette". It has a well-designed AireServices borne with two large drainage platforms either side of it.*
Facilities: *Water•Grey Drain•Black Drain*
No. of spaces: *60*
Parking: *7.5€/24hrs*
Services: *Incl.*
Opening times: *All year*
GPS Coordinates: *N48.64271   W01.99482*
Alternative: *Camping Alet, Allee Gaston Buy, St Servain, 35400 St Malo   Open: 01/07 – 14/09*

DAY 5
CROSS THE RANCE RIVER ON D168 & D266 TO:
Dinard: A charming family seaside resort with its very beautiful 19th C British-style villas. There are guided boat trips of the valley of the Rance (wooden boat with viewing deck), where you can enjoy a meal at the bar, bring along a picnic, or select from one of the gourmet menus.
TAKE D768 & D786 WEST TO:
Le Cap Frehel: Lying at the end of 400 hectares of moorland, "Cap Frehel" towers over the sea from its pink sandstone cliffs. Boasting outstanding flora and fauna, it is home to a large, nesting seabird reserve, with shags, gulls and guillemots being easy to spot.
FOLLOW D786 WEST AROUND THE COAST TO:
Binic: Sheltered by a jetty, this delightful little fishing and yachting harbour is always bustling with life. Binic is a pleasant little port with a nice beach, swimming pool, museum, good selection of shops, eating places and a SuperU supermarket. An excellent market is held on the quay on Thursday mornings.
STAY AT: *the Municipal aire in* **Binic***, located in* **Rue de l'Ic***, a large gravel parking area just off the* **D786***, about 1/2km west of the town. Bordered by trees and hedges that offer shade in places, and with some lighting at night, this aire is on the edge of town and a short*

walk from the nearby countryside. Artisanal service point with drainage grid; free wifi is available at the Office de Tourisme.
Facilities: Water•Grey Drain•Black Drain•Rubbish
No. of spaces: 25
Parking: Free
Services: Free
Opening times: All year
GPS Coordinates: N48.60083   W02.83500
Alternative: Camping Les Fauvettes, Rue des Fauvettes, 22520 Binic
Open: 31/03 – 30/09

DAY 6
CONTINUE NORTH ON D786 TO:
Saint-Quay: This seaside resort, with its 5 beaches, large villas and a casino, has retained all of its charm. A coastal footpath offers innumerable walks with beautiful views of the sea and the island of Saint-Quay.
CONTINUE NORTH ON D786 TO:
Paimpol: Wander the quays lined with ancient ship owners' houses, visit the Maritime Museum or the Breton Costume Museum, stroll around the narrow streets and take a few minutes to soak up the atmosphere of the bustling harbour quays. From the Pointe de l'Arcouest you can embark for Bréhat island (10 minute crossing) and a visit to the glass-making centre of Bréhat.
CONTINUE WEST ON D786 & D788 NORTH TO:
Perros Guirec has much to offer. Enjoy the fishing harbour and yachting marina, the village centred around the 12th C St Jacques church and the beaches of Trestaou. The coastal path will take you past magnificent rocky vistas to Ploumanac'h.
CONTINUE WEST ON D788 TO:
Tregastel:
STAY AT: The Municipal aire in **Tregastel** is situated in **Rue Poul Palud**, in a large tarmac car park next to the tennis courts, on the coast at Tregastel-Plage. It is about 100m from the beaches and 100m from the Super U supermarket. The aire is about 1km from the centre of Tregastel-Plage in quite a pleasant position but offering little shade. There is an artisanal service point and a large platform drain.
Facilities: Water•Grey Drain•Black Drain
No. of spaces: 35
Parking: 4-8€/24 Hrs

Services: Free
Opening times: All year
GPS Coordinates: N48.82441   W03.49858
Alternative: Camping Tourony, Rue Poul Palud, 22730 Tregastel
Open: 01/04 – 27/09

Above: Binic by I, Semnoz
Below: Paimpol

KEY TO MAP
(Opposite):

1) Rennes   2) Mont St Michel   3) Cancale
4) St Malo   5) Dinard   6) Le Cap Frehel
7) Binic   8) St Quay   9) Paimpol
10) Perros Guirec   11) Tregastel

Page 53

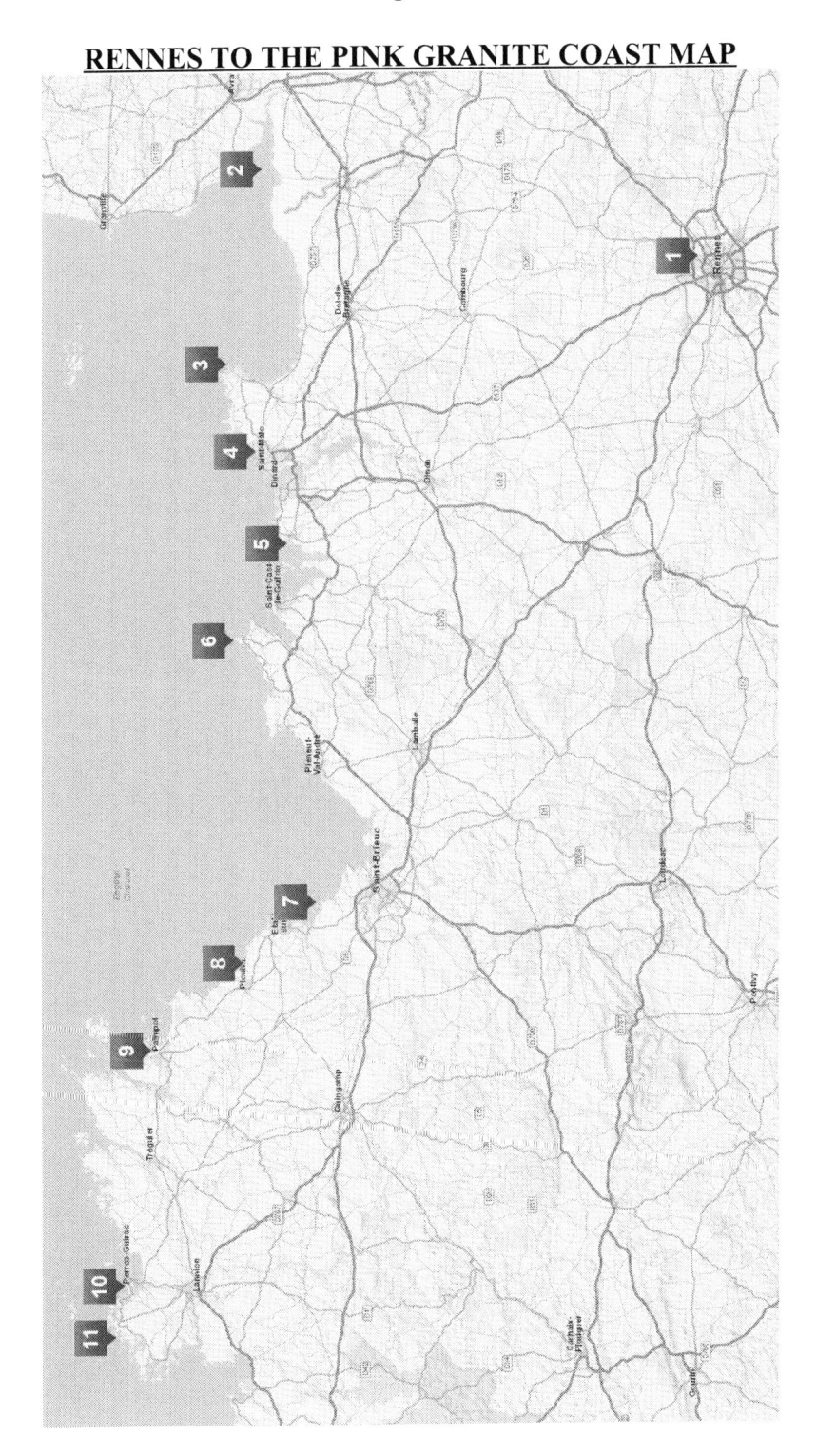

RENNES TO THE PINK GRANITE COAST MAP

BRITTANY TOUR 7
NANTES TO CARNAC & QUIMPER

This 4-Day Tour starts from the historic city of Nantes, going to Vannes on the Gulf of Morbihan and visiting the 6,000 year old megaliths of Carnac and the artists' village of Pont Aven. Continuing west to the sandy beaches of Concarneau, along the coast to the historic town of Quimper, the tour ends in the quaint village of Locronan.

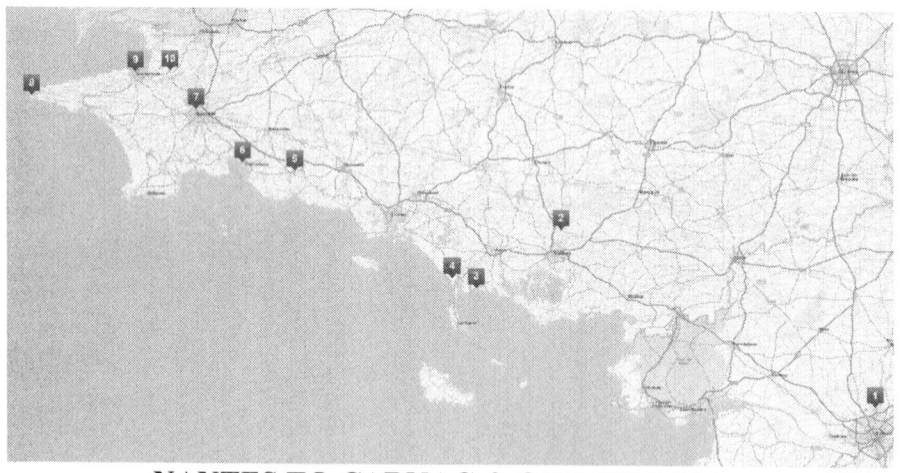

NANTES TO CARNAC & QUIMPER MAP

KEY TO MAP :

1) Nantes
2) Vannes
3) Carnac
4) Plouharnel
5) Pont Aven
6) Concarneau
7) Quimper
8) La Pointe du Raz
9) Douarnenez
10) Locronan

DAY 1
Nantes

STAY AT: *the private aire located on* **Boulevard Petit Port** *in* **Nantes,** *next to the campsite "Nantes Camping" where there are 15 spaces, shaded by trees and lit at night. Managed by the CampingCarPark company, the aire is in a medium-sized parking area, with access via an automatic barrier operated by the CCP membership card or by credit card at the machine at the entrance. There are 15 large (50m2) spaces on grass separated by trees, accessed by a tarmac track. The*

Euro Relais service point with drainage platform is outside the aire, and the pitches have access to 10A ehu's and wifi.
Facilities: *Water•Grey Drain•Black Drain•Electric•Wifi*
No. of spaces: *15*
Parking: *12€/24Hrs*
Services: *Incl*
Opening times: *All year*
GPS Coordinates: *N47.24333   W01.55673*
Alternative: *Nantes-Camping, 21 Bvd Petit Port, 44300 Nantes Open: all year*
Nantes: The architectural heritage of Nantes reflects the town's wealth and importance over the centuries. The mediaeval remnants of the town are still visible around the Gothic cathedral and in the tiny streets of Bouffay, a pedestrian area near the moated chateau des Ducs de Bretagne, where the famous Duchess Anne, twice Queen of France, was born. The Grand Elephant is a 50 ton giant mechanical elephant that carries passengers along the quayside, and the Galerie des Machines is a museum with brilliant mechanical creations on display.

DAY 2
TAKE N165 WEST TO:
Vannes on the Gulf of Morbihan area is a very old town, its rampart encircling one of the most beautiful examples of perfectly preserved and richly decorated architecture in Brittany, including a 16th C Renaissance cathedral. Boat trips can be enjoyed on the adjacent Gulf of Morbihan - a vast inland sea covering more than 12 000 hectares, sheltered from the Atlantic winds and containing over 350 islands.

CONTINUE ON N165 WEST & TAKE D768 SOUTH TO:
Carnac: An enjoyable visit for its five sandy beaches sheltered from the wind, the traditional rural architecture of its small village, and especially for the famous 6,000 year old megaliths, one of the most extensive Neolithic standing stone collections in the world.

TAKE D768 SOUTH TO:
Plouharnel
<u>STAY AT:</u> *The Municipal aire in* **Plouharnel,** *on* **Route de Quiberon,** *is next to the entrance to the campsite, Les Sables Blancs. There are about 40 level spaces on grass overlooking the sea, with little shade to offer, but in a quiet spot with walks and cycle tracks adjacent. About 20 spaces have hook ups available. The aire is accessed via an*

automatic barrier entered with a credit card. Artisanal service point and drainage grid.
Facilities: Water•Grey Drain•Black Drain•Electric
No. of spaces: 40
Parking: 10€/24Hrs
Services: 4€ Electric
Opening times: All year
GPS Coordinates: N47.57178   W03.12625
Alternative: Camping des Sables Blancs, Route de Quiberon, 56340 Plouharnel Open: 01/04 – 30/09

DAY 3
TAKE D781 ALONG THE COAST & N165 WEST TO:
Pont Aven, a former home of Gauguin, is a lovely village devoted to art, which can be discovered through its museum (housing famous works), galleries, bridges and footbridges - making up the Xavier Grall walk - and via its former wash houses and harbour quays. In the woods north of the village is the Tremalo Chapel located in a rural spot, close to the setting for Gauguin's famous painting, "The Yellow Christ".

TAKE D783 WEST TO:
Concarneau: This former Breton stronghold, today the third largest fishing harbour and premier tuna harbour in France, has a bustling port, fish market and splendid coast road overlooking its many sandy beaches. Visitors can explore this beautiful town and its many shops in the fully pedestrianised town centre.

STAY AT: the Municipal aire in **Rue de la Gare, Concarneau** - a very large tarmac car park next to the old railway station with marked spaces and lighting, but little shade. It is a 500m walk to the town centre and shops, and 300m to the Port. AireServices borne with drainage grid is easily accessible.
Facilities: Water•Grey Drain•Black Drain•Electric•Toilets
No. of spaces: 46
Parking: 6€/24Hrs, Free in winter
Services: 4€ Electric
Opening times: All year
GPS Coordinates: N47.87859   W03.92054
Alternative: Camping Les Sables Blancs, Ave du Dorlet, 29900 Concarneau Open: 01/04 – 31/10

DAY 4
CONTINUE WEST ON D783 TO:

Quimper: The historic capital of Finistere, standing majestically on the banks of the River Odet, has timber framed façades of fine medieval dwellings and the charming old districts of Loc Maria to explore. The Henriot pottery, which displays the golden age of the ceramic industry, is worth a visit, and it is possible to enjoy a sail on one of the many comfortable boats (with panoramic viewing decks) from the harbour.

TAKE D785 SOUTH TO PENMARCH &:

The Bay of Audierne encompasses dunes, marshes and a lake. This route also passes the oldest Calvary in Brittany, that of Notre Dame de Tronoën chapel.

CONTINUE NORTH ON THE D2/D784 COAST ROAD TO:

La Pointe du Raz is known as the 'end of a mythical world', this long narrow, rocky outcrop stands 70m above the water and stretches into the sea as a chain of coral reefs.

TAKE D784/ D765 EAST TO:

Douarnenez: Where you can visit the Boat Museum before continuing on the D7 East to:

Locronan: This pretty village is characterised by its unique architectural style, with cobbled streets, renaissance dwellings, the magnificent St Ronan Church, the Bonne Nouvelle Chapel, a wash house and a museum to enjoy.

STAY AT: *The pleasant Municipal aire in* **Rue du Prieure, Locronan,** *is situated in a park-like area with spaces on grass under trees and accessed by a gravel track. The aire is on the west side of the village surrounded by farmland, yet only 250m from the village centre. AireServices borne with 2 drainage platforms either side, and an adjacent toilet block.*

Facilities: *Water •Grey Drain •Black Drain •Toilets*
No. of spaces: *25*
Parking: *6€/24Hrs, Summer only*
Services: *2€ Water*
Opening times: *All year*
GPS Coordinates: *N48.09826   W04.21257*
Alternative: *Camping Locronan, Rue de la Tromenie, 29180 Locronan Open: 02/04 – 30/09*

Top: Nantes   Middle: Pont Aven by Moreau   Bottom: Quimper by Falk Koop

BRITTANY TOUR 8
THE MOST BEAUTIFUL TOWNS & VILLAGES – 8 DAYS

Brittany is a region with very picturesque scenery and has several villages classed as the 'Most Beautiful Villages in France' as well as some towns that are classed as a 'Petit Cite de Caractere.' This 8-Day Tour starts at Mont St Michel before heading into Brittany, visiting St Suliac, Dinan, Moncontour and Paimpol. Continuing west, the tour stops at St Renan, Locronan, Pont Aven and Josselin, before ending at Rochefort en Terre.

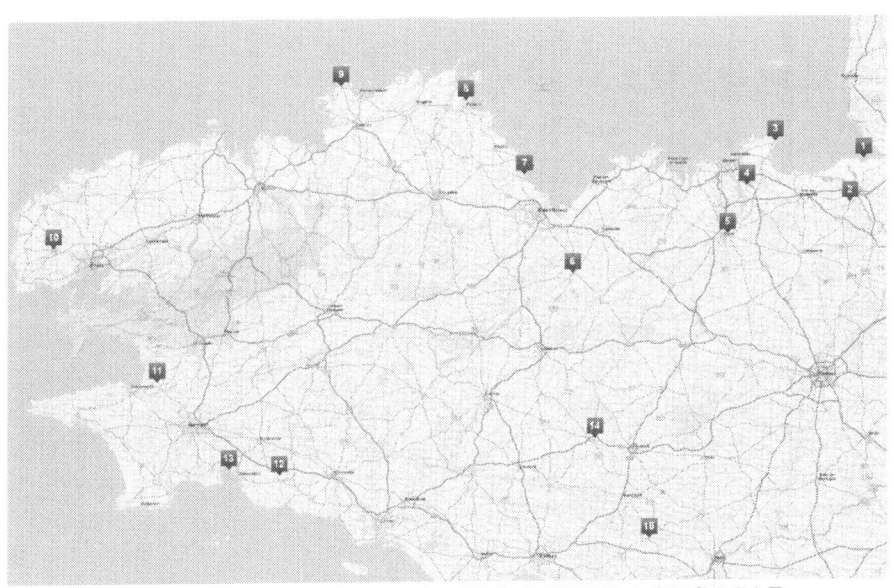

MOST BEAUTIFUL TOWNS & VILLAGES MAP

KEY TO MAP:

1) Mont St Michel
2) Fougeres
3) Cancale
4) St Suliac
5) Dinan
6) Moncontour
7) Binic
8) Paimpol
9) Tregastel
10) St Renan
11) Locronan
12) Pont Aven
13) Concarneau
14) Josselin
15) Rochefort en Terre

DAY 1
Mont St Michel

STAY AT: *the large purpose-built private aire on **Route Mont St Michel** in **Mont St Michel**, with 190 level spaces (each is 100 sq m, all with 10A hook ups and free wifi) on tarmac; rows are separated by grass strips and lit at night but have no shade. The aire is about 2kms from the departure point of the shuttle buses for Mont St Michel (so about 4kms from the Mont). There is a restaurant and boulangerie adjacent, with shops in the village as well as a cycle hire depot. AireServices borne with drainage platform.*

Facilities: *Water•Grey Drain•Black Drain•Electric*
No. of spaces: *190*
Parking: *13-18€/24hrs*
Services: *Incl.*
Opening times: *All year*
GPS Coordinates: *N48.61383   W01.50142*
Alternative: *Camping Mont St Michel, La Caserne, Mont St Michel Open: 30/03 – 01/11*

Mont-St-Michel is not in Brittany, but being one of the most beautiful towns in France and so close, it is a good place to start this tour. Classified as a World Heritage Area by UNESCO, Mont St Michel is a medieval fortified town standing proudly in the middle of the vast mud flats of the bay of Mont-Saint-Michel, which boasts the strongest tides in Europe. The town has many fine old buildings, 3 museums, tourist shops, restaurants, an Abbey with its cloister garden - "The Wonder of the Western World" - as well as a light display show. A visit to the town and Abbey takes 2-3 hours.

TAKE D776/ D975 SOUTH & D155 EAST TO:

Fougeres, a "Town of Art and History," possesses the oldest medieval fortress in Europe, a well preserved and imposing building that dominates the town and is one of the fortresses of the Brittany Marches that hosts concerts and outdoor displays in the summer. The picturesque streets of the medieval quarter have half-timbered houses, the oldest belfry in Brittany, mansions with grand facades, rich religious buildings and wash-houses. The town museum, located in an ancient dwelling, displays impressionist paintings, whilst there are colourful public gardens in the lower town and a good weekly market held here on Saturday mornings.

TAKE D155 NORTH-WEST & D76 TO:

Cancale

STAY AT: *The Municipal Aire in* **Cancale** *in* **Rue Ville Ballet***, is sited in a large gravel parking area, with plenty of available spaces on grass but not much shade. Parking is close (½ km) to the old port, whilst the aire has two AireServices bornes, platform drainage and lighting at night. A nice, well managed location sited above the Old Port, with good walks and a footpath down through to the port, its shops and restaurants.*

Facilities: *Water•Grey Drain•Black Drain*
No. of spaces: *80*
Parking: *10€/24Hrs (Free in winter)*
Services: *3.5€ Water*
Opening times: *All year*
GPS Coordinates: *N48.67017   W01.86591*
Alternative: *Camping Grouin, Ave Cote d'Emeraude, 35260 Cancale Open: 05/03 – 19/10*

DAY 2

TAKE D76/ D29 SOUTH & D7 WEST TO:

St Suliac offers a panoramic viewpoint of the Rance estuary, and for a long time it was a village of trawler men who fished off Newfoundland. In the narrow streets there are magnificent houses, a marvellous church, a tide mill, old salt marshes and a standing stone, all set in an unspoilt location.

TAKE D7/ D74 SOUTH & D795 WEST TO:

Dinan is a medieval citadel encircled by ramparts that tower over the Rance valley and are amongst the most important and oldest fortifications North of the Loire. One of the oldest medieval towns in Brittany, Dinan has the Basilica of Saint-Sauveur, with its four styles of architecture and a 15th C Belfry, plus the Convent of the Cordeliers and the Saint-Malo church. There are also many shopping streets lined with half-timbered houses, with the port area and buildings along Jerzual Street being particularly attractive. A large market is held on Thursday mornings in the town.

TAKE D12 SOUTH TO:

Lehon

STAY AT: *The Municipal Aire in* **Lehon** *in* **Rue de Port** *is located on the southern edge of Dinan, on the western side of the small village of Lehon, close to the river. Situated in the large tarmac parking area outside the Tennis Club, it offers half a dozen level spaces (with shade*

in places) and is lit at night. Artisanal service point with drainage grid. The aire is close to the Abbey of Lehon, as well as the chateau. A boulangerie, restaurant and bar can be found nearby, as well as a swimming pool.
Facilities: Water•Grey Drain•Black Drain
No. of spaces: 6
Parking: Free
Services: Free
Opening times: All year
GPS Coordinates: N48.44195   W02.04262
Alternative: Camping Municipal, Rue Chateaubriand, 22100 Dinan Open: 01/06 – 30/09

DAY 3
TAKE DN176 & N12 WEST TO LAMBALLE & D768 SOUTH TO:
Moncontour: Situated 25 kms south of Saint-Brieuc, is a medieval village that has retained the imposing 13th C ramparts that protected this ancient capital of the region. Known prior to the Industrial Revolution for its sailcloth production, Moncontour exported as far away as the Indies - a flourishing period that has left a rich heritage of beautiful houses, the Town hall and St Mathurin's church. The village Museum is devoted to the French Revolution, as well as having an exhibition of costumes.

TAKE D765/ N12 & D786 NORTH TO:
Binic
STAY AT: the Municipal aire in **Binic**, located in **Rue de l'Ic,** just off the **D786,** about ½ km west of the town. This large gravel parking area is bordered by trees and hedges, offering shade in places, and has some lighting at night. The aire is on the edge of town, a short walk from the nearby countryside. Artisanal service point with drainage grid. Free wifi is available at the Office de Tourisme.
Facilities: Water•Grey Drain•Black Drain•Rubbish
No. of spaces: 25
Parking: Free
Services: Free
Opening times: All year
GPS Coordinates: N48.60083   W02.83500
Alternative: Camping Les Fauvettes, Rue des Fauvettes, 22520 Binic Open: 31/03 – 30/09

Binic : Sheltered by a jetty, this delightful little fishing and yachting harbour is always bustling with life. Binic is a pleasant little port with a nice beach, swimming pool, museum, a good selection of shops, eating places and a SuperU supermarket. An excellent market is held on the quay on Thursday mornings.

DAY 4
CONTINUE ON D786 NORTH TO:

Paimpol is a charming port, having an historic centre with ancient ship owners' houses, and many shops, galleries and art workshops. Nearby is the Maritime Abbey of Beauport, founded in 1202, and the Chateau de Roche-Jagu, on the edge of the Trieux estuary. The largest market of the region is held in the town on Tuesday mornings.

CONTINUE ON D786 & D6/ D788 WEST TO:

Tregastel

STAY AT: *The Municipal aire in* **Tregastel** *is situated in* **Rue Poul Palud***, in a large tarmac car park next to the tennis courts, on the coast at Tregastel-Plage. The aire, in quite a pleasant position but having little shade, is about 100m from the beaches, 100m from the Super U supermarket and approximately 1km from the centre of Tregastel-Plage. There is an artisanal service point and a large platform drain.*

Facilities: *Water•Grey Drain•Black Drain*
No. of spaces: *35*
Parking: *4-8€/24 Hrs*
Services: *Free*
Opening times: *All year*
GPS Coordinates: *N48.82441   W03.49858*
Alternative: *Camping Tourony, Rue Poul Palud, 22730 Tregastel Open: 01/04 – 27/09*

DAY 5
TAKE D11 SOUTH & D786 & N12 WEST TO BREST & D67 TO:

St Renan, a small town founded in 500AD by the hermit St Ronan, soon became an important centre for its court and its market, which led to the building of many fine houses and market halls. The medieval town was important for its nearby tin mines and is still a lively location today, with a 300-stall market on Saturdays, although it is now more popular with walkers, fisherman and cyclists.

TAKE D5 SOUTH TO BREST & N165 SOUTH TO CHATEULIN, THEN D7 WEST TO:

Locronan gets its name from Saint Ronan, the hermit who lived here in the 5th C. Thanks to the sailcloth industry, Locronan reached its peak in the 16th C, with one of its biggest customers being the East India Company. The granite village has been wonderfully preserved and still boasts some very fine Renaissance houses, the magnificent 15th C church of St Ronan and two Chapels. The village also possesses an Art and History museum, displaying fine paintings, engravings, earthenware and weaving artefacts.

*<u>STAY AT:</u> The pleasant Municipal aire in **Rue du Prieure, Locronan** is situated in a park-like area with spaces on grass under trees, accessed by a gravel track. Surrounded by farmland on the west side of the village, the aire is only 250m from the village centre. AireServices borne with 2 drainage platforms either side and an adjacent toilet block.*

Facilities: *Water•Grey Drain•Black Drain•Toilets*
No. of spaces: *25*
Parking: *6€/24Hrs, Summer only*
Services: *2€ Water*
Opening times: *All year*
GPS Coordinates: *N48.09826   W04.21257*
Alternative: *Camping Locronan, Rue de la Tromenie, 29180 Locronan Open: 02/04 – 30/09*

DAY 6
TAKE D63/ D39 SOUTH & N165 WEST TO JCN 50 & D24 TO:
Pont Aven: The School of Pont-Aven Artists (centred around Paul Gauguin) was born in this small town in southern Finistère, and consequently the town features a museum of Fine Arts, as well as over 60 galleries and artists' studios. Remnants of 14 mills line the River Aven (as do wash houses, narrow alleys and granite houses), whilst the town is a popular shopping place with numerous small boutiques, gift shops and a varied selection of eating places.

TAKE D783 WEST TO:
Concarneau
*<u>STAY AT:</u> the Municipal aire in **Rue de la Gare, Concarneau**, 500m from the town centre/shops and 300m from the Port. The aire sits in a very large tarmac car park next to the old railway station, with marked spaces and lighting, but little shade. AireServices borne with drainage grid is easily accessible.*
Facilities: *Water•Grey Drain•Black Drain•Electric•Toilets*

No. of spaces: 46
Parking: 6€/24Hrs, Free in winter
Services: 4€ Electric
Opening times: All year
GPS Coordinates: N47.87859   W03.92054
Alternative: Camping Les Sables Blancs, Ave du Dorlet, 29900 Concarneau Open: 01/04 – 31/10

DAY 7
TAKE N165 & N24 WEST TO:
Josselin is an historic town (Petit Cite de Caractere) sitting alongside the Oust canal, with many 16th C half-timbered buildings and a Basilique with beautiful 15th C stained glass windows to appreciate. Its chateau offers a surprising contrast between its exterior, which is a remainder of the former medieval fortress, and its Renaissance-style, sculpted granite interior. The museum, in the former stables of the castle, houses the family collection of dolls.

STAY AT: *the Municipal aire in* **Josselin,** *located in* **Place St Martin,** *in a very large tarmac parking area within a short walk of the town centre (150m). The parking has some shade around the sides and has some adjacent grass areas. There is an AireServices service point with drainage grid, and toilets nearby. Shops, cafes and 2 supermarkets (Carrefour and Super U) can be found in the town, and a weekly market is held on Saturdays.*

Facilities: Water •Grey Drain •Black Drain •Toilets
No. of spaces: 50
Parking: Free
Services: 2€ Water
Opening times: All year
GPS Coordinates: N47.95611   W02.54958
Alternative: Domaine de Kerelly, Bas de la Lande, 56120 Josselin Open: 30/03 – 28/09

DAY 8
TAKE D4/ D764 SOUTH & D774 TO:
Rochefort en Terre lies 35 kms East of Vannes, on a rocky hill surrounding the valley of Gueuzon. The ancient stone construction of this little Breton village gives it a picturesque appearance despite the different architectural styles of half-timbered houses, gothic monuments, Renaissance hotels and 19th C architecture. Highlights of

this village are the Chateau and its gardens, as well as the Collegiate Church.

STAY AT: *the Parking in* **Rochefort**, *located in* **Rue de Souvenir (D21),** *in a very large gravel parking area within a short walk of the town centre (150m). The parking has good shade around the sides, with adjacent large grass areas, but has no services, apart from rubbish bins. There are a couple of shops (boulangerie and tabac), cafes and restaurants in the village.*
Facilities: *Rubbish bins*
No. of spaces: *30*
Parking: *5€/24 Hrs*
Services: *None*
Opening times: *All year*
GPS Coordinates: *N47.69921   W02.33368*
Alternative: *Camping Gre des Vents, Chemin de Bogeais, 56220 Rochefort   Open: 30/03 – 30/09*

Mont St Michel by Usan

Dinan

Pont Aven by Moreau

Josselin by Jolivet

Josselin aire

BURGUNDY TOUR 9
CATHEDRALS & CHURCHES - 4 DAYS

This 4-Day Tour lets you enjoy some of the finest Gothic Churches and Cathedrals in northern Burgundy. The Cistercians used stone, a building material typical of the Yonne area, in combination with the hugely important architectural invention of the pointed, "Gothic" arch, to give Gothic Art in Burgundy the splendour we see today. In addition, the stained glass workers and the sculptors of Ile-de-France, Burgundy and Flanders have all added their own personal touches to these impressive buildings.

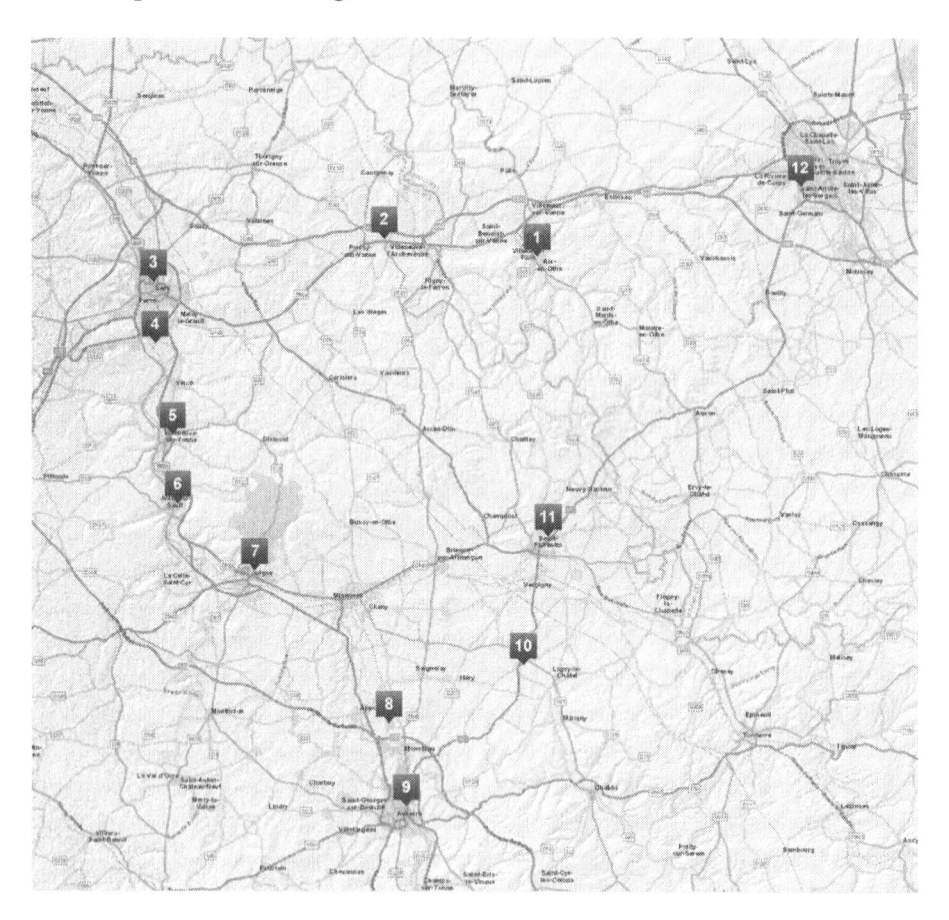

CATHEDRALS & CHURCHES MAP

KEY TO MAP (Left):

1) Aix en Othe	2) Villeneuve l'Archeveque
3) Sens	4) Gron
5) Villeneuve-sur-Yonne	6) St Julien du Sault
7) Joigny	8) Gurgy
9) Auxerre	10) Pontigny
11) St Florentin	12) Troyes

DAY 1
Aix en Othe

STAY AT: *the private aire at* **Rue du Moulin a Tan** *in* **Aix en Othe**. *The aire is not signposted in the village, but can be found on the northern side of this large village in a rural location next to a small river, in the grounds of a former mill. The aire is about 600m from the village centre. There are half a dozen level spaces on grass, with shade, accessed by a gravel drive. Equipment includes picnic tables, showers, laundrette, kitchenette, wifi, toilets and washing up sinks. Electric hook up is available for an extra charge. Artisanal service point and drainage grid with easy access. There is a reasonable range of shops in the village.*

Facilities: *Water•Grey Drain•Black Drain•Toilets•Wifi*
No. of spaces: *6*
Parking: *6€/24 Hrs*
Services: *2.5€ Electric*
Opening times: *01/04 – 15/10*
GPS Coordinates: *N48.22901   E03.72302*
Alternative: *Ferme des Hautes Frenes, D111, 10130 Eaux-Puiseaux*
Open: All year

TAKE D660 WEST TO:

Villeneuve l'Archeveque: The town is laid out in a diamond pattern characteristic of new towns built in the Middle Ages. At the centre of the town, surrounded by a group of old buildings, is the Gothic-style Church dating from the 13th C. Its portals are especially remarkable, as is the superb 16th C tomb attributed to the Master stonemason from the nearby Vauluisant Abbey.

TAKE D660 28KM WEST TO:

Sens, the former capital of the Gallic Senon tribe, has also been variously a Roman province, a powerful metropolis and an ecclesiastical centre. With this interesting history it's fortunate that it has held onto some outstanding remains of its lively past. The narrow streets house medieval half-timbered buildings, and the beautiful Market hall still holds weekly markets on Monday and Friday. Construction of the first major Gothic Cathedral in France began here around the year 1130; the impressively large Saint-Etienne Cathedral is designed with harmonious lines and benefits from the natural light let into the building through its beautiful 13th C windows. The treasury, which is now attached to the Musée de Sens, is one of the richest in Europe, containing ivory reliquary, plated ornaments, old fabrics, gold and silk altar facings, sumptuous tapestries, and 16th century objects from Flemish workshops.

TAKE D1060 WEST TO:
Gron
STAY AT: *The Municipal aire on* **Rue des Petits Pres** *in* **Gron** *is located on the western side of this small rural village. It is a small tarmac car park in a residential area next to a park, with half a dozen spaces available. There is no shade here, and no lighting apart from street lighting. It is a 400m walk to the centre of the village with its small range of shops (boulangerie, butcher, Bar-Tabac, pharmacy and Poste/news). There is a Euro Relais borne with drainage grid and adjacent toilets.*
Facilities: *Water•Grey Drain•Black Drain•Toilets*
No. of spaces: *6*
Parking: *Free*
Services: *Free*
Opening times: *All year*
GPS Coordinates: *N48.15996   E03.25658*
Alternative: *Camping Entre Deux Vannes, Ave de Senigallia, 89100 Sens Open: 15/05 – 15/09*

DAY 2
TAKE D72 & D606 15KM SOUTH TO:
Villeneuve-sur-Yonne: This walled town, constructed by King Louis VII on the border of his estate in 1163, has preserved the regular pattern and fortified doors typical of the period, with the surrounding moat making ideal gardens and the beautiful 17th C houses reflecting the town's prosperous past that is rooted in trade. From the River Yonne, you can walk uphill to Our Lady of the Assumption Church to admire its Renaissance façade and vast, well-lit nave that is a wonderful example of architectural unity. There are also windows and statues that pay testimony to the Troyes school of sculpture that

thrived in the 16th C. Many local walking and cycling routes start in the town.

TAKE D3 8KM SOUTH TO:

St Julien-du-Sault: The Archbishop of Sens' former chapel, erected in the 12th C on a hill overlooking the Yonne Valley, gave its name to the town that still exists today. At the centre of the town, the restored former 13th C collegiate church of Saint-Pierre offers an outstanding collection of 13th and 16th C stained-glass windows.

TAKE D3/ D959 SOUTH TO:

Joigny: On the edge of Othe Forest, this old riverside town is the ideal departure point for a trip on the Burgundy canal and is home to the celebrated Côte Saint-Jacques vineyard. There are 3 ancient quarters in the town, populated with timber-framed houses and cobbled streets, whilst near to the former Château des Gondi is the Saint-Jean church, which features a superb stone barrel arch in the Renaissance style.

TAKE D606/ N6 SOUTH TO:

Gurgy

STAY AT: *The Municipal aire on* **Chemin de Halage in Gurgy,** *is in a nice location on the banks of the River Yonne at the southern edge of this village, backing onto open farmland. Parking is on gravel/grass, with some trees providing shade, and is 400m from the centre of the village and its shops (boulangerie, grocer, Bar-Tabac, pharmacy and restaurant). A Raclet borne with drainage grid and electric hook-ups (but only 12 ehu's for 35 spaces).*

Facilities: Water •Grey Drain •Black Drain •Electric
No. of spaces: *35*
Parking: *8€/24 Hrs   (Council official collects)*
Services: *Incl.*
Opening times: *All year*
GPS Coordinates: *N47.86412   E03.55479*
Alternative: *Camping Municipal, Quai d'Epizy, 89300 Joigny Open: 15/04 – 30/09*

DAY 3

TAKE D606/ N6 SOUTH TO:

Auxerre: From one of the most splendid urban panoramas in France, on the right bank of the Yonne river, visitors can see the three imposing churches around the old town. The 13th C Saint-Etienne Cathedral is a masterpiece of Gothic art, modest in size but very elegant, it was the fifth church built on this outstanding urban site overlooking the Yonne River. The crypt and the chapel, decorated with frescoes (including an extremely rare 11th C representation of Christ on horseback), are remains of the 11th C church. Construction of the Cathedral began in 1215, took three centuries to build and features a large treasury, with particularly interesting 13th C windows. Next to the Cathedral is a former 12th C Abbey.

TAKE N77 NORTH 20KM TO:
Pontigny: Founded in 1114, Pontigny Abbey underwent rapid growth. The abbey-church is an imposing white stone structure offering the earliest example of the Gothic style in Burgundy, and is also the largest Cistercian church in existence in France. Three exiled archbishops from Canterbury, including Thomas Becket, took refuge there in the 13th C. Surrounding the Abbey are 3 water mills, a washhouse and a hay barn.

<u>***STAY AT:***</u> *the **Municipal aire**, situated on **Rue St Thomas** in **Pontigny**. A pleasant location on the northern side of this small rural village, 200m from the centre, where there are 13 designated parking spaces on tarmac, separated by low shrubs (with little shade) and lit at night. There is an Urba Flux service point with a large drainage platform and toilets adjacent, whilst access to the aire is via an automatic barrier operated by a credit card. This is a well laid out, modern aire, with boulangerie, grocer, bar/tabac and 2 restaurants available in the village.*

Facilities: *Water•Grey Drain•Black Drain•Electric•Toilets*
No. of spaces: *13*
Parking: *7€/24 Hrs*
Services: *3€ Water or Electric*
Opening times: *All year*
GPS Coordinates: *N 47.91085   E 03.70971*
Alternative: *Camping Municipal, D91, 89144 Ligny-le-Chatel Open: 01/05 – 30/09*

DAY 4
CONTINUE NORTH ON N77 13KM TO:
Saint-Florentin, erected on a hill at the confluence of two rivers, Saint-Florentin is on the border of Burgundy and Champagne. The 15th C Saint-Florentin Church is particularly noteworthy thanks to its rich collection of Renaissance sculptures and its windows, attributed to the Troyes school, depicting scenes from the Creation.

CONTINUE NORTH ON N77 TO:

Troyes: Few other French towns have as much to see as Troyes. The town itself is compact and is ideal for walkers, whilst the Old Town is a network of pedestrian streets, timber framed houses, fine churches and interesting museums. The Basilique is one of the most remarkable in France with its' impressive stained glass, whilst the nearby 13th C Cathedral is a fine example of Gothic architecture. There are two museums; the Modern Art museum, containing paintings and Art Deco glassware, and the St Loup museum, with a superb collection of paintings, archaeological finds, stuffed birds and medieval statues.

STAY AT: *the private Aire at* ***Rue du Moulin a Tan*** *in* ***Aix en Othe*** *or Camping de Troyes, Rue Roger Salengro, 10150 Pont Ste Marie Open: 01/04 – 15/10*

Joigny by Finot

Auxerre by By Finot

Above: Troyes by ParDXR

Right: Villeneuve sur Yonne by Goglins

Below: Aire at Gron

BURGUNDY TOUR 10
CHATEAUX AROUND AUXERRE – 5 DAYS

This 5-Day Tour of the Tonnerre region in Northern Burgundy visits some of the most prestigious historic sites in the region, which with their beautiful white stone and the particular quality of light it reflects, are often also used as venues for exhibitions. Contemporary art is displayed in the Renaissance chateau in the superb medieval village of Noyers, as well as in the village of Tanlay and at Quincy Abbey.

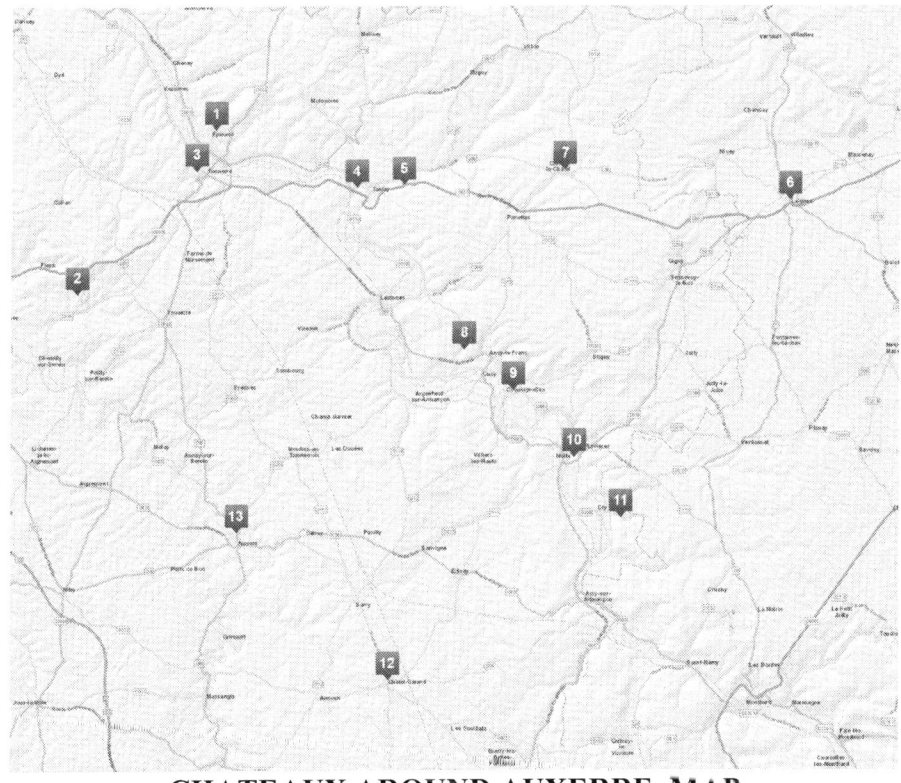

CHATEAUX AROUND AUXERRE MAP

KEY TO MAP:
- 1) Epineuil
- 2) Beru
- 3) Tonnere
- 4) Tanlay
- 5) Commissey
- 6) Laignes
- 7) Cruzy le Chatel
- 8) Ancy le Franc
- 9) Chassignelles
- 10) Nuits sur Armancon
- 11) Cry
- 12) Chatel Gerard
- 13) Noyers-sur-Serein

DAY 1
Epineuil

STAY AT: *The Municipal aire in* **Rue des Relichiens, Epineuil**, *is located on the Eastern edge of this small rural village, in a small grass parking area. Set in a residential area, the aire offers half a dozen spaces with some shade provided by trees, has picnic tables adjacent, and is lit by street lighting. It is 200m to the centre of the village with its small range of shops. An Aireservices borne with drainage platform.*

Facilities: *Water•Grey Drain•Black Drain*
No. of spaces: *6*
Parking: *Free*
Services: *Free (Jetons from shops)*
Opening times: *All year*
GPS Coordinates: *N47.87356   E03.98638*
Alternative: *Camping Municipal, Off Ave A. Briand, 89700 Tonnerre*
Open: 01/04 – 15/10

TAKE D188 WEST TO TONNERRE & D965 WEST 9KM TO:

Château de Béru: Belonging to the Counts of Béru since the 16th C, this beautiful residence has a splendid view over the Chablis vineyards. On the premises are a rare sun and moon dial from the 15th C, a 12th C door and tower, and a 1,000 hole dovecote dating from the 13th C. The estate also produces fine Clos-Béru Chablis wines.

TAKE D965 EAST 9KM BACK TO:

Tonnerre: The tour of Fontenilles Hospital or the Hôtel-Dieu (General hospital) begins with the main sick ward where you can see outstanding timber framework, an astronomical instrument engraved in the floor, a royal mausoleum and tomb, a 14th C sculpture of the Virgin and Child, and a tomb from the 15th C. The museum is contained in a 17th C building adjoining the main sick ward where there are rooms dedicated to displays on various themes; the religious art room, the Hospital from the 13th to the 19th C, the Hôtel-Dieu foundation, a reconstruction of an operating theatre from the early 20th C and a sick room from 1850.

STAY AT: *the Municipal aire in* **Rue des Relichiens, Epineuil**, *or Camping Municipal, Off Ave A. Briand, 89700 Tonnerre*

DAY 2
CONTINUE EAST 11KM ON D965 TO:

Tanlay: Surrounded by moats and set in a splendid park, the Château de Tanlay is one of Burgundy's finest Renaissance residences. Built in the 16th C, it was an important meeting place for the Huguenot leaders during the Religious Wars. Completion of the sumptuous interior décor, the trompe-l'œil room and the Tour de la Ligue, with its fabulous frescoes, were carried out under the ownership of the Marquis de Tanlay's family from 1705, and are particularly worth seeing. You can also walk around the park, designed by the famous French architect Le Muet, and along his 525 m long canal which is enhanced by a Renaissance monument.

TAKE MINOR ROAD 2KM EAST TO:

Commissey: Our Lady of Quincy Abbey, a daughter Abbey of Pontigny Abbey, was founded in 1133 in a sheltered valley and has conserved its authentic roots. It boasts a hostelry, a section of monastic buildings dating from the 12th C, and the Renaissance-style abbey lodgings, all of which testify to the sobriety of Cistercian art. There is also a boxwood maze by the artist Conrad Loder, and from June to September, a contemporary art exhibition is put on by the Art Centre of l'Yonne.

CONTINUE EAST ON D965 TO:

Laignes

<u>**STAY AT:**</u> *The Municipal aire in* **Chemin du Moulin Neuf in Laignes** *is pleasantly situated in a rural setting next to the river This well arranged aire has tree-shaded pitches on grass accessed by a gravel track; note that the ground is liable to become muddy in wet weather. The aire is about 1km from the town centre and its shops. Artisanal service point and rubbish bins.*

Facilities: *Water•Grey Drain•Black Drain*
No. of spaces: *6*
Parking: *Free*
Services: *Free*
Opening times: *All year*
GPS Coordinates: *N47.84849   E04.36133*
Alternative: *Camping Les Grebes, Rue Pont Neuf, 21330 Marcenay Open: 01/05 – 30/09*

<u>**DAY 3**</u>
RETURN ONTO D965 & HEAD WEST TO PIMELLES & THEN D12 NORTH TO:

Cruzy-le-Châtel: The Renaissance Château de Maulnes, overlooks its surroundings of the plateaux of the Tonnerrois and Cruzy-le-Châtel Forest. It is a pentagonal structure, built around a central well and an imposing spiral staircase, that has always been somewhat of a mystery and has generated many legends.

The construction of the Château, undertaken by the Count of Tonnerre between 1566 and 1573, was an ambitious architectural project that seems to have been abandoned before its completion and neglected since the early 18th C, but nonetheless, is classified as an Historic Monument. Acquired by the Department of Yonne, the chateau became the focus of a research programme that provided answers to its enigmatic history and enabled it to be restored to its near-original state.

TAKE D12 14KM SOUTH TO:

Château d'Ancy-le-Franc: A superb example of Renaissance architecture, Château d'Ancy-le-Franc was built around plans drawn by a celebrated architect in the 16th C. The building harbours some of France's rarest treasures, such as wall paintings, panelled ceilings, finely sculpted mouldings, colourful ornaments, remarkable marquetry and harmonious architecture – a journey through five centuries of history. In the summer, the Château also organises concerts. The Tourist Office, contained in the old pottery at the Château, offers an exhibition on the history of this pottery, which was in operation between 1765 and 1807. There are also the results of archaeological digs and a collection of pieces of earthenware produced by local manufacturers between the 18th and 19th C.

TAKE D17 2KM SOUTH TO:

Chassignelles

<u>***STAY AT:***</u> *The parking in* **Le Patis** *in* **Chassignelles**, *is pleasantly situated in a rural setting next to the Canal and the village football pitch, about 200m west of the village centre. There are pitches on gravel accessed by a tarmac track, with shade provided by numerous trees. There are no services in the parking area, but there is a restaurant opposite and a boulangerie in the village.*

Facilities: *Rubbish*
No. of spaces: *4*
Parking: *Free*
Services: *Free*
Opening times: *All year*
GPS Coordinates: *N47.75949 E04.17333*

Alternative: Camping La Graviere, Route de Frangey, 89160 Lezinnes
Open: 01/04 – 05/10
DAY 4
TAKE D905 10KM SOUTH TO:
Château de Nuits-sur-Armançon: This Renaissance Château, built around 1560, has a fine west façade and was originally protected by a fortified enclosure, whilst the east façade, overlooking the Armançon Valley, is a reminder of the château's military past. The "noble" floor, reserved for the richer families, has preserved its 18th C panelling and 16th C fireplaces with emblazoned plaques, whilst outside there is a 6-ha park with ancient trees and 17th C outbuildings.
TAKE D210 2KM EAST TO:
Cry: The beautiful white stone extracted from the Ravières quarries is known as marcasite and has been used since the 10th C for the construction of the large Cistercian abbeys of Pontigny and Fontenay in Burgundy, for the construction of the Basilica in Vézelay, and the Church in Saulieu. In the second half of the 19th C, the construction of the Burgundy Canal enabled transport of the stone for the construction of countless Parisian monuments. Today the stone is mainly used for its aesthetic properties and is shipped around the world for the construction of major contemporary projects.
TAKE D905 SOUTH TO ROUGEMONT (9KM) & D68 WEST TO:
Châtel-Gérard: At the heart of Châtel-Gérard Forest, in the middle of a glade cleared by monks in the 13th C and cultivated ever since, the Vausse Priory appears like a mirage. Founded in 1200, the priory was owned by Val-des-Choues Abbey in Côte d'Or until it was sold as a national property during the French Revolution, after which it housed an earthenware manufacturing concern until 1858. Today, you can visit the 14th C chapel and the fine cloister that encircles a charming priest's garden.
TAKE D101 NORTH & THEN D49 WEST TO:
Noyers-sur-Serein
STAY AT: *the parking in* **Promenade Pre de l'Echelle** *in* **Noyers-sur-Serein**. *This is pleasantly situated in a semi-rural setting next to the river and the village campsite, where there are pitches on grass/gravel accessed by a tarmac track and shade provided by numerous trees. The parking is about 200m south of the village centre. There are no services in the parking area but the village has a small selection of shops and eating-places.*

Facilities: Rubbish bins
No. of spaces: 4
Parking: Free
Services: Free
Opening times: All year
GPS Coordinates: N47.69449   E03.99483
Alternative: Camping Municipal, Promenade Pre de l'Echelle, 89310 Noyers Open: July/August

DAY 5

Noyers-sur-Serein: This medieval village and the site of its old Château are ranked as one of the "Most Beautiful Villages in France" and are magnificently located on a loop of the River Serein. The village has retained its fortified gates, towers, ramparts, half-timbered houses, narrow streets and squares with picture-postcard views. Archaeological, historical and cultural features make the site of this château of Miles de Noyers, a Commander at the Battle of Crecy, a journey through history, and the discovery of a forgotten heritage. The Musée de Noyers houses a collection of more than 100 paintings of naïve art - one of the most beautiful collections of naïve art in France donated by the painter Yankel, in tribute to his father, the painter Kikoïne, who once holidayed here in the 1930's.

STAY AT: *the parking in* **Promenade Pre de l'Echelle** *in* ***Noyers-sur-Serein*** *or the Camping Municipal, Promenade Pre de l'Echelle, 89310 Noyers*

Tanlay by Par Pline

Above: Ancy le Franc by Finot

Left: Noyers sur Serein by Alès

Below: Tonnere by Espirat

BURGUNDY TOUR 11
POTTERIES OF NORTH BURGUNDY – 2 DAYS

This 2-Day Tour retraces the prosperous pottery heritage of this area through its many restored murals, pottery workshops and exhibitions. Forests, clay and ochre lie at the heart of this rural region, something that its inhabitants have long appreciated. Whilst their expert hand craft and the heat of the fire from a plentiful wood supply transformed the clay in their soil into pottery and porcelains, their ochre was perfect for creating colourful frescoes on the walls of their churches and houses.

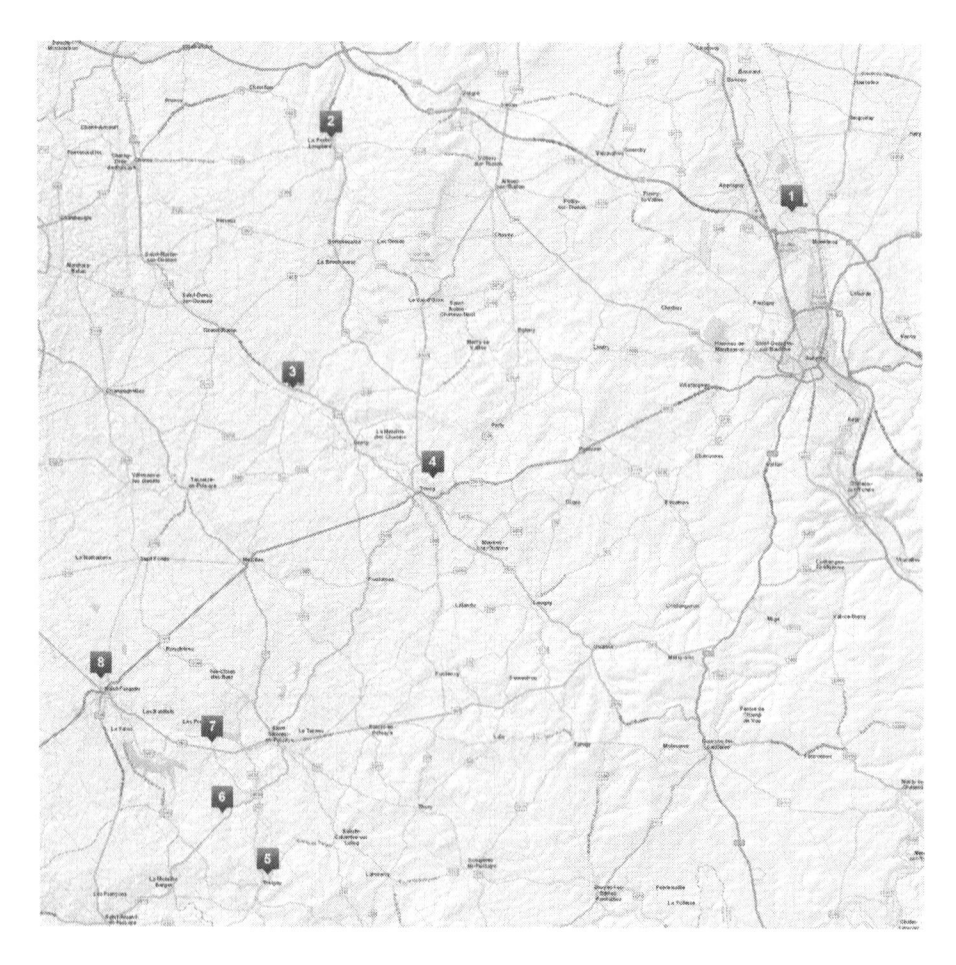

POTTERIES OF NORTH BURGUNDY MAP

KEY TO MAP (Left):

1) Gurgy
3) Villiers-St-Benoit
5) Treigny
7) Moutiers

2) La Ferte Loupiere
4) Toucy
6) Guedelon
8) St Fargeau

DAY 1
Gurgy

STAY AT: *The Municipal aire on* **Chemin de Halage** *in* **Gurgy,** *is in a nice location on the banks of the River Yonne at the southern edge of this village, backing onto open farmland. Parking is on gravel/grass, with some trees providing shade, and is 400m from the centre of the village and its shops (boulangerie, grocer, Bar-Tabac, pharmacy and restaurant). A Raclet borne with drainage grid and electric hook-ups (but only 12 ehu's for 35 spaces).*

Facilities: *Water•Grey Drain•Black Drain•Electric*
No. of spaces: *35*
Parking: *8€/24 Hrs (Council official collects)*
Services: *Incl.*
Opening times: *All year*
GPS Coordinates: *N47.86412   E03.55479*
Alternative: *Camping Les Platanes, Route de la Mothe, 89120 Charny Open : 01/04 – 30/10*

TAKE A6 NORTH TO JCN 18 & D3 SOUTH TO:

La Ferte Loupiere: Saint-Germain Church was built in the late 15th C on the remains of a building dating from the 12th C, of which the portal and the nave pillars still remain. The church offers a rare collection of late 15th C wall paintings that feature the "three dead and the three living", a theme regularly featured in the churches in Puisaye. There is also an immense 'Danse Macabre' that shows, over a length of nearly 25 m, a procession of mortals escorted by Death. Having this rare 'Danse Macabre', of which only 6 exist in France, and the quality of its work, make the church of La Ferté one of the major attractions in the region.

TAKE D3 SOUTH 11KM & D99 WEST TO:

Villiers-St-Benoit: The Museum of Art and History, has rich collections of utility stoneware, 15th C Puisaye blue stoneware and 18th C earthenware. The Museum also pays tribute to the history of the area, especially the exploitation of sandstone and ochre.

TAKE D950 SOUTH TO:
Toucy: This beautiful 17th C private mansion is the venue for one-off exhibitions of ceramic pieces all year long, a tribute to the grand pottery tradition in Puisaye.

TAKE D955 SOUTH 11KM TO ST SAUVEUR & THEN D955/ D66 SOUTH TO:
Treigny
STAY AT: *The Municipal aire in* **Rue Champs de Foire, Treigny**, *is located on the western side of this small rural village, next to the cemetery in a large, level gravel parking area. It is only 200m from the village centre but there is little shade here and no lighting at night. Artisanal service point with large drainage platform and WC's nearby. Boulangerie, supermarket and café in village.*
Facilities: *Water•Grey Drain•Black Drain•Toilets*
No. of spaces: *10*
Parking: *Free*
Services: *Free*
Opening times: *All year*
GPS Coordinates: *N47.54982   E03.18169*
Alternative: *Camping Municipal, Rue de la Mairie, 89520 Saints Open: 01/04 – 30/10*

DAY 2
Treigny: The medieval fortress of Chateau de Ratilly, decorated in the Renaissance style, consists of four corner towers and two further towers defending the bridge that is overlooked by a keep dating from the early 17th C. Inside can be found a traditional stoneware workshop and arts centre, with a permanent exhibition of 16th C Puisaye stoneware. Treigny Priory is the venue of the local Ceramic Artists Association and is where they showcase their original pieces and those of guests. In the summer, the programme features technical demonstrations, conferences and other special events.

TAKE MINOR ROAD WEST TO:
Guedelon: Not really pottery related, but the Chateau of Guedelon is remarkable in so far as it was only started 10 years ago - being built by stonemasons and carpenters using only medieval building techniques. Now part finished, with imposing sandstone walls that rise up out of the red Burgundy soil, it's a living history lesson and a successful tourism project. Each year, 250,000 visitors admire the work of

Guedelon's stonecutters, carpenters, potters, rope-makers and blacksmiths.

RETURN NORTH ON D955 TO:
Moutiers: Saint-Pierre Church dates from the 12th C, with a single nave behind a 13th C porch enclosed by a stone screen wall. The scale and style of the wall paintings inside make this a rare collection. Nearby, the La Bâtisse Pottery is owned by one of the oldest pottery dynasties in Puisaye, and this authentic and touching site offers the visitor a chance to discover the heart and soul of an old pottery in action. In the workshop, today's potters continue their ancestral techniques; the kneading of the earth, operating the dowel lathe, turning-engines, on-floor drying, sprinkling, and traditional baking in the wood-fired oven. The earthenware oven from 1930 and the large insulated oven from the 18th C, used for baking the salt and ash glazed stoneware, are the last remaining witnesses of a glorious past. There is a permanent exhibition of blue stoneware from Puisaye that was used at the tables of the high and powerful lords of the 16th C.

TAKE D85 WEST TO:
St Fargeau
STAY AT: *the Municipal aire in* **Rue Lavau, St Fargeau,** *next to the D965 through town. The aire is in a medium-sized tarmac car park in the centre of town, bordered by mature trees, and is close to the shops (150m) and the famous chateau (200m), with its' large gardens being directly behind the aire. Artisanal borne with drainage platform. A very pretty little village with an excellent chateau to visit, plus its' "Spectacle Historique" pageants (with 600 actors involved) are worth seeing on Friday and Saturday nights in the summer (14/7 – 25/8), but note that parking is not allowed here at these times. There is a supermarket, shops and restaurants in town.*
Facilities: *Water •Grey Drain •Black Drain •Toilets*
No. of spaces: *12*
Parking: *Free*
Services: *Free*
Opening times: *All year*
GPS Coordinates: *N47.64015   E03.07017*
Alternative: *Camping Municipal, Lac du Bourdon, 89170 Saint Fargeau Open: 15/04 – 30/09*

St Fargeau Chateau by Finot

Gurgy by Villafruela

Guedelon Chateau by Anderson

Aire at Gurgy

BURGUNDY TOUR 12
ABBEYS AROUND AUXERRE – 3 DAYS

The community of the Cistercian Order, founded in 1114 by Robert de Molesmes, reached its peak in the 12th C with a total of 700 abbeys aspiring to the ideal of absolute poverty and withdrawal from the world. This 3-Day Tour visits Pontigny Abbey, one of the most important treasures bequeathed to us by this medieval Christian order, as well as Fontenay, the secret abbeys of Quincy and Reigny, and the charming Vausse Priory.

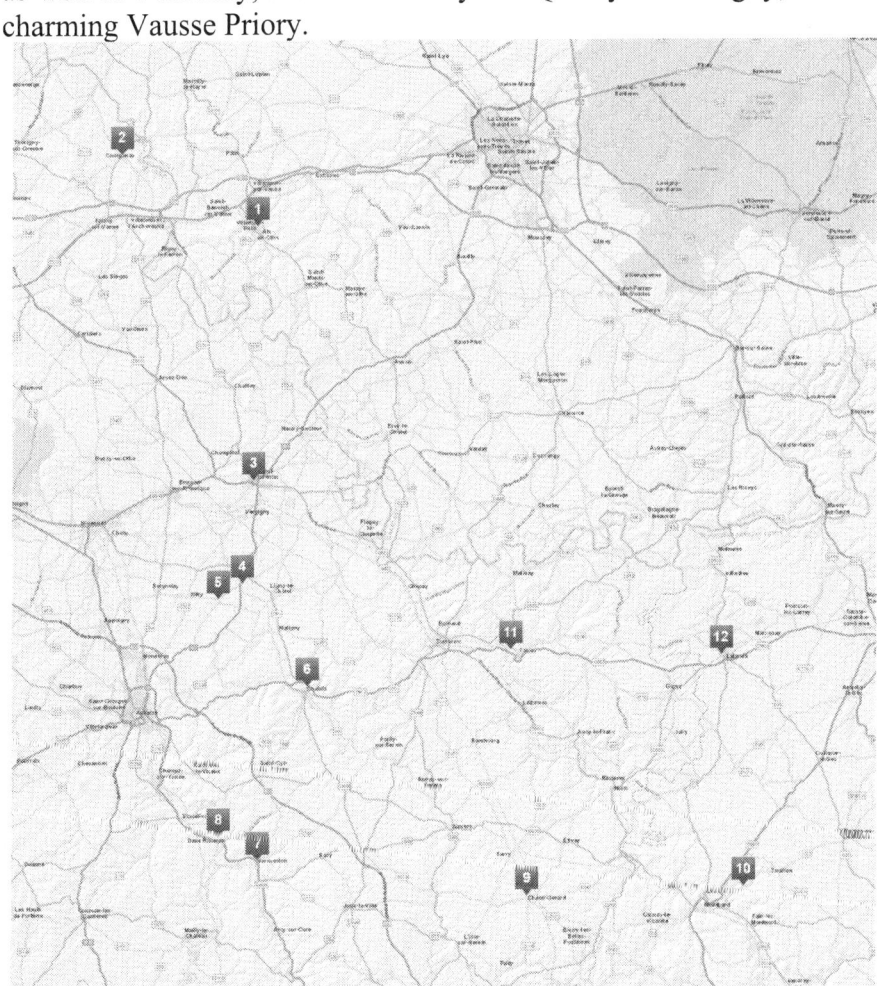

ABBEYS AROUND AUXERRE MAP

KEY TO MAP (Above):
1) Aix en Othe   2) Courgenay   3) St Florentin   4) Pontigny   5) Venouse
6) Chablis   7) Vermenton   8) Cravant   9) Chatel Gerard
10) Fontenay   11) Commissey   12) Laignes

DAY 1
Aix en Othe

STAY AT: *the private Aire at* **Rue du Moulin a Tan** *in* **Aix en Othe**. *The aire is not signposted in the village, but can be found on the northern side of this large village in a rural location next to a small river in the grounds of a former mill. The aire, about 600m from the village centre, offers half a dozen level spaces on grass with shade, accessed by a gravel drive. The site includes picnic tables, showers, laundrette, kitchenette, wifi, toilets and washing up sinks. Electric hook up available for an extra charge. Artisanal service point and drainage grid with easy access. There is a reasonable range of shops in the village*

Facilities: *Water •Grey Drain •Black Drain •Toilets •Wifi*
No. of spaces: *6*
Parking: *6€/24 Hrs*
Services: *2.5€ Electric*
Opening times: *01/04 – 15/10*
GPS Coordinates: *N48.22901   E03.72302*
Alternative: *Ferme des Hautes Frenes, D111, 10130 Eaux-Puiseaux*
Open: All year

TAKE D660 WEST & D79 NORTH TO:
Courgenay: Vauluisant Abbey, founded in 1127, is located between the forests of Othe and Lancy, on the border with Burgundy and Champagne. It was plundered and destroyed several times during the Hundred Years' War, but was fully restored in the 16th C. The buildings that are standing today, scattered around the magnificent park, were built or entirely renovated in this period - including the portals, tithe barn, dovecotes, mill, chapel, guest houses and the Francis I building. The château was converted from the original monastic building.

TAKE D84 SOUTH ONTO D660 & HEAD WEST 14KM, THEN TAKE D905 SOUTH TO:
Saint Florentin: Crécy Barn, acquired in 1138 by the monks of Pontigny, has always maintained its agricultural roots and despite many trials and tribulations it has survived the centuries (together with two buildings that date from the Middle Ages). The chapel – quite rare for a Cistercian barn – stands to the east, with its structure and the shape of the windows most likely dating from the late 12th C, while its beautiful roof framework, in the form of an upside-down ship's hull, is

a remnant from the 15th C. The second, much larger building stands north to south and features bays characteristic of the Gothic period. Both buildings now form part of the Crécy farm, along with other buildings constructed later.

TAKE N77 11KM SOUTH TO:

Pontigny Abbey is one of the most beautiful examples of a Cistercian church in France, and rarely have the finesse, purity and fervour of Cistercian architecture reached such heights of perfection. A daughter abbey of Cîteaux Abbey, Pontigny Abbey, was founded on the banks of the River Serein bordering Burgundy and Champagne. The abbey-church, however, was built in two stages between 1137 and 1150, with its style being typical of the transitional period from Roman to Gothic. A groined vault covers the front porch, aisles and transept, and the nave boasts the first cross-ribbed vault to be constructed in Burgundy. In the late 12th C, the apse was destroyed and replaced by the elegant Gothic choir that remains today. The Abbey went on to found 19 daughter Abbeys, which in turn created 45 more. Over the course of the 12th and 13th C, Pontigny gave refuge to three exiled English bishops, including Thomas Becket.

STAY AT: *The Municipal aire, situated on **Rue St Thomas in Pontigny**, is in a pleasant location on the Northern side of this small rural village, 200m from the centre. There are 13 designated parking spaces on tarmac (separated by low shrubs, but with little shade), lit at night. Urba Flux service point with a large drainage platform and toilets adjacent. Access to the aire is via an automatic barrier operated by credit card. This is a well laid out, modern aire with a few facilities in the village: boulangerie, grocer, bar/tabac and two restaurants.*

Facilities: *Water•Grey Drain•Black Drain•Electric•Toilets*
No. of spaces: *13*
Parking: *7€/24 Hrs*
Services: *3€ Water or Electric*
Opening times: *All year*
GPS Coordinates: *N 47.91085   E 03.70971*
Alternative: *Camping Municipal, D91, 89144 Ligny-le-Chatel Open: 01/05 – 30/09*

DAY 2
TAKE D5 3KM SOUTH TO:

Venouse: Beauvais Barn, founded in 1237 on the outskirts of the commune of Venouse, was part of the Cistercian Pontigny Abbey, and stands on a still-intact site between cereal fields and woods planted with a variety of trees. The undulating terrain offers a panoramic view of the Serein Valley and the Abbey. The Barn was used up to the 14th C by lay brothers, and then by farmers until the French Revolution.
RETURN TO PONTIGNY & TAKE D91 16KM SOUTH TO:
Chablis: Petit Pontigny is a former outbuilding at Pontigny Abbey, of which a cellar supported by groin-vaulted bays remains (not open for tours). There is a wonderful example of an old wine press standing covered in the courtyard and the site is also the head office of the Chablis Wines Bureau.
TAKE D91 SOUTH & D144 WEST TO:
Vermenton: Reigny Abbey, set in picturesque surroundings on the banks of the Cure, was founded in 1134 by the Abbot of Clairvaux and a community of disciples. The abbey became very powerful and prosperous in the Middle Ages under the protection of Pope Eugene III, being home to as many as 300 monks before becoming a Royal Foundation in 1493. Unfortunately, the Hundred Years' War, the Huguenots and the French Revolution all took their toll on the building, but nevertheless some interesting remains of its prestigious past can be admired today; the exceptional 14th C Cistercian refectory (one of three remaining in France) with its superb nave in its original colours; the Monks' hall and dormitory, refurbished and magnificently furnished by monks in the 18th C; the 18th C portal; and a fine example of a 17th C dovecote. You can also just make out the foundations of long-demolished buildings where excavations have revealed the base of the abbey-church, showing the original scope of the abbey and the Cistercian hydraulic system, which has been conserved intact.
TAKE D606 NORTH TO:
Cravant
<u>STAY AT:</u> *the **Municipal aire**, situated on the Western edge of **Cravant** in a small gravel parking area next to the canal marina, where there are 4 spaces (with electricity available from the Port office). The aire is next to the canal moorings area, where there is some shade under trees, and is lit by nearby street lighting. It is 300m to the centre of the village and its small range of shops: boulangerie, grocer, butcher, fishmonger and a couple of restaurants. Free wifi is available at the OT, and an Artisanal borne with drainage platform is*

located separately at the southern end of the village, on the Industrial Estate just off the main D606. There is additional parking in the village at Place du Donjon, next to the Chateau.
Facilities: Water •Grey Drain •Black Drain •Electric •Rubbish
No. of spaces: 4
Parking: 6€/24 Hrs
Services: Incl
Opening times: All year
GPS Coordinates: N47.68206   E03.68378
Alternative: Camping Municipal, Route de Bazarnes, 89460 Accolay
Open: 01/04 – 30/09

DAY 3
TAKE D11/ D49 EAST TO NOYERS & THEN D101 SOUTH TO:
Châtel-Gérard: At the heart of Châtel-Gérard Forest, in the middle of a glade cleared by monks in the 13th C and cultivated ever since, the Vausse Priory appears like a mirage. Founded in 1200, the priory was owned by Val-des-Choues Abbey in Côte d'Or and then sold as a national property during the French Revolution. It housed an earthenware manufacturing concern until 1858, pieces of which are still very much sought after, whilst today you can visit the 14th C chapel and the fine cloister that encircles a charming priest's garden.

TAKE D68 EAST TO ROUGEMONT & D905/ D32 EAST TO:
Fontenay Abbey: A UNESCO World Heritage Site, almost entirely intact since its foundation by St Bernard in 1118, is the most faithful example of a Cistercian abbey as envisaged by the major reformer of the Benedictine Order. The small, isolated community set in the middle of a wood includes inside its walls all the various buildings required by the monks for their physical and spiritual tasks: the cloister is surrounded by the church, capitulary room, dormitory, scriptorium, warming room, forge and former 17th C Abbey palace, as well as a French-style garden.

TAKE D905 NORTH TO TONNERRE & D965 11KM EAST TO TANLAY, THEN MINOR ROAD 2KM WEST TO:
Commissey: Our Lady of Quincy Abbey was a daughter Abbey of Pontigny, founded in 1133 in a sheltered valley. The Abbey has conserved its authentic roots, boasting a hostelry, a section of monastic buildings dating from the 12th C. and the Renaissance-style Abbey lodgings, all of which testify to the sobriety and rigour of Cistercian art.

TAKE D965 24KMS EAST TO:
Laignes
STAY AT: *the Municipal aire in* **Chemin du Moulin Neuf** *in* **Laignes***, which is pleasantly situated in a rural setting next to the river. This well arranged aire has pitches on grass accessed by a gravel track and shade provided by numerous trees. The ground is liable to become muddy in wet weather. The aire is about 1km from the town centre and its shops. Artisanal service point and rubbish bins.*
Facilities: *Water •Grey Drain •Black Drain*
No. of spaces: *6*
Parking: *Free*
Services: *Free*
Opening times: *All year*
GPS Coordinates: *N47.84849   E04.36133*
Alternative: *Camping Les Grebes, Rue Pont Neuf, 21330 Marcenay Open: 01/05 – 30/09*

Pontigny by Schneider & Aistleitner

Reigny by Patrick89

Fontenay Photo by Myrabella

Aire at Aix en Othe

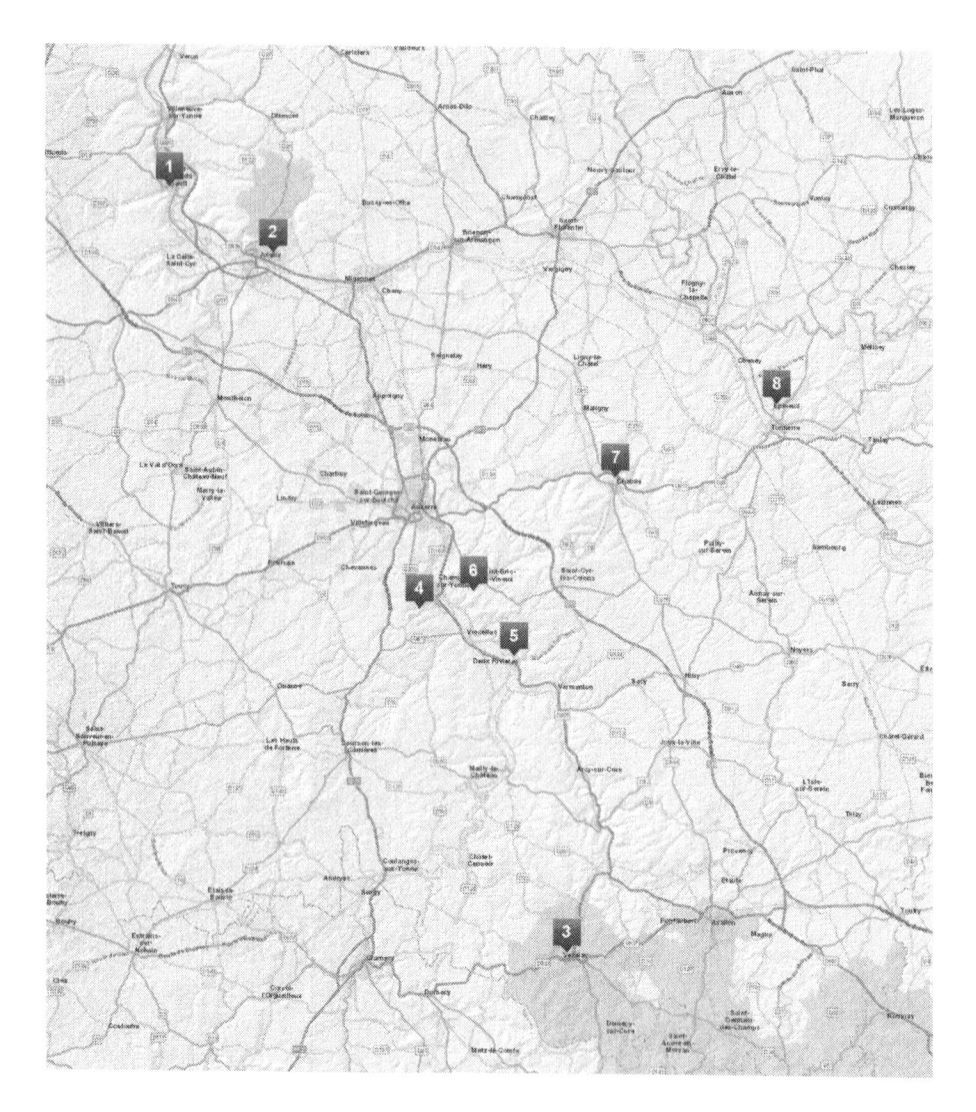

BURGUNDY VINEYARDS MAP

KEY TO MAP:

1) St Julien du Sault
3) Vezelay
5) Cravant
7) Chablis

2) Joigny
4) Jussy
6) Irancy
8) Epineuil

BURGUNDY TOUR 13
BURGUNDY VINEYARDS – 2 DAYS

The 2-Day Burgundy Vineyards Trail enables you to get a real feel for the various vineyards in the Yonne department, which produce some of the great Burgundy wines. The vineyards of Chablis, whose name is famous around the world, and its neighbours in the Auxerre and Tonnerre regions, as well the slightly less central vineyards of Joigny, to the north, and Vézelay, to the south are all producers of fine Burgundy wines.

Above: Irancy by Colas   Below: Aire at St Julien

DAY 1
St Julien du Sault

<u>STAY AT:</u> the Municipal aire on **Rue du Stade** in **St Julien du Sault**, located on the eastern side of this large rural village, next to the sports centre in a purpose built level tarmac parking area. It is 400m from the village centre, has 13 individual level spaces separated by hedges and offers some shade but no lighting. This is a quiet location, despite there being a children's play area nearby. Artisanal service point with large drainage platform. Boulangerie, supermarkets and café in the village, as well as a museum.

Facilities: Water•Grey Drain•Black Drain•Rubbish
No. of spaces: 13
Parking: Free
Services: Free
Opening times: All year
GPS Coordinates: N48.02901   E03.30194
Alternative: Camping des Iles, Route de Villeyallier, 89330 St Julien du Sault Open: 15/04 – 30/09

TAKE N6/ D606 SOUTH TO:

Joigny: The first Burgundian vineyard on the route is the Côte Saint-Jacques, overlooking the town and with a few hectares in Volgré and Champvallon. It traditionally produces the Côte-Saint-Jacques red and rosé Burgundy wines, whose reputation goes back hundreds of years, and, for the last few decades, a much-appreciated white Burgundy.

TAKE N6/ D606 SOUTH PAST AUXERRE TO GIVRY & THEN D951 TO:

Vézelay: In Vézelay, on the slopes of the Eternal Hill and the lovely neighbouring villages of Saint-Père, Tharoiseau and Asquins, this celebrated vineyard dating from the Middle Ages produces an excellent variety of white Burgundy made from Chardonnay grapes, plus an interesting red Burgundy. For those with a taste for discovery, there is also a Bourgogne Grand-Ordinaire made from old Burgundy grape varieties that have almost entirely disappeared.

RETURN NORTH ON N6/ D606 & D239 TO:

Jussy: The wine route crosses the winemaking villages of Jussy and Escolives-Sainte-Camille on the Yonne's left bank, where you must not miss a visit to the Gallo-Roman site, the small Roman church, and Migé with its windmill. Here, the Pinot Noir produces a remarkable red Burgundy and the Bourgogne-Coulanges with its red fruit aromas.

TAKE D239 / D606 SOUTH TO:
Cravant
STAY AT: the Municipal aire, situated on the Western edge of **Cravant** in a small gravel parking area next to the canal marina, with 4 spaces available (with ehu possible from Port office). The aire is next to the canal moorings area, with some shade under trees and having nearby street lighting. It is 300m to the centre of the village and its small range of shops: boulangerie, grocer, butcher, fishmonger and a couple of restaurants. Free wifi is available at the OT and there is an Artisanal borne with drainage platform located separately at the southern end of the village, on the Industrial Estate, just off the main D606. There is additional parking in the village at Place du Donjon, next to the Chateau.
Facilities: Water •Grey Drain •Black Drain •Electric •Rubbish
No. of spaces: 4
Parking: 6€/24 Hrs
Services: Incl
Opening times: All year
GPS Coordinates: N47.68206   E03.68378
Alternative: Camping Municipal, Route de Bazarnes, 89460 Accolay
Open: 01/04 – 30/09

DAY 2
TAKE D606 NORTH TO:
Irancy: The route enters Palotte Hill, the best vineyard in Irancy. This is a winemaking village dotted with old houses, including the house where Jacques Germain Soufflot, the architect of the Pantheon, was born in 1710. The house is wonderfully set at the bottom of a horseshoe hill surrounded by vines and cherry trees. In Irancy, and across a few hectares of the neighbouring villages of Cravant and Vincelottes, 150 hectares of Pinot Noir and a few hectares of the rare Cesar variety (an ancient grape that may well go back to the Gallo-Roman era) produce Irancy, a superb red Burgundy that keeps very well, and is a top vintage. Via **Vincelottes**, on the Yonne's right bank at the foot of Irancy, you can make your way to **Bailly** and its vast underground cellars where a wonderfully fine Crémant de Bourgogne is produced, and then to **Saint-Bris-le-Vineux**, with its Renaissance houses, large, beautiful church and astonishing medieval cellars. The Pinot Noir and Chardonnay here give us splendid red and white Bourgognes-Côtes-d'Auxerres, and the Aligoté produces a wonderful

Bourgogne-Aligoté. A 60-ha patch of Sauvignon, the only area of this variety in the whole of Burgundy, creates a delicately flavoured white, Saint-Bris, that is soon to have its own appellation in acknowledgement of its superb quality. Wending between the hills, the route reaches **Chitry-le-Fort**, with its strange fortified church and the hillsides where Pinot and Chardonnay grow side by side to produce wonderfully fine red and white Bourgognes-Chitry. It then climbs the hill to leave the Yonne Valley, passing under the A6 motorway, and descends into the Serein Valley.

TAKE D2 NORTH:
Past **Préhy** and its church, standing alone in the middle of vines, the road descends to the **Serein**, giving wonderful views over the Montmains and Butteaux premiers crus before arriving at the small town of **Chablis**: Here you can explore the vineyard of Chablis, the biggest Blanc de Bourgogne vineyard that spreads across 4,300 ha planted exclusively with Chardonnay, producing wines celebrated the world over: the Petit Chablis, produced on the top of the hills, to drink young, Premiers Crus Chablis, and the greeny-gold Grands Crus Chablis, that are both in a class of their own.

In the background, the seven grands crus - Blanchot, Les Clos, Valmur, Grenouille, Vaudésirs, Preuses and Bougros - huddle on their slope, surrounded by hills cloaked with the premiers crus of Montée-de-Tonnerre and Mont-de-Milieu to the right, Fourchaume and Homme-Mort to the left.

After a trip around Chablis and its beautiful 13th C Saint-Martin Church, you can take the route through some of the most splendid vineyards before leaving the Serein Valley, climbing to plains covered in forests and vast cereal crops before dropping into the Armançon Valley.

TAKE D965 EAST:
The wine route crosses **Tonnerre**, with its outstanding 13th C General hospital and amazing Fosse Dionne, the source of the Vaucluse, and then presses on to **Molosmes**, an old village lost in the surrounding sloping hills. Tonnerre and Molosmes produce principally a white Burgundy and, from just recently, the white Bourgogne-Tonnerre appellation.

Epineuil: The final leg; Pinot Noir dominates with the Bourgogne-Epineuil, a wine with very particular aromas specific to the land. On a few hills only, those of Grisées in particular, Chardonnay produces a white Burgundy that is on a par with Chablis. As the trip comes to an end, take a trip to Epineuil's church to see its wonderful furniture.

STAY AT: *The Municipal aire in* **Rue des Relichiens, Epineuil**, *is located on the eastern edge of this small rural village. The aire is in a residential area and consists of a small grass parking area with half a dozen spaces available, some shade under trees, and street lighting. It is 200m to the centre of the village and its small range of shops. An Aireservices borne with drainage platform. Picnic tables are adjacent.*

Facilities: *Water•Grey Drain•Black Drain*
No. of spaces: *6*
Parking: *Free*
Services: *Free (Jetons from shops)*
Opening times: *All year*
GPS Coordinates: *N47.87356   E03.98638*
Alternative: *Camping Municipal, Off Ave A. Briand, 89700 Tonnerre Open: 01/04 – 15/10*

Left : Chablis by Finot

Right: Vezelay Photo by Krieger

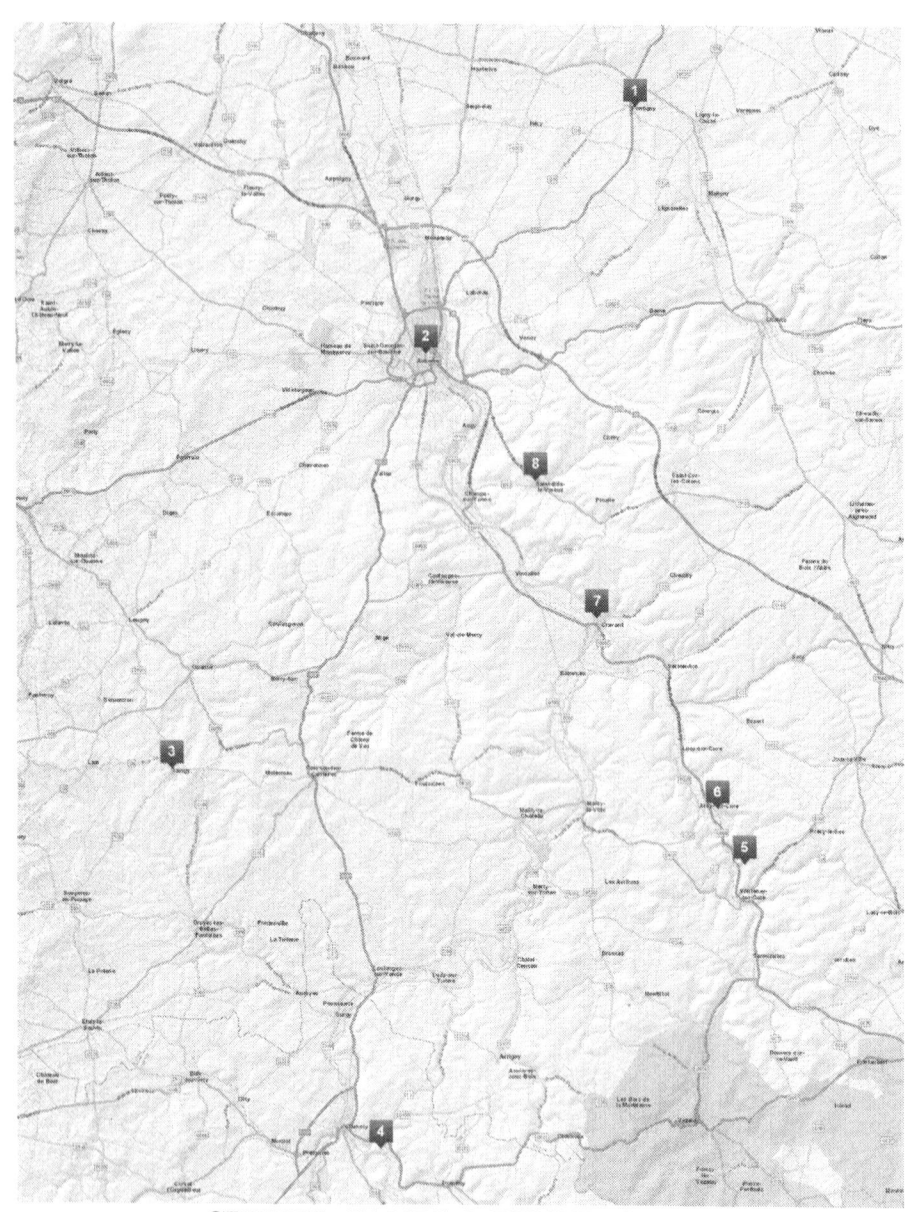

CRYPTS, CAVES & TUNNELS MAP
KEY TO MAP:
- 1) Pontigny
- 2) Auxerre
- 3) Taingy
- 4) Chevroches
- 5) St More
- 6) Arcy sur Cere
- 7) Cravant
- 8) St Bris le Vineux

BURGUNDY TOUR 14
CRYPTS, CAVES & TUNNELS – 3 DAYS

An unusual, 3-Day Tour in Burgundy that explores the many impressive underground places existing in the region. These include: an impressive Underground Quarry of white stone, still bearing traces of the master stonecutters of yesteryear; Caves with their 28,000-year-old wall paintings; an amazing labyrinth of Wine Cellars where Crémant wine is stored; and crypts in an Abbey – all unmissable.

Top: Cravant by Lapointe   Bottom: Auxerre by Vicente

DAY 1
Pontigny

STAY AT: _the Municipal aire, situated on_ **Rue St Thomas** _in_ **Pontigny**, _in a pleasant location on the northern side of this small rural village, 200m from the centre. There are 13 designated parking spaces on tarmac separated by low shrubs, having little shade but lit at night. Urba Flux service point with a large drainage platform and toilets adjacent. Access to the aire is via an automatic barrier operated by credit card. This is a well laid out, modern aire and there are a few shops in this little village; boulangerie, grocer, bar/tabac and two restaurants._

Facilities: _Water•Grey Drain•Black Drain•Electric•Toilets_
No. of spaces: _13_
Parking: _7€/24 Hrs_
Services: _3€ Water or Electric_
Opening times: _All year_
GPS Coordinates: _N 47.91085   E 03.70971_
Alternative: _Camping Municipal, D91, 89144 Ligny-le-Chatel Open: 01/05 – 30/09_

TAKE N77 19KM SOUTH TO:

Auxerre: The Carolingian crypts built around the tomb of St Germain and their extremely rare 9th C frescoes, the oldest known in France, together with the Abbey church itself, make up the main attraction of Saint-Germain Abbey. The pre-Roman nave, demolished in the 19th C, located under the current nave of Saint-Germain Church, is an astonishing group of excavations, now accessible to the public. This collection of monuments offers visitors a chance to explore 1,500 years of Auxerre's underground history.

Saint-Etienne Cathedral: A masterpiece of Gothic art from the 13th C, modest in size but grand in its elegance, the cathedral was the fifth church built on this outstanding urban site overlooking the Yonne River. The first three constructions were destroyed by fire. The fourth, the stone Roman church erected in the 11th C, was torn down to make way for the Gothic structure and only the crypt and the chapel remain today. The chapel is decorated with frescoes, including an extremely rare representation of Christ on horseback dating from the 11th C.

TAKE N151 SOUTH 25KM & THEN D9 WEST TO:

Taingy: The stone extracted from this splendid Underground Quarry has been exploited for centuries, and was used for the construction of the Paris Opera House, Paris Town Hall, the National Conservatory, the Cathedrals of Auxerre, Sens, and numerous public buildings. The extraction of blocks of stone created impressive caves showing marks left by chisels and iron bars, the only tools used by quarry men for centuries.

RETURN ONTO N151 & HEAD SOUTH TO CLAMECY, TAKE D951 EAST TO:

Chevroches

STAY AT: *the Municipal aire, situated in a medium sized gravel parking area next to the **Canal basin** in **Chevroches**, a small rural village. The aire is 100m from the village centre, overlooks the canal (with rural views beyond) and offers some level spaces, lit at night but without shade. Artisanal service point with drainage grid. A pleasant, quiet aire with views over the canal, walks along the towpath and only a short walk into the village (but there are no shops there).*

Facilities: *Water•Grey Drain•Black Drain*
No. of spaces: *6*
Parking: *Free*
Services: *Free*
Opening times: *All year*
GPS Coordinates: *N47.44981   E03.54631*
Alternative: *Camping Municipal, Rue de Chevroches, 58500 Clamecy Open: 01/04 – 30/09*

DAY 2

TAKE D951 EAST TO GIVRY – THEN D606 NORTH 8KM TO:

Saint-Moré: Head to Camp de Cora, the site of a Gallo-Roman fort on the Agrippa Way that linked Lyon and Boulogne-sur-Mer, a strategic site overlooking the Cure Valley. Visitors can take the path at the entrance to the Saint-Moré tunnel to climb up the Saint-Moré rocks for a magnificent view, and to see the nearby caves that were occupied by hermits in the 19th C - an ideal spot for a picnic.

CONTINUE NORTH 2KM ON D606 TO:

Arcy-sur-Cure: Hollowed out of a coral limestone massif that emerged at the end of the Mesozoic era by the River Cure, the caves are a major prehistoric location that is classified as a National Archaeological Site. Eleven prehistoric caves were found to contain the remains of past human occupants, the caves having been in continuous use for 200,000 years. In addition to the exceptional richness of these former habitats, the site also boasts two painted caves. Their age (particularly the 33,000 year old "Grande Grotte") ranks the site in Arcy as the second oldest for painted caves, after the "Grotte Chauvet" in the Ardèche. It is also possible to stroll along the banks of the River Cure that formed these prehistoric caves.

CONTINUE NORTH ON D606 15KM TO:

Cravant: On the right banks of the River Yonne, between Cravant and Vincelotte under the much-visited Palotte Hill, lie former quarries that have been exploited intensively since the 12th C and where the soft limestone has been eroded into vast spaces. One of these quarries provided shelter during the Second World War, right up until June 1944, for the assembly workshops of the German army's famous Focke-Wulf 190. The French later took over the factory for the construction of planes, and the first NC 900 plane, which took part in the Normandy-Niemen squadron, left the Cravant factory in March 1945.

STAY AT: *The Municipal aire is situated on the Western edge of* **Cravant** *in a small gravel parking area next to the* **canal marina***, and has 4 spaces (with ehu available from the Port office). The aire is next to the canal moorings area, with some shade under trees and nearby street lighting. It is 300m to the centre of the village and its small range of shops: boulangerie, grocer, butcher, fishmonger and a couple of restaurants. Free wifi is available at the OT and an Artisanal borne with drainage platform is located separately at the southern end of the village, on the Industrial Estate, just off the main D606. There is additional parking in the village at Place du Donjon, next to the Chateau.*

Facilities: *Water•Grey Drain•Black Drain•Electric•Rubbish*
No. of spaces: *4*
Parking: *6€/24 Hrs*
Services: *Incl*
Opening times: *All year*
GPS Coordinates: *N47.68206   E03.68378*
Alternative: *Camping Municipal, Route de Bazarnes, 89460 Accolay Open: 01/04 – 30/09*

DAY 3
CONTINUE NORTH ON D606 13KM TO CHAMPS-SUR-YONNE & TAKE D62 EAST TO:
St Bris-le-Vineux: The exploitation of the underground quarries in Bailly dates back to the 12th C and this excellent quality limestone was

used until the 20th C for the construction of monuments, including châteaux and churches such as Pontigny Abbey. Transportation of the stone was made easier by utilising the River Yonne that ran along the foot of the quarries. Since 1972, these quarries have housed the Bailly-Lapierre wine cellars, founded by the winegrowers in the Auxerre region to produce Burgundy Crémant, the 4 ha of cellars hold 5 million bottles.

STAY AT: the **Municipal aire**, *situated on the Western edge of* **Cravant** *or the Camping Municipal, Route de Bazarnes, 89460 Accolay*

Top: Taingy by Goglins   Bottom: Aire at Pontigny

BURGUNDY TOUR 15
APOTHECARIES & OLD HOSPITALS – 3 DAYS

A 3-Day Tour that visits some of the network of 20 old apothecaries and Hôtel-Dieu historic hospitals located in Burgundy and nearby surroundings that have opened their doors for visitors to discover the mysteries and secrets of these ancient hospitals and pharmacies.

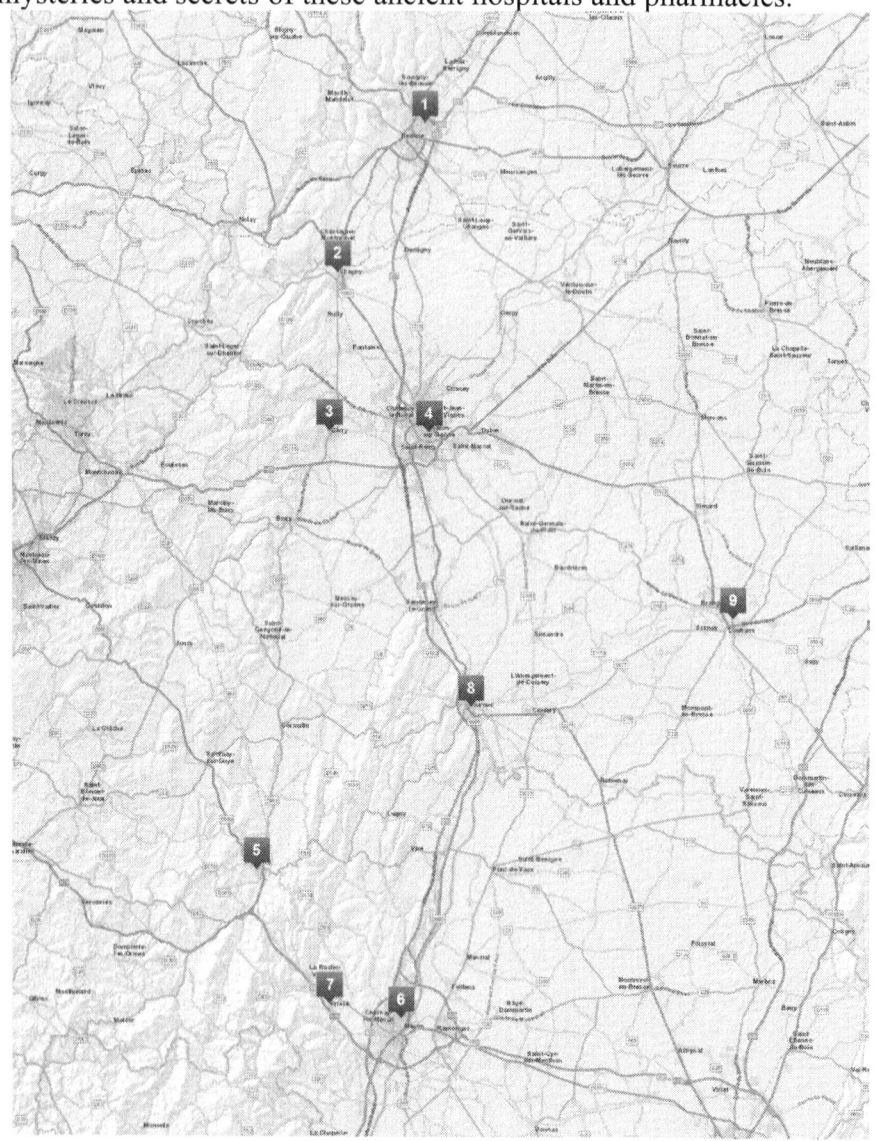

APOTHECARIES & OLD HOSPITALS MAP

KEY TO MAP (Left):
1) Beaune
2) Chagny
3) Givry
4) Chalon sur Saone
5) Cluny
6) Macon
7) Prisse
8) Tournus
9) Louhans

DAY 1
Beaune
STAY AT: *the Municipal aire in* **Ave Charles DeGaulle, Beaune** *which is in a large tarmac car park behind the Police Station, with parking in marked spaces. Only 6 spaces are reserved for motorhomes but it's a good sized car park so finding a space shouldn't be difficult. The aire is well lit at night but there is no shade here, whilst the parking is quite convenient for the town centre and shops (10 mins on foot), with a Carrefour supermarket and a café nearby. Flot Bleu service point, drainage grid and 4 ehu's.*
Facilities: *Water•Grey Drain•Black Drain•Electric*
No. of spaces: *6*
Parking*: Free*
Services: *4€ Water or Electric*
Opening times: *All year*
GPS Coordinates: *N47.01805   E04.83597*
Alternative: *Camping Municipal, Rue Auguste Dubois, 21200 Beaune. Open: 15/03 – 30/10.*
Beaune: The Hospices de Beaune were founded in 1443 and are one of Frances' most prestigious Gothic monuments, consisting of a pair of two-storied buildings arranged around a stone courtyard. The building wings are well preserved, containing half-timbered galleries and having ornate rooftops with dormer windows. The hospital museum contains many 15th C medical instruments and a collection of tapestries.
TAKE D974 SOUTH 13KM TO:
Chagny: The hospital was founded in 1700, by the Baron of Chagny, and its apothecary, at 16, Rue de la Boutière, was built in 1715. It features some outstanding period wood panelling and a fine collection of Parisian ceramic jars from the beginning of the 19th C, in addition to mortars, herb jars and containers.
TAKE D981 SOUTH 18KM TO:

Givry
STAY AT: *The municipal aire in* **Rue de la Gare, Givry**, *is in a large gravel car park with plenty of spaces but no shade. It is near to the centre of town (250m), with shops and eating-places also found nearby, and is situated next to the "Voie Verte", a 22km cycle track along the old railway line from Givry to Le Gengoux. The aire has a Raclet borne with a small drainage grid next to the public toilets. This is a fairly quiet location away from any roads on the east side of town and there is an information board in the car park.*
Facilities: *Water•Grey Drain•Black Drain•Electric*
No. of spaces: *10*
Parking: *Free*
Services: *2€ Water or Electric*
Opening times: *All year*
GPS Coordinates: *N46.78045   E04.74835*
Alternative: *Camping Municipal, Rue Julien Leneveu, 71380 St Marcel. Open: 01/04 – 30/09*
DAY 2
TAKE D69 EAST TO:
Chalon-sur-Saone: The Saint-Laurent Hospital at 7 Quai de l'Hôpital, founded in 1529, is located on the "Ile Saint-Laurent". There is a guided visit of the pharmacy (that boasts a very beautiful collection of 18th C ceramic jars), the 16th C convent, the Tin Room with decorative tinwork, and the 18th C nun's refectory, along with its' chapel.
TAKE N80 WEST & D981 SOUTH 43KM TO:
Cluny: Hôpital de Cluny, at 13 Place de l'Hôpital, has an apothecary with early 19th C wooden houses and collections of jars dating from the 17th C.
TAKE N79 SOUTH TO:
Macon: The Apothecary at 344, Rue des Epinoches is located on the ground floor of the "Hôtel Dieu" hospital and displays an outstanding combination of Louis XV-period woodwork along with a superb collection of pharmacy jars in a fine local ceramic.
TAKE D17 WEST TO:
Prisse
STAY AT: *the private aire (closed during the grape harvest) in* **Rue de l'Ancienne Gare, Prisse**, *situated in the grounds of the local wine cooperative "Terres Secretes" on the east side of this small town. The*

aire has just 6 spaces next to the co-op, with parking on tarmac bordered by grass areas and hedges/shrubs, some shade under trees and lighting at night. The aire is about 500m from the small selection of shops and a SuperU. There is an Artisanal service point with grey drainage platform. There is no charge for a stay or services if you buy some wine; tastings are possible and the wine shop is also open Sundays. Cycle track adjacent.

Facilities: Water•Grey Drain•Black Drain
No. of spaces: 6
Parking: Free
Services: 2€ Water
Opening times: All year
GPS Coordinates: N46.88311   E05.26758
Alternative: Camping Municipal, Rue des Grandes Varennes, 71000 Sance. Open: 15/03 – 30/10

DAY 3
TAKE D17 EAST & D906 NORTH TO:

Tournus: Hôtel-Dieu and Musée Greuze, at 21, rue de l'Hôpital, is an historic hospital built between the 17th and 19th C, and is classified as an historical landmark. It has preserved all of its former rooms (three patient wards and two chapels) with their original furnishings: enclosed wooden beds, dishes, silver and pottery. It also houses a well-equipped apothecary, complete with Dijon-style ceramics and hand-blown flasks. A wing of the Hôtel Dieu building houses the Greuze Museum.

TAKE D975/ D971 EAST 30KM TO:

Louhans: The Hôtel-Dieu Apothecary, at 3 Rue du Capitaine Vic, displays a rare example of exceptional quality in its furnishings and architectural detail. The well-decorated main courtyard provides access to the patient wards, whose furniture has been well preserved. This site had been operational in its current state until 1977 and the apothecary is an architectural marvel of the "Hôtel Dieu" hospital. The fine collection of earthenware demonstrates the history of the pharmacy jar, from the brown and blue Spanish model of the late 15th C, to the "Nevers" style in bright blue. The hospital's ceramics and blown glass still contain products of animal, vegetable and mineral composition - a collection unique in all of Europe.

At 400m long, the main Grande Rue is lined with over 150 arcades that are unique in France; it has 15th C houses, as well as the Saint

Pierre church with its roof of glazed tiles, the "Bailli's House", and the Saint Pierre and Saint Paul towers. A market is held in town on Monday mornings.

STAY AT: *The Municipal aire, next to the Marina on* **Rue du Port, Louhans**, *is in a gravel parking area next to the river on the west side of town, with various parking spaces along the river bank (many under trees). The Aire is about 600m from the town centre and shops, with a modern Artisanal service point and large platform drain. Showers are available in the adjacent Capitainerie.*

Facilities: *Water•Grey Drain•Black Drain•Toilets*
No. of spaces: *25*
Parking: *4€/24 Hrs*
Services: *2€ Water*
Opening times: *All year*
GPS Coordinates: *N46.62948   E05.21510*
Alternative: *Camping Municipal, Rue de la Chapellerie, 71500 Louhans Open: 01/04 – 30/09*

Left: Beaune Hospice by Gzen92

Below: Aire at Givry

Above: Cluny by NonOmnisMoriar   Below: Louhans by By Chabe01

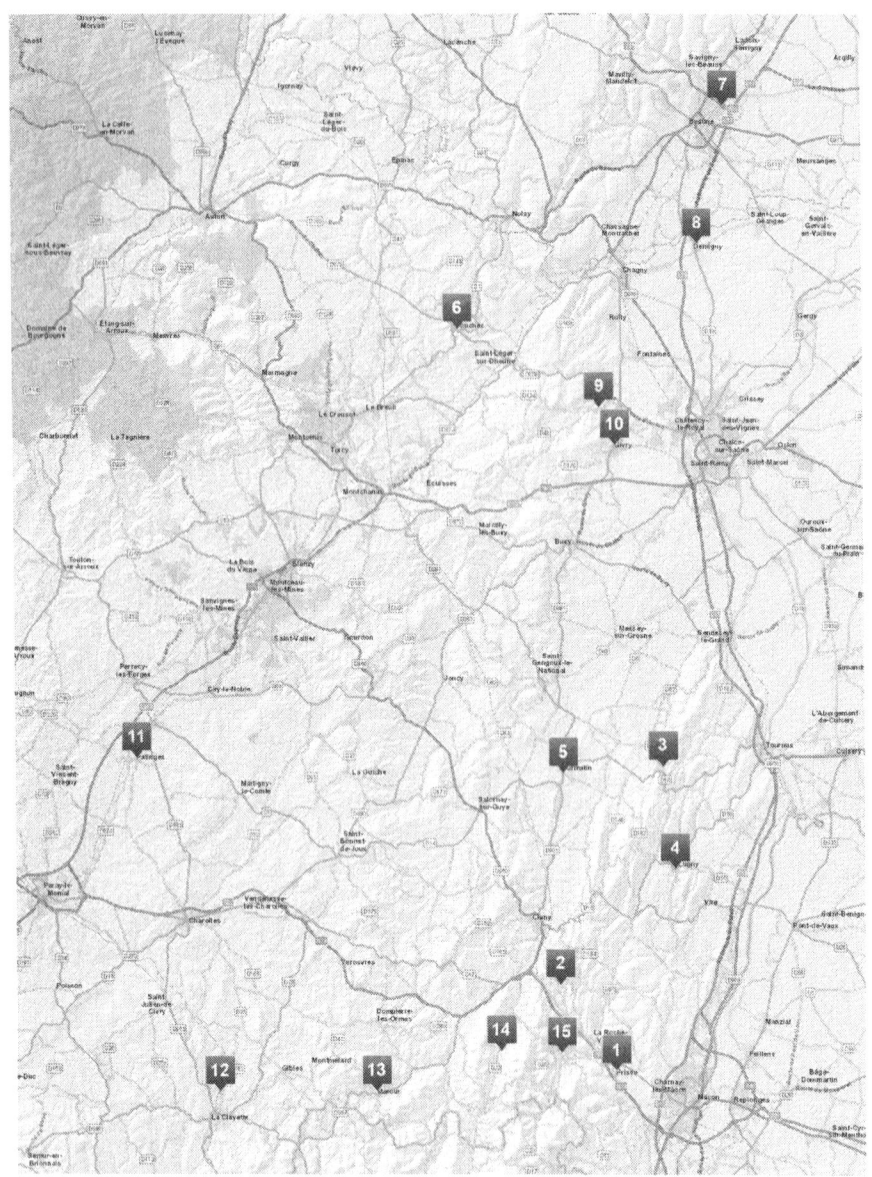

CHATEAUX OF SOUTHERN BURGUNDY MAP

KEY TO MAP:
- 1) Prisse
- 2) Berze le Chatel
- 3) Brancion
- 4) Lugny
- 5) Cormatin
- 6) Couches
- 7) Beaune
- 8) Demigny
- 9) Mellecey
- 10) Givry
- 11) Palinges
- 12) Curbigny
- 13) Matour
- 14) St Point
- 15) Pierreclos

BURGUNDY TOUR 16
CHATEAUX OF SOUTHERN BURGUNDY – 5 DAYS

This 5-Day Tour follows the "Southern Burgundy Châteaux Trail" which was devised by the owners of châteaux throughout the Saône-&-Loire department, who have joined efforts in order that visitors can see and better appreciate the historical and architectural attributes of these monuments.

Brancion by Finot

DAY 1
Prisse

STAY AT: *the private aire (closed during the grape harvest) in* **Rue de l'Ancienne Gare, Prisse**, *situated in the grounds of the local wine cooperative "Terres Secretes" on the east side of this small town. The aire has just 6 spaces next to the co-op, with parking on tarmac bordered by grass areas and hedges/shrubs, with some shade under trees and lighting at night. The aire has a cycle track adjacent and is about 500m from the small selection of shops and a Super U. There is an Artisanal service point with grey drainage platform. There is no charge for a stay or services if you buy some wine; tastings are possible and the wine shop is also open Sundays.*

Facilities: Water•Grey Drain•Black Drain
No. of spaces: 6
Parking: Free

Services: *2€ Water*
Opening times: *All year*
GPS Coordinates: *N46.88311   E05.26758*
Alternative: *Camping Municipal, Rue des Grandes Varennes, 71000 Sance Open: 15/03 – 30/10*
TAKE D17 WEST TO:
Berzé-le-Châtel: With its 13 towers dominating the Mâconnais valley, Château de Berzé-le-Châtel is a handsomely preserved 13th C medieval fortress. Renowned as being invulnerable to assailants under Louis XI, the castle's ingenious defensive systems are still found within its three-walled enclosure. Predating the castle, a 10th C Carolingian chapel is hidden among the terraced gardens that offer an exceptional view overlooking Lamartine country.
TAKE D85 NORTH TO AZE & D82 NORTH TO:
Brancion: Set within the medieval village of Brancion, Château de Brancion is the largest in all of Southern Burgundy and a living example of medieval military architecture. It features a wonderful view from the castle keep to the village and far beyond, to the valley of the Grosne River. The village has buildings from the 12th C including the Romanesque church and a 14th C marketplace.
TAKE D161 SOUTH TO:
Lugny
STAY AT: *The Municipal aire in* **Rue de la Folie** *in* **Lugny** *is located behind the Post Office on the eastern side of this small town. It offers half a dozen level spaces on gravel/grass in a large parking area with good views, and has toilets and a children's playground nearby. Artisanal service point with drainage platform. There is a small selection of shops in town within a short walk.*
Facilities: *Water●Grey Drain●Black Drain*
No. of spaces: *6*
Parking: *Free*
Services: *Free*
Opening times: *All year*
GPS Coordinates: *N46.47126   E04.81177*
Alternative: *Camping Hameau des Champs, Route de Chalon, 71460 Cormatin Open: 01/04 – 30/09*
DAY 2
TAKE D161 NORTH & D14 WEST TO:

Cormatin: Begun in 1605, the Château of Cormatin is unique in France for its exceptionally well-preserved interiors from the reign of Louis XIII. The guided tour includes turn-of-the-century sitting rooms, the kitchens and a grand "open" staircase. The 12-ha grounds feature: wide moats, a fine boxwood maze, gardens of flowers, an old-style vegetable garden, an outdoor theatre and a myriad of lakes and fountains. The "Allée Lamartine" landscaped walk is shaded by 130 two hundred-year-old lime trees and a tearoom is open from July to August.

TAKE D981/ D28 NORTH TO MONTCHANIN & TAKE D974/D978 NORTH TO:

Couches: The Château of Marguerite de Bourgogne, with its 12th C keep and walls, serves as a reminder that this was one of the most important defensive sites in the region. The Gothic chapel and the main house, with its polychrome tiles, complete this picturesque setting.

TAKE D1 14KM NORTH TO NOLAY & D973 20KM NORTH TO:

Beaune

<u>**STAY AT:**</u> *the Municipal aire in* **Ave Charles DeGaulle, Beaune** *which is in a large tarmac car park behind the Police Commissariat, with parking in marked spaces. Only 6 spaces are reserved for motorhomes but as it is a good sized car park finding a space shouldn't be difficult. The aire is well lit at night but there is no shade here. The parking is quite convenient for the town centre and shops (10 mins on foot), with a Carrefour supermarket and a café nearby. Flot Bleu service point, drainage grid and 4 ehu's.*

Facilities: *Water•Grey Drain•Black Drain•Electric*
No. of spaces: *6*
Parking: *Free*
Services: *4€ Water or Electric*
Opening times: *All year*
GPS Coordinates: *N47.01805   E04.83597*
Alternative: *Camping Municipal, Rue Auguste Dubois, 21200 Beaune Open: 15/03 – 30/10*

Beaune: The Hospices de Beaune were founded in 1443 and are one of Frances' most prestigious Gothic monuments, consisting of a pair of two-storied buildings arranged around a stone courtyard. The building wings are well preserved, containing half-timbered galleries and having ornate rooftops with dormer windows. The hospital museum contains many 15th C medical instruments and a collection of tapestries. Beaune is an interesting old town where you can visit one of the many wine-cellars for wine-tasting and also has the last traditional mustard factory in Burgundy.

DAY 3
TAKE D19 12KM SOUTH TO:
Demigny: The Château de Demigny, rebuilt at the end of the 18th C on the site of a former fortress, was the home of the Marquis de Foudras and this monument features a magnificent wrought iron entrance gate. The interior staircase and the sitting rooms open onto a panoramic view over the Côtes de Beaune vineyards, whilst a wine press, dating back to 1777, can be found in the chateau's outbuildings. Foudras Museum is devoted to Hunting and Nature, hunting with hounds having taken place in Burgundy from the 18th C to modern times. You can also visit the grounds and vegetable garden.

TAKE D62 WEST TO CHAGNY & D981 SOUTH 13KM TO:
Mellecey: A 13th C fortified manor, the Château de Germolles became the favourite residence of Marguerite of Flanders in the 14th C, and of the first Duke of Burgundy during the Valois dynasty. In addition to the 13th C entrance towers, chapel and cellar, the main building's three-storied Gothic architecture is definitely worth seeing. Also of note are the painted murals and sculptures, the private chapel for the Royal couple, and a collection of decorated paving tiles that had previously been laid on the manor's floor. The castle grounds have been planted according to the romantic 19th C English style.

TAKE D981 SOUTH TO:
Givry

STAY AT: the municipal aire in **Rue de la Gare, Givry**, which is in a large gravel car park with plenty of spaces but no shade. It is near to the centre of town (250m), with shops and eating-places also found nearby, and is situated next to the "Voie Verte", a 22km cycle track along the old railway line from Givry to Le Gengoux. The aire has a Raclet borne with a small drainage grid next to the public toilets. This is a fairly quiet location away from any roads on the east side of town, and there is an information board in the car park.

Facilities: Water•Grey Drain•Black Drain•Electric
No. of spaces: 10
Parking: Free
Services: 2€ Water or Electric

Opening times: All year
GPS Coordinates: N46.78045   E04.74835
Alternative: Camping Municipal, Rue Julien Leneveu, 71380 St Marcel Open: 01/04 – 30/09

DAY 4
TAKE D981 SOUTH ONTO N80, HEAD WEST ONTO N70 & FOLLOW N70/ D985 SOUTH TO:

Palinges: The 18th C Château de Digoine, a private historical monument, is characterised on the north side by a Louis XIVth-style facade, framed by two imposing towers, and on the south side by a grand architectural facade. On both sides lie monumental gates and an elegant courtyard. A guided tour is offered (in French) of the vestibule, sitting rooms, billiard room, library and the small Italian-style theatre, but you can make an unaccompanied visit around the English-style park, flower garden and greenhouse.

CONTINUE SOUTH ON D985 TO CHAROLLES & D985 17KM SOUTH TO:

Curbigny: The 17th C Château de Drée is also privately owned, with guided tours given around the kitchen, dining room, various sitting rooms and bedrooms, as well as the outbuildings; a pigeon house, jail and ice chamber. Two marked paths have been laid out and there is a self-guided tour of the chateau grounds (rose garden, French-style terraced gardens, fountains and statues).

TAKE D987 EAST TO :

Matour
STAY AT: The Municipal aire on **Route St Pierre (D211)** in **Matour** is in a medium-sized parking area screened by hedges, in a very quiet location on the south side of the village. Accessed by a concrete track, the aire has several spaces on grass but little shade and is not lit at night. The aire is convenient for the village centre (300m) and is adjacent to a large fishing lake. Artisanal borne with a drainage grid. This is a well-maintained and convenient aire, offering ample spaces in a very picturesque area with shops and services nearby; boulangerie, butcher, grocer, bar, pizzeria, restaurant and bank.

Facilities: Water •Grey Drain•Black Drain
No. of spaces: 10
Parking: Free
Services: Free
Opening times: All year

GPS Coordinates: N46.30329   E04.48233
Alternative: Camping Municipal, Rue de la Piscine, 71520 Matour
Open: 07/04 – 30/10

DAY 5

CONTINUE ON D987/ D95 EAST TO PONTCHARRAS & TAKE D45/ D22 NORTH TO:

Saint-Point: The 12th C Château de Lamartine is surrounded by two sets of ramparts and was built to defend the land held by the Abbey of Cluny. The poet and statesman Alphonse de Lamartine acquired the property for his wedding in 1820 and proceeded with renovation work along the lines of a Romantic Gothic style. The château is presently furnished from Lamartine's time and the visit includes the poet's bedroom, office, dining room and sitting room. The tour of the grounds features an English-style park with hundred-year-old trees, Lamartine's tomb and a 12th C church with frescoes.

TAKE D22 SOUTH & D45 EAST TO:

Pierreclos: An important landmark, the Pierreclos Chateau has borne witness to the major events shaping French history. The building is renowned for its magnificent glazed tile roof, which is so typical of historical Burgundian architecture, and the visitor enters the chateau by the gilded 17th C gate. From Medieval times there is the Romanesque church, the defence tower, distinctly Middle Age kitchens, bakery, dungeon and the remarkable 12th C cellars. Also of note is the exceptional spiral staircase, the only one of its kind in all of France. A tasting of this family estate's wines is possible, along with a wide selection of finely crafted Burgundy wines to purchase in the chateau wine shop. During the tourist season a restaurant is open in the castle armoury.

CONTINUE ON D45 EAST TO:

Prisse

<u>**STAY AT:**</u> the private aire in **Rue de l'Ancienne Gare, Prisse** or Camping Municipal, Rue des Grandes Varennes, 71000 Sance

Above: Beaune Photo by Jebulon

Right: Cormatin

Below: Lac de Matour

BURGUNDY TOUR 17
WINES OF THE COTE D'OR – 3 DAYS

The 3-Day "Côte de Nuits" Tour travels through this French wine region located on the limestone ridge at the heart of the Burgundy wine country. It goes from Beaune to Dijon, passing through Nuits-Saint-Georges, which gives its name to this area and is the regional centre. Dijon is the gateway to the "Côte de Nuits" wine route, the famous "touristic road of great Burgundy wines".

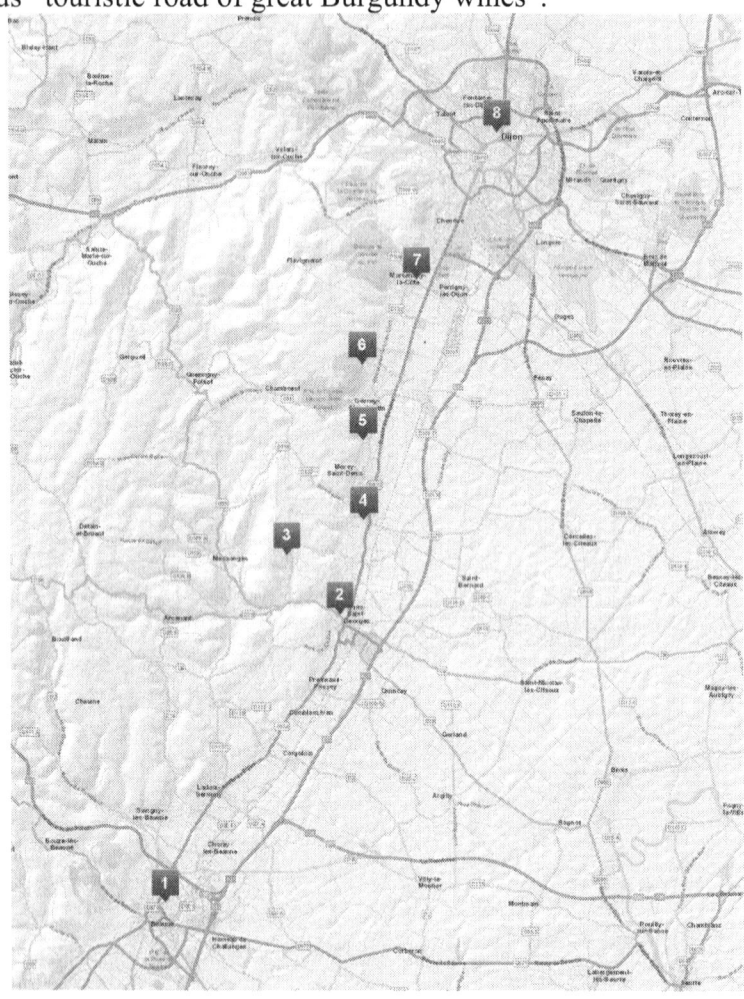

KEY TO WINES OF THE COTE D'OR MAP (Left):
1) Beaune
2) Nuits St George
3) Concoeur
4) Vougeot
5) Gevrey
6) Brochon
7) Marsannay-la-Cote
8) Dijon

DAY 1
Beaune

STAY AT: *the Municipal aire in* **Ave Charles DeGaulle, Beaune** *which is in a large tarmac car park behind the Police Commissariat, with parking in marked spaces. Only 6 spaces are reserved for motorhomes but as it is a good sized car park finding a space shouldn't be difficult. The aire is well lit at night but there is no shade here. The parking is quite convenient for the town centre and shops (10 mins on foot), with a Carrefour supermarket and a café nearby. Flot Bleu service point, drainage grid and 4 ehu's.*

Facilities: *Water •Grey Drain•Black Drain•Electric*
No. of spaces: *6*
Parking: *Free*
Services: *4€ Water or Electric*
Opening times: *All year*
GPS Coordinates: *N47.01805   E04.83597*
Alternative: *Camping Municipal, Rue Auguste Dubois, 21200 Beaune Open: 15/03 – 30/10*

Beaune is the capital of Burgundy wines, an interesting old town, with the Hospices de Beaune being one of Frances' most prestigious Gothic monuments. This medieval hospital with its multicolored rooftops is a masterpiece of flamboyant gothic architecture consisting of a pair of two-storied buildings arranged around a stone courtyard. The building wings are well preserved, containing half-timbered galleries and having ornate rooftops with dormer windows. The hospital museum contains many 15th C medical instruments and a collection of tapestries. Visit one of the many wine cellars in the town for a wine tasting, and also find the last traditional mustard factory in Burgundy.

DAY 2
TAKE D974 NORTH TO:

Nuits-Saint-Georges: The "Imaginarium", a museum devoted to the sparkling wines of the world, is an entertaining and interactive introduction to the world of "bubbly", leisure and wine tourism. The visit, lasting between 90 minutes and 2 hours, includes 14 film shows and numerous models.

TAKE D25 WEST & D109 NORTH TO:

Concoeur: You can visit the "Fruirouge" farm in Concoeur, where the famous blackcurrant cream is still made traditionally and new products are launched, such as blackcurrant ketchup or butter.

The farm has a shop selling their produce of jams, fruit juices, fruit and condiments – tastings are available.
CONTINUE ON D109 NORTH TO:
Vougeot: The Chateau Clos de Vougeot, standing in the middle of the vineyards, is a famous spot in Burgundy and one of its' finest architectural examples. After visiting the Château, a former wine storehouse of the Cistercian monks of Cîteaux, you can round off a pleasant trip with a visit to a wine cellar for a tasting session.
CONTINUE ON D974 NORTH TO:
The wine villages of Gevrey Chambertin, Brochon and Fixin are found on this route that is also known as the "Champs Elysées" of the Côte de Nuits on account of its red Grand Cru wines of world repute.
CONTINUE ON D974 NORTH TO:
Marsannay-la-Cote
STAY AT: *the Municipal aire in* **Rue du Rocher, Marsannay-la-Cote,** *which is in a large tarmac parking area with marked spaces outside the village hall. The Artisanal borne with platform drain is well-designed and easy to access. Overnight parking is quieter in the Tourist Office car park (opposite the Mairie) about 300m west of here on Rue de Mazy. Shops and services are also nearby.*
Facilities: *Water•Grey Drain•Black Drain*
No. of spaces: *12*
Parking: *Free*
Services: *Free*
Opening times: *All year*
GPS Coordinates: *N47.27088   E04.99259*
Alternative: *Camping du Lac, Bvd Chanoine Kir, 21000 Dijon Open: 01/04 – 01/11*
Marsannay-la-Cote is on the "Route des Grands Crus" and the domaine Chateau de Marsannay, which specialises in all three colours of Marsannay AOP but also produces four other varieties, offers a tour of its cellars, giving tastings of all seven wines.
DAY 3
CONTINUE ON D974 NORTH TO:
Dijon is the historical capital of Burgundy. To explore the city, take the "Owl" tour with 22 stopping places, or take the trip on an entertaining means of transport, The Segway. The Musée des Beaux-Arts in Dijon is one of the oldest museums in France, housing one of France's major art collections. It is also one of the most impressive,

not only in terms of its huge collections ranging from Egyptian art to artefacts of the 20th C, but also because of the historical interest of the museum building itself – the Palace of the Dukes of Burgundy. There are four more museums in the city, including an Archaeological museum and a Natural History museum. The Cathedral is also worth visiting with its' 11th C crypt and the city has 13 wine cellars that are open to the public – details are available at the Office de Tourisme in the city.

STAY AT: *the Municipal aire in* **Rue du Rocher, Marsannay-la-Cote** *or Camping du Lac, Bvd Chanoine Kir, 21000 Dijon.*

Left: Marsannay la Cote by Arnaud

Right: Parking at Marsannay la Cote

Above: Nuits-St-Georges by Palauenc   Below: Dijon

BURGUNDY TOUR 18
DIJON & SURROUNDINGS – 4 DAYS

This 4-Day Tour of the Cote d'Or department starts in the wine-producing town of Marsannay-le-Cote before moving on for a day in the historic city of Dijon. Three of the "Most Beautiful Villages in France" are visited, followed by a famous ancient battle site and then the majestic Fontenay Abbey. The tour finishes in Mirebeau-sur-Beze, after having stopped at two chateaux and two more medieval fortified villages.

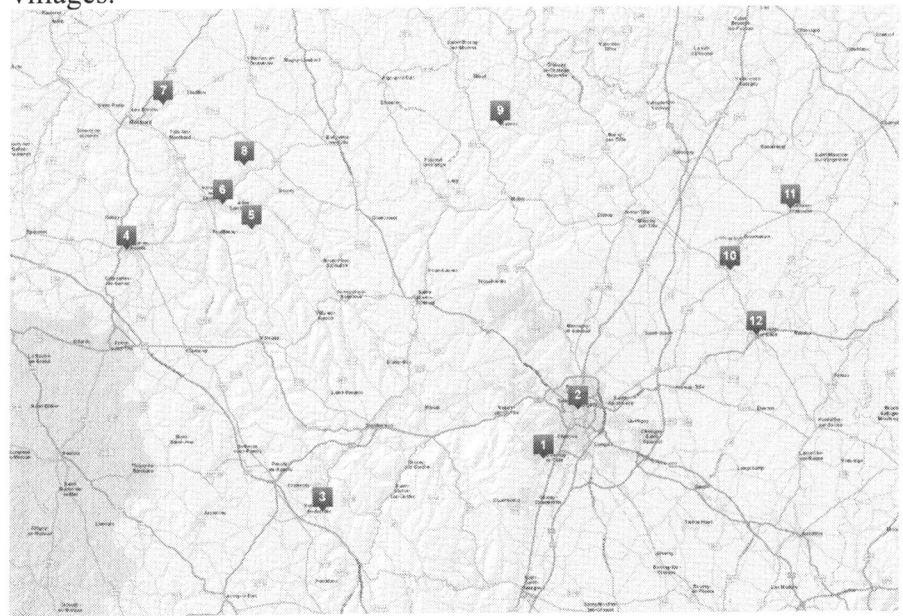

DIJON & SURROUNDINGS MAP

KEY TO MAP:
1) Marsannay-la-Cote
2) Dijon
3) Châteauneuf-en-Auxois
4) Semur-en-Auxois
5) Flavigny-sur-Ozerain
6) Alise-Sainte-Reine
7) Fontenay
8) Bussy-Rabutin
9) Salives
10) Beze
11) Fontaine-Francaise
12) Mirebeau-sur-Beze

DAY 1
Marsannay-la-Cote

STAY AT: *the Municipal aire in* ***Rue du Rocher, Marsannay-la-Cote,*** *which is in a large tarmac parking area with marked spaces outside the village hall. The Artisanal borne with platform drain is well-designed and easy to access. Overnight parking is quieter in the*

Tourist Office car park (opposite the Mairie) about 300m West of here on Rue de Mazy. Shops and services are also nearby.
Facilities: Water•Grey Drain•Black Drain
No. of spaces: 12
Parking: Free
Services: Free
Opening times: All year
GPS Coordinates: N47.27088   E04.99259
Alternative: Camping du Lac, Bvd Chanoine Kir, 21000 Dijon Open: 01/04 – 01/11

Marsannay-la-Cote is on the "Route des Grands Crus" and the wine producer Chateau de Marsannay, which specialises in all three colours of Marsannay AOP but also produces four other varieties, offers a tour of its wine cellars, giving tastings of all seven wines

TAKE D974 NORTH TO:

Dijon is the historical capital of Burgundy. To explore the city, take the "Owl" tour with 22 stopping places, or take the trip on an entertaining means of transport, The Segway. The Musée des Beaux-Arts in Dijon is one of the oldest museums in France, housing one of France's major art collections. It is also one of the most impressive, not only in terms of its huge collections ranging from Egyptian art to artefacts of the 20th C, but also because of the historical interest of the museum building itself – the Palace of the Dukes of Burgundy. There are four more museums in the city, including an Archaeological museum and a Natural History museum whilst the Cathedral is also worth visiting with its' 11th C crypt. The city has 13 wine cellars that are open to the public – details are available at the Office de Tourisme in the city.

From Dijon it is possible to take a boat trip along the Burgundy Canal and pass through the 3 kms long "Vault" tunnel.

<u>**STAY AT:**</u> *the Municipal aire in* **Rue du Rocher, Marsannay-la-Cote** *or Camping du Lac, Bvd Chanoine Kir, 21000 Dijon.*

<u>DAY 2</u>
TAKE D905 & D33 WEST ALONG THE CANAL TO:

Châteauneuf-en-Auxois is one of the "most beautiful villages in France" and one of the last remaining examples of 14th C Burgundian military architecture. During the Hundred Years War, towers and curtain walls were built to defend the village and the Auxois plains. A tour of the village combines narrow streets, medieval houses, buildings devoted to war and those devoted to aristocratic life.

TAKE D970 NORTH TO:
Semur-en-Auxois is also a fortified village, built on a pink granite hill, at a bend in the meandering Armanon river. This lovely old village has cobbled streets lined with half-timbered houses, the Gothic collegiate church, the keep and the ramparts as well as the Baudon washhouse - all are illuminated at night.

STAY AT: *the Municipal aire in* **Ave Louis Pasteur, Semur-en-Auxois,** *which is in the large tarmac car park at the sports complex. Parking is in marked spaces with no shade and is surrounded by the sports pitches/tennis courts. A quiet position with a small parade of shops nearby, but the town centre is about 800m distant. Artisanal borne with drainage grid.*
Facilities: *Water •Grey Drain •Black Drain •Toilets*
No. of spaces: *12*
Parking: *Free*
Services: *Free*
Opening times: *All year*
GPS Coordinates: *: N47.49501   E04.34998*
Alternative: *Camping Municipal, Rue du Lac, 21140 Pont-et-Massene Open: 01/04 – 05/10*

DAY 3
TAKE D954 & D9 EAST TO:
Flavigny-sur-Ozeain is another one of the "most beautiful villages in France". Built around a Benedictine Abbey founded in the 8th C, this Burgundian village displays its medieval history through its ramparts, fortified gates, cobblestone streets, houses and mansions. Its' famous aniseed-flavoured sweets called "Anis de Flavigny" are still made in the former Abbey, whilst it is possible to visit the Abbey crypt, the Church, the Maison des Textiles and its garden.

TAKE D9 NORTH 5KM TO:
Alise-Sainte-Reine, was the site of the famous battle of Alesia, fought between Julius Caesar and the Gauls. A visit to the interactive MuseoParc, and the orientation table, locates the famous 52 BC battlefield with the aid of videos and reconstructions of Roman forts and their war machines. On Mount Auxois (407m alt.), is a statue of the Gallic hero Vercingetorix. Saint Regina, martyred in the third

century by a Roman general, is another of the village's historical figures.

TAKE D905 NORTH 15KM TO:

Fontenay Abbey: a UNESCO World Heritage Site, almost entirely intact since its foundation by St Bernard in 1118, is the most faithful example of a Cistercian abbey as imagined by the major reformer of the Benedictine Order. The small, isolated community set in the middle of a wood includes all the various buildings required by the monks for their physical and spiritual tasks: the cloister is surrounded by the church, capitulary room, dormitory, scriptorium, warming room, forge and the former 17th C Abbey palace as well as a French-style garden.

FROM MONTBARD, TAKE D5 NORTH TO:

STAY AT: *the parking next to the* ***Abbey****, pleasantly situated in a rural setting next to woodland, with ample pitches on grass, accessed by a gravel track, and shade provided by the numerous trees. This is a very quiet location but has no facilities nearby and no lighting. It is a distance of 5kms to the shops/eating places in Montbard.*

Facilities: *None*
No. of spaces: *20*
Parking: *Free*
Services: *None*
Opening times: *All year*
GPS Coordinates: *N47.63809   E04.38523*
Alternative: *Camping Les Grebes, Rue Pont Neuf, 21330 Marcenay Open: 01/05 – 30/09*

DAY 4

TAKE D955 SOUTH & D954 EAST TO:

Bussy-Rabutin: The **Château de Bussy** is set in a magnificent wooded valley and features a remarkable décor, whilst the magnificent grounds have been restored in the 17th C style, featuring water fountains, a maze, and gardens in a star formation. Statues of mythological figures complete the landscaping and the grounds also have a beehive, icehouses, a dovecote, an orchard and a kitchen garden where old varieties of vegetables are grown.

TAKE D954 EAST TO ST BROING & D996 SOUTH TO:

Salives is a medieval village set in the green valley of the Tille river, still retaining its fortified walls, keep, wash house and wells.

TAKE D19 EAST & D959 SOUTH TO IS-SUR-TILLE, CONTINUE 16KM EAST ON D959 TO:
Beze: Another fortified medieval village with a Benedictine Abbey, granary and washhouses. You can also visit the cave "Grotte de Beze" by boat, a magical underground cruise on a crystal-clear river.
TAKE D960 12KM NORTH EAST TO:
Fontaine-Francaise: The chateau here is one of the most beautiful in Burgundy, a symbol of the Age of Enlightenment, having a vast park with its lime trees cut into porticos to the Louis XV style.
TAKE D960 WEST & D959 SOUTH TO:
Mirebeau-sur-Beze
STAY AT: *the Municipal aire located on the western edge of **Mirebeau** in **Chemin de la Tour**, in a medium-sized tarmac parking area, next to the towns' football pitch/tennis courts and about 250m from the town centre. There is some shade here and the aire is in a quiet spot, bordered by a residential area and farmland to the south. Euro-Relais service point with small drainage platform. Mirebeau is a small rural town with a good range of shops and eating-places.*
Facilities: *Water•Grey Drain•Black Drain•Electric*
No. of spaces: *6*
Parking: *Free*
Services: *2€ Water or Electric*
Opening times: *All year*
GPS Coordinates: *N47.399991   E05.31317*
Alternative: *Camping Trou d'Argot, Rte de Fontaine, 21610 Montigny sur Vingeanne Open: 01/05 – 01/10*

Below: Aire at Mirebreau

Above: Dijon

Right: Semur en Auxois by Pline

Chateauneuf en Auxoix by Finot

CENTRE TOUR 19
TOWNS & CHATEAUX AROUND TOURS – 4 DAYS

A 4 day tour of the Chateaux of the Loire valley, starting in Amboise with the Chateau Royal, before visiting the chateaux of Chenonceau, Villandry, Langeais, Azay-le-Rideau and Chinon.

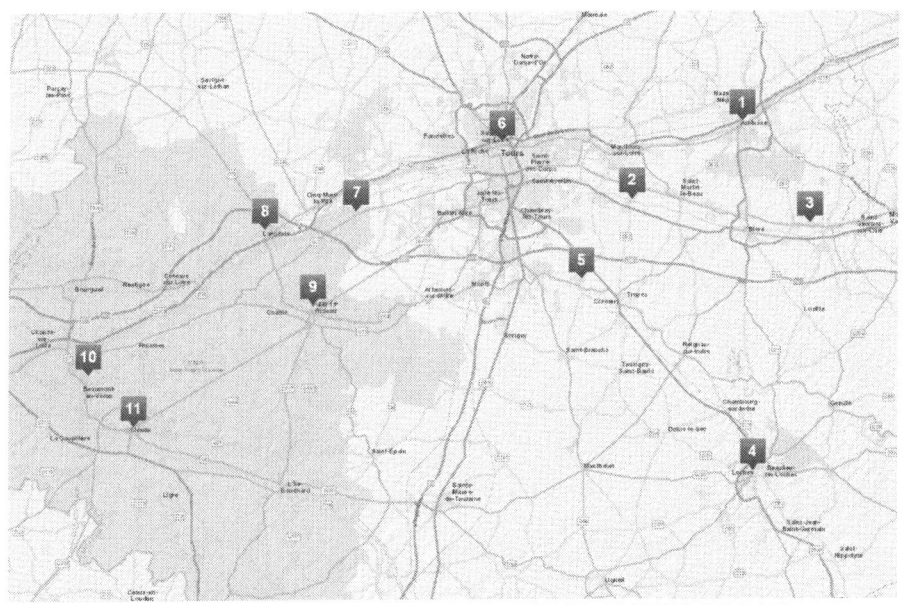

TOWNS & CHATEAUX AROUND TOURS MAP

KEY TO MAP (Above):

1) Amboise	2) Azay sur Cher
3) Chenonceau	4) Loches
5) Esvres sur Indre	6) Tours
7) Villandry	8) Langeais
9) Azay le Rideau	10) Avoine
11) Chinon	

DAY 1
Amboise

STAY AT: *the Municipal aire in **Amboise**, in **Allee de la Chapelle St Jean** situated on the north side of an island in the Loire river, opposite the Chateau of Amboise and next to the municipal campsite L'Ile d'Or. The parking has been purpose built for motorhomes and is about 1km from the town centre (across the river). Parking is on grass, shaded by trees, accessed by a tarmac track, with entry to the*

aire controlled by an automatic barrier (payable by credit card). Artisanal service point with drainage platform. There is a campsite and municipal swimming pool next to the aire. A good range of shops can be found in town and there is a market on Sunday morning.
Facilities: Water•Grey Drain•Black Drain•Electric •Rubbish
No. of spaces: *35*
Parking: *12€/24 Hrs*
Services: *3€ Water or Electric*
Opening times: *All year*
GPS Coordinates: *N47.41859   E00.98891*
Alternative: *Municipal Campsite, Rue de L'Ille d'Or, 37400 Amboise. Open 02/06 – 10/09*

Amboise: Solidly built on its pedestal of rock, the Château Royal affords a wonderful view of the old town of Amboise and the banks of the Loire. Built between the 15th and 16th C, the château is notable particularly for its sumptuous collection of furniture and the grounds. It also has La Chapelle Saint Hubert, containing the tomb of Leonardo da Vinci, and an unobstructed view of the old town from the ramparts.

Le Clos-Luce: Persuaded by King Francis I to come to France to continue his work, Leonardo da Vinci came to live at Le Clos-Lucé, where he died peacefully in 1519. The house now contains a number of recreated scenes, working models and computerised displays featuring da Vinci's incredible inventions and calculations.

Parc des Mini Chateaux: In this small park you can see all 44 of the Loire Valley's finest châteaux recreated at 1/25th scale.

<u>**STAY AT:**</u> *the Municipal aire* **in Amboise,** *in* **Allee de la Chapelle St Jean,** *or the Municipal Campsite, Rue de L'Ille d'Or, 37400 Amboise.*

DAY 2
TAKE D751 WEST ALONG THE LOIRE & D40 SOUTH TO:
Azay-sur-Cher: The Priory of St Jean du Grais, founded in 1127 by the founder of the Knights Templar, was once frequented by lords and pilgrims, some of them came here for the water in the well, the precious liquid being thought to have miraculous properties, with the power to restore sight. Visitors today can admire the priory's medieval architecture and the sweeping panoramic view.

TAKE D976 EAST TO:
Chateau de Chenonceau: is one of the classic Loire Valley châteaux. Built astride the river Cher, its famous gallery is one of its finest features, as are the gardens created by Catherine de Medici. There is a

plant nursery in the outbuildings which supplies the flowers used to decorate the château interior.

TAKE D976 WEST & D31 SOUTH TO:
Loches: In the gently meandering valley of the river Indre, the town of Loches offers some remarkable architecture and a panorama of the gently rolling countryside of Southern Touraine. The main features retained from the town's fascinating medieval past are the fortifications, the impressive keep (one of the tallest in France) and the Collegiate church of Saint Ours. With more peaceful times came the splendour of the Renaissance, when Loches gained the Royal Lodgings with its more intricate curves. There is in addition the lower town to explore, which includes the 16th C Town Hall and the Chancery. Every Wednesday the town comes to life with one of the finest markets in the area selling local produce.

TAKE D943 24KMS NORTH & D17 WEST TO:
Esvres sur Indre
STAY AT: *the Municipal aire in* **Rue Auguste Noyant,** *in* **Esvres sur Indre***. In a medium sized tarmac car park bordered by grass verges and hedges, on the south side of this small town. Parking is 200m from the town centre with its reasonable range of shops/eating places. The artisanal service point is easy to use and access. This is a well-maintained and quiet aire, with picnic table, swimming pool and tennis courts adjacent.*
Facilities: *Water•Grey Drain•Black Drain•Rubbish*
No. of spaces: *6*
Parking: *Free*
Services: *Free*
Opening times: *All year*
GPS Coordinates: *N47.28278   E00.78531*
Alternative: *Camping La Grange Rouge, D910, 37250 Montbazon Open: 30/03 – 30/10*

DAY 3
TAKE D943 NORTH TO:
Tours is a real experience, being a city with a lively student atmosphere that complements its cultured heritage. The old quarter stretches from the historical district of Place Plumereau and Rue Colbert to the square by the Cathedral. With its 13th C stained glass windows, Saint Gatian's Cathedral is one of the greatest churches in

the Loire valley. Tours has two major museums; the Museum of Fine Arts and the Guild Museum, housed in a 13th C church.
TAKE D7 WEST TO VILLANDRY:
Chateau de Villandry: When it comes to gardens, the 16th C gardens of Villandry are hard to beat. Every year the team of gardeners at the château produce new combinations of colours and plant creations in the five gardens on the estate: the vegetable garden, the ornamental garden, the water garden, the aromatic garden and the maze. The 'Night of a Thousand Lights' is held on the first weekend of July when the gardens are illuminated at night. The interiors of the chateau are decorated to match the style of this family château and are warmly welcoming, with a collection of 17th C paintings on display.
TAKE D7 WEST & D57 OVER THE LOIRE TO:
Langeais
<u>**STAY AT:**</u> *the Parking in* **Rue Foulques Nerra** *in* **Langeais** *opposite the Chateau, in a large tarmac car park with shade in places and lighting at night. As well as being adjacent to the Chateau, the car park is within a short (100m) walk of shops and eating-places in the town. No services here.*
Facilities: None
No. of spaces: 6
Parking: Free
Services: None
Opening times: All year
GPS Coordinates: N47.32478   E00.40531
Alternative: Camping du Lac, Rue de Tours, D953, 37130 Langeais Open: 01/06 – 15/09

Right: Chinon by Jolivet

DAY 4

Chateau de Langeais: A marvellous illustration of the architectural transition that took place during the Renaissance, this château has features that date from its days as a fortress in the Middle Ages - such as the parapet walk and fully-working drawbridge - to some early indications of the Renaissance period. It was here, in 1429, that Anne of Brittany wed king Charles VIII.

TAKE D947 & D7 EAST ALONG THE LOIRE TO:

Azay-le-Rideau: This magnificent Chateau, built during the reign of Francis I, is set within grounds designed to form a haven of greenery around this Renaissance gem, the facades of which are reflected in the still waters of the Indre. The château is in the centre of Azay-le-Rideau, offering visitors the opportunity for a pleasant stroll around the streets of the town. Throughout the summer, the night-time "Imaginaires" show lights up the château in a myriad of different colours.

Just a few kms from the Château, at 'The Cave Valley of Les Goupillieres', you can explore deep into the past, secret world of the cave dwellers during the Middle Ages. Communities of peasant farmers settled in these caves cut into the limestone when it was quarried for building materials for the châteaux.

TAKE D17/ D7 WEST TO:

Avoine

STAY AT: *the Municipal aire in* **Rue de la Republique** *in* **Avoine,** *located on the north western edge of the town, close to the Lac Mousseau. This is in a park area, with 10 large parking spaces on tarmac and bordered by grass areas. Access is by automatic barriers at the entrance, payable by credit card. The aire is about 800m from the town centre, close to a wooded area and backing onto farmland. AireServices service point with drainage platform.*

This is a very well laid out and maintained aire, but not very convenient for the town centre. There is a nice park-like area with woodland walks around a lake, a play area, boules and picnic tables. A reasonable selection of shops and services can be found in town, including a Shopi supermarket, four restaurants and a café/Tabac, plus a swimming pool.

Facilities: *Water •Grey Drain •Black Drain •Electric*
No. of spaces: *10*
Parking: *4€/24 Hrs*

Services: *2€ Water or Electric*
Opening times: *All year*
GPS Coordinates: *N47.21333   E00.17785*
Alternative: *Camping Municipal, Quai Danton, 37500 Chinon Open: 01/04 – 30/10*
DAY 5
TAKE D749 EAST TO:
Chinon: Keeping watch magnificently over the town, the Château de Chinon is one of the highlights of Touraine. Built in the Middle Ages, this fortress is a hugely imposing building of thick-walled ramparts. It also has a fascinating history (Joan of Arc recognised the heir to the throne here - the future Charles VII) and a first-class collection of tapestries, making it one of Touraine's finest attractions. The town is populated with half-timbered houses, noticeably along Rue Haute St Maurice where you can find the Art Museum at No 44.
<u>**STAY AT:**</u> *the Municipal aire in* **Rue de la Republique in Avoine** *or Camping Municipal, Quai Danton, 37500 Chinon*

Left: Amboise by Jalaudin

Below: Tours by Moroder

Below: Aire at Avoine

CENTRE TOUR 20
CHARTRES & SURROUNDINGS – 4 DAYS

A 4-Day Tour that starts at the Chateau d'Anet, north of Dreux, before visiting the Royal Chapel in Dreux, the gardens in Pierres and Maintenon, and the historic city of Chartres. The tour continues west to the childhood home of Marcel Proust, the beautiful town of Nogent-le-Rotrou, and finishes in the Parc Naturel of Perche.

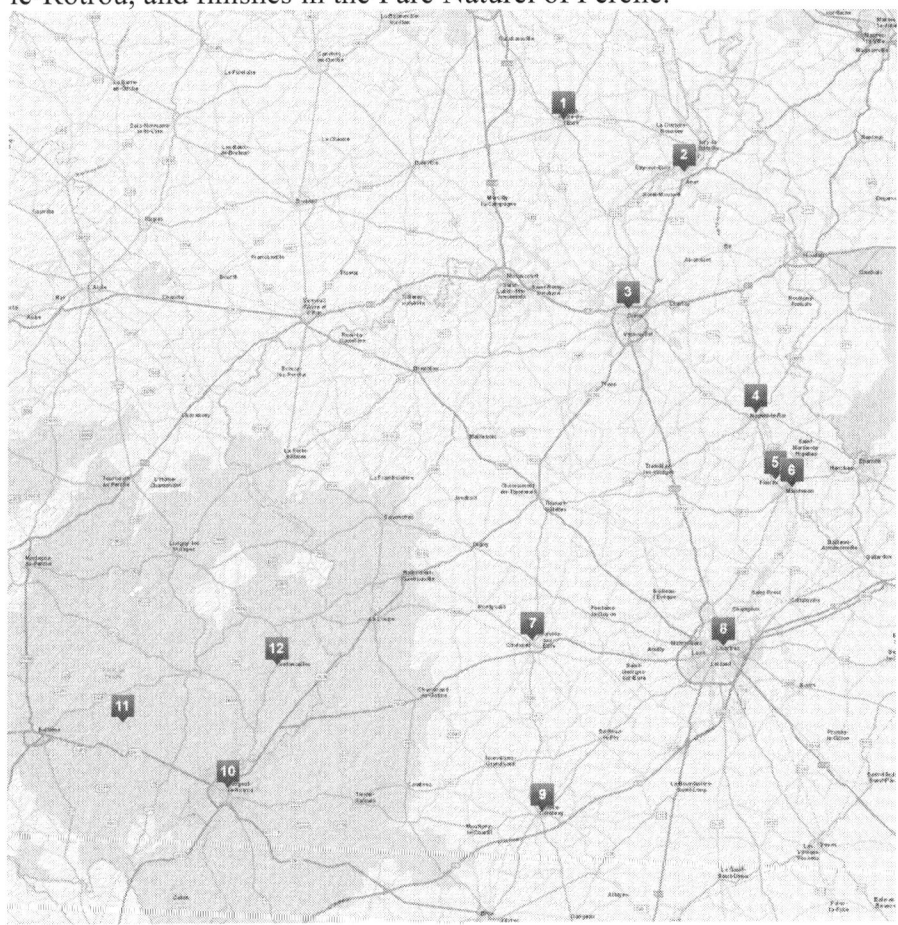

CHARTRES & SURROUNDINGS MAP

KEY TO MAP:
- 1) St Andre de l'Eure
- 2) Anet
- 3) Dreux
- 4) Nogent le Roi
- 5) Pierres
- 6) Maintenon
- 7) Courville sur Eure
- 8) Chartres
- 9) Illiers-Combray
- 10) Nogent le Rotrou
- 11) Noce
- 12) Bretoncelles

DAY 1
St Andre de l'Eure

STAY AT: *the purpose-built Municipal aire in* **Rue de Jumelles, St Andre de l'Eure**. *This is located on the western edge of this small town and offers 6 level spaces on tarmac, separated by low hedges and bordered by grass. Set next to the road, the aire overlooks a fishing lake, with open farmland to the west, and is within 200m of the town centre. Artisanal service point with drainage platform. This is a well-designed and maintained aire, lit at night but providing no shade. The town is pleasant, with a good range of shops, a Carrefour supermarket, and a market on Friday mornings.*

Facilities: *Water•Grey Drain•Black Drain• Rubbish*
No. of spaces: *6*
Parking: *Free*
Services: *Free*
Opening times: *All year*
GPS Coordinates: *N48.90681   E01.26925*
Alternative: *Municipal Campsite, Chemin des Trillots, 27530 Ezy sur Eure Open: 01/03 – 15/11*

TAKE D833 EAST & D163 SOUTH TO:

Anet: The best architects of the era worked on Chateau Anet, once owned by the beautiful Diane of Poitiers, which bears witness to its past splendour, despite being damaged during the Revolution. The Chateau has been extensively restored; both the interior and gardens can be visited.

TAKE D928 19KM SOUTH TO:

Dreux: Perched on a hill overlooking the town, the Gothic Royal Chapel has overlooked the burial grounds of Orléans since Louis-Philippe's time. Inside you can admire the stained glass windows and carved statues, but it's not only the history of Dreux that merits the visit, it's also its atmosphere and in December the "Festival des Flambarts" presents a carnival style parade and colourful street entertainment.

TAKE D929 SOUTH TO:
Nogent le Roi

STAY AT: *the Municipal aire in* **Rue Pont des Demoiselles** *in* **Nogent le Roi**. *Located in a large tarmac car park on the northern side of this small rural town, this aire has marked spaces, there is little shade here, but it is a quiet location overlooking the football pitch and is*

close to the swimming pool. Artisanal service point with a drainage grid, free electricity. A quiet location at night (but with some coming and going during the day), with a short walk (300m) to the town centre for the small selection of shops.
Facilities: Water•Grey Drain•Black Drain• Electric
No. of spaces: 6
Parking: Free
Services: Free
Opening times: All year
GPS Coordinates: N48.65048   E01.52902
Alternative: Camping Les Ilots, Le Haut Bourray, 28130 Villiers le Morhier   Open: 01/02 – 21/12

DAY 2
TAKE D983 SOUTH TO:
Pierres: Colour, odour and taste intertwine in the Clos de Bois Richeux Medieval Gardens. On one of the oldest manor farms in France, this is a very special botanical heritage composed of herb gardens with medicinal plants, aromatic inner courtyards and vegetable gardens full of very old varieties.

CONTINUE 2KM SOUTH TO:
Maintenon: This old feudal chateau was transformed in the 17th C, gaining richly decorated apartments, an aqueduct and extensive French formal gardens. Such improvements were required to satisfy the owner, the future mistress of Louis XIV, Madame de Maintenon. Crossing the grounds, the aqueduct's arches are reminders of the monumental project that was supposed to join the waters of the Eure to the Chateau of Versailles.

TAKE D906 19KM SOUTH & D923 15KM WEST TO:
Courville sur Eure
STAY AT: *the Municipal aire in Avenue Thiers, Courville sur Eure. The aire here is in the medium- sized gravel parking area outside the Municipal camping on the southern side of this small rural town. This is a quiet location next to the river and near some small lakes, but close to the town centre (300m) and its good range of shops and services. The Aireservices service point with a platform drain is near to the small toilet block. A quiet, well maintained aire with 6 level spaces on gravel and 6 on grass, set next to the Eure with walks adjacent, parking bordered by grass, some shade under mature trees, and lighting at night. The adjacent Camp site open 01/05 – 22/09.*

Facilities: Water•Grey Drain•Black Drain•Electric•Toilets
No. of spaces: 12
Parking: Free
Services: 2.5€ Water or Electric
Opening times: All year
GPS Coordinates: N48.44591 E01.24118
Alternative: Camping Bords de L'Eure, Rue de Launay (D339), 28000 Chartres Open: 01/03 – 31/10

DAY 3
TAKE D923 15KM EAST TO:
Chartres: Considered a masterpiece, the Cathedral is a listed UNESCO heritage site and the spires of this 12th C Gothic gem can be seen across the surrounding countryside. The cathedral has been well preserved, with the majority of the original stained glass windows having survived intact, while the architecture has seen only minor changes. Opposite the cathedral is The International Centre of Stained Glass Windows, which increases the influence of the art of stained glass through training courses and exhibitions. The city's School of Agriculture, housed in an engine shed built in 1905, is the largest French museum dedicated to agriculture - there are more than 100 exceptional agricultural machines on show, live, interactive temporary exhibitions and a multimedia area. From April until October "Chartres en Lumieres" takes place in the evenings, illuminating the city's buildings with stunning light and music displays. Also nearby, the Maison Picassiette, a house made of mosaics, merits its listed building status.

STAY AT: *the Municipal aire in* **Ave Thiers, Courville sur Eure,** *or Camping Bords de L'Eure, Rue de Launay (D339), 28000 Chartres*

DAY 4
TAKE D921 WEST 25KM TO:
Illiers-Combray was the childhood village of the famous French author Marcel Proust. Here you will find 'Aunt Léonie's' home, now the Proust Museum, and the charming Pré Catelan garden created by the author's uncle that became Swann's Park in Proust's novel.

TAKE D922 35KM WEST TO:
Nogent-le-Rotrou: Chateau St Jean is 1,000 years old and rises high above the Huisne valley on a rocky spur. The main structure includes a substantial square keep (amongst the oldest remaining keeps in France), a ring of fortified walls and towers added during the 12th C,

and an entrance with two large round towers. A converted museum in the heart of its old stone walls displays the history of the town and its region, whilst the town itself has many old buildings to discover.

CONTINUE WEST ON D955 FOR 13KM TO:

Nocé: The nearby Natural Regional Park of Perche is ideal for long walks, passing through a landscape of small valleys and farmland criss-crossed by hedges and trees. There is a rich rural architecture, built from a variety of natural materials that produce an amazing palette of colours, enhanced by the façades of the manor houses and churches, farms and abbeys.

TAKE D203 & D918 EAST TO:

Bretoncelles

*<u>STAY AT:</u> the Municipal aire in **Rue Garreau (D918), Bretoncelles**. This aire is situated in a small gravel parking area next to the village sports centre and swimming pool, about ½ km north of the village. Bordered by trees, with hedges separating the spaces, the parking area is next to the tennis pitches and backs onto open farmland. Euro-Relais service point with drainage grid. Superette, newsagent and a café can be found in the village.*

Facilities: *Water•Grey Drain•Black Drain•Electric*
No. of spaces: *6*
Parking: *Free*
Services: *2€ Water or Electric*
Opening times: *All year*
GPS Coordinates: *N48.43611   E00.88667*
Alternative: *Camping Bords de l'Huisne, Rue de l'Huisne, 61110 Bellou sur Huisne Open: 01/04 – 15/10*

Aire at Saint Andre

Above: Nogent-le-Rotrou by Ernesty

Right: Chartres by Urban

Below: Maintenon by Selbymay

CENTRE TOUR 21
VENDOME & LE LOIR – 3 DAYS

This 3-Day Tour begins in the picturesque village of Chateaudun before visiting the Chateau of Montigny, the Commandery in Arville and the town of "Art & History" – Vendome. Take a trip on the Loir valley railway, followed by visits to gardens in Sasnières and Couture, explore a troglodyte village and complete the tour in Montoire sur le Loir.

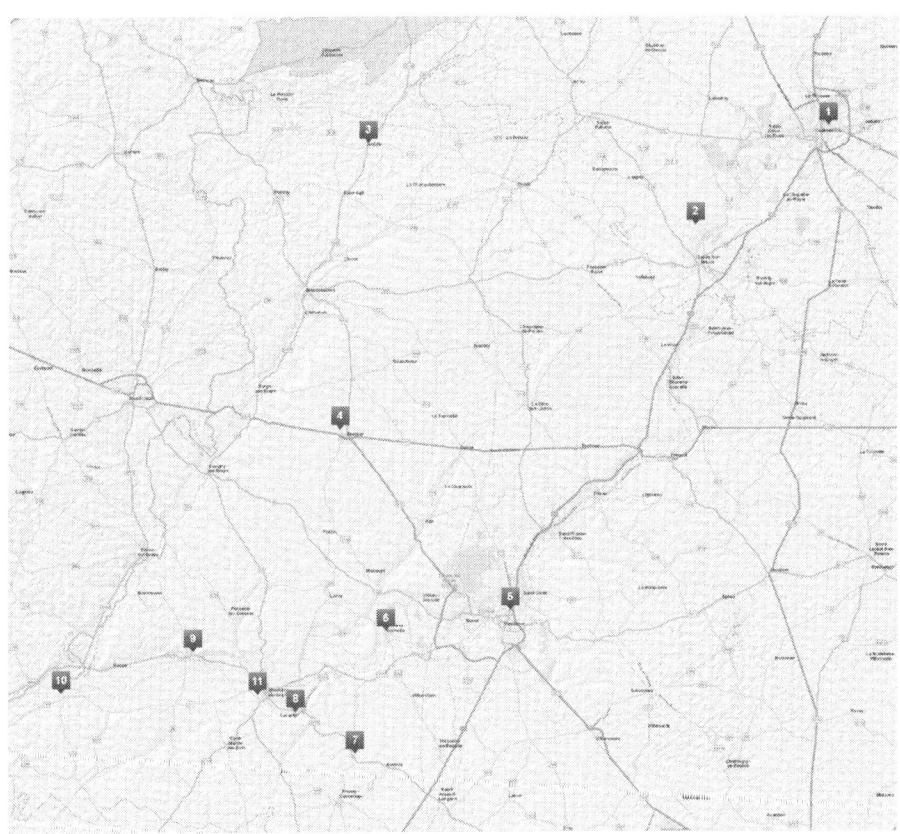

VENDOME & LE LOIR MAP

KEY TO MAP:
1) Chateaudun
2) Montigny-le-Gannelon
3) Arville
4) Epuisay
5) Vendome
6) Thore-la-Rochette
7) Sasnieres
8) Lavardin
9) Troo
10) Couture-sur-Loir
11) Montoire-sur-le-Loir

DAY 1
Chateaudun

STAY AT: the Municipal aire in **Rue des Fouleries, Chateaudun**. This pleasant aire, located in a public car park next to the chateau and the river Loir, offers 10 spaces on tarmac bordered by grass verges with shrubs/trees but no shade. The aire is in the town centre, close to a good range of shops/services and is lit at night. UrbaFlux service point with drainage platform and toilets adjacent. There is a museum, a château and gardens in the town, with caves nearby.

Facilities: Water•Grey Drain•Black Drain•Electric•Toilets
No. of spaces: 10
Parking: Free
Services: 2€ Water or Electric
Opening times: All year
GPS Coordinates: N48.07127   E01.32415
Alternative: Municipal Campsite, Rue de Chollet, 28200 Chateaudun
Open: 01/04 – 04/11

Châteaudun, The Château has an imposing cylindrical 12th C keep, a chapel, and two residential wings that form a comfortable residence of harmoniously combined Gothic and Renaissance styles. It also houses an impressive tapestry collection from the 16th C and has formal gardens to visit outside.

TAKE N10/ D35 12KM SOUTH TO:
Montigny-le-Gannelon: The Château here sits on top of a hill overlooking the River Loir, surrounded by a 15ha park and gardens. Having been restored in the 19th C and still inhabited today, visitors can see souvenirs from the post-Napoleonic era that combine the history of France with the history of the family. The cliff surrounding the château is full of troglodyte homes.

TAKE D23 26KM WEST TO:
Arville: The Commandery of the Knights Templars is the best-preserved Commandery in France and is a unique building where you can discover the era of the crusaders and their Knights through the interactive Museum. During a guided tour, one can experience life during this period by visiting the tithe barns, the garret, the church and the bread oven.

TAKE D921/ D151 SOUTH TO EPUISAY & D957 TO:
Les Petits Places

STAY AT: *the Private aire **"Escale"** on the **D957 between Epuisay and Aze**, easy to access and well sign-posted off the D957. This private aire is in an open, grassy area with no shade and has spaces on grass accessed by a gravel track. Shops, etc can be found either at Epuisay (4km) or Vendome (13km). Artisanal service point with drainage grid. This is a very well equipped, comfortable aire situated on an isolated farm where there are 6 spaces with electric for spending the night in complete calm surrounded by lawns and floral displays.*

Facilities: *Water•Grey Drain•Black Drain•Electric*
No. of spaces: *6*
Parking: *10€/ 24 Hrs*
Services: *Incl.*
Opening times: *All year*
GPS Coordinates: *N47.86414   E0.97662*
Alternative: *Camping Vendome, Rue Geoffroy martel, 41100 Vendome   Open: 07/04 – 28/10*

DAY 2
TAKE D957 SOUTH TO:
Vendôme, is a "Town of Art and History", the main places of interest being the Abbey church with its beautiful belfry and an exuberantly decorated facade, its cloisters and the Abbey gardens, the St Jacques Chapel and the Bourbon Vendôme Chateau with its ancient ramparts. The museum has many 16th to 19th C artefacts, including the harp of Marie Antoinette. Balzac also stayed here when he was a child. In July and August you can explore Vendôme by boat along the River Loir.

TAKE D917 10KM WEST & D82 NORTH TO:
Thore-la-Rochette: The Loir Valley train takes you along 36km of restored tracks with several stops on route. Gourmets can enjoy local specialities at the station on their return. The train runs in June, July and August.

CONTINUE WEST ON D917 & THEN D67 SOUTH TO:
Sasnières: The 3ha Garden of the Domaine de Sasnières was designed as a small green valley with a peaceful, fresh water pond, by a gardener that is passionate about plants and botany.

HEAD NORTH ON D108 6KM TO:
Lavardin
STAY AT: *the Parking in **Rue des Vaux Boyers** in **Lavardin**. This car park is on the western side of the village in a gravel area provided*

with good shade and spaces bordered by hedges. A restaurant and a local produce shop can be found in the village, with more shops in nearby Montoire.
Facilities: *Toilets*
No. of spaces: *6*
Parking: *Free*
Services: *None*
Opening times: *All year*
GPS Coordinates: *N47.74164   E0.88402*
Alternative: *Camping Reclusages, Ave des Reclusages, 41800 Montoire sur Loir   Open: 01/05 – 30/09*
Lavardin: One of the "Most Beautiful Villages of France", the village of Lavardin, with its troglodyte dwellings on the hillside and bridge over the River Loir, is a charming place to stop. You can still visit the remains of a chateau and its keep, which overlook the Loir. St Genest Church has some remarkable murals and there are beautiful old Gothic and Renaissance houses in the village, as well as a museum.

DAY 3
CONTINUE NORTH ON D108 FOR 3KM & TAKE D917 7KM NORTH TO:
Troo: This troglodyte village is an unusual and interesting place with medieval underground galleries, cellars, stone stairways, caves, remains of the ramparts and gateways, and an old stone quarry. The "Man and his knife" and the "Children of Trôo" exhibitions recount the unique aspects of life in an ancient troglodyte habitat.
CONTINUE WEST FOR 13KM ON D917 & D57 TO:
Couture-sur-Loir: The 15th C Possonnière Manoire, an interesting manor house with extensive rose gardens, was the birthplace of one of France's most prominent literary figures, Pierre de Ronsard, who spent the first twelve years of his life in this Italian Renaissance style residence.
TAKE D10 EAST TO:
Montoire-sur-le-Loir: There is a Second World War Museum next to the aire in the former railway station. The "Musikenfete" in August brings together 500 traditional musical instruments from all over the world, some of which you can try out whether you are a musician or just a beginner. Since 1973 the Montoire Festival has represented the different cultures of the world through top amateur dance troops and classical orchestras.

STAY AT: *the Municipal aire on* **Ave de la Republique** *in* **Montoire-sur-le-Loir**. *The aire is located on the north side of town, close to the town centre in a gravel car park with some shade from small trees. It is close to the shops (250m) and a Carrefour supermarket, and has some picnic tables available in the parking area. Raclet service point with drainage grid. A pleasant small town with a reasonable selection of shops, eating places and services.*
Facilities: *Water•Grey Drain•Black Drain•Electric*
No. of spaces: *6*
Parking: *Free*
Services: *Free*
Opening times: *All year*
GPS Coordinates: *N47.75756   E00.86935*
Alternative: *Camping Reclusages, Ave des Reclusages, 41800 Montoire sur le Loir   Open: 01/05 – 30/09*

Above: Arville by Freihalter

Page 148

Top: Vendome   Middle: Troo by Capper   Bottom Montoire aire

CENTRE TOUR 22
NANCAY TO BOURGES – 4 DAYS

This 4-Day Tour starts at the Observatory in Nancay, followed by a visit to the "Stuart" town of Aubigny, and then on to the chateaux at Blancafort and Oizon. The pottery village of La Borne is next, before visiting the medieval town of Sancerre, the "Most Beautiful" village of Apremont, then Villiers Chateau and ending in the city of Bourges.

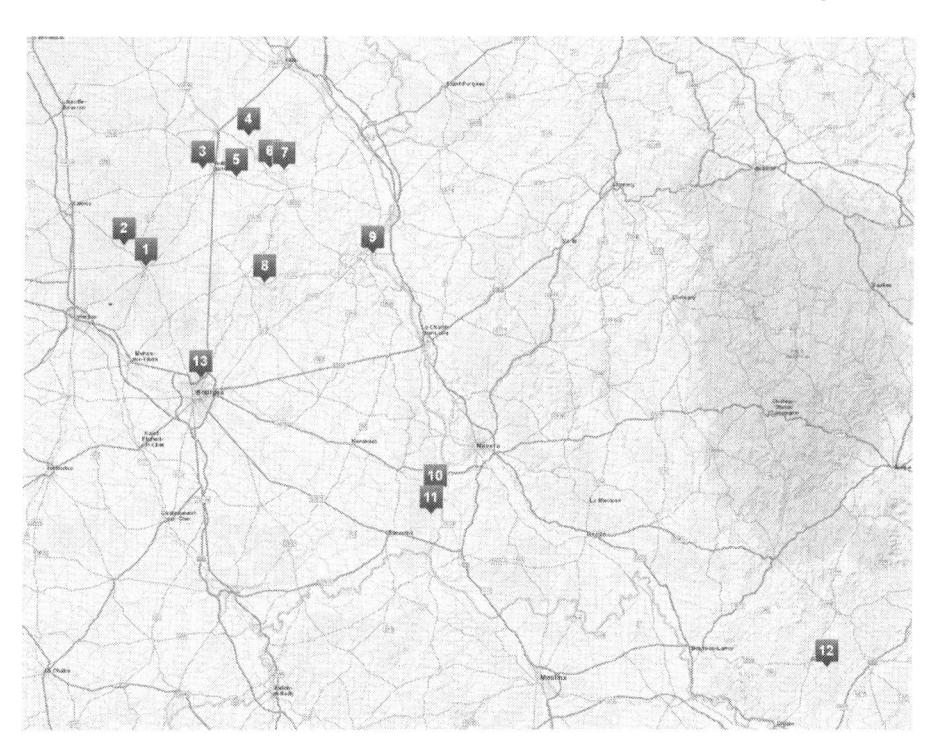

NANCAY TO BOURGES MAP

KEY TO MAP:

1) Neuvy sur Barangeon
2) Nancay
3) Aubigny-sur-Nere
4) Blancafort
5) Oizon
6) Concressault
7) Barlieu
8) La Borne
9) Sancerre
10) Apremont-sur-Allier
11) Neuvy le Barrois
12) Chassy
13) Bourges

DAY 1
Neuvy sur Barangeon

STAY AT: *the Parking next to the campsite and* ***Etang de la Noue,*** *off the* ***D944 at Neuvy sur Barangeon***. *This pleasant spot is located in a public car park, next to the lake, where there are 10 spaces on tarmac or grass accessed by a gravel track. The aire is 800m south from the town centre, close to the campsite, not lit at night but has good shade. NB: there are no services here and overnight parking is only allowed when the campsite is closed –September till Easter*
Facilities: *None*
No. of spaces: *10*
Parking: *Free*
Services: *None*
Opening times: *All year except 01/04 - 30/09*
GPS Coordinates: *N47.31267   E02.26535*
Alternative: *Municipal Campsite, Route de Bourges (D944), 18330 Neuvy   Open: 01 /04 – 30/09*

TAKE D944 NORTH TO:
Nancay: There is a modern art exhibition in the Capazza Gallery, which is next door to the "radio astronomy station" of Nançay, the "Open Skies Centre", with exhibitions, a planetarium, observation points and guided tours. Children can enjoy the nearby Adventure Park and walk amongst the trees in the heart of the 6ha forest, where you will find a circuit adapted to every age and ability.

TAKE D29/ D79/ D924 29KM NORTH TO:
Aubigny-sur-Nere: The Château here is located in the town centre, the entrance and turrets are centuries old but the interior has been restored, displaying Renaissance rooms and tapestries with gardens outside. The museum of the Old Scottish Alliance tells the fascinating story of how the town became linked with the House of Stuart in Scotland. The town centre itself is also worth a detour, in particular for its picturesque timbered houses built in the 15th C after a terrible fire had ravaged the town.

STAY AT: *the Municipal aire on* ***Route de la Chapelotte (D7)*** *in* ***Aubigny-sur-Nere***, *located on the south side of town, 800m from the centre. It offers level spaces on tarmac, some shaded by trees, is close to a lake and the football pitch, but has no lighting at night. Artisanal service point with a drainage platform. A good selection of shops in*

town and there is another aire on the north side of the town but it is shared with lorries and can be noisy.
Facilities: *Water•Grey Drain•Black Drain*
No. of spaces: *8*
Parking: *Free*
Services: *Free*
Opening times: *All year*
GPS Coordinates: *N47.48192   E02.44995*
Alternative: *Municipal Campsite, Route d'Oizon (D923), 18700 Aubigny Open: 01/04 – 30/09*

DAY 2
TAKE D30 9KM EAST TO:
Blancafort: 15th C Blancafort Château is a pink brick stronghold situated next to the Sauldre canal, with a formal French garden, galleries and arcades. Inside this noble domain one can admire the Aubusson tapestries and 17th C furniture.

TAKE D39 8KM SOUTH TO:
Oizon: The 15th C Renaissance Verrerie Château was built by the Stuarts in the heart of a forest next to a large lake. Theatrical tours of the chateau and grounds are organized from April till October, taking place every day in July and August.

TAKE D213 5KM EAST TO:
Concressault: Visit the world of Black Magic at the Museum of Witchcraft to see exhibits and learn about its history.

TAKE D8 WEST TO:
Barlieu
<u>**STAY AT:**</u> *The Municipal aire on the* **Base de Loisirs** *on* **D8** *in* **Barlieu** *is on fairly level ground (but soft when wet), surrounded by farmland. This aire is situated in a large gravel/grass parking area with a hedged surround offering a little shade in places, a children's play area, fishing and swimming can be found nearby in the Base de Loisirs. Euro-Relais borne with drainage grid but only a couple of ehu's.*
Facilities: *Water•Grey Drain•Black Drain•Electric*
No. of spaces: *10*
Parking: *3.5€/ 24 Hrs*
Services: *2.5€ Electric*
Opening times: *All year*
GPS Coordinates: *N47.47938   E02.63136*

Alternative: Municipal Campsite, Route des Aix (D12), 18250 Henrichemont   Open: 01/05 – 31/10

DAY 3

TAKE D8 SOUTH and D926 25KM SOUTH, THEN D39/ D12 TO HENRICHEMONT and D22 EAST TO:

La Borne is a hamlet where pottery has been made since the 13th C, reaching its peak in the 19th C when there were 21 workshops in operation. Today you can visit the Ivanoff ceramic workshops in outbuildings that have been converted into a museum, and in the village school you can also visit the Pottery museum, where you will find the work of potters over the years. Wandering through La Borne**,** you will come across potters, sculptors and ceramic artists at work who make this village the "fired clay" capital of the area.

TAKE D22 and D955 13 KM EAST TO:

Sancerre is a medieval town perched on top of a rocky hill, and is well known for its vineyards and wines with their reputation of excellence. In the historic town centre is the Maison de Sancerre, where 350 local winegrowers have created an imaginative display of the local wine area with 4D cinema, a garden, play area, shop and a panoramic terrace. The 30m high tower, Tour des Fiefs, is the last remnant of the 14th C chateau.

TAKE D920/ D45 62KM SOUTH TO:

Apremont-sur-Allier is one of the "Most Beautiful Villages of France", lying in the River Allier flood plains. The main features of the village are the floral park inspired by the English garden, the old chateau remodeled in the 19th C yet still crowned with 5 towers, and the old village of sailors and quarrymen, with its pink houses. There is also a permanent exhibition in the chateau stables.

CONTINUE ON D45, 3KM SOUTH TO:

Neuvy le Barrois

<u>**STAY AT:**</u> *the private aire located in the grounds of a farm,* **La Prairie**, *on* **Route de Mornay (D45)**, *½ km south of* **Neuvy le Barrois**. *There are 6 individual spaces separated by hedges, all with 16A hook ups, on hard standing bordered by grass verges with a little shade in places. There is lighting at night as well as a toilet block with sinks and showers, laundry facilities and farm produce for sale. Artisanal service point with large drainage platform. This is a very quiet rural aire located behind the barn of a small farm with views over the*

surrounding countryside. There are no facilities available in the nearby small village of Neuvy.
Facilities: *Water•Grey Drain•Black Drain•Electric•Toilets*
No. of spaces: *6*
Parking: *10€ / 24 Hrs*
Services: *Incl.*
Opening times: *All year except*
GPS Coordinates: *N46.86098   E03.03961*
Alternative: *Municipal Campsite, La Bruyere (D45), 18600 Mornay sur Allier   Open: 15/05 – 15/09*

DAY 4
TAKE D45 NORTH and D976 WEST TO NERONDES, THEN D6 NORTH TO:
Chassy: The charming Villiers Château garden lies between a vast man-made lake, with a 16th C windmill and the 15th C manor house. There is a display of clematis and perennial plants, a botanical collection of lilacs, a rose garden and a children's play area.
TAKE D12 and N151 WEST TO:
Bourges: The sumptuous St Etienne Cathedral is a UNESCO World Heritage Site; climb its 396 steps to contemplate the magnificent view of the old town. Jacques Coeur's Palace, commissioned by Charles VII's Master of the Mint is a Gothic masterpiece and reminiscent of the splendours of bygone times. This "Town of Art and History" can also be visited at night by following the spectacular, illuminated night walk and there are four museums in Bourges: Natural History, Local Heritage, Art, and a Craft and Industry Museum.
STAY AT: *the Municipal aire on* **Rue du Pre Doulet in Bourges**. *The aire is in a large gravel parking area next to the city retail park and the adjacent car parks, on the west side of the city. It is bordered by trees, which provide some shade. The UrbaFlux service point with platform drain is easily accessible. This is a quiet spot at night despite being near to the retail complex with a Cinema, Ice rink, LeClerc supermarket and fast food outlets. Shuttle buses run Mon – Sat into the city centre.*
Facilities: *Water•Grey Drain•Black Drain*
No. of spaces: *30*
Parking: *Free*
Services: *Free*
Opening times: *All year*

GPS Coordinates: N47.08308   E02.38318
Alternative: *Municipal Campsite, Bvd de l'Industrie,   18000 Bourges*
Open: 15 /03 – 15/11

Left: Blancafort by Stainier

Below: Sancerre by Taxiarchos228

Right: Aubigny sur Nere by Ji-Elle

Below: Neuvy le Barrois aire

CENTRE TOUR 23
MONTARGIS TO BEAUGENCY – 6 DAYS

This 6-Day Tour along the Loire starts at Montargis, the "Venice of Gatinais", following the river to Nogent, Briare, Gien, Sully and Chateauneuf-sur-Loire. The route then heads North to the Chateau Chamerolles, the museums in Pithiviers and Boynes before then returning to the Loire at Orleans. After staying in this historic city, the river towns of Meung and Beaugency are also visited.

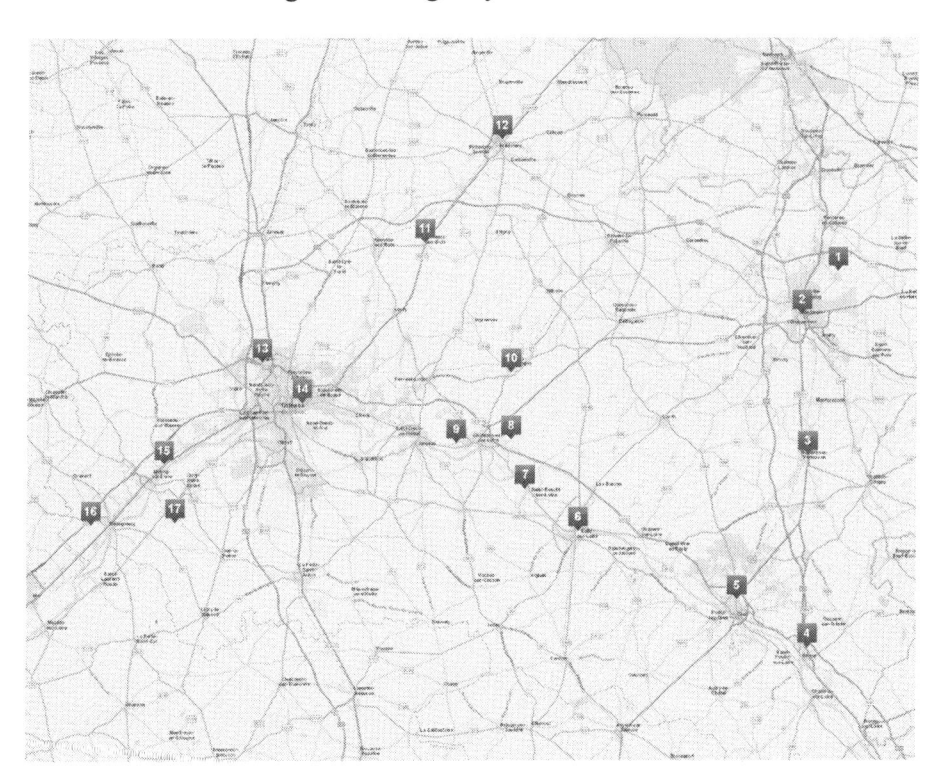

MONTARGIS TO BEAUGENCY MAP

KEY TO MAP:

1) Paucourt
2) Montargis
3) Nogent sur Vernisson
4) Briare
5) Gien
6) Sully sur Loire
7) Saint-Benoit-sur-Loire
8) Germigny des Pres
9) Chateauneuf sur Loire
10) Vitry aux Loges
11) Chilleurs aux Bois
12) Pithiviers
13) Saran
14) Orleans
15) Meung sur Loire
16) Beaugency
17) Dry

DAY 1
Paucourt
STAY AT: the Municipal aire in **Rue de l'Eglise in Paucourt,** *a small village situated in the centre of the large forest of Montargis. The aire is found in a medium sized tarmac parking area, with several unshaded, level parking spaces and is lit at night. Bordered by large grassy areas, including a play area, this is a quiet, well-kept aire in this small, rural village that has no shops and just one café. There is an artisanal service point with drainage grid.*
Facilities: *Water•Grey Drain•Black Drain*
No. of spaces: *12*
Parking: *3€/ 24 Hrs*
Services: *Free*
Opening times: *All year*
GPS Coordinates: *N48.03461   E02.79128*
Alternative: *Municipal Campsite, Ave L.M.Chautemps (D815), 45200 Montargis   Open: 01/02 – 30/11*
TAKE D815 SOUTH TO:
Montargis with its 130 bridges, footbridges and canal towpaths, the town has earned the nickname of the 'Venice of Gâtinais'. The Briare, Loing and Orléans canals feed into it, offering a variety of walks from which you can admire beautiful half-timbered houses leaning over the water in a more rural than urban setting.
TAKE D2007 SOUTH 19KM TO:
Nogent sur Vernisson: You will find the most beautiful collection of trees in Europe at the Barres Aboretum and a guided tour gives you the chance to identify the many species, whilst children can try the Tree Climbing area where they can enjoy flying on zip wires.
CONTINUE ON D2007 SOUTH 27KM TO:
Briare
STAY AT: The Municipal aire in **Rue des Vignes, Briare,** *is located in a large gravel parking area bordered by grassy areas, with several level parking spaces on offer. Parking is shaded in places by trees but is not lit at night. The aire is 100m south of the canal, on the east bank of the Loire, in a tree-lined spot about ½ km from the town centre and its shops. Flot Bleu service point with platform drain.*
Facilities: *Water•Grey Drain•Black Drain*
No. of spaces: *20*
Parking: *Free*

Services: 2€ Water
Opening times: All year
GPS Coordinates: N47.63167, E02.73995
Alternative: Camping Le Martinet, Val du Martinet, 45250 Briare
Open: 01/04 – 30/09

DAY 2

Briare: Monsieur Eiffel, of Eiffel Tower fame, also built the magnificent canal bridge that crosses the Loire; the bridge is the longest in Europe and a perfect example of its type. The pleasure port is a highlight of river tourism with Chatillon-sur-Loire on the opposite bank, and Mantelot Lock is a listed site. The Nautical Museum explores navigation on both the canal and the river, whilst the Mosaic and Enamel Museum is also linked with the activities of the river and recounts 150 years of the mass production of buttons, pearls, and mosaics in the name of art.

TAKE D952 WEST 10KM TO:

Gien: Overlooking the Loire River, the Château of Anne de Beaujeu, daughter of Louis XI, has an exhibition of the history of hunting with hounds, falconry, and other forms of "la chasse". These are all explained, and you can see the various instruments, clothing and art concerned with this subject. The production processes involved in making the famous Gien porcelain can be seen in the Porcelain Museum, along with its collection of rare and monumental pieces.

CROSS LOIRE and TAKE D951 WEST 25KM TO:

Sully-sur-Loire

STAY AT: *The Municipal aire in **Chemin Salle Verte, Sully-sur-Loire** is located at the edge of the Loire on the western side of this small town, in a large gravel parking area. There are large marked spaces with grass adjacent, and some shade under trees, the aire is lit at night and it is 1km from the centre of town. There is an Artisanal service point and drainage platform. There is a good range of shops in town as well as some eating-places. This is a very quiet location, being next to a forest with a chateau within 500m and several walks/cycle trails.*

Facilities: Water •Grey Drain •Black Drain
No. of spaces: 35
Parking: Free
Services: Free
Opening times: All year

GPS Coordinates: N47.77116   E02.38448
Alternative: Camping Hortus, Rte d'Orleans (D60), 45600 St Pere-sur-Loire   Open all year

DAY 3

Sully-sur-Loire: Composed of an imposing medieval keep and a wing added in the 18th C, this marvelous chateau was the residence of a famous minister of Henry IV.

CROSS LOIRE AGAIN and TAKE D60 NORTH 8KM TO:

Saint-Benoit-sur-Loire: The Benedictine Abbey here is a Roman masterpiece, sitting just a couple of feet from the Loire. The sounds of Gregorian chants can still be heard here, but the Basilica is the only remains of the original Abbey.

CONTINUE NORTH ON D60 6KM TO:

Germigny des Pres: The Carolingian Oratory, built by Theodulf, a close advisor to Charlemagne, was the first monument of Christian art to be built in the western hemisphere. Inside you can find the Byzantine dome covered in mosaics.

CONTINUE NORTH ON D60 TO:

Chateuneuf-sur-Loire

THEN TAKE D10 NORTH TO:

Vitry aux Loges

<u>STAY AT:</u> the Municipal aire in **Rue des Erables, Vitry aux Loges.** The separate Euro-Relais borne is in a lay-by on Rue des Erables, at the entrance to the town from the East - it is easy to access, having a drive-thru arrangement with platform drainage, and is lit at night. Continue 100m along this road and you will find a parking area facing the canal, with half a dozen level spaces on tarmac but no shade. This is a quiet spot and is convenient for the village centre - a short level walk to a small selection of shops (boulangerie, grocer, deli and restaurant). A good spot for walks along the canal.

Facilities: *Water•Grey Drain•Black Drain*
No. of spaces: *6*
Parking: *Free*
Services: *Free*
Opening times: *All year*
GPS Coordinates: N47.93939   E02.27089
Alternative: Municipal Campsite, Rte de la Plage, 45110 Chateuneuf-sur-Loire   Open: 01/04 – 30/10

DAY 4

TAKE D143 NORTH ONTO D921 NORTH, THEN D109 WEST TO:
Chilleurs-aux-Bois: Chateau Chamerolles, although built for pleasure, looks like a fort and is the former residence of a certain Lancelot of the Lake. Its grounds, where a vegetable garden rubs shoulders with a maze and numerous aromatic plants, will enchant you. Take the Perfume Tour through the Château's museum and see the exhibitions reconstructing the production of perfume through the ages.
CONTINUE NORTH ON D2152 47KM TO:
Pithiviers has a Transport Museum, where you can board an old locomotive and travel along 4 km of preserved track. The Saffron Museum, in nearby Boynes, reminds you of the importance of the region in respect to the history of this precious spice.
RETURN SOUTH ON D2152 47KM TO:
Saran
<u>**STAY AT:**</u> *the Municipal aire at* **Allee Claude Bernard** *in* **Saran**, *located close to the Mairie, on the northern edge of this small town (part of the Orleans suburbs). The aire is in a medium sized gravel parking area bordered by small trees /grass with lighting at night, and is adjacent to a small park/lake area. Modern artisanal service point with drainage platform. A pleasant quiet location conveniently situated 4km north from the centre of Orleans and 1km from Junction 14 of the A10 autoroute. The aire is within 200m level walk of Saran centre, where there is a good range of small shops.*
Facilities: Water•Grey Drain•Black Drain
No. of spaces: *10*
Parking: *Free*
Services: *Free*
Opening times: *All year*
GPS Coordinates: *N47.95094   E01.87321*
Alternative: *Municipal Campsite, Chemin de la Roche, 45140 St Jean de la Ruelle   Open: 01/04 – 04/09*
DAY 5
Orleans: Although Orléans owes much of its fame to Joan of Arc, the city today still has many other attractions on offer. Treasures such as the gothic Sainte-Croix Cathedral, and the Butterfly House at the 35 ha La Source Floral Park. Museums include the Campanaire Bollée Museum and the Orléans History and Archaeology Museum, which has an exceptional collection of Gallo-Roman bronze statues. The 16th

C Groslot Mansion where Charles IX, Henri III and Henri IV all stayed is also worth a visit, as is the Fine Arts Museum and its famous Pastels Cabinet.

STAY AT: *the Municipal aire at* **Allee Claude Bernard in Saran** *or Municipal Campsite, Chemin de la Roche, 45140 St Jean de la Ruelle*

DAY 6
TAKE D2152 WEST 21KM TO:
Meung-sur-Loire: The Château was the residence of the Bishops of Orléans for seven centuries and a tour takes you from the Middle Ages up to the splendours of the17th C. This tour is full of unusual surprises such as the Bishop's bathroom, the underground passages and the "oubliettes". Along the little rivers, better known as the "Mauves", you can walk past old mills used for flour, other grains and tanning.

CONTINUE WEST 9KM ON D2152 TO:
Beaugency occupies a strategic location, thanks to its medieval bridge on the Loire, and was captured by the English before being liberated by Joan of Arc. The town is fascinating with its small, peaceful, medieval streets.

TAKE D19 WEST and D951 NORTH TO:
Dry

STAY AT: *the Municipal aire on* **Route de Meung,** *in* **Dry.** *This aire is located close to the church and sits next to a park on the northern side of this rural village, providing a medium sized tarmac parking area with some shade, bordered by grass areas. The aire is next to a play area and is only 100m from the centre of the village. There is a toilet in the adjacent football club and a Euro-Relais service point with drainage grid. There are a few shops in village where you can buy the jetons: epicerie and a tabac/café/news.*

Facilities: *Water•Grey Drain•Black Drain*
No. of spaces: *10*
Parking: *Free*
Services: *2€ Water*
Opening times: *All year*
GPS Coordinates: *N47.79847 E01.71441*
Alternative: *Municipal Campsite, Rte de Lailly (D19), 45190 Beaugency   Open: 01 /04 – 30/09*

Below: Aire at Parcourt

Top: Montargis Photo
by Gzen92

Middle: Briare

Bottom: Sully sur Loire
by Pline

CENTRE TOUR 24
BLOIS TO CHAMBORD – 4 DAYS

This 4-Day Tour starts from the old town of Blois on the Loire and then visits the chateaux of Chaumont, Beauregard, Cheverny and Villesavin. After staying in Tour-en-Sologne, the tour also visits the Car Museum in Romorantin followed by chateaux at St Aubin and Talcy, finishing at the Royal Chateau of Chambord.

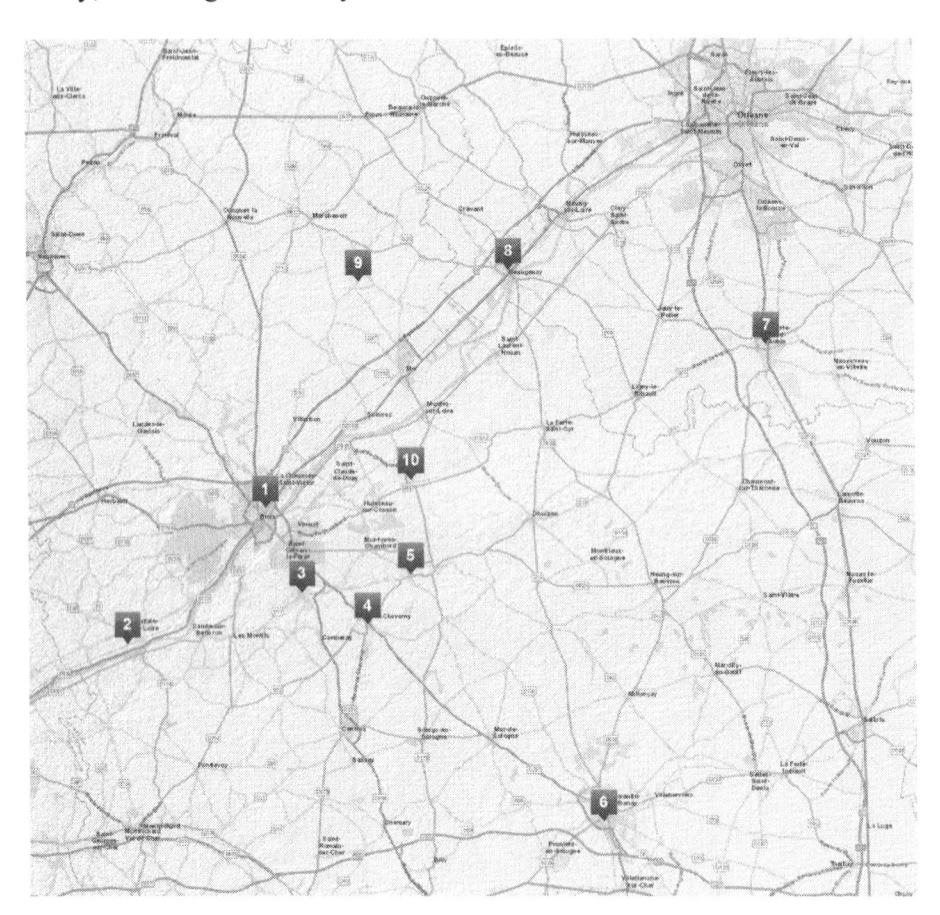

BLOIS TO CHAMBORD MAP
KEY TO MAP:
- 1) Blois
- 3) Cellettes
- 5) Tour en Sologne
- 7) La Ferté St Aubin
- 9) Talcy
- 2) Chaumont-sur-Loire
- 4) Cheverny
- 6) Romorantin
- 8) Beaugency
- 10) Chambord

DAY 1
Blois

STAY AT: *the Municipal aire in **Rue Jean Moulin, Blois.** This Aire is located in a large tarmac parking area reserved for motorhomes, accessed by an automatic barrier (accessible 0600 – 2300), which you pay for, when you leave, by credit card. The aire is located in the centre of town, about 500m from the Chateau, where there are 40 marked level spaces, with little shade available but lit at night. The artisanal borne with drainage grid, wifi, toilets and showers are adjacent. This is a well-located aire for visiting Blois, being fairly close to the centre, Cathedral and the Chateau (15 min walk). Blois is an interesting town to visit, with a wide range of shops, restaurants, museums, etc.*

Facilities: *Water•Grey Drain•Black Drain•Toilets*
No. of spaces: *40*
Parking: *8€ /24Hrs*
Services: *Incl.*
Opening times: *All year*
GPS Coordinates: *N47.58652   E01.32644*
Alternative: *Camping Val de Blois, Bas de Loisirs (D951), 41350 Vineuil Open: 01/05 – 30/09*

Blois, a beautiful old town on the banks of the Loire, is labelled as a "Town of Art and History". Visitors can take a boat trip to explore the river's abundant flora and fauna, or enjoy a ride around the grounds of Blois Château by horse and cart. The château itself is a masterpiece of Renaissance architecture, betraying aspects of a medieval style although five different types of architecture were used in its construction. Also in the town is the House of Magic, an entertaining place to visit for kids of all ages, as well as the Artefact Museum, which houses a stunning collection of works by Arman, Dali, Christo and Cesar.

TAKE D952 SOUTH TO:

Chaumont-sur-Loire: The château originally belonged to Catherine de Medici, but when her husband died, she pressured Diane de Poitiers into swapping Chaumont for the château at Chenonceau. Today you can still see the drawbridge, which has remained intact, and the 19th C Hermes saddlery in the courtyard. Between June and October, the château plays host to the International Garden Festival, with landscape gardeners arriving from all over the world to create beautiful gardens around a central theme, which changes from year to year.

TAKE D751 and D77 WEST TO:
Cellettes: Initially built by a statesman friend of Ronsard, Beauregard Château was extended in the 17th C adding particularly impressive interior decor and wood panelling. The château houses 327 portraits, including those of 15 French Kings, whilst the grounds boast a portrait garden.

CONTINUE SOUTH ON D765 TO:
Cheverny

STAY AT: *The Municipal aire in* **Rue des Combattants (D765), Cheverny,** *located on the northern edge of this large rural village, next to the tennis courts. Ample parking spaces are available in a large tarmac car park, with a little shade and lighting, bordered by a grass area to the north with picnic tables adjacent. Modern Euro Relais service point with platform drain. This is a fairly quiet aire, about 200m from the village centre, with a small parade of shops and restaurant opposite. There is also a gravel/grass parking area for motorhomes on the south side of the village (800m from centre), near to the Chateau on Rue du Boucher, a quiet spot but with no service point to offer.*

Facilities: *Water•Grey Drain•Black Drain•Rubbish*
No. of spaces: *20*
Parking: *Free*
Services: *2€ Water*
Opening times: *All year*
GPS Coordinates: *N47.51284   E01.45651*
Alternative: *Camping Cheverny, Les Saules, 41700 Cheverny Open: 01/05 – 17/09*

DAY 2
Cheverny: This magnificent 17th C château was the inspiration behind Captain Haddock's (of Tintin fame) Château at Moulinsart and Tintin fans will love Cheverny as there is a permanent exhibition called "The Secrets of Moulinsart". You can enjoy the park by boat on the lake, or in a buggy - a fun and original way to explore the leafy surroundings.

TAKE D102 EAST TO:
Tour-en-Sologne: Villesavin Château was home to François I's private secretary, and was built by the architects of Chambord Château. In the gardens, children can have a great time trying to find

out the identity of the ghost who has haunted Villesavin since 1919. Nearby is the Museum of Marriage, built in 1840, which contains everything you can imagine relating to conjugal rites in France.

STAY AT: *the Municipal aire in* **Rue de la Mairie (D102), Tour-en-Sologne.** *The aire is located on the southern side of this small village, in a medium sized tarmac parking area, near to the church and the Mairie. A grass area surrounds it, with shade available in a couple of places. A Euro-Relais borne with platform drain. This is a well-maintained, clean and quiet aire close to the centre of the village, having a toilet block with washing up sinks adjacent, and picnic tables on the grass. There is only a boulangerie (with some grocery) and a restaurant in the village.*
Facilities: *Water•Grey Drain•Black Drain•Rubbish •Electric•Toilets*
No. of spaces: *10*
Parking: *Free*
Services: *2.5€ Water or Electric*
Opening times: *All year*
GPS Coordinates: *N47.53765   E01.50015*
Alternative: *Camping Les Pres, Rue du Gue, 41250 Mont pres Chambord   Open all year*

DAY 3
TAKE D120/ D119 SOUTH and D765 EAST TO:
Romorantin: Car enthusiasts will love the Matra museum, which follows the history of the company from its three Le Mans victories during the 1970's, right up until the latest models. There is also the Sologne Museum, which is housed in an old mill.
TAKE D922 NORTH 50KM TO:
La Ferté St Aubin: St Aubin Château is a remarkable architectural complex where the visitor can explore 15 furnished rooms as well as a classroom, the stables and an Orangerie containing an old toys collection. The Chateau is also renowned for its old-style cuisine, and gives demonstrations and tastings of its historical cooking whilst the 'Enchanted Island' is a children's entertainment park with shows. The Château's Park covers more than 40ha, offering miniature golf, children's entertainment and play areas.
STAY AT: *the Municipal aire in* **Ave Lowendal, off D2020, La Ferte St Aubin.** *This aire is located in a medium sized gravel car park on the northern edge of this small town, close to the municipal campsite and about 400m from the town centre. The aire is in a quiet location,*

backing onto woods with picnic benches, and offers 10 spaces for motorhomes, shaded by mature trees but not lit at night. Mini Flot bleu service point with drainage grid. Facilities in town include restaurants, various shops and a Carrefour supermarket. The Chateau is within 200m of the aire.
Facilities: *Water•Grey Drain•Black Drain•Rubbish*
No. of spaces: *10*
Parking: *Free*
Services: *2 € Water*
Opening times: *All year*
GPS Coordinates: *N47.72651   E01.93938*
Alternative: *Camping du Cosson, Ave Lowendal, 45240 La Ferte St Aubin   Open: 26/04 – 28/09*

DAY 4
TAKE D18/ D103 WEST 25KM TO:
Beaugency occupies a strategic location, thanks to its medieval bridge on the Loire, and was captured by the English before being liberated by Joan of Arc. The town is fascinating with its small, peaceful, medieval streets.
TAKE D917WEST and D15 SOUTH TO:
La Beauce: Talcy Chateau, nestling in the village, is a 16th C fortress with a mixture of medieval ruggedness and Renaissance elegance.
TAKE D15 SOUTH TO MER, THEN D112 SOUTH ACROSS LOIRE TO:
Chambord: The Royal Château and its grounds cover almost 3,000 acres – an area almost the size of Paris, making it an ideal choice for rambling and discovering local nature, with deer and wild boar roaming freely in this great natural spot. There are hundreds of miles of cycling paths, and it's possible to enjoy barge trips on the River Cosson.
STAY AT: *the Municipal aire in* **Rue de la Mairie (D102), Tour-en-Sologne,** *or Camping Les Pres, Rue du Gue, 41250 Mont pres Chambord*

Right: Tour en Sologne aire

Top: Blois by Wmeinhart   Middle: Cheverny by GIRAUD
Bottom: Beaugency Photo by Le Letty

CENTRE TOUR 25
RICHELIEU TO AMBOISE – 5 DAYS

A 5-Day Tour that begins in the town built by Cardinal Richelieu before visiting a chateau at Lemere and continuing with an exploration of the historic town of Chinon. Next comes a visit to Candes St Martin, one of the "Most Beautiful Villages of France", followed by the Loire chateaux at Rigny-Usse, Vilandry and Chancy. The Loire towns of Tours and Amboise warrant a day each, interspersed with visits to the Beaumarchais Nature Reserve and the Loire Valley Aquarium.

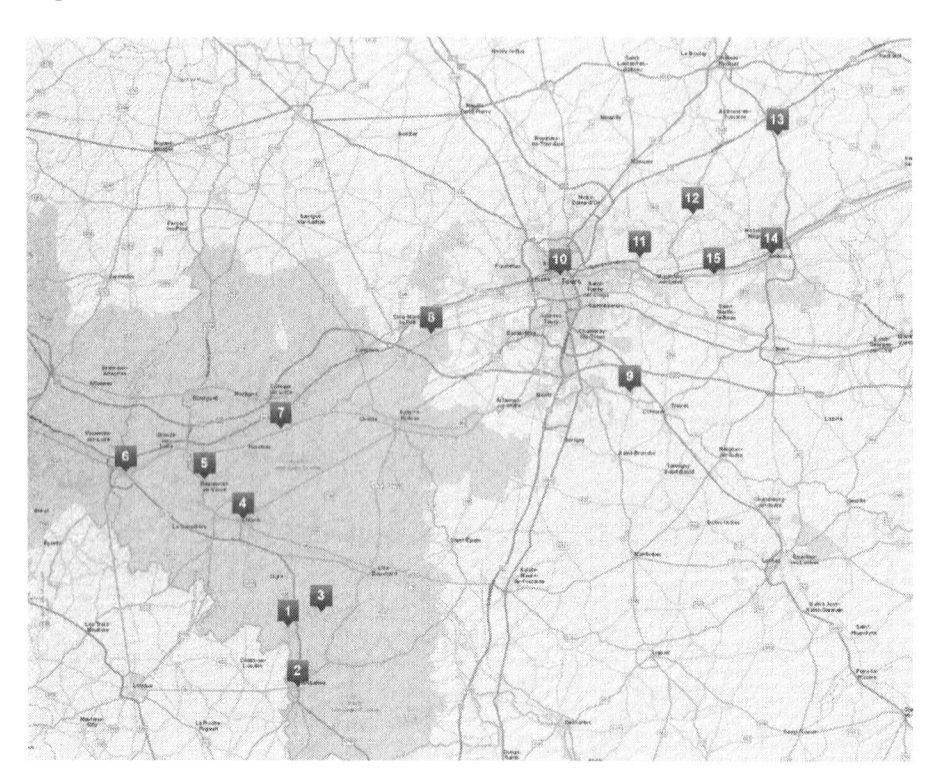

RICHELIEU TO AMBOISE MAP

KEY TO MAP:
1) Champigny sur Veude
2) Richelieu
3) Lemere
4) Chinon
5) Avoine
6) Candes St-Martin
7) Rigny Usse
8) Villandry
9) Esvres sur Indre
10) Tours
11) Vouvray
12) Chancay
13) Autreche   14) Amboise
15) Lussault-sur-Loire

DAY 1
Champigny sur Veude
STAY AT: *the Municipal aire in* **Rue Bonne Dame, Champigny sur Veude.** *The aire is located in a medium sized tarmac car park, shaded by trees, on the southern side of this small rural town, 300m from the town centre, where there is an artisanal service point with WC's adjacent. This is a pleasant, quiet spot next to a large park and lake, only a short level walk from town and its small range of shops (boulangerie, butcher, superette and café). There is a chateau and chapel to visit, and way-marked walks start from the aire.*
Facilities: *Water •Grey Drain •Black Drain •Toilets*
No. of spaces: *10*
Parking: *Free*
Services: *Free*
Opening times: *All year*
GPS Coordinates: *N47.06498   E00.31747*
Alternative: *Municipal Campsite, Ave de Schaafheim, 37120 Richelieu Open 15/05 – 15/09*
TAKE D749 4KMS SOUTH TO:
Richelieu: This unusual, innovative town was built by the famous Cardinal Richelieu and is a model of 17th C urbanism; the architectural plan was ahead of its time in terms of modern town-planning and its innovative grid style. An exhibition explains the history of the Cardinal and his town, whilst the church and the market hall are both worth a visit, together with the Palace gardens.
TAKE D749 NORTH TO:
Lemere: The restored 15th C. Le Rivau Château welcomes you into a world of fairy tales – the Chateau Gardens, with the "Gargantua vegetable garden" and its forest housing giant sculptures, whilst the chateau takes you back in time with all the recreated sounds of life in a medieval French chateau.
TAKE D749/ D751 NORTH TO:
Chinon is a "Town of Art and History" and it was at Chinon Château that Joan of Arc met her king, Charles VII. In the town you can learn more about the life of a Loire sailor by visiting the River House, where you will find model boats, an aquarium and an audio-visual presentation that unveils local life on the river. A trip on board a "futreau" boat along the River Vienne, or a wander past the half-timbered houses of the old town, are both great ways to explore the

town. North of Chinon is the Loire-Anjou Natural Regional Park with its tributaries of four rivers stretching between Angers and Tours. There are unusual troglodyte dwellings dug into the rocks, some of which house mushroom caves, and children can enjoy animated displays while learning about the natural heritage.

TAKE D749 NORTH TO:
Avoine
STAY AT: *the Municipal aire in* **Rue de la Republique** *in* **Avoine,** *located on the north western edge of the town, close to the Lac Mousseau in a park area where there are 10 large parking spaces on tarmac bordered by grass areas. Access is by automatic barrier at the entrance, payable by credit card and the parking is close to a wooded area and backs onto farmland, being about 800m from the town centre. AireServices service point with drainage platform. This is a very well laid out and maintained aire, but not very close to the town centre. There is a nice park like area, with woodland walks around the lake, a play area, a boules pitch and picnic tables. The town offers a reasonable selection of shops and a Shopi supermarket, 4 restaurants and a café/Tabac, plus a swimming pool.*
Facilities: *Water•Grey Drain•Black Drain•Electric*
No. of spaces: *10*
Parking: *4€/ 24 Hrs*
Services: *2€ Water or Electric*
Opening times: *All year*
GPS Coordinates: *N47.21333   E00.17785*
Alternative: *Camping Municipal, Quai Danton, 37500 Chinon*
Open: 01/04 – 30/10

DAY 2
TAKE D118 WEST FOR 8KM TO:
Candes St-Martin: This peaceful village, lying at the confluence of the Rivers Loire and Vienne, is one of the "Most Beautiful Villages of France". A former fishing and inland port, Candes St-Martin presents a scene of great contrast, with the black slate roofs and the white stone walls of its houses, and the Collegiate Church of Saint-Martin.

TAKE D7 19KMS EAST TO:
Rigny-Ussé Château is a fairy tale chateau, and was the inspiration behind Perrault's "Sleeping Beauty". Visitors can see the many furnished rooms, including a vault, the King's chamber, the Grand Staircase, and the Gallery with 17th C tapestries. The gardens were

designed by the King's gardener who laid out the grounds at Versailles.

TAKE D7 EAST 20KM TO:

Villandry: One of the last great Renaissance Châteaux in the Loire Valley, it is a rare example of a château whose gardens are in the same style as its architecture. The park including water and vegetable gardens, was re-designed at the beginning of the twentieth century and is considered to be exceptional, offering a display of colour throughout the year.

TAKE D121 SOUTH and D17 EAST TO:

Esvres sur Indre

<u>***STAY AT:***</u> *the Municipal aire in* **Rue Auguste Noyant** *in* **Esvres sur Indre***, which is in a medium sized tarmac car park bordered by grass verges and hedges. It is situated on the south side of this small town, where there is a reasonable range of shops and eating-places. The parking is 200m from the town centre, and the artisanal service point is easy to use and access. This is a well-maintained and quiet aire, with picnic table, swimming pool and tennis courts adjacent.*

Facilities: *Water•Grey Drain•Black Drain•Rubbish*
No. of spaces: *6*
Parking: *Free*
Services: *Free*
Opening times: *All year*
GPS Coordinates: *N47.28278   E00.78531*
Alternative: *Camping La Grange Rouge, D910, 37250 Montbazon*
Open: *30/03 – 30/10*

DAY 3

TAKE D943 NORTH TO TOURS:

Tours: In La Riche, on the West side of the town, the remains of St Cosme Priory lay within the walls of eight rose and iris gardens, and the 15th C Prior's bedroom and workshop are open to the public. Located between the Loire and the Cher, Tours is labelled as a "Town of Art and History", and is a place with a lively student atmosphere that complements its cultured heritage. When St Gatien Cathedral is lit up at night, you can appreciate its four centuries of architecture and the 18th C stained glass windows. The streets Rue Colbert, Rue Briçonnet, and Rue de Grand Marché, are lined with half-timbered houses, the wood panelled style also being in evidence on the buildings around the historic centre of Plumereau Square. Home to the world's only Guild

Museum, Tours also has a Museum of Fine Arts to visit, as well as Saint Martin's Basilica.

CROSS THE LOIRE and TAKE D952 EAST TO:
Vouvray
STAY AT: *the Municipal aire, off the* **D952** *in* **Vouvray.** *Located on the south side of the village, next to the municipal campsite and between the village and the Loire River, the aire is only 100m from the village centre's shops and eating-places. It comprises a small tarmac parking area overlooking fields and woodland, having 3 large spaces for motorhomes with picnic tables and a modern toilet block adjacent. There is a Euro-Relais service point with drainage platform.*
Facilities: *Water•Grey Drain•Black Drain•Electric•Toilets*
No. of spaces: *3*
Parking: *Free*
Services: *3€ Water or Electric*
Opening times: *All year*
GPS Coordinates: *N47.40916   E00.79735*
Alternative: Municipal *Camping, Off D952, 37210 Vouvray Open: 01/05 – 30/09*

DAY 4
TAKE D46 NORTH TO:
Chancay: The Valmer Château was built in 1640 amongst vineyards, by an advisor to Louis XIII. The château's 40-acre park is dotted with columns, terraced Italian gardens and vegetable gardens, where a range of beautiful and rare vegetables are grown.

CONTINUE ON D46 NORTH TO REUGNY and D55 EAST TO:
Autreche: The Beaumarchais Nature Reserve is a wildlife park, home to bison, wild boar, ostriches, deer and doe. The park stretches over 15 acres and the animals can be seen from the safety of the Safari Train.

TAKE D31 SOUTH 13KM TO:
Amboise
STAY AT: *the Municipal aire in* **Amboise,** *in* **Allee de la Chapelle St Jean** *situated on the north side of an island in the Loire river, opposite the Chateau of Amboise and next to the municipal campsite, L'Ile d'Or. The parking has been purpose built for motorhomes and is about 1km from the town centre (across the river). Parking is on grass, shaded by trees, and is accessed by a tarmac track with entry to the aire controlled by an automatic barrier (payable by credit card). Artisanal service point with drainage platform. There is a municipal*

swimming pool next to the aire and a good range of shops can be found in town where there is a market on Sunday morning.
Facilities: *Water •Grey Drain •Black Drain •Electric •Rubbish*
No. of spaces: *35*
Parking: *12€/ 24 Hrs*
Services: *3€ Water or Electric*
Opening times: *All year*
GPS Coordinates: *N47.41859   E00.98891*
Alternative: *Municipal Campsite, Rue de L'Ille d'Or, 37400 Amboise Open: 02 /06 – 10/09*

DAY 5

Amboise: The Chateau Royal d'Amboise is solidly built on a pedestal of rock and affords a wonderful view of the old town of Amboise and the banks of the Loire. The château contains an interesting collection of furniture (Gothic, Renaissance and 19th C) and is the resting place of Leonardo da Vinci. The Chapelle Saint Hubert, situated inside the château, contains the tomb of the Italian inventor, whilst outside are the Renaissance gardens in delightfully Italianate surroundings.

Le Clos-Luce: Leonardo da Vinci lived at Le Clos Lucé for the last three years of his life, and died there on 2 May, 1519. Today the Clos Lucé is a Leonardo de Vinci museum that reflects the prestigious history of the region, and includes forty models of the various machines made from the original sketches drawn by the Italian master of arts and sciences. The Chateau's park takes visitors on a journey through the Italian genius's art and visions. Standing nearby, at 44 metres tall, the 18th C Chanteloup Pagoda is the last remains of a former chateau and offers one of the finest views of the Loire Valley, there is also the Miniature Châteaux park - a collection of 44 scale models of Loire châteaux, with 9,000 bonsai trees, set in over an acre.

FOLLOW D751 WEST 5KM TO:

Lussault-sur-Loire: The Loire Valley Aquarium manages to display freshwater and saltwater fish specimens under the same roof. The collection includes everything from coral reef shark to piranha, cayman and river fauna.

<u>**STAY AT:**</u> *the Municipal aire in* **Amboise**, *in* **Allee de la Chapelle St Jean** *or Municipal Campsite, Rue de L'Ille d'Or, 37400 Amboise*

Amboise by Jalaudin

Candes St Martin Photo by Chbo91

Villandry

Aire at Voudray

CENTRE TOUR 26
AZAY LE RIDEAU TO MONTLOUIS SUR LOIRE – 7 DAYS

Starting at the Chateau of Azay-le-Rideau, this 7-Day Tour visits the villages of Villaine-les-Rochers and Sache, followed by the chateaux of Loches, Montpoupon and Valencay. The towns of Issoudun, Chateauroux, St Amand-Montrond and Vierzon are enroute, as well as Noirlac Abbey, Beauval Zoological Park and a troglodyte village.

Below: Beauval Zoo by Thesupermat   Above: Issoudun by Benjism89

DAY 1
Avoine

STAY AT: *the Municipal aire in* **Rue de la Republique** *in* **Avoine**, *located on the north western edge of the town, close to the Lac Mousseau. Situated in a park area, close to woodland and backing onto farmland, it offers 10 large parking spaces on tarmac bordered by grass areas. The parking is about 800m from the town centre and is accessed by automatic barriers at the entrance, payable by credit card. AireServices service point with drainage platform. Although it is a very well laid out and well maintained aire, it's not very close to the town centre. This is a nice park-like area, with woodland walks around the lake, a play area, boules pitch and picnic tables. There is a reasonable selection of shops in town, including a Shopi supermarket, 4 restaurants, and a café/Tabac as well as a swimming pool.*

Facilities: *Water•Grey Drain•Black Drain•Electric*
No. of spaces: *10*
Parking: *4€/ 24 Hrs*
Services: *2€ Water or Electric*
Opening times: *All year*
GPS Coordinates: *N47.21333   E00.17785*
Alternative: *Camping Municipal, Quai Danton, 37500 Chinon   Open 01/04 – 30/10*

TAKE D7/ D17 EAST TO:

Azay-le-Rideau: This magnificent Chateau was built during the reign of Francis I, and the surrounding grounds were designed to form a haven of greenery around it. The facades of this Renaissance gem are reflected in the still waters of the Indre. The château is in the centre of Azay-le-Rideau, offering visitors the opportunity for a pleasant stroll around the streets of the town. Throughout the summer, the night-time "Imaginaires" show lights up the château in a myriad of different colours.

Just a few kilometres from the Château d'Azay-le-Rideau, at the 'Cave Valley of Les Goupillieres', you can explore deep into the secret world of the cave dwellers. During the Middle Ages, communities of peasant farmers settled in caves cut into the limestone when it was quarried for building materials for the châteaux. Also nearby is the Maurice Dufresne museum, which shows off almost 3,000 different kinds of historic machinery, such as old cars, weapons and agricultural tools.

TAKE D57 5KM SOUTH TO:

Villaines-les-Rochers: As the area produces a third of all the basketwork in France, this industry has been central to life in Villaines-les-Rochers for a long time, and visitors today can still watch the wicker-weavers at work. The Wicker and Basketwork museum tells the story of this craft.
RETURN NORTH ONTO D17 and HEAD 6KM EAST TO:
Saché: This 16th C manor was the residence of the author, Balzac, the place where he drew inspiration for his work "Lis of the Valley" and where he spent so much of his time, away from the crowds of Paris. In the museum much of the décor remains unchanged, and you can find original manuscripts of Balzac's work.
CONTINUE ON D17 WEST TO:
Esvres sur Indre
STAY AT: *the Municipal aire in* ***Rue Auguste Noyant*** *in* ***Esvres sur Indre.*** *This is in a medium sized tarmac car park, bordered by grass verges and hedges, on the south side of this small town. Parking is 200m from the town centre, where there is a reasonable range of shops and eating-places. The artisanal service point is easy to use and access. This is a well-maintained and quiet aire, with picnic table, a swimming pool and tennis courts adjacent.*
Facilities: *Water•Grey Drain•Black Drain•Rubbish*
No. of spaces: *6*
Parking: *Free*
Services: *Free*
Opening times: *All year*
GPS Coordinates: *N47.28278   E00.78531*
Alternative: *Camping La Grange Rouge, D910, 37250 Montbazon Open 30 /03 – 30/10*
DAY 2
CONTINUE EAST ON D17 TO D943 and THEN SOUTH 25KM TO:
Loches: The keep of this château was used as a prison right up until 1926 and the 36-metre climb to its summit is hard work, but the view from the top is over the beautiful Chancery that houses a permanent exhibition; "A Town of Art and History". At the foot of the keep lies a secret garden, with aromatic plants and vegetable patches. In Vignemont, on the South side of Loches, you can find Troglodyte houses carved out of rock, with over 700 metres of tunnels to walk

through, the excavated limestone was used in the construction of many of the monuments in the region.
TAKE D764 NORTH 25KM TO:
Cere-le-Ronde: Montpoupon Château and its Museum, give an insight into the lifestyle of the hunting gentry, displaying hunting artefacts, a renovated hunting lodge, and various related arts and crafts.
TAKE D81 18KM SOUTH TO NOUANS and D960 25KM EAST TO:
Valençay: perches neatly on the sloping hillside, its 16th C château is a copy of Chambord Château, and was a gift from Napoleon to his chief diplomat, Talleyrand. The chateau has a themed visit, taking the visitor from a spectacular culinary display, through to duels to the death, all acted out by costumed actors. The park includes a children's château, a Grand Maze and a Car Museum, which holds over 60 vehicles, including a collection of bikes.
<u>STAY AT:</u> *the Municipal aire in* **Ave de la Resistance (D956)** *in* **Valencay.** *Located in a small gravel parking area behind the Tourist Office on the western side of town, about 300m from the town centre, with half a dozen level spaces. This is a fairly quiet location opposite the Chateau de Valencay, with only a short walk to the Automobile Museum. Euro-Relais borne with a platform drain. A good range of shops and eating-places can be found in town.*
Facilities: *Water•Grey Drain•Black Drain•Rubbish*
No. of spaces: *6*
Parking: *Free*
Services: *2€ Water*
Opening times: *All year*
GPS Coordinates: *N47.16041   E01.56171*
Alternative: *Municipal Camping, Rte de Loches, D960, 36600 Valencay Open 01/05 – 20/09*
DAY 3
TAKE D956 SOUTH 16KM and D34/ D37 EAST TO:
Bouges-le-Château: has a 40-acre park, French gardens, a museum of horse-drawn carriages and hunting lodges, as well as having an uncanny resemblance to the Petit Trianon, in Versailles. A night-time tour is led by guides dressed in period costumes.
TAKE D37 SOUTH and D8 EAST 33KM TO:

Issoudun: Explore the medieval history of the White Tower, or visit the St Roch Hospice Museum, which displays artefacts used in apothecary during the 17th and 18th centuries, and holds contemporary art exhibitions.

TAKE N151 WEST 30KM TO:
Chateauroux: The ancient Cordelier's Convent, looking out over the Indre Valley, houses the Fine Arts School - the site for various exhibitions of contemporary art and you can also visit the terrace gardens and superb washhouse. Taking its name from one of Napoleon's children, the 17th C Bertrand Mansion invites visitors to relive epic tales from the Napoleonic era, there is a spectacular aviary in the grounds, which was made for Napoleon by 18 Chinese workers during their incarceration on St Hélène.

TAKE D943 32KM SOUTH ONTO D69/ D951 EAST TO:
Le Chatelet
STAY AT: *the Municipal aire in* **Rue de la Gare, Le Chatelet.** *Located in a medium sized parking area to the west of this rural village, it offers level, tree-shaded spaces on tarmac/grass and is lit at night. The aire backs onto open countryside, is bordered by grass areas and overlooks a small lake, with a play area and benches nearby. Raclet service point with drain. There are way-marked walks around the village, which has shops and restaurants, and there is an Abbey and chateaux in the vicinity.*
Facilities: *Water •Grey Drain •Black Drain •Electric*
No. of spaces: *10*
Parking: *Free*
Services: *2€ Water or Electric*
Opening times: *All year*
GPS Coordinates: *N46.64498   E02.27849*
Alternative: *Municipal Camping, l'Etang Merlin, D80, 18370 Chateaumeillant Open 01/05 – 30/09*

DAY 4
RETURN ON D951 WEST 6KM TO:
Maisonnais: The medieval gardens of the Notre-Dame-d'Orsan Priory invite you to contemplate a variety of green spaces and ancient plants, discovering amongst other things a vegetable garden maze and a garden of vines.

TAKE D951 EAST and D65 SOUTH 13KM TO:

Culan: Located on a protected natural site, Culan chateau stands proudly on a rock overlooking magnificent medieval gardens. The chateau holds numerous events in the summer, including daily falconry shows and evening tours by candlelight.

TAKE D997 NORTH 15KM and D1 EAST 12KM TO:

Ainay-le-Vieil: Nicknamed "Little Carcassonne", Ainay-le-Vieil's medieval walls encircle a flamboyant gothic inner dwelling, surrounded by formal English style gardens.

*STAY AT: the Municipal aire in **Rue de la Tuilerie (D118), Ainay-le-Vieil**. Situated to the south of this small rural village, this aire is well signposted and located next to the village football pitch where there are 6 level spaces on grass, accessed by a gravel drive and bordered by high hedges. The aire is about 500m from the village centre (no shops or services in the village) and its magnificent chateau. Artisanal borne with platform drain and adjacent WC.*

Facilities: *Water•Grey Drain•Black Drain•Toilets*
No. of spaces: *6*
Parking: *Free*
Services: *Free*
Opening times: *All year*
GPS Coordinates: *N46.66098   E02.55599*
Alternative: *Municipal Camping, Rue de la Roche, 18200 St Amand-Montrond Open 01/04 – 30/09*

DAY 5
TAKE D2144 10KM NORTH TO:

St Amand-Montrond: The town is ranked third in France for the production of gold jewellery, and visitors can head to an iconic glass pyramid on the outskirts called 'Le Cité d'Or' (the city of gold). This is a museum dedicated to the global history of gold around the world, which helps you to discover the myth and reality of this precious metal. The town has a wide variety of shops, and small electric boats can be hired for short trips on the Berry Canal that bisects the town.

CONTINUE NORTH ON D2144 TO:

Bruere-Allichamps: Noirlac Abbey is one of the most well preserved monasteries in Europe and is almost entirely open to the public. Guided tours introduce you to the Cistercian world.

TAKE D92 7KM EAST TO:

Meillant Château, built at the end of the 15th C, was a masterpiece of the Loire Valley. With its Lion Tower, richly decorated by Milanese sculptors, the château depicts both the end of the Gothic era, in all its splendour, and the start of the Renaissance period. The chateau cellars host a permanent collection of reconstructed models of a medieval village, a Renaissance town, and a Gutenberg printing house – all displaying everyday life from the Middle Ages in miniature.

RETURN TO ST AMAND and JOIN A71 @ JCN 8, HEAD NORTH TO JCN 7. TAKE D400 and D2076 NORTH TO:

Mehun sur Yevre

STAY AT: *the Municipal aire off* **Rue de Jeanne d'Arc, Mehun sur Yevre.** *This aire is located near to the town centre, alongside the Canal du Berry (on the east side) in a small tarmac parking area shaded by tall trees. There are grass areas adjacent, and picnic tables/benches placed next to the canal. The aire has open countryside to the west with walks along the towpath. The Urbaflux service point with platform drain is located next to the parking, with payment for water available by credit card only. The aire is 400m from the town centre and its good range of shops/services, with the additional option of visiting the Chateau of Charles VII.*

Facilities: *Water •Grey Drain•Black Drain•Toilets*
No. of spaces: *6*
Parking: *Free*
Services: *2.5€ Water*
Opening times: *All year*
GPS Coordinates: *N47.14405   E02.21040*
Alternative: *Municipal Camping, Ave Champ de Foire, 18500 Mehun sur Yevre Open 08 /05 – 30/09*

DAY 6
TAKE D2076 NORTH TO:

Vierzon: has been a major railway junction since the 19th C, and more than 150 years of railway history are on display at the Laumônier Museum where you can see a unique collection of parts, models, and photos, etc. as well as a children's area.

TAKE D2076/ D976 61KM WEST TO:

Saint Aignan: Beauval Zoological Park (on the D675), is one of Europe's top animal parks, being home to tigers, gorillas, rhinoceros, white lions, crocodiles, manatees, birds of prey and a stud farm. An oasis where threatened species are protected and the animals grow up in a natural environment, included in the tour are sea lion shows and birds of prey demonstrations, as well as a visit to the animal nursery, where numerous baby animals can be found.

TAKE D976 WEST TO:

Ange

STAY AT: *the Municipal aire off the **D17**, in **Place de la Mairie**, Ange. This aire is located in a large gravel parking area in this small village, next to the Mairie. It is surrounded by open farmland with good views, but can only offer shade in a couple of places. There are 2 shops (epicerie and a boulangerie) and a café/bar in the village. The Raclet borne with drainage grid is lit at night.*

Facilities: *Water•Grey Drain•Black Drain•Electric*
No. of spaces: *20*
Parking: *Free*
Services: *3€ Water*
Opening times: *All year*
GPS Coordinates: *N47.33160   W01.24335*
Alternative: *Camping Couleurs du Monde, D764, 41400 Faverolles sur Cher Open 18/04 – 26/09*

DAY 7

TAKE D176 WEST TO:

Bourre: The stone used to build the Loire Valley Châteaux was mined in this picturesque "troglodyte" village, where today's visitors can see the underground town, quarrying methods from the past, homes carved into the rock, a stone mason's quarry and 17th C production of silk worms. Today mushroom cultivation flourishes in the humidity of the rocks, 40m underground.

TAKE D176 WEST TO:

Chateau de Chenonceau: is one of the classic Loire Valley châteaux. Built astride the river Cher, its famous gallery is one of its finest features, as are the gardens created by Catherine de Medici. In the outbuildings there is a plant nursery, which supplies the flowers used to decorate the château interior.

CONTINUE WEST ON D40 TO:

Montlouis-sur-Loire: Innumerable varieties of tomatoes are grown in the traditional vegetable gardens of Bourdaisière Château, a Tomato Hot House can be visited, as well as the park, arboretum, the stables and the château itself.

TAKE D751 13KM EAST TO:

Amboise

STAY AT: *the Municipal aire in **Amboise**, in **Allee de la Chapelle St Jean** situated on the north side of an island in the Loire river, opposite the Chateau of Amboise and next to the municipal campsite, L'Ile d'Or. The parking has been purpose built for motorhomes and is about 1km from the town centre (across the river). Parking is on grass, shaded by trees, and is accessed by a tarmac track with entry to the aire controlled by an automatic barrier (payable by credit card). Artisanal service point with drainage platform. There is a municipal swimming pool next to the aire and a good range of shops can be found in town with a market on Sunday morning.*
Facilities: *Water •Grey Drain •Black Drain •Electric •Rubbish*
No. of spaces: *35*
Parking: *12€/ 24 Hrs*
Services: *3€ Water or Electric*
Opening times: *All year*
GPS Coordinates: *N47.41859   E00.98891*
Alternative: *Municipal Campsite, Rue de L'Ille d'Or, 37400 Amboise Open 02/06 – 10/09*

Above: Vierzon Railway Museum by Cjp24

Page 184

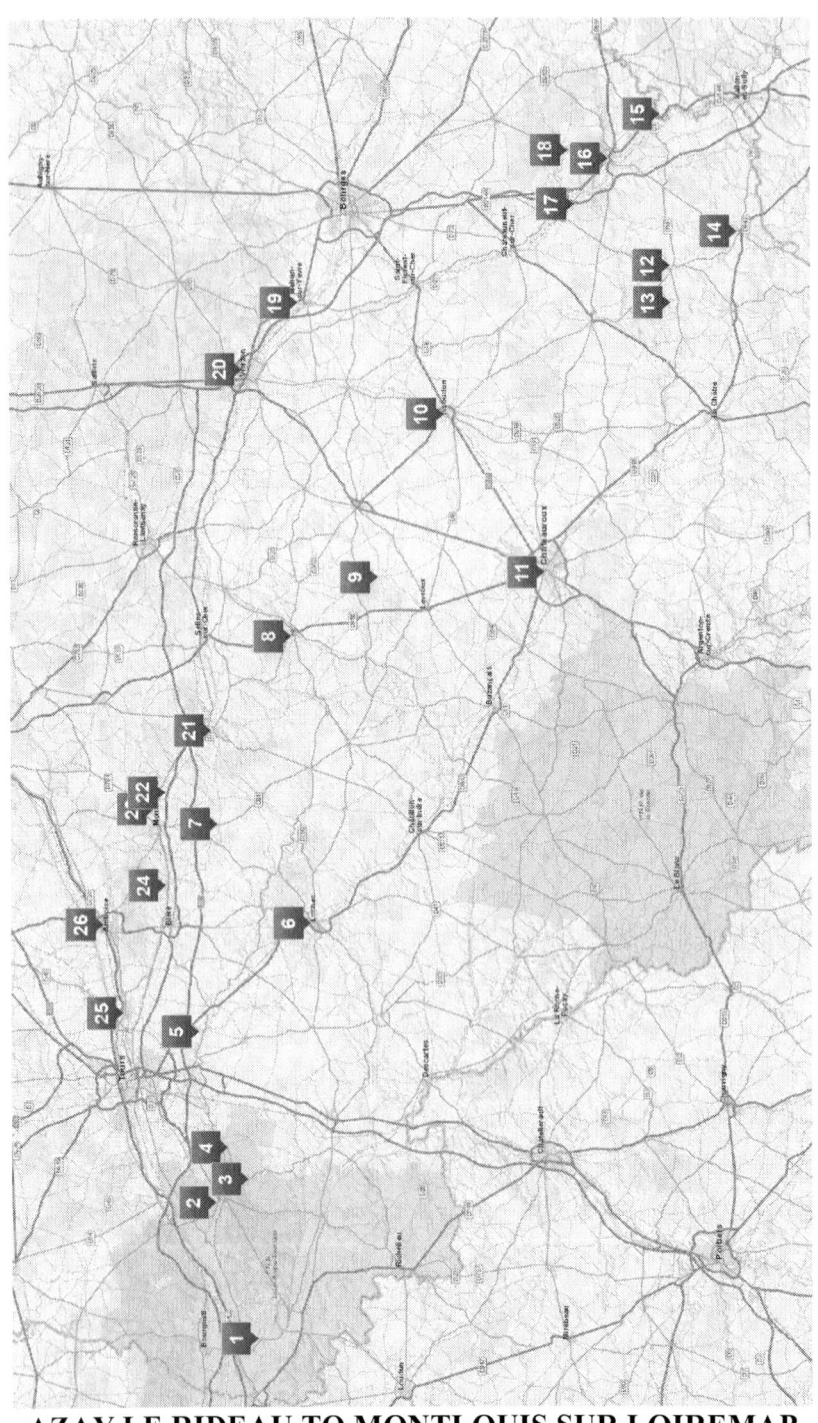

AZAY LE RIDEAU TO MONTLOUIS SUR LOIRE MAP

KEY TO MAP (Opposite):

1) Avoine
2) Azay le Rideau
3) Villaines-les-Rochers
4) Sache
5) Esvres sur Indre
6) Loches
7) Cere-le-Ronde
8) Valencay
9) Bouges-le-Château
10) Issoudun
11) Chateauroux
12) Le Chatelet
13) Maisonnais
14) Culan
15) Ainay-le-Vieil
16) St Amand Montrond
17) Bruere-Allichamps
18) Meillant
19) Mehun sur Yevre
20) Vierzon
21) Saint Aignan
22) Ange
23) Bourre
24) Chenonceau
25) Montlouis-sur-Loire
26) Amboise

Above: Aire at Esvres sur Indre

CENTRE TOUR 27
GRAND PRESSIGNY TO EGUZON – 3 DAYS

This 3-Day Tour starts at the Chateau of Le Grand Pressigny, visits the Haute-Touche Wildlife Park, the picturesque villages of Ingrandes, Gargilesse, and the large Gallo-Roman museum in St Marcel.

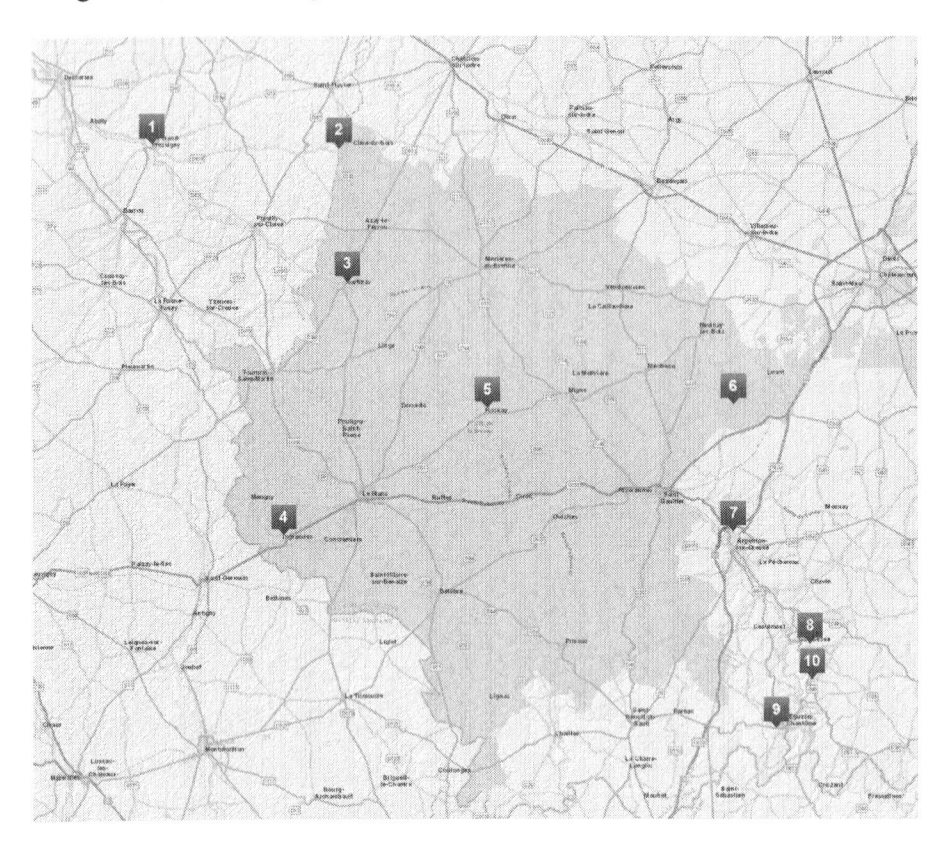

GRAND PRESSIGNY TO EGUZON MAP

KEY TO MAP:
- 1) Le Grand Pressigny
- 3) Martizay
- 5) Rosnay
- 7) St Marcel
- 9) Eguzon
- 2) Obterre
- 4) Ingrandes
- 6) La Perouille
- 8) Gargilesse
- 10) Cuzion

DAY 1
Le Grand Pressigny
STAY AT: *the Municipal aire in **Rue St Martin** in **Le Grand Pressigny**, in the large tarmac car park of the town's swimming pool next to the 2* municipal campsite "Croix Marron", on the outskirts of the town, about 350m south of the centre. The parking is close to open countryside, is bordered by hedges and provides some shade under trees. There is an Artisanal service point with drainage grid. Showers/ toilets are available in the campsite (in season) whilst the town's outdoor swimming pool is open June-August, as well as the tennis courts. Shops in town include a boulangerie, butcher, epicerie, tabac/ news, pharmacy and bank, 2 restaurants and a brasserie. A market is held on Thursdays and there is also a chateau and museum to visit.*
Facilities: *Water•Grey Drain•Black Drain•Electric*
No. of spaces: *10*
Parking: *Free*
Services: *Free*
Opening times: *All year*
GPS Coordinates: *N46.91722   E00.80667*
Alternative: *Camping Municipal, Rue St Martin, 37350 Le Grand Pressigny Open 09/04 – 30/09*

Le Grand Pressigny: The château, a mixture of medieval and Renaissance styles, houses a Prehistoric museum with beautiful collections of carved flint from this region, where great quantities of flint were exported from in the past, various videos and models give a fascinating insight into this period of history.
TAKE D103 EAST 21KM TO:
Obterre: The 100 ha Haute-Touche Nature Reserve is a wildlife park with over 1000 animals, including deer, birds, tigers, antelopes, zebra and giraffe, as well as wolves, which have been brought back into the area after a long absence.
TAKE D14 SOUTH TO AZAY-LE-FERRON and TAKE D975 6KM SOUTH TO:
Martizay
STAY AT: *the Municipal aire off the **D975** in **Martizay**. Located next to the river, on the south bank, about 400m from the centre of the village in a park/leisure area, where there are picnic tables, grass areas and a play area. There are about 10 spaces on tarmac with some shade in places, 3 separate hook-up points (also with water) and*

toilets adjacent, all in a pleasant location with open farmland to the west. An Artisanal service point with drainage platform. The village has a small selection of shops; boulangerie, butcher, bar/café/news, superette and a Museum, a market is held here on Wednesday mornings.
Facilities: *Water •Grey Drain •Black Drain •Electric •Toilets*
No. of spaces: *10*
Parking: *Free*
Services: *Free*
Opening times: *All year*
GPS Coordinates: *N46.80583   E01.03833*
Alternative: *Camping Municipal, D6, 36220 Tournon St Martin Open 15/06 – 15/09*

DAY 2
CONTINUE SOUTH ON D975 TO LE BLANC and TAKE D951 WEST 9KM TO:
Ingrandes: being the past home of Henry de Monfreid, the great French adventurer and writer, the village museum now houses the souvenirs of this famous Red Sea explorer, who settled here in 1948.
RETURN TO LE BLANC, THEN TAKE D27 13KM EAST TO:
Rosnay: Full of woods, moors, lakes and prairies, the Brenne Natural Regional Park has everything for nature lovers and walkers. The Information Centre here has guides for the area and makes a good starting point.
TAKE D27/ D14 EAST TO:
La Perouille
STAY AT: the Municipal aire at **l'Etang de la Roche, La Perouille.** *This aire is located 500m to the East of this small rural village, next to the village lake where there are a dozen level spaces on grass with picnic tables and benches. Note: it is also possible to park on the access road in places if the ground is wet. The aire is a bit isolated, and there is no lighting, but it is shaded by trees in places, has a Euro-Relais service point, drainage platform and an adjacent toilet block. This is a small village with just a bar/tabac/restaurant that also sells the jetons, the aire is signposted in the village.*
Facilities: *Water •Grey Drain •Black Drain •Electric •Toilets*
No. of spaces: *12*
Parking: *Free*
Services: *2€ Water or Electric*

Opening times: *All year*
GPS Coordinates: *N46.70582   E01.52271*
Alternative: *Camping Les Chambons, Rue des Chambons, 36200 Argenton sur Creuse Open all year*

DAY 3
TAKE D1 and THEN D927 SOUTH TO:
Saint-Marcel: The purpose-built museum here is located on the excavated site of Argentomagus, the Gallo-Roman name for this town. Covering an area of 2,400m2 the museum has many finds from the archaeological excavations, including artefacts from prehistoric times up to the end of the Roman Empire.

TAKE D48/ D36 SOUTH 17KM TO:
Gargilesse: is a small village of artists, one of the "Most Beautiful Villages of France", and was also home to the author George Sands. The church has beautiful 13th to 16th C frescoes on the walls of its crypt, as well as a collection of magnificent historic columns.

CONTINUE SOUTH ON D40/ D45 TO:
Eguzon: Chamboln Lake, created by the Eguzon dam, offers a variety of watersports from swimming to canoeing and water skiing. "Le Boucle du Pin" is a peaceful walk nearby with breathtaking views, whilst the Creuse Valley Museum displays the crafts and daily life of the area, as well as the history of the construction of the dam.

CONTINUE ON D45 TO:
Cuzion

<u>STAY AT:</u> *the parking at* **Point des Piles (D45)** *in* **Cuzion.** *Located in a small parking area next to the river and behind a cycle track, this car park is in a pleasant, quiet spot with some shade from trees, but unfortunately is not near to any facilities apart from an Auberge on the opposite bank. It is about 1km from Cuzion but close to the Eguzon dam, where parking is also available - although this was formerly an aire, the service facilities are no longer operational.*

Facilities: *None*
No. of spaces: *10*
Parking*: Free*
Services*: None*
Opening times: *All year*
GPS Coordinates: *N46.46025   E01.60417*
Alternative: *Camping Municipal, Les Morigeaux, 37270 Eguzon-Chantome*

Left: Ingrandes by Llann Wé[2]

Right: St Marcel by Repérant

Left: Gargilesse by Havang(nl)

Right: Aire at Martizay

CENTRE TOUR 28
THE JOAN OF ARC SITES ALONG THE LOIRE – 5 DAYS

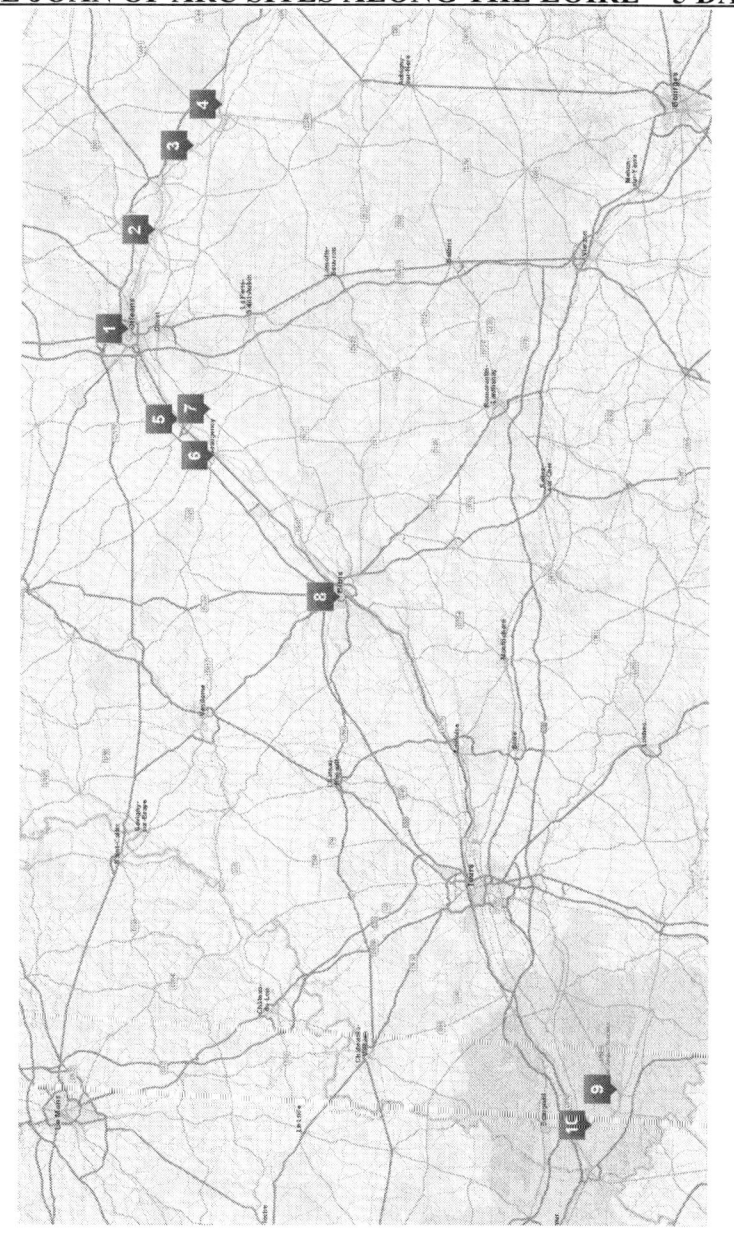

KEY TO JOAN OF ARC SITES MAP (Above):
1) Orleans
2) Jargea
3) St Benoit sur Loire
4) Sully-sur-Loire
5) Meung-sur-Loire
6) Beaugency
7) Dry
8) Blois
9) Chinon
10) Avoine

This is a 5-Day Tour around the famous sites in the Loire associated with the history of the French heroine, Joan of Arc. The sites visited relate to her military triumphs in lifting the sieges of towns along the Loire, which at that time were being occupied by the English army.

A brief history:

Joan of Arc was born in 1412 at Domremy, a small village in the Vosges region, to farmer, Jacques d'Arc and his wife, Isabelle. When Joan was 13 years old, she started to hear voices from God telling her that she must rid France of the English (who werc at the time occupying large areas of the country). As she grew older, the voices 'spoke' to her two or three times a week – now telling her that she must raise the siege of the city of Orléans (being besieged by the English army) and take the Dauphin to Reims, to be crowned king. In May 1428, at the age of sixteen, Joan left home and traveled to Vaucoleurs, a fortress in Champagne that was still in French hands, where she met the garrison commander and asked to be taken to see the Dauphin, in Chinon. She was initially refused this request, but after several attempts her story was eventually given some credence and she was taken for an interview with the Dauphin (the future Charles VII). Here, surprisingly, she managed to convince the future king to equip her with an army to relieve the siege of Orleans, with the result that in May, 1429 she successfully defeated the English army and lifted the 7 month siege.

DAY 1
Orleans

STAY AT: The Municipal aire at **Allee Claude Bernard in Saran**, located close to the Mairie on the northern edge of this small town (part of the Orleans suburbs). The aire is in a medium sized gravel parking area, is bordered by small trees and grass, and has lighting at night. Modern artisanal service point with drainage platform. This is a pleasant, quiet location adjacent to a small park/lake area, conveniently situated 4km north from the centre of Orleans and 1km from Junction 14 of the A10 autoroute. The aire is within a 200m level walk of Saran centre, where there is a good range of small shops.

Facilities: Water•Grey Drain•Black Drain
No. of spaces: 10
Parking: Free
Services: Free

Opening times: All year
GPS Coordinates: N47.95094   E01.87321
Alternative: Municipal Campsite, Chemin de la Roche, 45140 St Jean de la Ruelle   Open 01/04 – 04/09

Orleans is a very interesting and historic city with many fascinating old buildings. The Tourist Information in Place de l'Etape (close to the Cathedral) can provide plenty of info, including Discovery Trail maps, and there is also a guided Joan of Arc tour of the city available.

Maison de Jeanne d'Arc in Place de Gaulle: When Joan of Arc entered the City of Orléans (on 29 April, 1429) it had been besieged by the English for seven months. She stayed in the house of the king's Treasurer, Jacques Boucher - a house that was extensively extended at the end of the Middle Ages but was much later destroyed by bombing in 1940. Rebuilt in 1965, on a smaller footing than the original, it now appears as it would have looked in the 1400's and currently houses a museum dedicated to Joan of Arc. The ground, first, and second floors all contain models and items relating to the main stages in the life of the heroine.

Cathedral Sainte-Croix: Joan of Arc visited this cathedral many times during and after the 1429 siege. It has been substantially rebuilt following damage during the various wars since.

Tour Blanche: The wall that surrounded Orleans at the time of the siege was reinforced in places by towers, and the Tour Blanche is one of these last remaining towers. Its base, which can be seen in Rue Saint Flou, dates from the 14th C, but the uppers parts are more recent - modifications were made in the 15th C, as can be seen from the arrow slits and enlarged openings to take cannons. The tower ceased to be used for defensive purposes at the end of the 15th C.

STAY AT: *The Municipal aire at* **Allee Claude Bernard in Saran,** *or the Municipal Campsite, Chemin de la Roche, 45140 St Jean de la Ruelle*

DAY 2
TAKE D960 EAST 17KM TO:
Jargeau: After lifting the siege at Orleans, Joan turned her attention to Jargeau (17km east of Orleans), which was being occupied by the English, and after a two-day battle this town was captured by the French. Unfortunately there are few remains at Jargeau from this period and, apart from a statue to Joan, there is little to see here.

TAKE D960/ D60 EAST 17KM TO:

St Benoit sur Loire: The Romanesque Abbey of Fleury is where Joan and Charles prayed in June, 1429 before the shrine of St Benedict. The Abbey has marvellous carvings on the entrance pillars, 12th C church art and the relics of St Benedict in the crypt. Open 01/ 04 – 01/11
CONTINUE ON D60 EAST 8KM TO:
Sully sur Loire: Dating from 1102 and built on two small islands, the Chateau, with its thick walled towers, is an impressive fortress surrounded by a moat and has an elegant Renaissance interior. Joan visited Charles here on two occasions, and rumour has it that the owner, Georges de La Tremoille, actually tried to kill her by throwing her from the battlements. Visitors can see the medieval keep, the parapet walk, the remarkable 14th C wooden roof structure, the Duke of Sully apartments and the collections of paintings, tapestries and period furniture.
STAY AT: *The Municipal aire in* **Chemin Salle Verte, Sully-sur-Loire.** *Located at the edge of the Loire on the western side of this small town, the aire is in a large gravel parking area, surrounded by grass areas. There are large marked spaces with grass adjacent, trees provide some shade and the aire is lit at night. This is a very quiet location next to a forest (with several walks/cycle trails), 1km from the centre of town and within 500m of the chateau. There is an Artisanal service point and drainage platform. Good range of shops can be found in town, as well as some eating-places.*
Facilities: Water •Grey Drain•Black Drain
No. of spaces: 35
Parking: Free
Services: Free
Opening times: All year
GPS Coordinates: N47.77116   E02.38448
Alternative: Camping HORTUS, Rte d'Orleans (D60), 45600 St Pere sur Loire. Open all year
DAY 3
RETURN TO JARGEAU and TAKE D921 SOUTH THEN D14/ D951 EAST TO CLERY ST ANDRE and CROSS THE LOIRE TO:
Meung sur Loire became the scene of the next battle in Joan's campaign in June, 1429. This town was also occupied by English forces, using the chateau as their headquarters, but because Meung was so heavily fortified, the majority of the French army moved on after having only captured the bridge over the Loire.

The Château, an interesting building dating back to the 12th C, was the residence of the Bishops of Orléans for seven centuries. It is full of surprises - such as the Bishop's bathroom, the underground passages and the "oubliettes" - and it has 15 acres of gardens in the French formal style. Open 1/03 – 31/10. Also of interest is the Collegiate church, with remains from the 11th C. In the town you can walk along the little rivers, better known as the "Mauves," past old mills used for flour, other grains and tanning.

TAKE D2152 SOUTH TO:

Beaugency was the place for the next episode in Joan of Arc's campaign against the English. Arriving here on 15th June, 1429, she laid siege to the town, thereby forcing the demoralized English occupiers to surrender and leave on the 17th June, without many casualties on either side (a statue of Joan, in Place St-Firmin, commemorates this event). When the English garrison retreated on that evening of 17th June, they headed north to Patay, where the French army subsequently routed them.

The keep (or Donjon) at Beaugency is a 4 storey medieval fortress dating from the 11th C, which, together with some of the town walls, constitutes the chief remains from the 1429 siege. Le Pont is the 26-arch medieval bridge that, although restored, is the same bridge Joan would have used to cross the Loire into the town. Also to visit is the Abbey Notre Dame, where the Roman Catholic church made their decision (in 1152) to annul the marriage between Louis VII and Eleanor of Aquitaine (who subsequently married Henry II of England).

TAKE D19 EAST and D951 NORTH TO:

Dry

STAY AT: *The Municipal aire on* **Route de Meung** *in* **Dry***, located close to the church and next to a park on the northern side of this rural village. Set in a medium sized tarmac parking area (with some shade available) and bordered by grass areas, the aire is next to a play area and only 100m from the centre of the village. There is a toilet in the adjacent football club, and a Euro-Relais service point with drainage grid. There are a few shops in the village (epicerie and tabac/café/ news) where you can buy the jetons.*

Facilities: *Water•Grey Drain•Black Drain*
No. of spaces: *10*
Parking: *Free*
Services: *2€ Water*

Opening times: All year
GPS Coordinates: N47.79847   E01.71441
Alternative: Municipal Campsite, Rte de Lailly (D19), 45190 Beaugency   Open 01/04 – 30/09

DAY 4
TAKE D951 SOUTH TO:

Blois: Labelled as a "Town of Art and History," Blois is a beautiful old town on the banks of the Loire. It was here, in the Royal Chateau, that Joan went on 25th April, 1429 to be blessed by the Archbishop of Reims, before leaving with her army to defeat the English at Orleans. The Château itself is a masterpiece of Renaissance architecture and betrays aspects of medieval style, although five different types of architecture were used in its construction. There are 560 rooms, 100 bedrooms and 75 staircases in the chateau, with some beautifully decorated rooms featuring the ornate and colourful decoration and furnishings of the period. Visitors can take a boat trip to explore the river's abundant flora and fauna, or take a ride around the grounds of Blois Château by horse and cart.

STAY AT: *The Municipal aire in* **Rue Jean Moulin, Blois.** *This aire is located in a large tarmac parking area reserved for motorhomes, accessed by an automatic barrier (accessible 0600 – 2300), which you pay for when you leave. Situated in the centre of town, about 500m from the Chateau, the aire has 40 marked level spaces (with little shade) and is lit at night. An artisanal borne with drainage grid, wifi, toilets and showers adjacent. This is a well located aire for visiting Blois, being close to the centre, cathedral and the Chateau (a 15 min walk) and good value. Blois is an interesting town to visit, and has a wide range of shops, restaurants, museums, etc.*

Facilities: Water•Grey Drain•Black Drain•Toilets
No. of spaces: 40
Parking: 8€/24Hrs
Services: Incl
Opening times: All year
GPS Coordinates: N47.58652   E01.32644
Alternative: Camping Val de Blois, Bas de Loisirs (D951), 41350 Vineuil   Open 01/05 – 30/09

DAY 5
TAKE D751 WEST AROUND TOURS TO:

Chinon: was the scene of the first meeting between the Dauphin (the future king Charles) and Joan of Arc, in February, 1429, at the Royal lodge in Chinon castle.

Royal Fortress: In the 12th C, Henry II and Eleanor of Aquitaine established the Court of the Plantagenet in the fortress that would later become home to Richard the Lionheart. The various towers offer views of the city. In the Clock Tower, visitors can see four-room apartments with their Flemish tapestries, and the Tour de Coudray is where Joan stayed whilst in Chinon. There is a Joan of Arc Museum here that includes part of the 14th C royal apartments and the 12th C Round tower. The museum collections, displayed on four floors, feature paintings, engravings, sculptures, pottery, medals, coats of arms and weapons that retrace the amazing life and times of Joan of Arc.

Museum of Art and History: One of the most beautiful museums in Touraine. Situated in the heart of the old town, the museum presents rich collections of archaeology, arts of the Middle-Ages and Renaissance period, earthenware, masterpieces of the various guilds, and paintings from the 16th to the 20th C.

La Chapelle Sainte-Radegonde: This underground chapel was a place of worship in pre-Christian days, and was inhabited by a hermit in the 6th C. There is an 11th C wall painting of a royal riding party, believed to represent King Henry II leading Eleanor of Aquitaine into captivity.

TAKE D749 NORTH TO:
Avoine

<u>**STAY AT:**</u> *the Municipal aire in* **Rue de la Republique** *in* **Avoine***, located on the north western edge of the town, close to the Lac Mousseau. About 800m from the town centre, it is situated in a park area, providing 10 large parking spaces on tarmac bordered by grass areas. Access is by automatic barriers at the entrance (payable by credit card) and the parking is close to a wooded area, backing onto farmland. AireServices service point with drainage platform. Although not very close to the town centre, this is a very well laid-out and well-maintained aire in a nice park-like area, with woodland walks around the lake, a play area, boules and picnic tables. There is a reasonable selection of shops in the town, a Shopi supermarket, 4 restaurants and a café/Tabac, plus a swimming pool.*

Facilities: *Water•Grey Drain•Black Drain•Electric*

No. of spaces: 10
Parking: 4€/24 Hrs
Services: 2€ Water or Electric
Opening times: All year
GPS Coordinates:
N47.21333   E00.17785
Alternative: Camping Municipal, Quai Danton, 37500 Chinon   Open 01/04 – 30/10

Above : Chinon by Jolivet

Above Left: Blois by Wladyslaw Sojka   Right: Beaugency Photo by Rouzet

Aire at Sully sur Loire

Page 199

CHAMPAGNE-ARDENNES TOUR 29
FORTRESSES OF THE ARDENNES – 4 DAYS

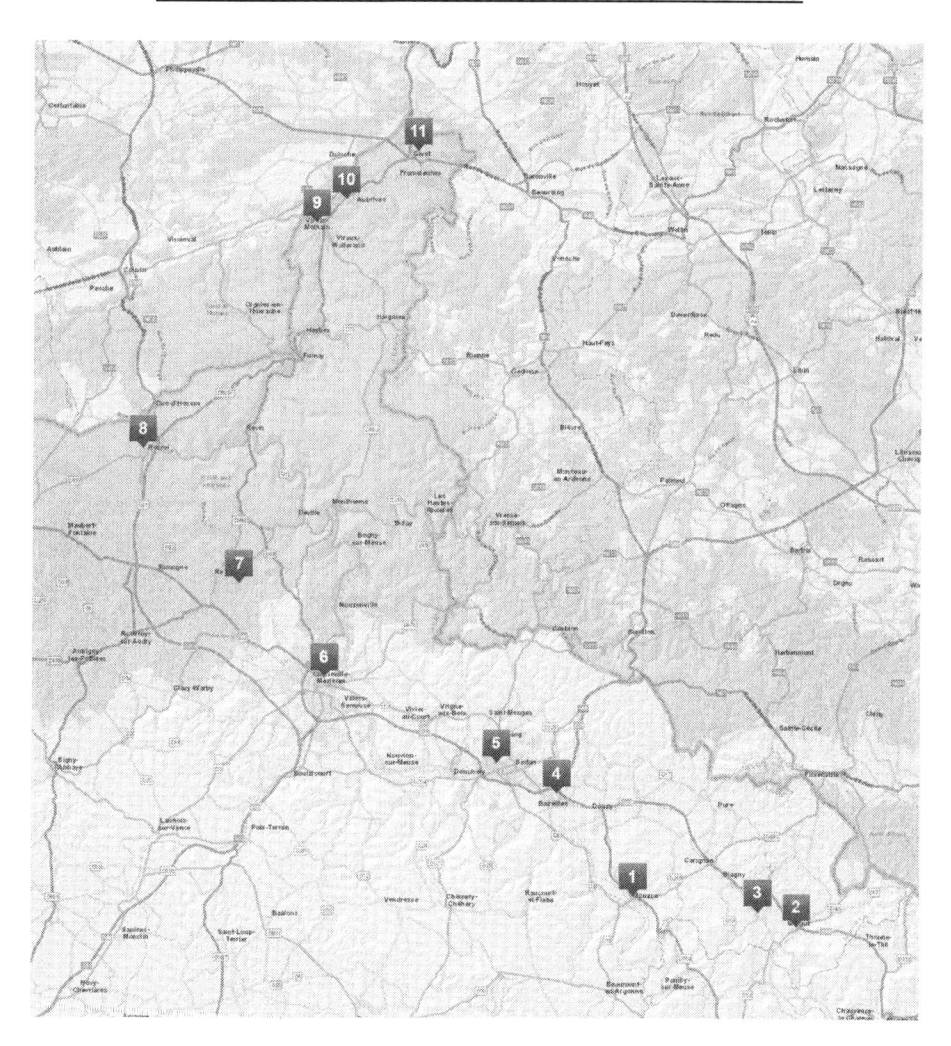

FORTRESSES OF THE ARDENNES MAP

KEY TO MAP:
1) Mouzon
2) Margut
3) Villy la Ferte
4) Bazeilles
5) Sedan
6) Charleville-Mezieres
7) Montcornet
8) Rocroi
9) Vireux-Molhain
10) Hierges
11) Givet

This 4-Day Tour follows the signposted "Fortifications Route" from the Meuse Valley to the Rocroi Plateau, travelling back through 2,000 years of history from the WWII fort on the Maginot Line to the 3rd C Roman encampment of Vireux. On the way, it visits the 11th C Montcornet chateau, Europe's largest fort at Sedan, the star-shaped fortified town of Rocroi, and in Bazeilles - the "Maison de la Dernière Cartouche" recalls the heroic resistance of a handful of soldiers during the Franco-Prussian war of 1870.

DAY 1
Mouzon
STAY AT: *the Municipal aire* **in Mouzon,** *in* **Ave de la Vigne.** *The aire is located next to the river on the north side of Mouzon, with parking on tarmac overlooking the Meuse river, having little shade but lit at night. The aire is only 100m from the centre of the village where there is a reasonable selection of shops and restaurants. There are showers and toilets adjacent on the harbour at the Capitainerie, where electric hook ups and wifi are also available as well as an artisanal service point.*
Facilities: *Water•Grey Drain•Black Drain•Electric•Wifi•Rubbish*
No. of spaces: *6*
Parking*: 10€/ 24 Hrs*
Services: *Incl*
Opening times: *All year*
GPS Coordinates: *N49.60695   E05.07722*
Alternative: *Camping les Bouleaux, Rue de L'Ecluse, 55700 Inor*
Open all year
Mouzon: is situated on the thoroughfare of the great Gallo-Roman highway running from Reims to Trier, and the town boasts an abbey church - a superb Gothic edifice that is allied with the Cathedral in Laon. Constructed by the Benedictines in the 13th C on the site of a Romanesque abbey, it has a remarkable interior and it also houses superb 18th C organs. There is also a museum, ramparts and the remains of a chateau to see.
TAKE D19 and D8043 WEST TO:
Margut: This museum is located only a few kilometres away from the Maginot Line and exhibits the life of French and German soldiers during the fighting in the Ardennes.
TAKE D44 SOUTH and D52 WEST TO:

Villy la Ferte: On May 18th, 1940, this fort came under attack both from the air and from a German infantry division, backed up with heavy artillery and anti-tank weapons. The position, although heavily damaged, was not breached and would not surrender but after further bombardment the garrison eventually went quiet. No return fire came from the fort and after a while, the Germans attacked the position, reached the outer doors and blew their way in. Once inside, they found that the entire 105-man garrison had been asphyxiated after the fume extractor fans had been damaged - there were no survivors on the French side. The tour will take you 35 metres underground as you explore the life of a soldier in a fortress of the Maginot Line.
CONTINUE WEST ON D52 and D8043 TO:
Bazeilles: The Maison de la Dernière Cartouche (Last Cartridge Museum) commemorates the sacrifice of 200 heroic defenders of the town of Bazeilles, during the Franco-Prussian War of 1870, when the soldiers defended the town until they were down to their last bullet.
FOLLOW THE ROAD 3KM NORTH TO:
Sedan
<u>*STAY AT:*</u> *the **Parking next to the Chateau**. The large level parking area is located next to the Chateau close to the centre of town, with parking on tarmac shaded by the chateau walls and lit at night. The parking is only a short walk from the centre of the town where there is a good selection of shops and restaurants, with a Brasserie opposite the parking. There are no services on the parking.*
Facilities: *None*
No. of spaces: *10*
Parking: *Free*
Services: *None*
Opening times: *All year*
GPS Coordinates: *N49.70075   E04.95072*
Alternative: *Municipal Camping, Bvd Fabert, 08200 Sedan   Open 01/04 – 30/09 or return to the Municipal aire in **Mouzon**, in **Ave de la Vigne**.*
<u>**DAY 2**</u>
Sedan: is Europe's largest fortified chateau, and the 2 hour guided tour (with audio-guide) takes the visitor back to the Middle Ages. It follows the lives of the princes, men-at-arms and servants of the fortress, with a multimedia centre that recounts the great moments of the chateau and its main characters.

TAKE A203 OR D5 WEST TO:
Charleville-Mezieres: The stronghold here was victoriously defended during the siege of 1521, and a tour of the ramparts takes in the imposing Tour du Roy. There are also 3 museums in the town to visit.
STAY AT: *the Municipal aire in* **Rue des Paquis, Charleville-Mezieres.** *The aire is in a large tarmac car park, close to the Municipal Campsite and next to the Port de Plaisance, being well situated next to the river, overlooking the yacht marina and near to a swimming pool. Spaces here, in this fairly quiet location, are well marked and are lit at night but have little shade. Raclet service point, but no adjacent grey drainage grid. It's only a 10-minute walk to the centre of town to find a good range of shops and services.*
Facilities: *Water•Grey Drain•Black Drain•Electric •Rubbish*
No. of spaces: *6*
Parking: *Free*
Services: *2€ Water or Electric*
Opening times: *All year*
GPS Coordinates: *N49.77917   E04.72008*
Alternative: *Municipal Camping Rue des Paquis, 08000 Charleville-Mezieres Open 01/04 – 15/10*

DAY 3
TAKE N43 WEST and D988/D22 NORTH TO:
Montcornet: this medieval fortress is perched on a rocky spur, it was rebuilt and extended during the 15th C, but the fortress was dismantled in 1760, leaving the ruins that are visible today. Visitors can explore the site and see the small museum inside.

TAKE D8043 and N51 NORTH TO:
Rocroi: Henry II of France built a stronghold here in 1555 that was altered in 1675 by the military architect Vauban, who retained the star-shaped ground plan. In 1643, the chateau was the setting for a battle against the Spanish that was won by the famous French general, Grand Condé. The town has a first, defensive, fortified wall with five bastions (all of them different), and a second defensive and offensive wall with half-moon batteries. The last guardhouse in the garrison is a fine example of 17th C military architecture built by Vauban that now houses the Museum of the Battle and the Thirty Years' War. Further on, on the left-hand side is a huge military arsenal, built in 1692, with walks around the ramparts.

STAY AT: the Municipal aire in **Rue Tour de Ville, Rocroi.** Situated on the southern outskirts of the town, the aire is found in a small tarmac parking area. There are 6 individual spaces on tarmac separated by strips of grass, with additional parking on grass, shaded by trees with grass areas and lighting at night. There is an UrbaFlux service point with a drainage grid and rubbish bin. There is a slope on the spaces of this pleasant, quiet little aire, but it is well shaded and lit at night. It is located about 400m from the centre of this fortified town where there is a small selection of shops: butcher, grocer, boulangerie and a few eating places.
Facilities: Water •Grey Drain•Black Drain•Electric •Rubbish
No. of spaces: 6
Parking: Free
Services: 2€ Water or Electric
Opening times: All year
GPS Coordinates: N49.92351   E4.51695
Alternative: Camping La Muree, Rue Catherine de Cleves, 08230 Bourg-Fidele   Open 15/01 – 15/12

DAY 4
CONTINUE NORTH ON D8051 (30KM) TO:
Vireux-Molhain: During ancient Roman times, when the Meuse formed the border with the Frankish empire, the castrum of Vireux was erected, in the 3rd C, at the confluence of the Meuse and Viroin rivers, marking the Northern border of Roman Gaul and protecting the empire from Germanic invaders. This marvellous viewpoint is an ancient fortification, defended on its four sides by a thick wall, still having the remains of the two corner towers of the enclosure, a bread oven, a circular fireplace and a cemetery, as well as some medieval remnants.
CONTINUE NORTH ON D8051 (4KM) TO:
Hierges: The Chateau, although it served as a stately home during the Renaissance, the structure that was built around 1560 still retains a feudal appearance, offering protection against the unrest troubling the region at that time. The ruins here retain the walls and four round towers whilst two interior rooms have a permanent art display and the artist's village of Hierges is picturesque, with cobbled streets and 17th C houses.
CONTINUE NORTH ON D8051 (7KM) TO:

Givet: In 1555, under threat from the French, the Spanish King Charles V built an impregnable citadel on a rocky spur at Givet, to which he gave his name, Charlemont. The Spanish fortress passed into French hands in 1678, and improvements to the fortifications continued with the construction of hundreds of metres of underground tunnels. Audio guides are available in English for a tour of the Fort, and a shuttle bus runs from the Tourist Office in Givet to the fort.

STAY AT: *the Municipal aire in* ***Givet****, in* ***Rue Berthelot.*** *The aire, located near to the river on the north side of Givet, outside the municipal camping, offers parking on tarmac in a large car park, having little shade but is lit at night. The aire is in a residential area, 600m from the centre of Givet, where there is a reasonable selection of shops and restaurants. A Euro-Relais service point with drainage platform. This is a quiet location close to the Meuse river, as well as a leisure lake, being about 15 mins level walk from the centre of town with an Aldi supermarket nearby.*

Facilities: Water •Grey Drain •Black Drain •Electric •Rubbish
No. of spaces: 6
Parking: Free
Services: 3€ Water or Electric
Opening times: All year
GPS Coordinates: N50.14371   E04.82569
Alternative: Camping Ballastiere, Rue Berthelot, 08600 Givet Open all year

Below: Villy la Ferte by Adri08

Above: Sedan by Rabich   Middle: Givet by Bulach   Bottom: Rocroi aire

Page 206

ABBEYS OF THE ARDENNES FORESTS MAP

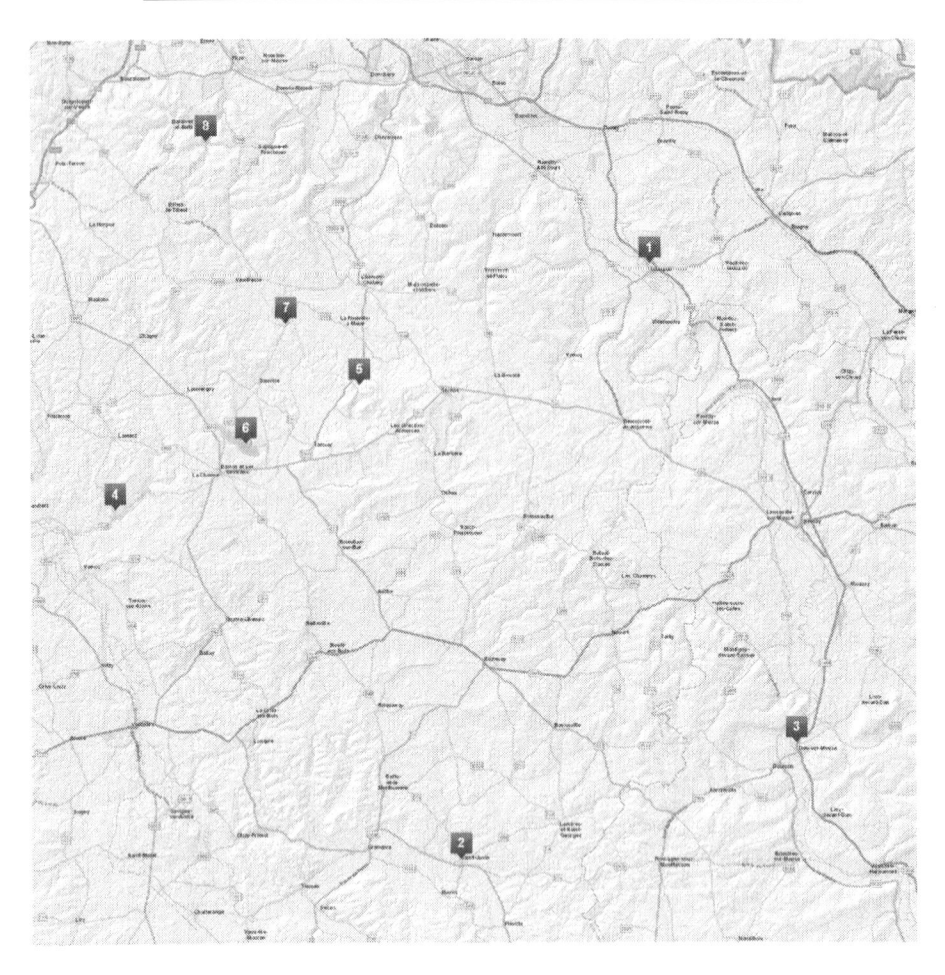

KEY TO MAP:

1) Mouzon
3) Dun sur Meuse
5) Le Mont Dieu
7) La Cassine Cordelier

2) St Juvin
4) Neuville Day
6) Lac de Bairon
8) Elan

CHAMPAGNE-ARDENNES TOUR 30
ABBEYS OF THE ARDENNES FORESTS – 3 DAYS

As a forested frontier territory, the Ardennes has for centuries represented a place of insecurity to the monasteries, which were prize targets for looters and armed bands during the Middle Ages. This is a 3-Day Tour of religious centres in the region that were fortified against raiders, the construction of which was mainly undertaken by the Benedictine monks.

DAY 1
Mouzon
STAY AT: *the Municipal aire in **Mouzon**, in **Ave de la Vigne** The aire is located next to the river on the north side of Mouzon, with parking on tarmac overlooking the Meuse river, having little shade but lit at night. The aire is only 100m from the centre of the village where there is a reasonable selection of shops and restaurants. There are showers and toilets adjacent on the harbour at the Capitainerie, where electric hook ups and wifi are also available as well as an artisanal service point.*
Facilities: *Water•Grey Drain•Black Drain•Electric •Rubbish*
No. of spaces: *6*
Parking: *10€/ 24 Hrs*
Services: *Incl*
Opening times: *All year*
GPS Coordinates: *N49.60695   E05.07722*
Alternative: *Camping les Bouleaux, Rue de L'Ecluse, 55700 Inor Open all year*

Mouzon is situated on the thoroughfare of the great Gallo-Roman highway running from Reims to Trier, and the town boasts an abbey church - a superb Gothic edifice that is allied with the Cathedral in Laon. Constructed by the Benedictines in the 13th C on the site of a Romanesque abbey, it has a remarkable interior and it also houses superb 18th C organs. There is also a museum, ramparts and the remains of a chateau to see.

TAKE D964 17KM SOUTH TO STENAY and D947 21KM WEST TO BUZANCY and THEN TAKE D6 SOUTH and D946 EAST TO:
Saint Juvin: One of the strangest fortified churches in the Ardennes can be found here - having no bell-tower, it is unmistakably a church-fortress with high, 2m thick walls and narrow windows. The church is

square in plan with turrets at each corner, each turret having small openings at the top.

TAKE D946 15KM SOUTH and D998 24KM EAST TO:
Dun sur Meuse

STAY AT: the Municipal aire in **Dun sur Meuse**, in **Rue du Vieux Port.** This modern aire is nicely situated next to and overlooking a mooring basin on the banks of the Meuse canal. Parking is on a dozen gravel spaces bordered by grass verges and small trees, accessed off a tarmac road. This is a pleasant location (300m north of the centre of village), with nice views and some shade. There are toilets/ showers, picnic tables, tourist info, laundry, rubbish bins and an UrbaFlux borne with a drainage platform. The spaces (slightly sloping) have hook up points – 3 posts each with 4 sockets (included in fee). It is a short walk into the village for a few shops and a restaurant, with walks/cycling along the canal.

Facilities: Water•Grey Drain•Black Drain•Electric•Rubbis•Toilets
No. of spaces: 12
Parking: 7€/ 24 Hrs
Services: Incl
Opening times: All year
GPS Coordinates: N49.38852 E05.17838
Alternative: Camping Lac vert, Off D998, Place de la Gare, 55110 Doulcon   Open 01 /04 – 31/10

DAY 2

Dun sur Meuse was a Gallo Roman settlement, but unfortunately it has few remains from this time. The massive church, built in 1346, is worth viewing both for its architecture and its 18th C furnishings inside.

5kms North of Dun, in Mont devant Sassey, there is a 12th C Church that is considered to be one of the most beautiful in Northern France, with remarkable Romanesque and Gothic architecture and a unique crypt.

TAKE D964 NORTH TO STENAY, THEN D30 WEST ONTO D977/ D25 TO:

Neuville Day: A priory belonging to the Carthusian Monastery of Le Mont-Dieu. Its vaulted bell-shaped medieval cellars, three storeys high, were designed to preserve the wine throughout its production, each floor having a different temperature.

HEAD EAST ON D25 TO LE CHESNE and TAKE D977 NORTH TO:
Le Mont Dieu: Founded in 1132, the Carthusian monastery of Mont-Dieu was rebuilt in the 17th C after the ravages of the wars of religion. The abbey buildings date from this time and are remarkable for their Louis XIII architecture as well as for their harmonious proportions. One can also visit the clearing where there is a Charterhouse, the oldest in France, a focal point in the beautiful forest of Mont Dieu.
RETURN SOUTH ON D977 and THEN D12/ D312 NORTH TO:
Lac de Bairon
STAY AT: *the Parking next to* **Lac de Bairon**, *North of* **Le Chesne.** *This large car park is situated next to and overlooking the large lake, with parking on a dozen tarmac spaces screened by hedges and accessed off the D312. This is a pleasant location on the North side of the lake, having nice views, street lighting adjacent and some shade, 'Le Panoramic' bar and brasserie is adjacent, with the lake beach opposite. There are no services here.*
Facilities: *None*
No. of spaces: *12*
Parking: *Free*
Services: *None*
Opening times: *All year*
GPS Coordinates: *N49.52681 E04.78414*
Alternative: *Camping du Lac de Bairon, Off D312, 08390 Le Chesne Open 01/04 – 31/10*
TAKE D12 NORTH TO:
DAY 3
La Cassine Cordelier: In 1571, the Duke of Rethel built a chateau in La Cassine and later in 1585, he founded a Cordelier convent there. Today the chateau is in ruins, but in the ancient convent one can still see the monks' dormitory and the cloisters. The Cultural Association of La Cassine Chateau organizes sound and light shows here every summer.
TAKE D12 NORTH TO:
Elan: Cistercian monks founded the Abbey of Elan in the 12th C, their first abbot being Saint Roger. Whilst the abbey church, built on the ruins of the old abbey, is somewhat modest, the 15th C abbey manor, flanked by four imposing towers, is remarkable for its chestnut wood roof structure in the shape of an upside-down ship's hull. Inside is an

exhibition about Cistercian abbeys in France and a tourist information point and close by is the site of Saint Roger's Chapel, with its ponds - a pleasant departure point for a forest walk.

STAY AT: *the Municipal aire in* **Mouzon***, in* **Ave de la Vigne** *or the Camping du Lac de Bairon, Off D312, 08390 Le Chesne.*

Above Le Mont Dieu by GOGLINS

Top Right: Dun surr Meuse by Ketounette

Bottom Right: Mouzon Cathedral by Mattana

Below: Dun sur Meuse aire

CHAMPAGNE-ARDENNES TOUR 31
FORTIFIED CHURCHES TOUR – 2 DAYS

This 2-Day Tour follows a sign-posted route through this landscape of hills and hedged farmlands, between the Rocroi plateau and the Aisne river, in which churches, strongholds, chateaux and abbeys have all been fortified. History left the population with no other choice than to fortify their churches and houses as protection from the soldiers who pillaged this region during the Hundred Years' War.

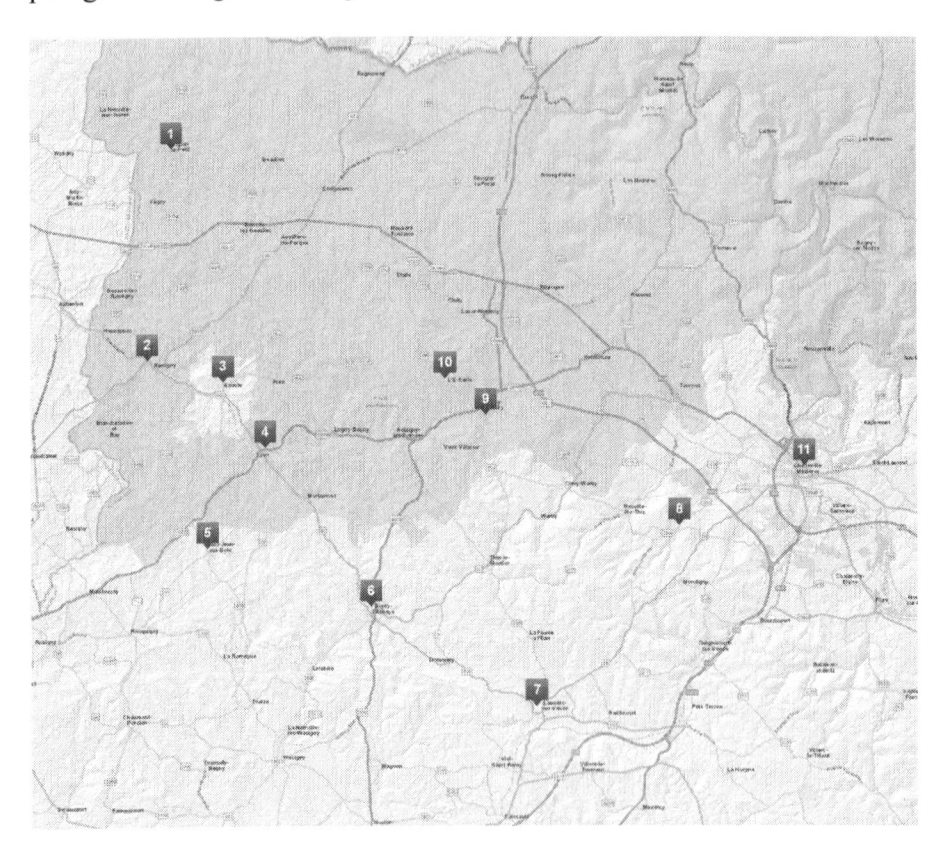

FORTIFIED CHURCHES MAP

KEY TO MAP:
1) Signy le Petit
2) Rumigny
3) Aouste
4) Liart
5) St Jean aux Bois
6) Signy l'Abbaye
7) Launois sur Vence
8) Fagnon
9) Servion
10) L'Echelle
11) Charleville-Mezieres

NOTE: Unfortunately this area is sadly lacking in aires, so the majority of stopovers are either in parking places with few services, or the local campsites, if open.

DAY 1
Signy le Petit
STAY AT: the Parking in **Signy le Petit***, in* **Place de l'Eglise***. This large level car park is situated next to the church in the centre of the village, with ample parking on tarmac, being lit at night and having a little shade. There are no services here but the parking is close to a good range of shops and eating-places in the village.*
Facilities: None
No. of spaces: 12
Parking: Free
Services: None
Opening times: All year
GPS Coordinates: N49.90331 E04.27923
Alternative: Camping Domaine de la Motte, Base de Loisirs, 08380 Signy-le-Petit. Open all year
Signy le Petit: The church was built at the end of the 17th C with quartz walls, 3m thick at the base of the tower. The square tower-porch, flanked by two pepper-pot lookouts with arrow slits, leads on to the vaulted nave, which is built of bricks with a ribbed vault made of yellow stone. **GPS:** N49.90331 E04.27923
TAKE D20 EAST and D877 12 KM SOUTH TO:
Rumigny: La Cour des Prés Chateau is situated amongst the great hundred-year-old beech trees at the entrance to the village. It is an ancient stronghold that was built in 1546 in response to King Francis I's appeal to fortify the region to protect the population from the invasions of the Spanish. A guided tour will lead you through the history of the residence to appreciate its charm, and in the summer baroque musical evenings and candlelit dinners take place.
GPS: N 49.80920 E 4.26724
TAKE D27 4KM EAST TO:
Aouste: The architectural features of this beautiful fortified church date from the 15th C, the gothic style having a square tower/ keep, pierced with arrow slits. The well (currently covered) and immense chimney inside were used in the case of long periods of siege.
GPS: N49.79922 E 4.31747
CONTINUE ON D27 4KM EAST TO:

Liart: The church of Notre-Dame, fortified in the 15th C, has a rectangular tower-porch resembling a keep on two levels, having arrow slots/ firing orifices that were used to defend the narrow western entrance. With its unusual roof, the tower looks like a chateau, and its two turrets give access to a converted attic, situated above the chancel, which was used as a refuge in times of trouble. There is also an animal park in the village.

TAKE D978 and D10 SOUTH TO:
St Jean aux Bois: The market hall of Saint Jean aux Bois was built in the 18th C and has the appearance of a thatched cottage.
RETURN TO LIART and TAKE D27 EAST 10KM TO:
Signy l'Abbaye
<u>STAY AT:</u> *the Parking in* **Signy l'Abbaye***, in* **Rue de l'Abbaye***. This large level car park is situated next to the football field, 300m North of the centre of the village. It offers ample parking on tarmac and is lit at night, but has little shade. This is a quiet spot outside the Municipal campsite, but there are no services here when the campsite is closed. The picturesque village has a reasonable range of shops and eating-places, as well as a small Carrefour supermarket.*
Facilities: *None*
No. of spaces: *12*
Parking: *Free*
Services: *None when adjacent campsite is closed*
Opening times: *All year*
GPS Coordinates: *N49.70161 E04.41943*
Alternative: *Camping Municipal, Rue de l'Abbaye, 08460 Signy-l'Abbaye Open 01/04 – 30/09*

DAY 2
CONTINUE ON D27 EAST 11KM TO:
Launois sue Vence: The former Post Relay House of Launois consists of a set of buildings that have remained intact since the 17th C. The Postmaster's residence has an inner courtyard flanked by an immense hall for stagecoaches - a true masterpiece of the Ardennes carpenters, a series of stables covering 80m2, and a former sheep barn. There is also a wine press in the vaulted cellars and a 12th C church in the village. Every second Sunday of the month (except August), bric-a-brac traders, antique dealers and collectors hold a market here, with many other events taking place throughout the year
TAKE D3 NORTH and D34 WEST TO:

Fagnon: This beautiful building, named the "Abbey of Seven Fountains", is all that remains of an abbey that was founded in 1129. The building was used as a casino during the First World War, and in later years General De Gaulle enjoyed strolling in the parklands of the abbey, which he visited frequently. Today, a 4 star hotel, restaurant and golf course have been set up in these exceptional surroundings.

CONTINUE WEST ON D34 TO NEUFMAISON and THEN NORTH TO:

Servion: The 16th C fortified church has a square porch with two round corner towers, which form its defensive system. The north tower contains two holding rooms, while the south tower contains a spiral staircase leading to the two floors of the tower-porch. Currently, the church is not used as a place of worship, but serves as a small cultural centre and holds an art exhibition every summer.

TAKE D9 WEST TO:

L'Echelle: The Chateau de l'Echelle, an impressive 14th C stronghold faced by two huge towers, saw action during the thirty years war, when a quarter of the village population was executed here. Also in the village is the 18th C Hôtel Beury, a former inn that has been altered to accommodate resident artists, with several exhibition halls, studios and bedrooms, as well as having magnificent gardens.

TAKE D978 and N43 17KM EAST TO:

Charleville-Mezieres

<u>**STAY AT:**</u> *the Municipal aire in* **Rue des Paquis, Charleville-Mezieres,** *in a large tarmac car park, close to the Municipal Campsite and next to the Port de Plaisance. This fairly quiet location is well situated, being next to the river, overlooking the yacht marina and near to a swimming pool. The spaces here are well marked and lit at night but have little shade. Raclet service point but no adjacent grey drainage grid. It is a 10-minute walk to the centre of town for a good range of shops/ services.*

Facilities: *Water •Grey Drain•Black Drain•Electric •Rubbish*
No. of spaces: *6*
Parking: *Free*
Services: *2€ Water or Electric*
Opening times: *All year*
GPS Coordinates: *N49.77917   E04.72008*
Alternative: *Municipal Camping Rue des Paquis, 08000 Charleville-Mezieres Open 01/ 04 – 15/10*

Aouste by Adri08

Liart by michiel1972

Launois sur Vence by Docquin

Charleville Mezieres aire

CHAMPAGNE-ARDENNES TOUR 32
REIMS and SURROUNDINGS – 3 DAYS

A 3-Day Tour of Reims and the surrounding region, an area that has been closely connected to the history of the city and the coronations of the French kings. The Saint-Thierry Massif and the Ardre Valley have preserved traces of this illustrious past, blending nature with some architectural gems.

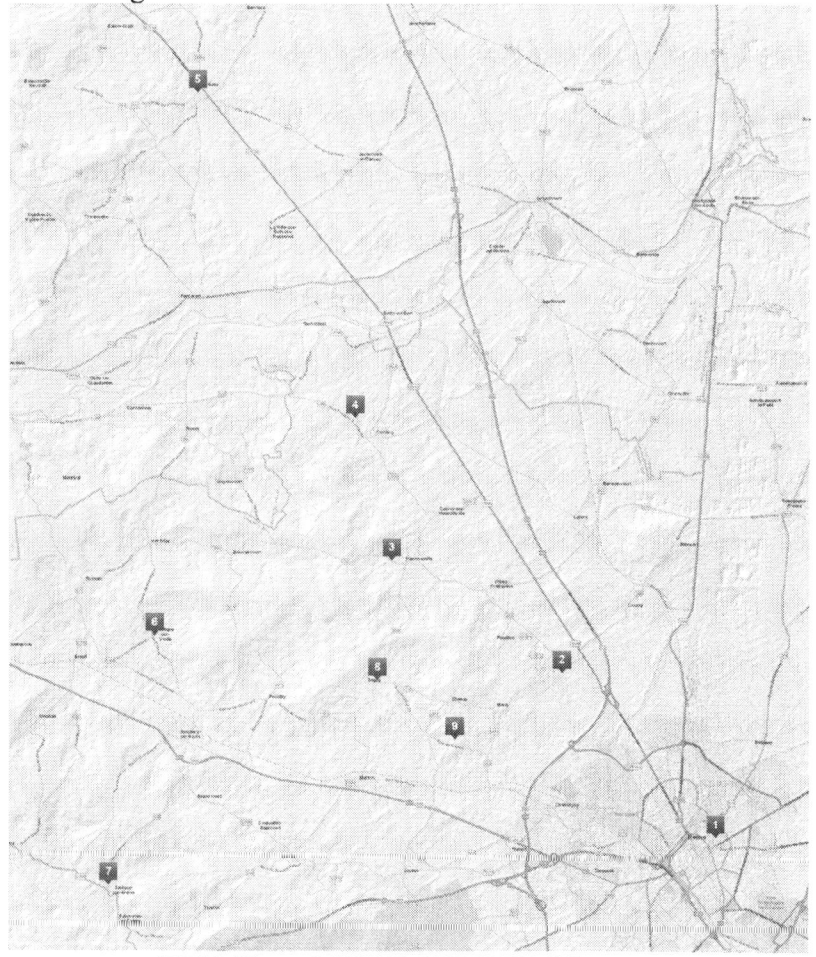

REIMS and SURROUNDINGS MAP

KEY TO MAP:
1) Reims
2) St Thierry
3) Hermonville
4) Cormicy
5) Corbeny
6) Montigny-sur-Vesle
7) Savigny-sur-Ardres
8) Trigny
9) Chalons-sur-Vesle

DAY 1
Reims

STAY AT: *the Municipal aire in* **Chaussee Bocquaine, off D980, Reims.** *The aire is in the small tarmac parking area next to the CIS Youth Hostel in the city and behind the theatre "La Comedie". Providing marked spaces and some shade under trees, this is a secure location backing onto a small park area and is accessed by a security barrier. There are toilets in the hostel (Open 08.00 – 22.00) as well as a restaurant. The aire is situated 100m from the River Vesle and about 1km from the cathedral and city centre, but there are shops and services nearby. An artisanal service point with platform drainage. This is a very good location for visiting Reims, being a level walk over the river to the Cathedral and the centre of the city. Access to the parking is via an automatic barrier for which you need a 4-digit code (available from CIS reception) – you can ring up beforehand (depending on your French) for the code, as parking outside can be awkward. Cycle hire is available from the hostel. Tel: 03 26 40 52 60*

Facilities: *Water•Grey Drain•Black Drain•Toilets*
No. of spaces: *9*
Parking: *Free*
Services: *Free*
Opening times: *All year*
GPS Coordinates: *N49.24895   E04.02167*
Alternative: *Municipal Camping, Rue du Routoir, 51360 Val de Vesle Open 01/04 – 15/10*

Reims: The cathedral is a 13th C Gothic masterpiece, where 30 French kings were crowned over the centuries and where Joan of Arc brought the Dauphin to be crowned. The famous statue of the Smiling Angel is above the North door, and you can climb to the top of the towers to see inside the breathtaking roof. Nearby Tau Palace houses the cathedral's treasury and some of its original statuary. The magnificent Saint Remi's basilica has a 4 storey Gothic choir and 12th C stained glass windows whilst there is also a museum showing the history of the abbey and of Reims. The Basilica is, like the cathedral and Tau Palace, on UNESCO's World Heritage List. The Musee des Beaux-Arts has an excellent collection of paintings, whilst champagne can be tasted at the Ruinart or Taittinger cellars in the city.

STAY AT: *the Municipal aire in* **Chaussee Bocquaine, off D980, Reims** *or the Municipal Camping, Rue du Routoir, 51360 Val de Vesle Open 01/04 – 15/10*

DAY 2

TAKE D944 NORTH and TURN WEST AFTER 5KM TO:

Saint-Thierry: The village, surrounded by over 50ha of vineyards, sprouted up around the monastery founded by Saint Thierry in the year 500. It was enlarged over the ages before being torn down during the French Revolution. The remains of the abbey include the 12th C chapel, the former chapter room with its beautiful carved capitals and the terraced gardens with views of Reims.

CONTINUE ON D30 NORTH 6KM TO:

Hermonville was an important small town in the Middle Ages, and boasts the beautiful 12th C Saint-Sauveur church. The houses on the narrow village streets and small square are decorated with statues, bas-reliefs and old porches whilst there is also a British WWI cemetery in the village and a ruined chateau nearby. The early 12th C church of neighbouring Cauroy-lès-Hermonville is worth a look because of its wooden Romanesque nave and the region's oldest porch.

TAKE D530 NORTH TO:

Cormicy: The Maison Bleue national cemetery, with over 14,000 French graves, recalls the fierce fighting of 1914 and offers a view over the port of the Aisne and Marne canal.

TAKE D944 11KM NORTH TO:

Corbeny

STAY AT: *the Municipal aire in* **Corbeny** *in* **Rue Marc Lavetti (D18),** *situated in a small gravel parking area with 3 individual spaces separated by shrubs but having no shade. The parking is next to, and overlooks, a lake on the East side of the village where there are a few shops. The spaces are reserved for motorhomes but there is no service point here.*

Facilities: *None*
No. of spaces: *3*
Parking: *Free*
Services: *None*
Opening times: *All year*
GPS Coordinates: *N49.46465   E03.82737*
Alternative: *Municipal Camping, Rue des Godins, 02190 Guignicourt Open 01/04 – 31/10*

DAY 3
TAKE D19 and D28 SOUTH TO:
Montigny-sur-Vesle: to see the "Holy Virgin's Grotto" 500 m from the village. There is also a very nice 14km way marked walk starting from Montigny to the villages of Pevy and Prouilly.

CONTINUE SOUTH ON D28:
The scenic route runs alongside vineyards, market gardens and former peat bogs in the Vesle Valley until reaching **Jonchery-sur-Vesle**.

TAKE D28 6KM SOUTH TO:
Savigny-sur-Ardres: A plaque on the house opposite the village church marks the site where, on 28th May 1940, Charles de Gaulle made the first radio broadcast calling on the French to form an armed resistance to the Nazis.

RETURN NORTH ON D28 TO JONCHERY and TAKE D75 NORTH TO:
Trigny with its washhouses, fountains and stone houses was the starting point of the route taken by French kings to their coronations in Reims. A nearby viewpoint offers a beautiful view of the area, and a marked walk through the streets below reveals the charm of this flower-bedecked village with its medieval ramparts.

CONTINUE SOUTH ON D26 TO:
Châlons-sur-Vesle: Where you can see some superb quarries, before proceeding on to **Gueux**, a stopping point for the kings of France on the way to their coronations.

TAKE D27 EAST TO:
Reims

STAY AT: the Municipal aire in **Chaussee Bocquaine, off D980, Reims** or Municipal Camping, Rue du Routoir, 51360 Val de Vesle

St Thierry by Potrowl

Above: Reims by Sémhur GFDL   Middle: Reims by Chis   Bottom: Reims aire

CHAMPAGNE-ARDENNES TOUR 33
REIMS and THE CHAMPAGNE VINEYARDS - 5DAYS

This 5-Day Circuit takes you from the historic city of Reims into the heart of the vineyards of the Champagne country, with vines stretching as far as the eye can see on these undulating hillsides dotted with villages, chateaux and churches.

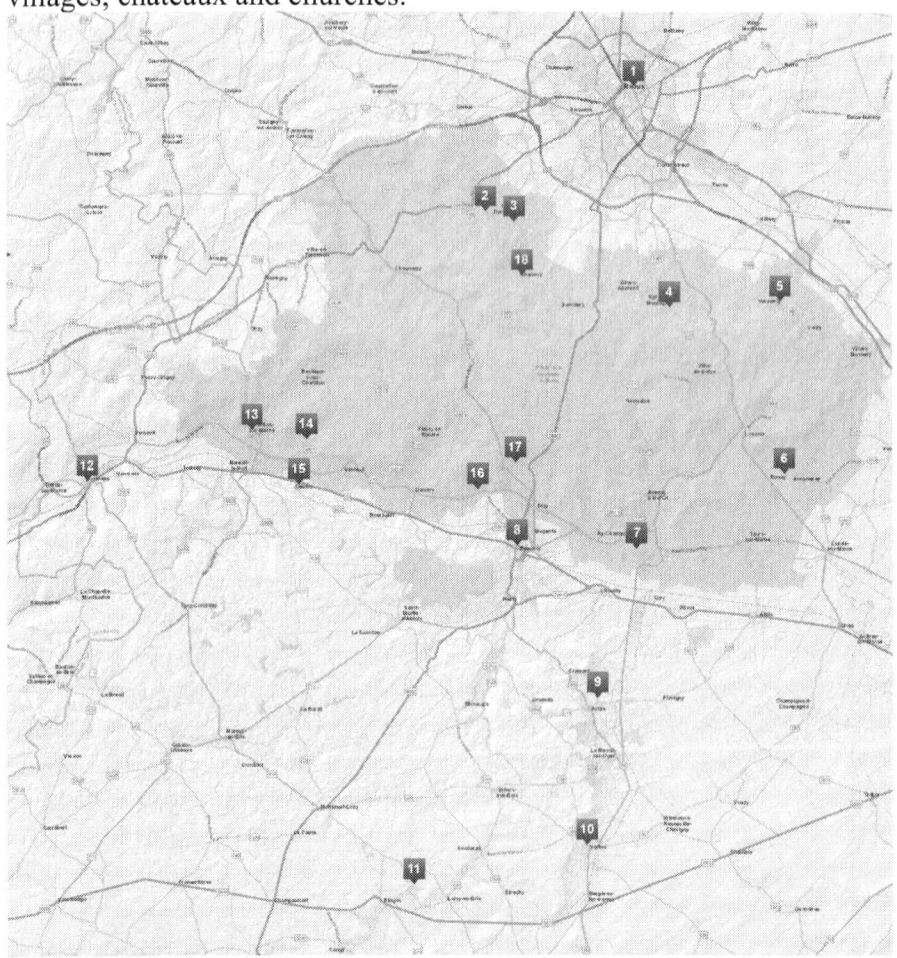

REIMS and THE CHAMPAGNE VINEYARDS MAP

KEY TO MAP:
1) Reims
2) Villedommange
3) Sacy
4) Chigny-les-Roses
5) Verzenay
6) Bouzy
7) Mareuil-sur-Aÿ
8) Epernay
9) Avize
10) Vertus
11) Beaunay
12) Dormans
13) Châtillon-sur-Marne
14) Villers sous Chatillon
15) Oeuilly
16) Cumières
17) Hautvillers
18) Chamery

DAY 1
Reims

STAY AT: *the Municipal aire in* **Chaussee Bocquaine, off D980, Reims.** *The aire is in the small tarmac parking area next to the CIS Youth Hostel in the city and behind the theatre "La Comedie". Providing marked spaces and some shade under trees, this is a secure location backing onto a small park area and is accessed by a security barrier. There are toilets in the hostel (Open 08.00 – 22.00) as well as a restaurant. The aire is situated 100m from the River Vesle and about 1km from the cathedral and city centre, but there are shops and services nearby. An artisanal service point with platform drainage. This is a very good location for visiting Reims, being a level walk over the river to the Cathedral and the centre of the city. Access to the parking is via an automatic barrier for which you need a 4-digit code (available from CIS reception) – you can ring up beforehand (depending on your French) for the code, as parking outside can be awkward. Cycle hire is available from the hostel. Tel: 03 26 40 52 60*

Facilities: *Water•Grey Drain•Black Drain•Toilets*
No. of spaces: *9*
Parking: *Free*
Services: *Free*
Opening times: *All year*
GPS Coordinates: *N49.24895   E04.02167*
Alternative: *Municipal Camping, Rue du Routoir, 51360 Val de Vesle Open 01/04 – 15/10*

Reims: The cathedral is a 13th C Gothic masterpiece, where 30 French kings were crowned over the centuries and where Joan of Arc brought the Dauphin to be crowned. The famous statue of the Smiling Angel is above the North door, and you can climb to the top of the towers to see inside the breathtaking roof. Nearby Tau Palace houses the cathedral's treasury and some of its original statuary. The magnificent Saint Remi's basilica has a 4 storey Gothic choir and 12th C stained glass windows whilst there is also a museum showing the history of the abbey and of Reims. The Basilica is, like the cathedral and Tau Palace, on UNESCO's World Heritage List. The Musee des Beaux-Arts has an excellent collection of paintings, whilst champagne can be tasted at the Ruinart or Taittinger cellars in the city.

STAY AT: *the Municipal aire in Chaussee Bocquaine, off D980, Reims or the Municipal Camping, Rue du Routoir, 51360 Val de Vesle*

Open 01/04 – 15/10
DAY 2
TAKE D980 WEST and D26 SOUTH TO:
Villedommange: The squat bell tower crowning the 12th C church was originally planned to be so huge that it was never finished. This is the heart of the "Petite Montagne", where the scenic D26 route passes through the beautiful Champagne vineyards dotted with many historic villages and their churches.
CONTINUE SOUTH ON D26 TO:
Sacy, to see the Church and its tall, elegant spire, then on to **Chamery** and its 57m bell tower, before proceeding to the church at **Sermiers**, with its onion-domed bell tower. This is the "Grande Montagne" region, the heart of the growing area for the Pinot Noir grape, one of the three varieties used to make champagne.
CONTINUE EAST ON D26:
Chigny-les-Roses is the village where Madame Pommery, the founder of the famous Pommery Champagne company, lived and had her rose garden. This area grew many varieties of roses, which once helped in the prevention of vine-threatening diseases.
CONTINUE EAST ON D26:
Shortly before **Mailly-Champagne**, a sculpture by Pages can be seen right in the middle of the vines.
The road partly follows the contours of the Natural Regional Park, which preserves a 50,000 ha forest with its many walking paths.
CONTINUE EAST ON D26:
Verzenay is an unusual village, nestling at the bottom of a valley, bounded by a mill and a lighthouse built in 1909, which is also a wine museum. Further on is **Verzy**, a very old wine making village. The Faux de Verzy forest boasts nearly 1,000 beech trees with their umbrella-shaped crowns. This is the Montagne de Reims, stop here to visit the observation post of Mount Sinaï at 283m alt.
CONTINUE SOUTH ON D26:
Following the scenic route along back roads crossing plains, vineyards and forests, until reaching **Ambonnay** with its century-old wine press, fountain, old signs and the church of Saint Réol.
TAKE D19 WEST TO:
Bouzy which, although famous for its red wine, has over 30 champagne cellars, each of which sell a CD tour guide of the

"vineyard route" giving information about grape-growing and how these outstanding wines are made.

TAKE D34 NORTH:
You can catch a glimpse of a private 17th C Chateau and grounds designed by Le Nôtre behind an imposing gate at **Louvois**.

TAKE D9 SOUTH:
Mareuil-sur-Aÿ: Entering the village, you'll drive alongside the very steep "Clos des Goisses", one of Champagne's few enclosed vineyards.

STAY AT: *the Municipal aire in **Mareuil-sur-Ay**, in **Place du Grand Jard**, sited next to and overlooking the canal marina. This is a nice situation, with parking on tarmac, shaded by tall trees, and only a short 200m walk to the village centre. The Artisanal borne has all services available, with a drainage grid for grey water. This very quiet position offers lovely walks along the towpath, but there is only a Casino superette (jetons available here), a boulangerie, and some wine cellars in the village.*

Facilities: *Water •Grey Drain •Black Drain •Toilets •Electric*
No. of spaces: *8*
Parking: *Free*
Services: *5€ Water or Electric*
Opening times: *All year*
GPS Coordinates: *N49.04525   E04.03485*
Alternative: *Municipal Camping, Allee de Cumieres, 51200 Epernay Open 01/04 – 15/09*

DAY 3
Mareuil-sur-Aÿ: Thick ramparts once surrounded this important small town, where French kings, as well as the rulers of other lands, owned estates and presses. A beautiful half-timbered building, known as Henry IV's press-house, stands behind Saint Brice's church with its Gothic portal.

CONTINUE WEST ON D1 TO:
Epernay, the capital of Champagne, whose "above-ground" activity contrasts with the peaceful 100 kms of cellars below ground, where millions of bottles lie resting. The famous Avenue de Champagne has many 18th and 19th C buildings that are home to interminable underground galleries and sumptuous wine cellars, including the most prestigious names such as Moet and Chandon, Mercier and De Castellane. The Castellane cellars also have a museum with a display of winemaking equipment, as well as a tour of the bottling plant.

From **Epernay to Vertus**, the Côte des Blancs runs from north to south, leaning up against the Brie plateau. The vineyards are almost exclusively Chardonnay (white grape), and produce a Champagne that is a blend of finesse and elegance: the Blanc de Blancs.

TAKE D40 SOUTH and THEN D10 EAST:
Through **Cuis,** with its beautiful Romanesque church, before passing close to some cliffs to reach **Cramant** and its giant 8m long bottle. Continue to the little village of **Avize,** with its fresco decorations and a wine-growing academy, and then on to **Oger,** one of "France's Most Beautiful Villages", famous for its floral decorations and its "Museum of Champagne". There is also a "Museum of Vines and Wine" at **Mesnil-sur-Oger.**

CONTINUE ON D9 SOUTH TO:
Vertus, a picturesque village full of narrow streets and fountains, plus an 11th C church built on stilts. The cliffs that overlook the village are popular for rock climbing and walking.

CONTINUE ON D9 SOUTH:
After **Bergères-lès-Vertus**, the road runs alongside Mont Aimé. This hill, for long the fortress of Queen Blanche of Navarre, is steeped in history, but all that is left to see today are a handful of scattered ruins and pale souvenirs of the massacre of the 183 Cathars who were burned here in 1239.

TAKE D933 and D37 WEST TO:
Beaunay
STAY AT: the aire in **Beaunay**, on **Ferme de Bel Air** (also one of the farms of the France Passion scheme). Signposted in the village, this private aire is in a very rural location on a vineyard just outside the village, in a nice, quiet position with good views of the countryside and surrounded by vineyards. The medium-sized, gravel parking area is bordered by grass areas, with little shade but with lighting and picnic tables. Artisanal service point with drainage grid and 3 electric hook ups. The very friendly owners, Beatrice and Michel Jaquesson, offer tastings and champagne for sale. Tel: 0326593494
Facilities: Water•Grey Drain•Black Drain•Electric
No. of spaces: *15*
Parking: *8€/ 24 Hrs*
Services: *Incl*
Opening times: *All year*
GPS Coordinates: *N48.88170   E03.87479*

Alternative: Municipal Camping, Allee de Cumieres, 51200 Epernay Open 01/04 – 15/09

DAY 4
TAKE D18 WEST:
Passing the Renaissance chateau at **Montmort Lucy**, then on through **Orbais l'Abbaye** with its remains of a 7th C abbey. Continue on to:

Dormans is a small holiday resort and within the vast gardens of its Louis XIII chateau, (free admission) stands the Memorial to the Victories of the Marne with an unbeatable view. There is also the chateau mill with an 8 m bucket wheel and another Champagne museum to visit.

TAKE D3 and D1 EAST TO:
Châtillon-sur-Marne: This small village, with its fortifications dating back to the 11th C, boasts a colossal 33m statue, set up in honour of Pope Urban II, who was born in the village and is best known as the initiator of the first Crusade. An internal staircase leads up to the statue's arm, and a viewing table enables visitors to identify the 22 villages in the valley.

TAKE D1 and D501 EAST TO:
Villers sous Chatillon

STAY AT: *the Municipal aire in* **Rue du Parc (off D501), Villers sous Chatillon**. *This aire is positioned in a wide lay-by in a cul-de-sac on the North side of Villers, close to the village centre (150m). It is edged with mature trees providing shade, is a tranquil spot at night, and has a Euro-Relais service point with a drainage grid. It is easy to find the aire in this small village, and jetons are available from the Bar-Epicerie or Mairie.*

Facilities: *Water•Grey Drain•Black Drain•Toilets•Electric*
No. of spaces: *4*
Parking: *Free*
Services: *3€ Water or Electric*
Opening times: *All year*
GPS Coordinates: *N49.09642   E03.80072*
Alternative: *Camping Rural, Rue de Bailly, 51700 Vandieres   Open 01/04 – 01/11*

DAY 5
TAKE D501 and D1 SOUTH TO:
Oeuilly: The open air museum "Maison Champenoise" in this "timeless" village demonstrates how wine growers have lived and

worked since the 18th C, with an original 1900 schoolhouse and a Photography museum displaying photos of the area from 1902 to 1980.

TAKE D222 EAST:
Passing by **Boursault Chateau**, built by Veuve Clicquot in 1845, standing high over the valley.

RETURN ONTO D3 and TAKE D1 EAST TO:
Cumières: From this small village on the right bank of the Marne, the boat "Champagne Vallée" can take you on a cruise along the river to discover the Marne Valley, with trips ranging from 2 to 4 hours.

TAKE Route d'Hautvillers NORTH TO:
Hautvillers: This charming village is most famous for its Benedictine abbey, where one of the monks, the blind Dom Pérignon, invented Champagne and his tomb can be found in the Abbey. Wrought iron shop signs decorate the village, serving as a reminder of the centuries-old professions that once existed here. There is a permanent exhibition to visit in the tourist office and a remarkable viewpoint to be found in the village whilst another fine viewpoint exists at nearby **Champillon**, where you can enjoy the spectacular views over Epernay, the first hills of the Côte des Blancs, and the banks of the Marne.

TAKE D951 NORTH and D26 EAST TO:
Chamery

<u>**STAY AT:**</u> *the Municipal aire in* **Chamery**, *in* **Rue du Chateau Rouge**. *The aire here is in a medium- sized gravel car park, next to the village hall on the western edge of the small village. It overlooks vineyards, has little shade but is set in a pleasant, peaceful location. There are no shops in the village, although farm produce is available locally, and there is a nice 12th C Church to visit. The AireServices service point with a drainage channel is easy to access.*

Facilities: *Water •Grey Drain •Black Drain •Electric*
No. of spaces: *5*
Parking: *Free*
Services: *2€ Water or Electric*
Opening times: *All year*
GPS Coordinates: *N49.17399   E03.95413*
Alternative: *Municipal Camping, Rue du Routoir, 51360 Val de Vesle Open 01/04 – 15/10*

Top: Reims by Victorgrigas   Middle: Mareuil sur Ay by Garitan
Bottom: Epernay by Fab5669

Aire at Chamery

Aire at Mareuil sur Ay

CHAMPAGNE-ARDENNES TOUR 34
CISTERCIAN ABBEYS OF HAUTE-MARNE – 3 DAYS

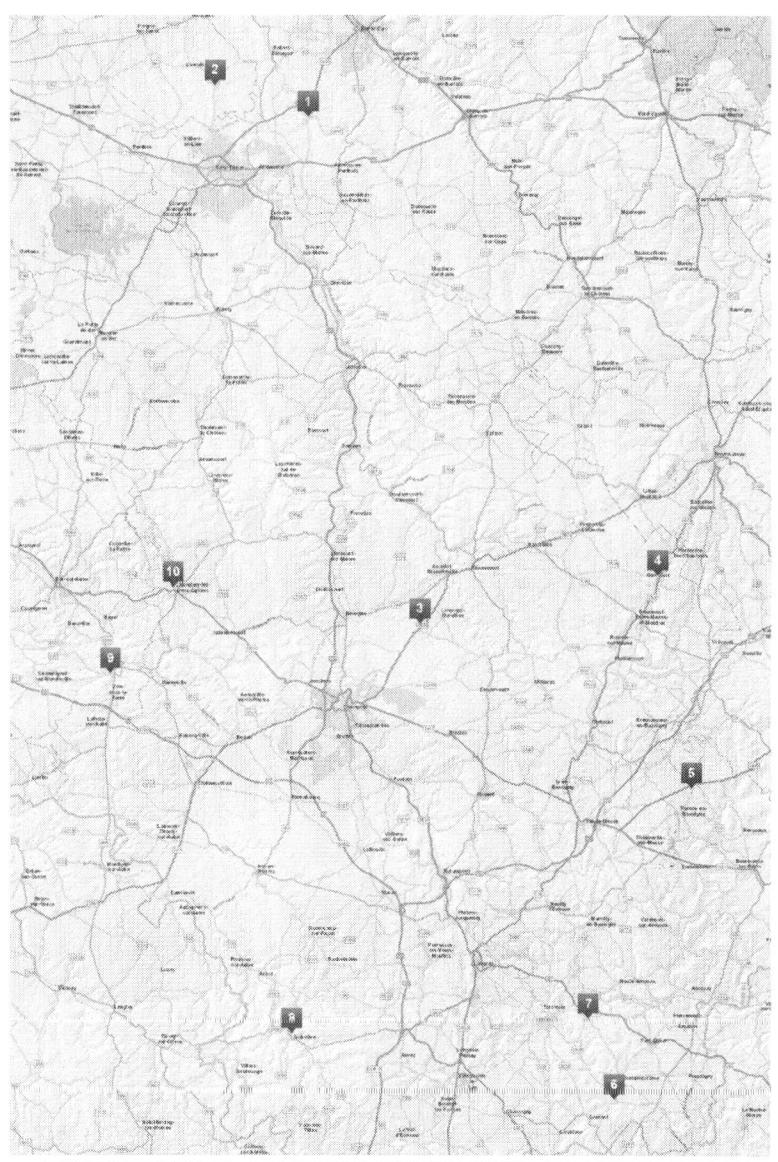

CISTERCIAN ABBEYS OF HAUTE-MARNE MAP

KEY TO MAP:
1) Haironville 2) Trois Fontaines 3) La Crête 4) Goncourt
5) Parnoy en Bassigny 6) Belmont 7) Corgirnon
8) Auberive 9) Clairvaux 10) Colombey les Deux Eglises

This 3-Day Tour explores the Abbeys of the Cistercian order that spread widely and rapidly thanks to the arrival in Cîteaux, in 1112, of St Bernard of Clairvaux. Langres became one of the most important dioceses in France, mainly due to the first two of its daughter abbeys - the Clairvaux and Morimond Abbeys - which in turn founded several hundred monasteries across Europe.

DAY 1
Haironville

STAY AT: *the Municipal aire in* **Haironville,** *in* **Rue Charles Collet (D4),** *located immediately outside the village hall, just south of the village. It offers 4 spaces on gravel (next to the service point) in a medium sized car park with picnic tables that is lit at night and has some shade. There is an AireServices borne with a drainage platform in a drive-through arrangement, making access simple. This is a fairly modern aire outside the Salle des Fetes in a pleasant spot off a side road, about 250m from the centre of the small rural village. It is quiet at night and overlooks the small river Saulx, whilst shops (boulangerie and Proxi grocer) and a bar are nearby. Jetons are available from the 2 shops but they are both closed on Sundays.*

Facilities: Water•Grey Drain•Black Drain• Electric
No. of spaces: *4*
Parking: *Free*
Services: *2€ Water or Electric*
Opening times: *All year*
GPS Coordinates: *N48.68447   E05.08618*
Alternative: *Camping Chateau, Rue du Stade, 55000 Bar le Duc Open 01/ 05 – 15/10*

TAKE D635 WEST and D16 NORTH TO:

Trois Fontaines: Clairvaux's first daughter abbey, the Abbaye de Trois Fontaines, was founded by St Bernard in 1118. It was spared both the ravages of war and civil or religious troubles because of its isolated position far away from major thoroughfares. It was, nonetheless, rebuilt in the 18th C, with the entrance and its monumental door dating from this period. There are also some very fine remains of the 12th C church as well as extensive and lovely parkland to enjoy.

TAKE D16 SOUTH TO ST-DIZIER and N67 SOUTH TO BOLOGNE. THEN TAKE D44 EAST 14KM TO ANDELOT-BLANCHEVILLE and THEN HEAD SOUTH 5KM TO:

La Crête: Tucked away in a small valley on the banks of the River le Rognon, the Abbaye de La Crête was founded in 1121 by monks who had come from Morimond. Due to its size, the abbey was able to later found in turn four daughter abbeys but none of the original buildings remain now although there are 18th C replacements, which fortunately were not destroyed during the Revolution. There is a very beautiful listed concierge's lodge, as well as an abbey house, the large stables, a pigeon house and the outer walls.

RETURN TO ANDELOT and TAKE D674 EAST TO ST-BLIN. THEN TAKE D16/ D249 EAST 17KM TO:

Goncourt

STAY AT: *the Municipal aire in* **Goncourt, in Rue des Lottes**, *close to the village centre (with a boulangerie in the village). This is a very nice, peaceful waterside location next to the Meuse River and is a good place to fish, with parking alongside the road on tarmac and shaded by trees. Picnic tables are provided on the grassy areas next to the road. The basic Artisanal service point functions well.*

Facilities: *Water•Grey Drain•Black Drain•*
No. of spaces: *30*
Parking: *Free*
Services: *3€ Water*
Opening times: *All year*
GPS Coordinates: *N48.23681   E05.60992*
Alternative: *Camping Hirondelles, Rue du Foulon, 52150 Bourg Ste Marie   Open 15/ 02 – 15/12*

DAY 2

TAKE D148 EAST TO SOMMERECOURT and D5/ D122 SOUTH TO DAMBLAIN. THEN TAKE D232/ D108 SOUTH TO:

Parnoy en Bassigny: Morimond Abbey, the 4th daughter abbey of Cîteaux, was founded in 1115 on the banks of the river Flambard at the outer limits of the Germanic empire, so that the Cistercian order could expand throughout these areas. Its influence also spread widely in the Iberian Peninsula, but it was destroyed several times, in particular by the Imperial forces during the Thirty Years war, and the buildings had to be rebuilt. Demolished during the French Revolution, you can still see one section of the church walls, a few remains of the library, one side of the Concierge's Lodge and the Chapel of St. Ursula, where cultural events are now held.

TAKE D139/ D130 SOUTH TO BOURBONNE-LES-BAINS and THEN D460 33KM SOUTH TO GENEVRIERES BEFORE TURNING WEST ON D306 TO:

Belmont is the only female monastery that retains some remnants from the past. Founded in 1127, it was the second of several hundred female monasteries in Europe and was originally built on a hillside, before moving to the village in the 17th C. The monastic house remains, a lovely building with a central section and two wings.

TAKE D125 NORTH 11KM TO:

Corgirnon

<u>STAY AT:</u> *the Municipal aire in* **Corgirnon,** *in* **Rue Belle Fontaine**. *Located a short walk to the north of this small rural village (with its fishing lake), this well equipped aire has 8 individual spaces on tarmac, separated by hedges and well shaded by trees. Each pitch has an ehu and the price includes use of showers/ toilets and electricity, as well as the artisanal service point with drainage grid. A boulangerie van passes each morning, except for Monday. The Council official calls at about 7pm to turn on the electric and water, and he also provides a code number for the combination lock to the toilet/shower.*

Facilities: *Water•Grey Drain•Black Drain•Electric•Toilet*
No. of spaces: *6*
Parking: *7€/ 24 Hrs*
Services: *Incl*
Opening times: *All year*
GPS Coordinates: *N47.80715   E05.50313*
Alternative: *Camping Navarre, Bvd Marechal de Lattre, 52200 Langres   Open 15/ 03 – 13/10*

DAY 3

TAKE N19 17KM WEST TO LANGRES, THEN D974 SOUTH 6KM and D428 24KM WEST TO:

Auberive: Founded in 1135 by St Bernard, the Abbaye d'Auberive was the 24th abbey of the Clairvaux federation. The 12th C apse of the abbey church remains intact, but some buildings were rebuilt in the 18th C, including three of the cloister wings (with an imposing facade facing the gardens) and a magnificent gate at the entrance. Auberive later became a women's prison and is now a centre for culture and music for the Haute-Marne region.

TAKE D20 NORTH ONTO D965 WEST FOR 5KM and THEN D996 29KM NORTH TO:

Clairvaux: St. Bernard founded the Abbaye de Clairvaux, the third daughter abbey of Cîteaux, on the left bank of the river Aube (at the very edge of the Aube and Haute-Marne regions) in 1115, remaining abbot there until his death in 1153. After being famous throughout Christendom for centuries, Clairvaux was turned into a prison in 1808. The house for lay brothers is the magnificent but sole remainder from the 12th C, and the great cloister is an 18th C remnant. At the entrance, the Hôtellerie des Dames houses an exhibition room, a bookshop and the visitor reception area.

TAKE D12/ D15 and D23 NORTH 16KMS TO:
Colombey les Deux Eglises
STAY AT: *the Municipal aire in* ***Colombey les Deux Eglises,*** *in* ***Rue General DeGaulle (D23).*** *Located in the centre of this rural village, the aire is in a medium sized gravel parking area next to the Mairie. It offers 10 level spaces bordered by grass verges and partial shade under mature trees. Artisanal service point with drainage grid. It's a short walk to the shops and services: boulangerie, restaurants, Poste, grocer and souvenir shops, there is also a Charles De Gaulle Museum in this village where he was born. Nearby you can find a petanque pitch, tennis courts, tourist info, toilets and showers*
Facilities: *Water•Grey Drain•Black Drain•Toilet*
No. of spaces: *10*
Parking: *Free*
Services: *Free*
Opening times: *All year*
GPS Coordinates: *N48.22320   E04.88621*
Alternative: *Camping Municipal, Rte d'Aubepierre, 52210 Arc en Barrois   Open 01/04 – 30/09*

Auberive by Boulay

Above: Clairvaux by KBWEi

Left: Colombey by Boulay

Right: Aire at Corgirnon

FRANCHE-COMTE TOUR 35
THE MOST BEAUTIFUL TOWNS and VILLAGES - 6 DAYS

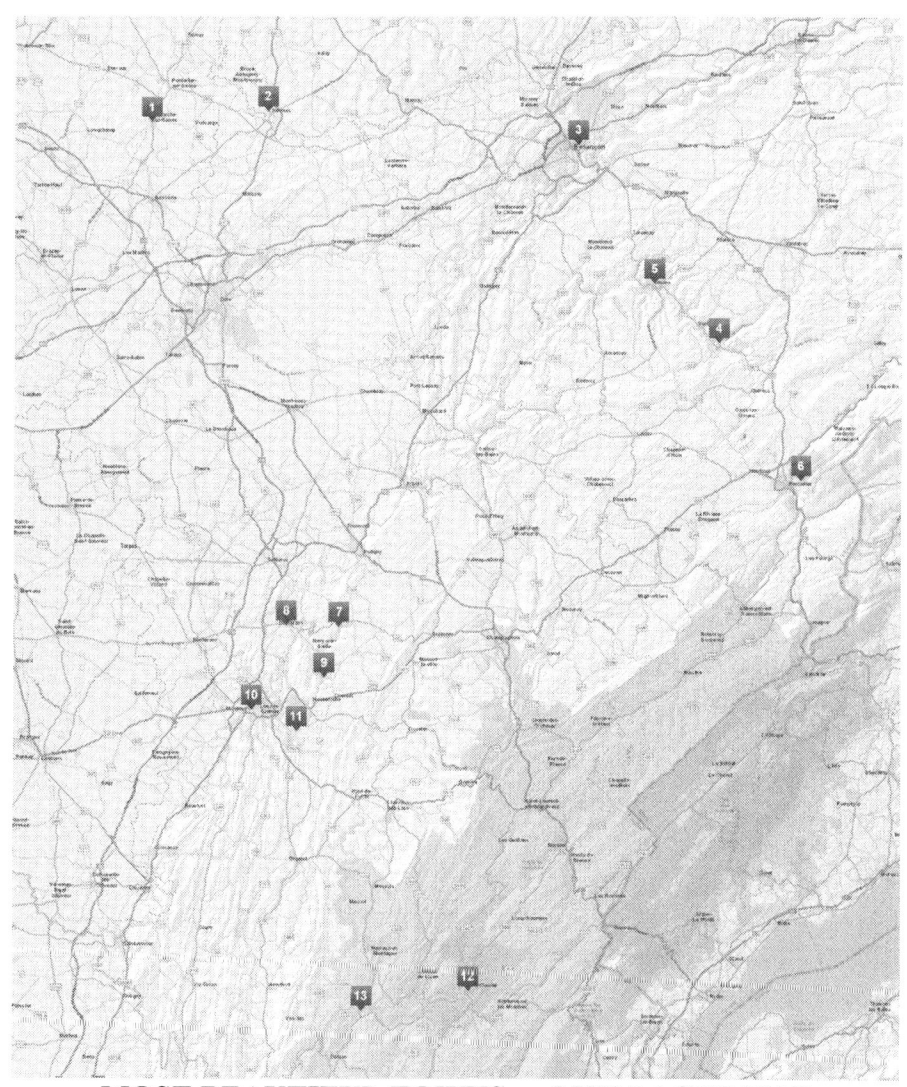

MOST BEAUTIFUL TOWNS and VILLAGES MAP

KEY TO MAP:
1) Lamarche sur Saone
2) Pesmes
3) Besancon
4) Lods
5) Ornans
6) Pontarlier
7) Chateau Chalon
8) Voiteur
9) Baume les Messieurs
10) Lons le Saunier
11) Conliege
12) St Claude
13) Jeurre

The 6-Day Tour starts in the beautiful village of Pesmes, on the edge of the Doubs department, before travelling South to the UNESCO listed town of Besancon. Continuing South through the Doubs, the tour visits the villages of Lods and Baume les Messieurs and the small towns of Ornans, Pontarlier, and Chateau Chalon, before arriving in the thermal spa resort of Lons le Saunier. The tour continues on through the Jura before finishing in the mountain town of St Claude.

DAY 1
Lamarche sur Saone

STAY AT: *The Municipal aire in* **Lamarche sur Saone***, located in* **Rue de la Marchotte***. This aire is pleasantly located next to the Saone river in a large parking area with spaces on grass accessed off a gravel track. The parking has little shade or lighting, but is next to the moorings on the river, with adjacent grass areas, and is about 150m north of the village centre and its shops. A Flot Bleu service point with large drainage platform that requires payment by credit card. Shops in the village include; boulangerie, grocer/news, butcher, 2 restaurants and a pizzeria. This is a very peaceful position, with the river to the east (and open countryside beyond) and lakes to the west. It is possible to fish in the river, or in the nearby lakes (payable by the day), and there are walks/ cycling alongside the river.*

Facilities: *Water•Grey Drain•Black Drain*
No. of spaces: *12*
Parking: *Free*
Services: *3€ Water*
Opening times: *All year*
GPS Coordinates: *N47.27250   E05.38667*
Alternative: *Camping Colombiere, Rte de la Dole, 70140 Pesmes Open 24/04 – 30/09*

TAKE D116 and D959/ D459 EAST, THEN D112 EAST TO:

Pesmes used to be a strategic site on the way from Gray to Dole and has had a turbulent history because of the various occupations it underwent before it became French in 1678. Despite that fact the village has preserved a wealth of heritage, including the remains of the chateau, the Church of Saint Hilaire (dating back to the 13th C) and fortified gates. There are 16th C dwellings along the River Ognon that used to belong to wealthy citizens, and the wine grower's houses are reminders of the village's wine producing past.

TAKE D12 12KMS NORTH and D67 30KMS EAST TO:

Besancon

STAY AT: *the Municipal aire in* **Besancon**, *located in* **Rue des Arenes**. *The aire is located in a medium sized tarmac car park, next to the river and close to the old quarter of the city. It offers a dozen level spaces, is lit at night but has little shade, and there is an AireServices borne with a platform drain. The aire is convenient for visiting this interesting city and there is a cycle route along the river. NOTE: This may be a difficult aire to access due to the one-way system, although it is signposted in town. Head for the large Church "Eglise de la Madeleine" on the North side of the river and Rue d'Arenes is the one-way street next to it. There is also a large car park to the East of the Citadelle at Parking Rodia - no services but OK for an overnight stay and is free.*

Facilities: *Water•Grey Drain•Black Drain*
No. of spaces: *12*
Parking: *7€/24 Hrs*
Services: *Incl*
Opening times: *All year*
GPS Coordinates: *N47.23701   E06.01651*
Alternative: *Camping La Plage, Rte de Belfort, 25000 Besancon Open 14/03 – 30/10*

DAY 2

Besancon: Overlooked by its commanding Vauban Citadel, that covers an area of 11ha and has previously been voted 'Tourist Attraction of the Year', Besancon is a UNESCO listed fortified town, whilst in the old quarter, is the 12th C Cathedral. Museums include the Museum of Fine Arts, with collections of Egyptian, Greek and Etruscan antiquities as well as magnificent Gallo-Roman mosaics and a Fine Art Collection; the Time Museum, in Granvelle Palace, which explores the measurement of time; a Natural History Museum and a Vauban exhibition in the Citadel. Another highlight of Besancon is the house where Victor Hugo was born (containing many of his possessions). Charles Nodier and the Lumière brothers were born in the same square, and the artist Gustave Courbet lived there also.

STAY AT: *The Municipal aire in* **Besancon**, *located in* **Rue des Arenes** *or Camping La Plage, Rte de Belfort, 25000 Besancon*

DAY 3

TAKE N57 EAST 38KMS and D32 SOUTH TO:

Lods: 45 kms South of Besançon, Lods, with the River Loue cascading through it, is a village where blacksmiths and vine growers long governed the pace of life. The village has retained the wine producers' houses of yesterday and has set up a Wine and Vineyard Museum, along with a Museum relating the history of its former commercial past. Also worth a visit in the village is St Theodules Church.

TAKE D67 WEST TO:

Ornans on the River Loue, has a rich past and is one of the towns classified as a "Small Town of Character." Along with its old stone dwellings, it has beautiful 16th, 17th and 18th C buildings - including mansions, halls, hospitals and churches. The museum, located in the house of the artist Gustave Courbet, displays several paintings by the artist.

Just North of Ornans is the 30 acre landscaped Dino-Zoo park, where a 2.5 km walk invites you to discover the evolution of life on earth, with about a hundred dinosaur reproductions presented in their habitat. Dinosaur fossils have been found in this region of the Jura and you will find an explanatory board (in English) along the route, which is set in the heart of a small valley crossed by a stream. Open Feb – Oct.

STAY AT: *The Municipal aire in* **Ornans***, located in* **Rue des Essarts***. The aire is located in a medium sized tarmac car park on the North East edge of this small town, near to the river and close to the OT. There are over a dozen level spaces (7x5m), lit at night but with little shade, and an artisanal borne with a platform drain. This is a pleasantly situated aire overlooking this historic little town. Access is via an automatic barrier, payable by credit card only, and the rate varies according to the season (price includes hook-up plus wifi). A short walk takes you into town for shops and eating places, whilst the aire is also close to the Via Ferrata climbing route.*

Facilities: *Water•Grey Drain•Black Drain•Electric•Wifi*
No. of spaces: *16*
Parking: *5 to 10€/24 Hrs*
Services: *Incl*
Opening times: *All year*
GPS Coordinates: *N47.10755   E06.14790*
Alternative: *Camping La Roche, Allee de la Tour, 25290 Ornans Open 04/04 – 10/10*

DAY 4
TAKE D67 EAST 20KMS and N57 SOUTH TO:
Pontarlier is a former Gallo-Roman town, sitting at an altitude of 837m. It is famous for its former Absinthe distillery and the Chateau de Joux, a medieval fortress that was reinforced by Vauban and later converted into a WWI fort. The museum, housed in a 15th C house, has a collection of stained glass.

TAKE D471 40KMS WEST TO CHAMPAGNOLE and THEN D5 31KMS WEST TO:
Chateau Chalon: Towering over its vineyards from the top of the cliff on which it is perched, the village of Chateau Chalon is the birthplace of the famous Vin Jaune (yellow wine), made from late harvest grapes. The village grew up around the chateau (that it took its name from) and the Benedictine abbey, but all that remains of these today are the keep and the Romanesque church of Saint Pierre. In the village there is a reconstruction of a 19th C schoolhouse, and an old cheese dairy.

TAKE D5 WEST TO:
Voiteur

STAY AT: *the Parking in* ***Voiteur***, *located in* ***Rue du Cimetiere***. *The parking is situated in a medium sized tarmac car park on the Eastern edge of this village, next to the cemetery, and offers half a dozen level spaces with shade in places. There are no services here apart from a water tap and toilets nearby. It's a short walk into the pleasant little village, where there are shops, a bank, supermarket, petrol station, restaurant and pizzeria. This is a quiet spot next to the football field, with picnic tables, petanque and a grass area.*

Facilities: *Water*
No. of spaces: *6*
Parking: *Free*
Services: *None*
Opening times: *All year*
GPS Coordinates: *N46.75507   E05.61408*
Alternative: *Camping Municipal, Place de la Toupe (D70), 39210 Baume les Messieurs Open 01 /04 – 30/09*

DAY 5
TAKE D70 SOUTH TO:
Baume les Messieurs is nestled in a cirque formed where three valleys meet and boasts an exceptional vista. The village houses cluster around a Benedictine abbey, which is one of the most

magnificent examples of Romanesque art in the Jura and houses one of the greatest altarpieces in Europe. Nearby are the Baume underground caves and a spectacular waterfall.

CONTINUE SOUTH ONTO D471 WEST TO:

Lons le Saunier is a nice, large town centred around a thermal spa centre that offers various treatments as well as massages, saunas and a 32C swimming pool. The town also has a casino, a bowling alley, and is home to the Bel cheese factory with its 'Laughing Cow House' – a children's museum dedicated to the cheese.

TAKE D678 TO:

Conliege

<u>STAY AT:</u> *the Municipal aire in* **Conliege***, located in* **Rue du Saugeois, off D678***. This Aire is in a small tarmac parking area off the D678 at the southern end of this small rural village. Situated next to a children's play area, it only has 1 space that has some shade from nearby trees. The parking is about 200m from the village centre, where there is a mini Flot Bleu borne with a platform drain, toilets and rubbish bin. The place is fairly quiet, being set back from the D678 through the village, and despite it only having one allocated space for camping cars, there are other spaces adjacent. There are views to the west, picnic tables nearby, and the parking is a starting point for marked walks. The village has a few shops, plus a couple of bars/eating places.*

Facilities: *Water • Grey Drain • Black Drain • Rubbish*
No. of spaces: *1*
Parking: *Free*
Services: *Free*
Opening times: *All year*
GPS Coordinates: *N46.65265   E05.59978*
Alternative: *Camping La Marjorie, Bvd de l'Europe, 39000 Lons le Saunier Open 01/04 – 15 /10*

<u>DAY 6</u>

TAKE D678/ D52 TO ORGLET and D470/ D436 SOUTH-EAST TO:

St Claude is an historic mountain town, with the remains of an abbey and a Gothic cathedral. It is also the departure point for visiting the Flumen Gorges, and the departure point for the touristic 'Swallow Line' railway that crosses the Jura, connecting Dole to Saint-Claude -

a journey of more than 120 km (2h30) through plains, mountains and the forest of Chaux.
TAKE D436 WEST TO:
Jeurre
STAY AT: *the Private aire in **Jeurre**, located in **Rue Principale**, off D27. This aire is next to the Rue Principale leading into Jeurre, with parking in a large level field surrounded by a tall hedge and trees – giving good privacy. There are over a dozen spaces on grass, accessed by a gravel track, but no lighting or much shade. The small rural village has no shops but this is a good area for walking. There is an artisanal borne with platform drainage.*
Facilities: *Water•Grey Drain•Black Drain•Electric*
No. of spaces: *15*
Parking: *5€/24 Hrs*
Services: *2€ Water, 3€ Electric*
Opening times: *01/05 - 31/10*
GPS Coordinates: *N46.36725   E05.70865*
Alternative: *Camping le Martinet, Rue du Martinet, 39200 St Claude Open 01/04 – 30/09*

Pesmes by By G CHP

Above: Besancon

Middle: Ornans

Below: Chateau Chalon
(All by Arnaud 25)

Bottom: Aire at Besancon

NORMANDY TOUR 36
THE IMPRESSIONISTS TOUR – 4 DAYS

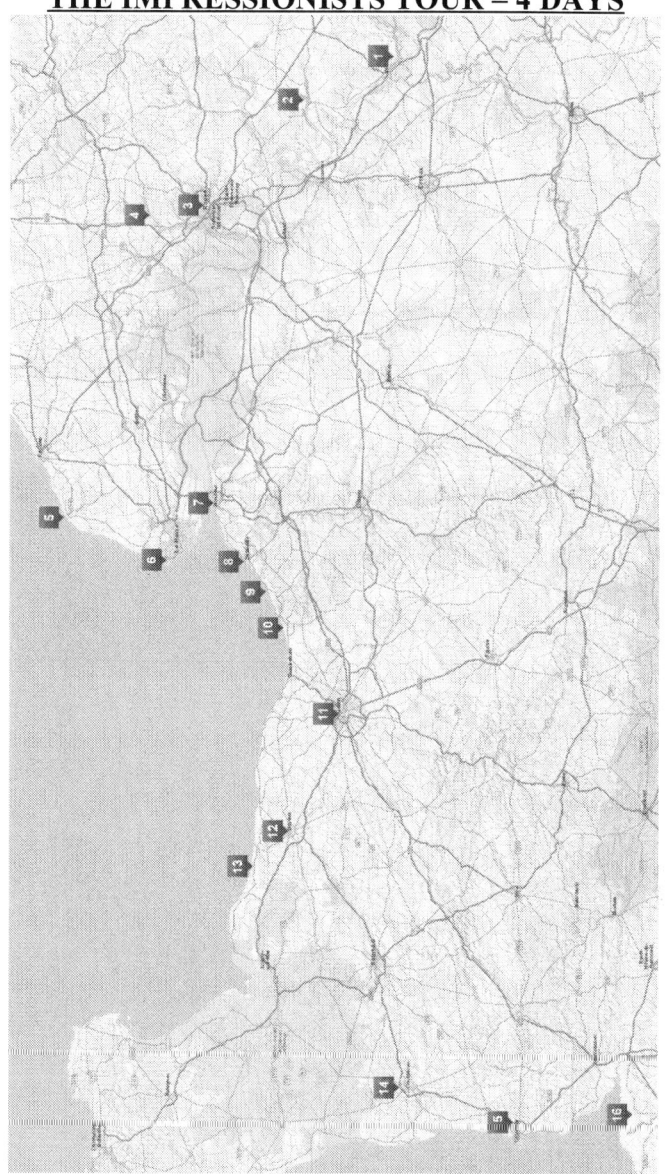

THE IMPRESSIONISTS TOUR MAP

KEY: 1) Giverny 2) Les Andelys 3) Rouen 4) Montville
5) Etretat 6) Ste Adresse 7) Honfleur 8) Deauville
9) Villers sur Mer 10) Cabourg 11) Caen 12) Bayeux
13) Ste Honorine des Pertes 14) Coutances 15) Granville
16) Mont St Michel

This 4-Day Tour visits the Normandy area whose beautiful light inspired the Impressionists and where many of its masterpieces were painted. Monet's "Impression Sunrise" (that gave birth to the name Impressionism) was painted in Sainte Adresse, near Le Havre, and this tour visits the important locations related to Monet and other artists, such as Renoir, Courbet and Pissaro, who were also attracted to the region.

DAY 1
Giverny
STAY AT: *the large parking area on* **Chemin du Roy (D5)** *in Giverny, with 40 level spaces on grass, accessed by a gravel track. It has no lighting and little shade, but is only 200m from the centre of the village and the Monet house. There is a restaurant and boulangerie adjacent, with shops in the village as well as a cycle hire depot. This is a quiet spot but is just a parking area with no services; there are eating places and souvenir shops in the village.*

Facilities: *Toilets*
No. of spaces: *40*
Parking: *Free*
Services: *None*
Opening times: *23/03 - 01/11*
GPS Coordinates: *N49.07333 W01.53002*
Alternative: *Camping les Fosses, Chemin de Reanville, 27950 St Marcel Open: 01/03 – 31/10*

Giverny in the Seine Valley, is the birthplace of Impressionism, with Claude Monet, the father of modern painting, being the leader of this movement. Monet lived in Giverny for 43 years and his house here is now a museum, with its famous 5-acre gardens that he painted so often. There is also the American Impressionist Art Museum, with its gardens, restaurant and tearooms, and the famous 19th C Hotel Baudy (just down the road), popular with the impressionist artists, including Cezanne.

TAKE D313 22KM NORTH TO:
Les Andelys: A magnificent setting deep in one of the great loops of the Seine River, overlooked by high chalk hillsides and the ruins of the 12th C Chateau Gaillard. In the town are two historic churches and the Nicholas Poussin museum, which traces the history of the town together with a section devoted to art. Riverboat trips are available along the Seine.

TAKE D126 and D138 NORTH TO:
Rouen: Monet rented rooms (located opposite the Cathedral) in Rouen for two consecutive winters; and the Museum of Fine Arts has the second largest Impressionist collection in France. Whilst in Rouen Monet painted his famous series of "Cathedrals" and it was here that the "Rouen School" of artists was conceived. The must-see highlights of Rouen include the Cathedral, the Abbey, Tour Jeanne d'Arc and the Old Town whilst there are numerous art galleries in the town.

TAKE D927 10KM NORTH TO:
Montville
STAY AT: *the Municipal aire,* **off D155 in Montville,** *is found in the town's Leisure area car parking (in a motorhome only section), next to a lake and an indoor swimming pool. The parking is on a gravel surface bordered by grass and is only 200m from the town shops. A restaurant (L'Hexagone - open from 15/3 – 31/10) is adjacent, as well as a play area, boules, mini-golf, and pedaloes on the lake. The Euro-Relais service point with a platform drain is in the adjacent car park - jetons can be purchased in the restaurant, museum or at the Marie. An interesting Fire Engine museum can be found in the town, and free wifi is available at the Tourist Office.*

Facilities: *Water•Grey Drain•Black Drain•Electric*
No. of spaces: *8*
Parking: *Free*
Services: *3€ Water or Electric*
Opening times: *All year*
GPS Coordinates: *N49.54749 E01.07248*
Alternative: *Camping Les Nenuphars, Rte des 2 Tilleuls, 76480 Roumare   Open: 30/03 – 15/12*

DAY 2
TAKE A150/ A29 (Jcn 6) WEST and D39 NORTH TO:
Etretat is famous for its cliffs, painted by many artists including Monet, Courbet and Isabey. Richard the Lionheart's ruined Aygues Chateau is open to visitors, as is the 11th C Notre Dame church.

FOLLOW D940 COAST ROAD SOUTH TO:
Sainte Adresse: Having grown up in Le Havre, Monet frequently went to the seaside resort of Sainte-Adresse to paint the beach and the cliffs. His work "Impression Sunrise" was painted here, and subsequently gave birth to the term Impressionism.

TAKE A131/ A29 ACROSS THE SEINE TO:

Honfleur: With half-timbered houses and stylish shops, especially around the old harbour, Honfleur is a picturesque seaside town. When Monet was 16 years old he met the local artist Eugène Boudin, a painter who was already well established, and Jongkind (who was also staying in the same area) often worked with them. During his studies in Paris, Monet brought many of his contemporary artists with him to Saint-Simeon Farm in Honfleur. Highlights of a visit include the Salt Cellars, Eugène Boudin Museum and the timber 15th C St-Catherine's Church next to the harbour.

HEAD WEST ALONG D513 COAST ROAD TO:

Deauville/Trouville are two popular, adjoining, seaside resorts that also boast a fishing port where many of the impressionists have painted. Boudin and Mozin famously painted the fine beach, and Eugène Boudin eventually died in Trouville. Art collections are housed in the Montebello museum (Trouville), whilst there are the promenades, expensive boutiques, many famous villas, hotels and the Casino to visit in Deauville.

CONTINUE WEST 8KM ALONG D513 COAST ROAD TO:
Villers sur Mer

STAY AT: *The Municipal aire in* **Rue des Martois** *in* **Villers sur Mer***. Pleasantly situated on the eastern edge of this small town, next to the countryside, near the beach, wetlands and hiking trails, but also not far from the shops. 14 places are available to accommodate motorhomes - the spaces are on gravel hard-standing separated by small hedges, and the aire is accessed off the main road by means of a gravel track. UrbaFlux service point with drainage grid. This aire is well located for the beach and walks, with a Prehistoric museum adjacent and wifi is also available at a charge.*

Facilities: *Water•Grey Drain•Black Drain•Electric•Wifi*
No. of spaces: *14*
Parking: *Free*
Services: *2€ Water, Electric incl.*
Opening times: *All year*
GPS Coordinates: *N49.32932   E0.01356*
Alternative: *Camping Les Ammonites, Rte de la Corniche, 14640 Auberville   Open: 01/04 – 18/10*

DAY 3
FOLLOW D513 COAST ROAD 10KM WEST TO:

Cabourg is popular for its casino and shops, and is home to numerous fine villas built during the "Belle Epoque". Monet painted the resort and its "Grand Hotel", which has glorious views onto the 4kms of sandy beach.

CONTINUE ON D513 TO:

Caen has little connection with the Impressionists, but a tour around the town founded by William the Conqueror is still worthwhile. Highlights include the cathedral-like Abbaye aux Hommes, founded in 1066, the Abbaye aux Dames, William's ruined Chateau Ducal and its gardens (also housing the Museum of Fine Arts), and the WWII museum - the Memorial de Caen.

TAKE N13 WEST TO:

Bayeux: following in William the Conqueror's foot-steps, the highlight here is the Bayeux Tapestry (which recalls the story of William the Conqueror's conquest of England) and the Gothic Cathedral, whilst also nearby are Château Fontaine Henry and the WWII Landing Beaches.

TAKE D6 NORTH TO:

Ste Honorine des Pertes

STAY AT: the Private aire **in Route Omaha Beach** *in* **Ste Honorine des Pertes**. *This aire is owned by the village 'Elan' petrol station and is quietly situated behind the garage (next to the campsite) in a large grass parking area, bordered on either side by farmland but offering little shade. The garage is ½ km west of the village centre, on the D514 road, but the village itself has few facilities. The spaces each have an electric hook up (included in tariff) and a Euro-Relais service point with double drainage platform. The garage owner is very friendly and the aire is well positioned on the coast road for visiting the various WWII sites, with it also being possible to walk to the coast from here (about 1km).*

Facilities: *Water •Grey Drain •Black Drain •Electric*
No. of spaces: *20*
Parking: *10€/24Hrs*
Services: *Incl*
Opening times: *All year*
GPS Coordinates: *N49.34833   W00.81722*
Alternative: *Camping Municipal, Bvd Eindhoven, 14400 Bayeux Open: 01/04 – 05/11*

DAY 4

TAKE D6 SOUTH and CONTINUE WEST ON D572/ D972 TO:
Coutances: this old town has kept its rich architectural patrimony, and the Cotentin region is the home of Millet, one of the initiators of Impressionism, who painted his famous "Angelus" here. Highlights of the town include the Cathedral, the oldest plant gardens in Normandy and the nearby 13th C Chateau de Gratot.
TAKE D971 SOUTH TO:
Granville is located in a beautiful site and was the birthplace of the artist Christian Dior. It is possible to visit the Christian Dior estate next to the promenade, whilst the town has the historic Abbey of Lucerne nearby.
TAKE D973/ N175 SOUTH and D43/ D275 WEST TO:
Mont-St-Michel: Fascinating to artists, Mont-St-Michel was captured many times by the impressionists,
including a famous painting by Paul Signac. Classified as a World Heritage Area by UNESCO, the medieval fortified town stands proudly in the middle of the vast mud flats of the bay of Mont-Saint-Michel, which boasts the strongest tides in Europe. The town has many fine old buildings, 3 museums, tourist shops, restaurants, an Abbey - "The Wonder of the Western World" - as well as a light display show. A visit to the town and Abbey takes 2-3 hours.
<u>STAY AT:</u> the large purpose-built private aire on **Route Mont-St-Michel** *in* **Mont-St-Michel***, with 190 level spaces (each is 100 sq m, all with 10A hook ups and free wifi) on tarmac. Grass strips separate the rows and the aire is lit at night, but there is no shade. The aire is about 2kms from the departure point of the shuttle buses for Mont St Michel (so about 4kms from the Mont). There is a restaurant and boulangerie adjacent, with shops in the village as well as a cycle hire depot. AireServices borne with drainage platform.*
Facilities: *Water•Grey Drain•Black Drain•Electric*
No. of spaces: *190*
Parking: *13-18€/ 24hrs*
Services: *Incl.*
Opening times: *All year*
GPS Coordinates: *N48.61383   W01.50142*
Alternative: *Camping Mont St Michel, La Caserne, Mont St Michel Open 30/03 – 01/11*

Page 251

Left: Giverny by Main

Right: Honfleur By Txllxt

Left: Deauville

Aire at Montville

CHATEAUX, PARKS and GARDENS MAP

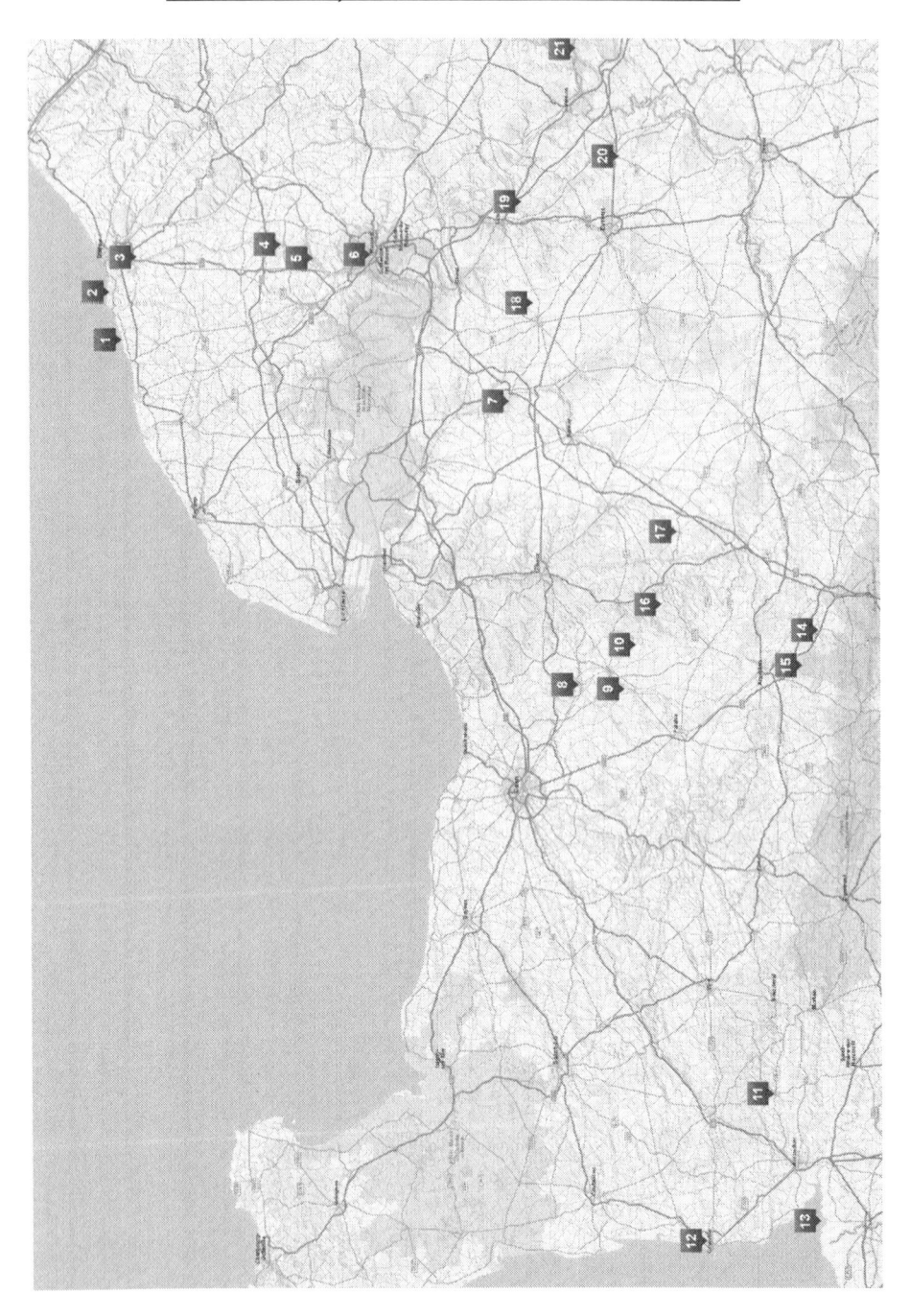

KEY TO MAP (Left):
1) St Aubin sur Mer   2) Varengeville sur Mer   3) Miromesnil
4) Cleres   5) Montville   6) Rouen   7) Harcourt
8) Mezidon-Canon   9) Vendeuvre   10) L'Oudon   11) Brecey
12) Granville   13) Mont-St-Michel   14) Mortree
15) Saint-Christophe Le Jajolet   16) Crouttes   17) Le Sap
18) Sainte Opportune   19) Acquigny   20) Vernon   21) Giverny

NORMANDY TOUR 37
CHATEAUX, PARKS and GARDENS – 5 DAYS

Normandy has some of the nicest gardens in France, many of which lie in the grounds of magnificent chateaux. This 5-Day Tour starts on the coast at the famous Parc des Moutiers near Dieppe, stopping at various chateaux and parks. It passes through Rouen, visits the chateaux gardens of Canon, Vendeuvre and Brecey before calling at Mont St Michel, and after viewing more gardens on the way, it finishes at Monet's famous garden in Giverny.

Miromesnil by Westerveld

DAY 1
St Aubin sur Mer
STAY AT: *The Municipal aire in **Val St Aubin** in **St Aubin sur Mer**, positioned about 300m north of the village, next to the beach and the*

campsite, is in a very large gravel parking area bordered by grass and having good views. Raclet service point with drainage grid. It is a level walk to the village and convenient for the beach, but has no shade and can be a bit exposed in windy weather. The manager from the adjacent Grand Sable campsite collects the parking fee, there are no facilities in the village, apart from a cafe selling bread, cakes, drinks and beach goods.

Facilities: *Water•Grey Drain•Black Drain*
No. of spaces: *60*
Parking: *8€/ 24 Hrs*
Services: *2€ Water*
Opening times: *All year*
GPS Coordinates: *N49.89371   E00.87366*
Alternative: *Camping Municipal, Rue de la Saane, 76860 Quiberville sur Mer   Open: 01/04 – 31/10*

TAKE D75 EAST TO:

Varengeville-sur-Mer: The house and garden of Parc des Moutiers, which are in the "Arts and Crafts" style, were created between 1898 and 1940 in a vast valley overlooking the sea by the architect Sir Edwin Lutyens and the gardener Gertrude Jekyll. Open 15/03 – 15/11. Nearby are the gardens of Parc de Vastérival that cover 9ha with over 10,000 species of plants. Open all year.

TAKE D55 SOUTH TO:

Miromesnil: The author Guy de Maupassant was born in the Château de Miromesnil. The well-groomed walled French gardens here grow vegetables and flowers in harmony, and there is a lovely gothic chapel to be found under the huge beech trees in the park. The 16th C chateau has various architectural features dating from Henry IV to the Renaissance.

TAKE N27 SOUTH TO D2 Jcn and D2 SOUTH TO:

Cleres: Between the charming chateaux of Clères and Bosmelet, lie the gardens of Clos du Coudray, Le Plume, Angelique and Bellevue. The 20,000 sq m Clos du Coudray in **Etaimpuis** won Best Park in France in 2006 and has a series of themed gardens. Open 01/04 - 31/10. Jardins de Bellevue in **Beaumont le Hareng** are botanical gardens, with various themes including golden, summer and hydrangea. Open all year. Le Jardin Plume in **Azouville** is a contemporary garden with Summer and Winter gardens, a vegetable garden and a garden centre. Open 01/05 – 30/10. The much smaller

Jardins d'Angélique in **Montmain** have been created around a lovely manor house and have the feel of an English Country Garden. Open May to Oct. There is also the vegetable garden at **Chateau Bosmelet,** which is open from June till September.

TAKE D155 SOUTH TO:
Montville
<u>*STAY AT:*</u> *: The Municipal aire, **off D155** in **Montville**, is found in the town's Leisure area car park (in a motorhome only section), next to a lake and an indoor swimming pool. The parking is on a gravel surface bordered by grass and is only 200m from the town shops. A restaurant (L'Hexagone - open from 15/3 – 31/10) is adjacent, as well as a play area, boules, mini-golf, and pedaloes on the lake. The Euro-Relais service point with a platform drain is in the adjacent car park - jetons can be purchased in the restaurant, museum or at the Marie. An interesting Fire Engine museum can be found in the town, and free wifi is available at the Tourist Office.*
Facilities: *Water•Grey Drain•Black Drain•Electric*
No. of spaces: *8*
Parking: *Free*
Services: *3€ Water or Electric*
Opening times: *All year*
GPS Coordinates: *N49.54749 E01.07248*
Alternative: *Camping Les Nenuphars, Rte des 2 Tilleuls, 76480 Roumare Open : 30/03 – 15/12*

DAY 2
TAKE D155/ D927 SOUTH TO:
Rouen: In the city are the gardens of Parc Vandrimare. The must-see highlights of Rouen include the Cathedral, the Abbey, Tour Jeanne d'Arc and the Old Town. The Museum of Fine Arts has the second largest Impressionist collection in France.
TAKE D938/ A13 WEST and A28 SOUTH TO JCN 13 and D26 TO:
Harcourt: The medieval Chateau is a fine example of Norman military architecture, with a 12th C keep, a "Jardin Remaquable" and its large arboretum. Open 01/03 – 15/11
TAKE D613 53KM WEST and D16 SOUTH TO:
Mezidon-Canon: The Chateau de Canon dates back to the mid 18th C and is famous for its ten "chartreuses" or walled gardens, as well as its French and English gardens. Open July and August.

TAKE D16/ D511 13KM SOUTH TO:
Vendeuvre: The Château de Vendeuvre has an 18th C interior with a miniature furniture museum, whilst the gardens consist of "Water Surprise", topiary, romantic and exotic gardens, as well as mazes. Open 01/04 – 30/09.
TAKE D251/ D39 EAST TO:
L'Oudon
STAY AT: *the Municipal aire* **in Le Billot, East of L'Oudon Montville.** *This is a rural location, sited in a medium sized gravel parking area on the outskirts of this village. A lovely spot with fine views, it offers pitches on grass with picnic tables nearby and is surrounded by farmland. Euro-Relais service point with large platform drain. The public toilets can be found nearby, as well as the tap for the water. The village is nice but a bit remote.*
Facilities: *Water•Grey Drain•Black Drain•Electric•Toilets*
No. of spaces: *15*
Parking: *Free*
Services: *3€ Water or Electric*
Opening times: *All year*
GPS Coordinates: *N48.96810   W00.07435*
Alternative: *Camping Municipal, Rue d'Ante, 14700 Falaise   Open: 01/ 05 – 30/09*
DAY 3
TAKE D511/D562 and D512 WEST TO VIRE and D524 TO VILLEDIEU THEN D999 18KM SOUTH TO BRECEY:
Brecey: Château de Brécey is a 17th C chateau with Italian style gardens laid out over four terraces. Open 01/04 – 30/10.
RETURN NORTH TO VILLEDIEU and TAKE D924 WEST TO:
Granville: The 19th C "Belle Epoque" style house and gardens of Christian Dior overlook the sea, with a small museum inside the house. Open February till November.
TAKE D973/ N175 SOUTH and D43/ D275 WEST TO:
Mont-St-Michel: is a medieval fortified town, classified as a World Heritage Area by UNESCO, standing proudly in the middle of the vast mud-flats of the bay of Mont-Saint-Michel, which boasts the strongest tides in Europe. The town has many fine old buildings, 3 museums, tourist shops, restaurants, an Abbey - "The Wonder of the Western World" - as well as a light display. There is a small 13th C

cloister garden with herbaceous plants and lovely views. A visit to the town and Abbey takes 2-3 hours. Open all year.

STAY AT: *the large purpose-built private aire on* **Route Mont-St-Michel** *in* **Mont-St-Michel**, *with 190 level spaces (each is 100 sq m, all with 10A hook ups and free wifi) on tarmac. Grass strips separate the rows and the aire is lit at night, but there is no shade. The aire is about 2kms from the departure point of the shuttle buses for Mont St Michel (so about 4kms from the Mont). There is a restaurant and boulangerie adjacent, with shops in the village as well as a cycle hire depot. AireServices borne with drainage platform.*

Facilities: *Water•Grey Drain•Black Drain•Electric*
No. of spaces: *190*
Parking: *13-18€/ 24hrs*
Services: *Incl.*
Opening times: *All year*
GPS Coordinates: *N48.61383   W01.50142*
Alternative: *Camping Mont St Michel, La Caserne, Mont St Michel Open: 30/03 – 01/11*

DAY 4
TAKE N175/ D976/ D908 EAST TO CARROUGES and 14KMS FURTHER ONTO D26 NORTH TO:

Mortree: The fairytale 15th C Gothic and Renaissance style Château d'O stands in the midst of a lake in a forest. Open June till Sept.

TAKE D958 NORTH 5KM TO:

Saint-Christophe Le Jajolet: The 18th C Château de Sassy has prestigious French formal gardens, surrounded by a moat, with an Orangery bordered by pruned lime trees, as well as box, yew, laurel and other slow-growing evergreen plants.

TAKE D958 TO ARGENTAN and D916 30KM NORTH TO:

Crouttes: Near Vimoutiers, you will find the ancient Priory of Crouttes nestling in a green valley with its orchard, medicinal plants, iris, roses and water-gardens. Open May till Sept

FROM VIMOUTIERS, TAKE D979 SOUTH and D12 7KM EAST TO:

Le Sap

STAY AT: *the Municipal aire on* **Route de Vimoutiers (D12)** *in* **Le Sap**. *The aire is located about 500m west of the small village of Le Sap, off the D12. Situated in a small cul-de sac next to a factory surrounded by farmland, there are parking spaces on gravel, and no*

shade. An easy to access AireServices borne with drainage platform. There are shops in the village, plus a cider-making museum. There is also another aire nearby with 3 spaces outside the campsite in Vimoutiers.
Facilities: Water•Grey Drain•Black Drain•Rubbish
No. of spaces: 3
Parking: Free
Services: Free
Opening times: All year
GPS Coordinates: N48.89531   E00.33031
Alternative: Camping la Campiere, Rue du Docteur Dentu, 61120 Vimoutiers   Open: 30/03 – 01/11

DAY 5
TAKE D438 NORTH and D613 EAST TO LE NEUBOURG and D39 NORTH TO:
Sainte Opportune: The Chateau du Champ de Bataille, known as the "Norman Versailles", has been restored to its 18th C splendour, complete with parks, gardens and period furniture. The interiors are richly decorated and furnished, whilst the gardens have also been completely restored. Open 01/03 till 31/12

TAKE D133 and D82 EAST TO:
Acquigny on the Eure river, has a fine 16th C château and park. The garden is surrounded by brick walls and is filled with medicinal and culinary plants as well as ornamental flowerbeds, under old pear trees. The Orangery has a collection of citrus and other trees from around the world. Open 04/04 till 30/10

TAKE D82 EAST and D6015 13KM SOUTH TO:
Vernon: Château Bizy, a jewel of 18th C architecture, has magnificent French and English style gardens, decorated with antique sculptures and fountains. Open 01/04 till 01/11.

TAKE D5 SOUTH TO:
Giverny: in the Seine Valley, is the birthplace of Impressionism, with Claude Monet, the father of modern painting, being the leader of this movement. Monet lived in Giverny for 43 years and his house here is now a museum, with its famous 5-acre gardens that he painted so often. Open 24/03 till 01/11.
Visit also the American Impressionist Art Museum, with its gardens, restaurant and tearooms, and the famous 19th C Hotel Baudy (just down the road), popular with the impressionist artists, including

Cezanne.

STAY AT: *the large parking area on* **Chemin du Roy (D5)** *in* **Giverny**, *with 40 level spaces on grass, accessed by a gravel track. It has no lighting or shade, but is only 200m from the centre of the village and the Monet house. There is a restaurant and boulangerie adjacent, with shops in the village as well as a cycle hire depot. This is a quiet spot but is just a parking area with no services - there are eating-places and souvenir shops in the village.*
Facilities: *Toilets*
No. of spaces: *40*
Parking: *Free*
Services: *None*
Opening times: *23/03 - 01/11*
GPS Coordinates: *N49.07333   W01.53002*
Alternative: *Camping les Fosses, Chemin de Reanville, 27950 St Marcel   Open : 01/03 – 31/10*

Mortree by Unozoe

Above: Granville by Nikater   Below: Aire at St Aubin

KEY to CATHEDRALS and ABBEYS MAP (Right):
1) Montville
2) Rouen
3) Lisieux
4) Caen
5) Ste Honorine des Pertes
6) Bayeux
7) Coutances
8) Mont-St-Michel
9) Sees
10) Le Sap
11) Evreux
12) Nonancourt

NORMANDY TOUR 38
CATHEDRALS and ABBEYS – 5 DAYS

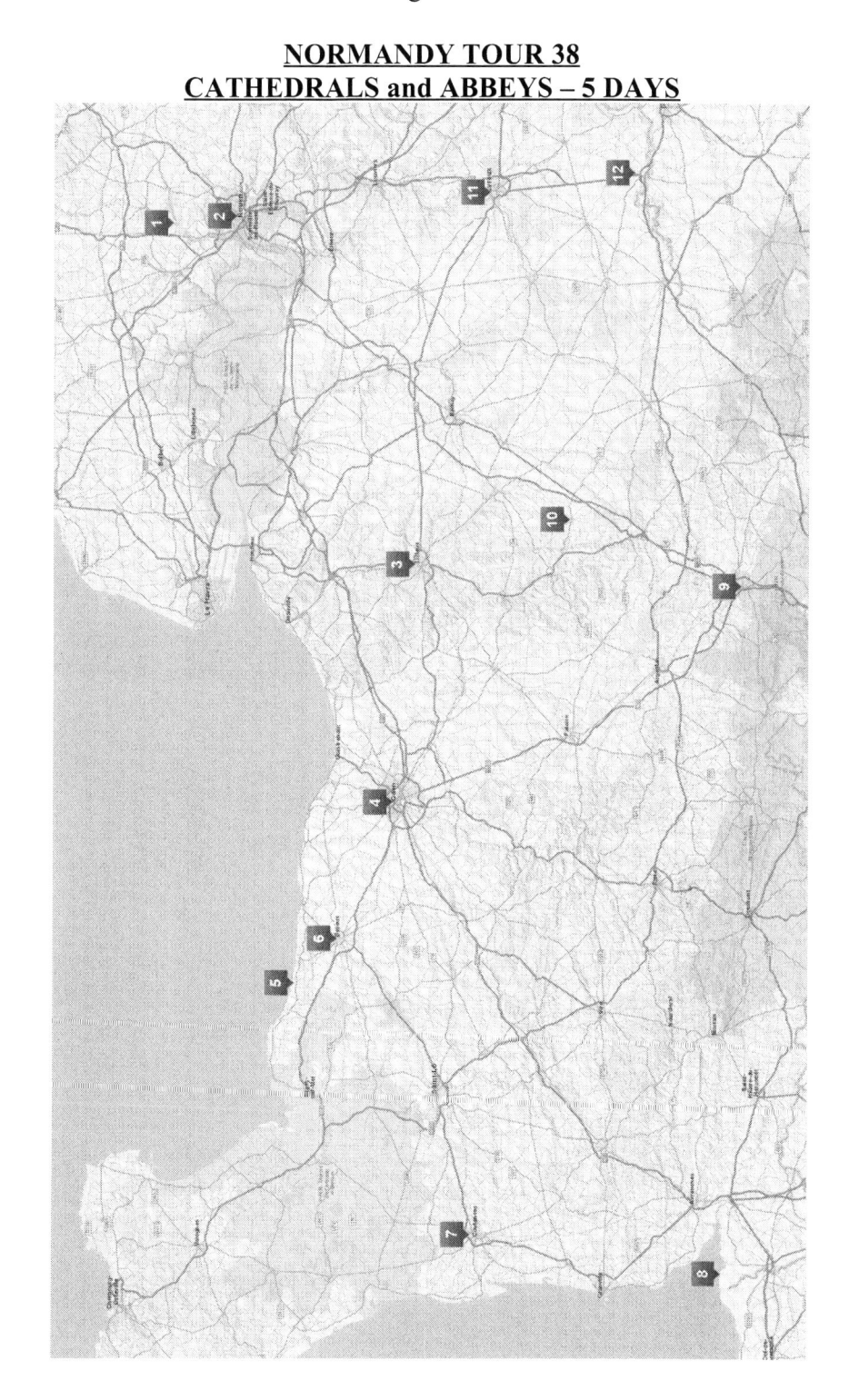

With its numerous Cathedrals, Abbeys and churches, Normandy is one of the richest regions for religious art, the stained glass in its Cathedrals making up the largest surface area of medieval glass in France. This 5-Day Tour starts at Rouen Cathedral before visiting those in Lisieux, Bayeux, Coutances, Sees and Evreux, interspersed with Abbeys at Caen and Mont Saint Michel.

DAY 1
Montville

STAY AT: The Municipal aire *off D155* in **Montville** *is found in the town's Leisure area car park (in a motorhome only section), next to a lake and an indoor swimming pool. The parking is on a gravel surface bordered by grass and only 200m from the town shops. A restaurant (L'Hexagone, open from 15/3 – 31/10) is adjacent, as well as a play area, boules, mini-golf and pedaloes on the lake. The Euro-Relais service point with a platform drain is in the adjacent car park - jetons can be purchased in the restaurant, museum, or at the Marie. An interesting Fire engine museum can be found in the town, and free wifi is available at the Tourist Office.*

Facilities: Water •Grey Drain •Black Drain •Electric
No. of spaces: 8
Parking: Free
Services: 3€ Water or Electric
Opening times: All year
GPS Coordinates: N49.54749 E01.07248
Alternative: Camping Les Nenuphars, Rte des 2 Tilleuls, 76480 Roumare Open: 30/03 – 15/12

TAKE D155 and D927 SOUTH TO:

Rouen: There has been a religious building on this site since 270 AD. The remains of a 4th C Cathedral have been discovered on the North side of the present 12th C Cathedral, and the gothic Notre Dame Cathedral shows the evolution of Norman architecture over the past 1,000 years. Inside you will find a 13th C choir, wonderful stained glass windows and some massive stone columns. The other must-see highlights of Rouen include the Abbey of St. Ouen, Tour Jeanne d'Arc & the Old Town, whilst the Museum of Fine Arts has the second largest Impressionist collection in France.

RETURN TO: **Montville**
STAY AT: The Municipal aire *off D155* in **Montville** or Camping Les Nenuphars, Rte des 2 Tilleuls, 76480 Roumare

DAY 2
TAKE A151/A150 SOUTH and A13 WEST ONTO D579 SOUTH TO:
Lisieux: The 19th C basilica dedicated to Saint Theresa is a famous place of pilgrimage, but the ancient St Pierre Cathedral is less well known. The greater part dates back to the 12th C, with early Norman gothic architecture dominating, Joan of Arc's judge, the Bishop of Lisieux, lies buried in the Lady Chapel. The town has many half-timbered houses, one of them housing the Museum of Art and History, and the Chateau of St Germain de Livet, with its fine museum, is a short drive from the town.
CONTINUE WEST ON D613 TO:
Caen: Although Caen has never had a cathedral it does have two abbeys of cathedral proportions - Abbaye aux Hommes, built by William the Conqueror in 1066, and Abbaye aux Dames, founded by William's wife in 1059 and rebuilt in the 18th C. Also worthy of a visit are William's ruined Chateau Ducal and its gardens (also housing the Museum of Fine Arts), and the WWII museum - the Memorial de Caen.
CONTINUE WEST ON N13 TO BAYEUX and TAKE D6 NORTH TO:
Ste Honorine des Pertes
STAY AT: : *The Private aire* **in Route Omaha Beach** in **Ste Honorine des Pertes**. *This aire is owned by the village petrol station (Elan) and is quietly situated behind the garage, next to the campsite, in a large grass parking area, bordered on either side by farmland but offering little shade. The garage is ½ km West of the village centre, on the D514 road, but the village itself has few facilities. The spaces each have an electric hook up (included in tariff) and a Euro-Relais service point with double drainage platform. The garage owner is very friendly and the aire is well positioned on the coast road for visiting the various WWII sites, with it also being possible to walk to the coast from here (about 1km).*
Facilities: *Water•Grey Drain•Black Drain•Electric*
No. of spaces: *20*
Parking: *10€/24Hrs*
Services: *Incl*
Opening times: *All year*
GPS Coordinates: *N49.34833   W00.81722*

Alternative: Camping Municipal, Bvd Eindhoven, 14400 Bayeux
Open: 01/04 – 05/11

DAY 3
RETURN TO:
Bayeux: The famous Bayeux Tapestry relates William's conquest of England, this masterpiece having been commissioned by William's half-brother Odo (the bishop of Bayeux) to be hung in his newly built Cathedral. In the Cathedral, a mixture of Norman and Gothic architecture, you can visit the crypt, the choir, and also the lace-museum in the nearby Bishop's Palace. Near to Bayeux are Château Fontaine Henry and the WWII Landing Beaches.

TAKE D572/ D972 WEST TO:
Coutances: Built on a hill, the Cathedral can be seen from as far away as Jersey. Its dimensions are modest but the beauty of its architecture, and its lantern-tower in particular, are outstanding. Inside are 15th C stained glass windows, medieval floor tiles and a 13th C chapel.

TAKE D971/ D973/ N175 SOUTH and D43/ D275 WEST TO:
Mont-St-Michel

STAY AT: *the large purpose-built private aire on **Route Mont-St-Michel** in **Mont-St-Michel**, with 190 level spaces (each is 100 sq m, all with 10A hook ups and free wifi) on tarmac. Grass strips separate the rows of spaces and the aire is lit at night, but there is no shade. The aire is about 2kms from the departure point of the shuttle buses for Mont St Michel (so about 4kms from the Mont). There is a restaurant and boulangerie adjacent, with shops in the village as well as a cycle hire depot. AireServices borne with drainage platform.*

Facilities: Water •Grey Drain •Black Drain •Electric
No. of spaces: 190
Parking: 13-18€/24hrs
Services: Incl.
Opening times: All year
GPS Coordinates: N48.61383 W01.50142
Alternative: Camping Mont St Michel, La Caserne, Mont St Michel
Open: 30/03 – 01/11

DAY 4
Mont-St-Michel: Classified as a World Heritage Area by UNESCO, is a medieval fortified town standing proudly in the middle of the vast mud flats of the bay of Mont-Saint-Michel, which boasts the strongest tides in Europe. The town has many fine old buildings, 3 museums,

tourist shops, restaurants, an Abbey - "The Wonder of the Western World" - as well as a light display show. A visit to the town and Abbey takes 2-3 hours.

TAKE D275/ D43/ D976 TO DOMFRONT and D908 EAST TO:
Sees: A mighty Cathedral, that was built around the year 1300 and is one of the masterpieces of Norman Gothic architecture, dominates this small town. The sculptures, 14th C stained glass, the tombs and altars are of particular note, and in the summer there are sound and light shows illustrating medieval life and the construction of the Cathedral. Nearby is the 12th C "Chapelle Canonialle" which originally served as a dormitory for Canons in the cathedral.

TAKE D438 NORTH 38KM ONTO D12 WEST TO:
Le Sap
STAY AT: *the Municipal aire on* **Route de Vimoutiers (D12)** *in* **Le Sap**. *The aire is located about 500m West of the small village of Le Sap, off the D12. Situated in a small cul-de sac next to a factory and surrounded by farmland, there are parking spaces on gravel but no shade. AireServices borne with drainage platform, easy to access and clean. There are shops in the village, plus a cider-making museum and there is also another aire with 3 spaces outside the campsite in Vimoutiers.*
Facilities: *Water •Grey Drain•Black Drain•Rubbish*
No. of spaces: *3*
Parking: *Free*
Services: *Free*
Opening times: *All year*
GPS Coordinates: *N48.89531   E00.33031*
Alternative: *Camping la Campiere, Rue du Docteur Dentu, 61120 Vimoutiers   Open: 30/03 – 01/11*

DAY 5
TAKE D12/ D438 NORTH TO BERNAY and D133/ D31 EAST TO:
Evreux: is not one of the largest cathedrals but it is probably one of the most beautiful. Its nave dates back to the 12th C, whilst the seventy 14th C stained glass windows are still complete and are regarded as one of the finest examples of French craftsmanship, whilst the Lantern-tower and Choir are late gothic. Nearby are the 13th C Abbey of St Taurin, and the beautiful Bishop's Palace, housing a very fine Art, History and Archeology museum.

TAKE N154 SOUTH 27KM TO:

Nonancourt
STAY AT: *the Municipal aire on* **Rue de l'Arsenal** *in* **Nonancourt**. *A modern aire located on the north-west side of town between the Mairie and the fire station. It is a small tarmac parking area with 6 marked, allocated spaces for motorhomes, and there is an AireServices service point with drainage platform. This is a pleasant, quietly situated aire next to a nice park and close to the river, the aire is well maintained but has little shade and no lighting at night. There is a children's play area adjacent with walks along the river and it is a short walk into the interesting old town for a good range of shops and an InterMarche supermarket.*
Facilities: *Water•Grey Drain•Black Drain•Electric•Rubbish*
No. of spaces: *6*
Parking: *Free*
Services: *Free*
Opening times: *All year*
GPS Coordinates: *N48.77248   E01.19226*
Alternative: *Camping Domaine de Marcilly, Rte St Andre, 27810 Marcilly sur Eure   Open all year*

Rouen Photo by Cephoto

Left: Caen by SennaParis

Middle: Evreux by Theoliane

Bottom: Ste Honorine aire

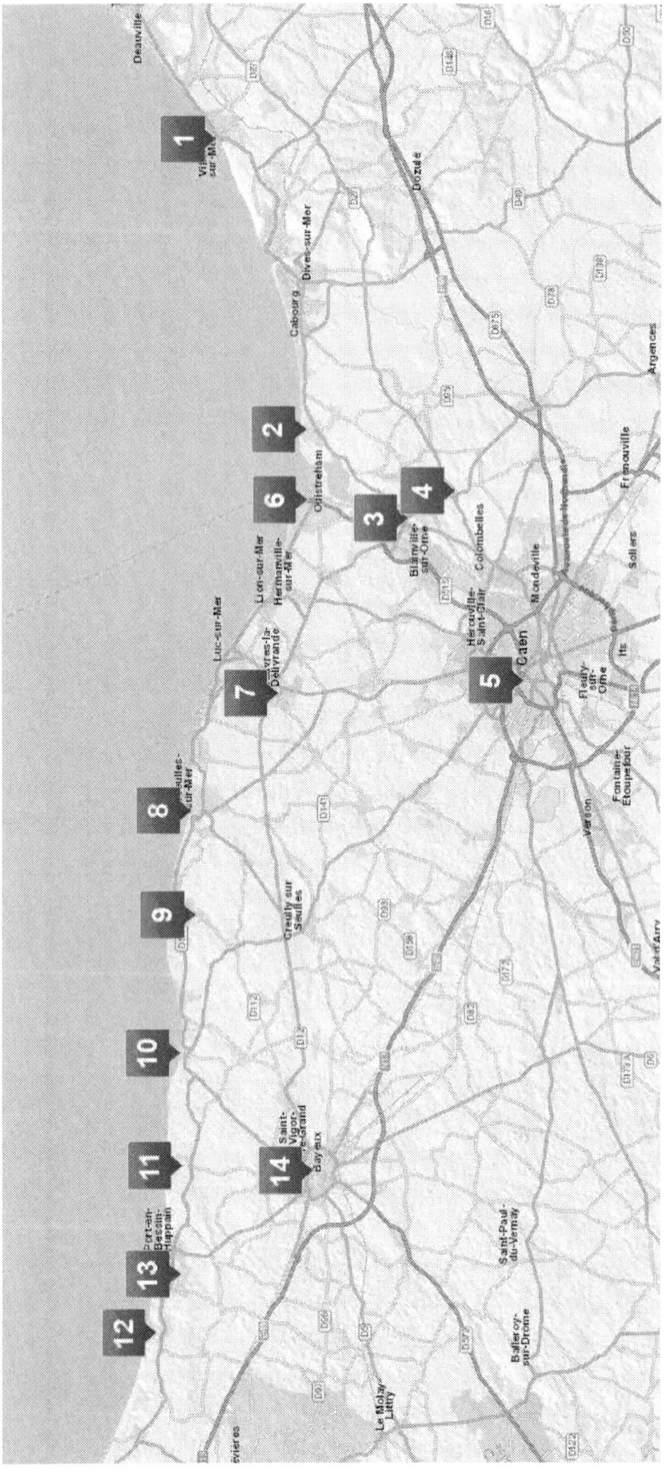
Deauville
1
Dives-sur-Mer
Cabourg
Dozulé
Argences
2
6
Ouistreham
3
4
Blainville-sur-Orne
Colombelles
Lion-sur-Mer
Hermanville-sur-Mer
Luc-sur-Mer
Hérouville-Saint-Clair
Mondeville
Caen
5
7
Fleury-sur-Orne
Fontaine-Étoupefour
Verson
8
9
Creully sur Seulles
10
11
14
Saint-Vigor-le-Grand
Bayeux
13
12
Saint-Paul-du-Vernay
Balleroy-sur-Drome
Le Molay-Littry

KEY TO "OPERATION OVERLORD" MAP (Left):

1) Villers sur Mer	2) Merville-Franceville
3) Ranville-Benouville	4) Herouvillette
5) Caen	6) Ouistreham
7) Douvres-la Delivrande	8) Courseulles sur Mer
9) Ver sur Mer	10) Arromanches les Bains
11) Longues sur Mer	12) Ste Honorine des Pertes
13) Port en Bessin	14) Bayeux

NORMANDY TOUR 39
"OPERATION OVERLORD" TOUR – 4 DAYS

Overlord was the name used by the Allies for the D-Day Landings, and this 4-DayTour explores the many places and events that marked the 6th June 1944, in the British and Canadian sector. The Allied operations were organised on 2 main fronts; the invasion carried out by British and Canadian troops planned to capture the area between Bayeux, Caen and the sea, whilst the other offensive carried out by the Americans had the objective of liberating Cherbourg. This tour extends from the River Orne in the East taking in the renowned Pegasus Bridge, and then following the coast westwards along the Landing beaches and on to Arromanches, before finally ending in Bayeux, the first French town to be liberated.

DAY 1
Villers sur Mer

STAY AT: *the Municipal aire on* ***Rue des Martois*** *in* ***Villers sur Mer***. *Pleasantly situated on the eastern edge of this small town, it's next to the countryside, near the beach, wetlands and hiking trails, but also not far from the shops. The aire is accessed off the main road by means of a gravel track, with 14 places available for motorhomes on gravel hard standing separated by small hedges. UrbaFlux service point with drainage grid. This is a good location for the beach and walks, with a Prehistoric museum adjacent and wifi is available.*
Facilities: *Water•Grey Drain•Black Drain•Electric•Wifi*
No. of spaces: *14*
Parking: *Free*
Services: *2€ Water, Electric incl*
Opening times: *All year*
GPS Coordinates: *N49.32932 E0.01356*
Alternative: *Camping Les Ammonites, Rte de la Corniche, 14640 Auberville   Open: 01/04 – 18/10*

TAKE D513/ D514 COAST ROAD WEST TO:
Merville-Franceville: The Museum of the Battery, set up in a German bunker of the Merville coastal battery, retraces the operation carried out by the British 6th Airborne Division to neutralise the guns defending the coast. The museum site consists of 4 bunkers with anti-aircraft guns, trenches, ammunition magazines, a command post and an aircraft used in the parachute drop. Open from 15/03 to 31/10

TAKE D514 7KM SOUTH TO:
Ranville-Bénouville: At dawn on 6th June, 1944, the first allied troops arrived in Ranville-Bénouville to liberate the region. The Pegasus Memorial museum contains hundreds of authentic objects, all emotive souvenirs, and features the famous Pegasus Bridge, which was the first bridge to be liberated on the French mainland. An actual-size model of a glider from that period is also exhibited in the museum's grounds, and Café Gondree, the first building to be recaptured, is next to the bridge and still trading. The museum is open from 1/02 to 30/11

TAKE D37 EAST TO:
Herouvillette
<u>**STAY AT:**</u> *the Municipal aire in* **Ave de Caen** *in* **Herouvillette.** *Parking is in a small tarmac car park, close to the centre of the village, in a quiet, open location. There are 4 marked spaces on tarmac and 4 places on grass, but little shade. Shops can be found within a short walk. A Euro-Relais service point with a large platform drain.*
Facilities: *Water•Grey Drain•Black Drain*
No. of spaces: *8*
Parking: *Free*
Services: *2€ Water*
Opening times: *All year*
GPS Coordinates: *N49.22007   W00.24494*
Alternative: *Camping Les Capucines, Rue Cote Fleurie, 14860 Ranville   Open all year*
<u>**DAY 2**</u>
TAKE D513 NORTH TO:
Caen: The Caen Mémorial museum was built on top of an underground gallery that contained the command post of General Wilhelm Richter, commander of the 716th German infantry division, which guarded the coastal sector. The museum covers all aspects of

WWII, including the history of the Nazi's rise to power, and has a section highlighting the D-Day landings. Open 01/02 to 31/12

TAKE D515/ D514 SOUTH TO:

Ouistreham: The Museum of No.4 Commando retraces the epic story of the first commandos to land on Sword Beach on 6th June, led by the French Commandant Philippe Kieffer. Open 15/03 to 31/10. The Atlantic Wall Museum is located inside the old German headquarters, a stones throw from the beach and the Ferry terminal, this building was in charge of the gun batteries covering the entrance to the river Orne and the canal. The 52ft high, 6 storey concrete tower has been fully restored to its appearance on the 6th of June 1944, with recreations of the dormitory, sick bay, gun emplacements and radio room, whilst there is a panoramic view from the top. Open 04/02 to 30/12.

TAKE D514 COAST ROAD WEST and D83 TO:

Douvres-la Delivrande: The first museum devoted to the history of radar is in the former German radar station at Douvres, where two remarkably preserved bunkers and an original layout help you to understand the role of radar and how the technique was developed. Open 26/05 to 16/09

TAKE D7 and D514 WEST TO:

Courseulles-sur-Mer

<u>***STAY AT:***</u> *the Municipal aire in **Ave de la Liberation, Courseulles-sur-Mer**. This Aire is quietly situated in a residential area, near to the seafront (only 50m from the beach) on a tarmac parking area next to the Municipal campsite. It is lit at night but there is a lack of shade; the town centre is about 500m away. Raclet service point with drainage channel*

Facilities: *Water•Grey Drain•Black Drain*
No. of spaces: *12*
Parking: *7€/ 24 Hrs*
Services: *2€ Water*
Opening times: *All year*
GPS Coordinates: *N49.33451   W00.44554*
Alternative: *Camping Champ de Courses, Ave de la Liberation, 14470 Courseulles-sur-Mer Open: 01/04 – 30/09*

<u>**DAY 3**</u>

Courseulles-sur-Mer: The Juno Beach Centre explains the role of Canada in the Second World War (also giving an insight into Canadian culture) and Canadian tour guides offer tours of Juno Park to explain the history of D-Day and the Atlantic Wall defences. Temporary exhibitions complement the permanent display. Open 01/02 to 31/12

TAKE D514 WEST 5KM TO:

Ver-sur-Mer: The Gold Beach Museum recounts the first airmail flight between the USA and France, together with a retrospective of the D-Day Landing and the British beachhead on Gold Beach. Open 1/05 to 31/10.

CONTINUE 8KM WEST ON D514 TO:

Arromanches les Bains: This beach resort was a strategically vital site in the Landings, and the artificial harbour - nicknamed Port Winston and assembled in a matter of weeks - was to play a crucial role in enabling 500,000 tonnes of equipment to be brought ashore between June and the end of August. The 360 Cinema shows the 18 minute long film "The Price of Freedom" displayed on 9 curved screens - a mixture of pictures of the D-Day Landings in 1944 and of Normandy as it is today. Open 1/02 to 31/12.

Musee du Debarquement is located right in front of the actual remains of the artificial "Mulberry B" harbour, this museum is devoted to the incredible feat of technology achieved by the British in building and setting up the artificial harbour - models, photographs and a video show. Open 1/02 to 30/12.

CONTINUE 5KM WEST ON D514 TO:

Longues-sur-Mer: This German artillery battery, covering Omaha and Gold beaches, gave the Allied ships a pounding on the morning of D-Day, and is the only coastal battery to have kept its guns intact, giving an impressive picture of what an Atlantic Wall long-range gun emplacement was really like. Open all year.

CONTINUE WEST ON D514 10KM TO:

Ste Honorine des Pertes

*__STAY AT:__ the Private aire in **Route Omaha Beach** in **Ste Honorine des Pertes**. This aire is owned by the village petrol station (Elan) and is quietly situated behind the garage, next to the campsite, in a large grass parking area, bordered on either side by farmland but offering little shade. The garage is ½ km West of the village centre, on the D514 road, but the village itself has few facilities. The spaces each have an electric hook up (included in tariff) and a Euro-Relais service point with double drainage platform. The garage owner is very friendly and the aire is well positioned on the coast road for visiting*

the various WWII sites, with it also being possible to walk to the coast from here (about 1km).
Facilities: *Water•Grey Drain•Black Drain•Electric*
No. of spaces: *20*
Parking: *10€/ 24Hrs*
Services: *Incl.*
Opening times: *All year*
GPS Coordinates: *N49.34833   W00.81722*
Alternative: *Camping Municipal, Bvd Eindhoven, 14400 Bayeux*
Open: 01/04 – 05/11
DAY 4
TAKE D514 4KM EAST TO:
Port-en-Bessin: The Museum has some of the impressive remains, documents and personal items, found in the vessels sunk on or around D-Day, that twenty-five years of underwater operations have brought up from the seabed. Through unique film and photo material the visitor gets a good impression of the underwater explorations. Open 1/06 to 30/09
TAKE D6 SOUTH TO:
Bayeux : Battle of Normandy Museum is located in the first town in France to be liberated, this museum displays equipment, artefacts and a film to offer a better understanding of the Landings in the context of the liberation of Western Europe. Open 15/02 to 24/12.
Commonwealth Cemetery and Memorial: This cemetery is the largest Commonwealth WWII cemetery in France and holds 4,868 graves of soldiers killed in the D-Day offensive. The Memorial opposite honours the memory of 1,837 missing servicemen.
<u>**STAY AT:**</u> *The Private aire in* **Route Omaha Beach** *in* **Ste Honorine des Pertes** *or Camping Municipal, Bvd Eindhoven, 14400 Bayeux*

Ouistreham by Archangel12

Above: Arromanches by Myrabella

Right: Juno Beach by Dr Wilson

Left: Aire at Villers sur Mer

NORMANDY TOUR 40
OMAHA BEACH TOUR – 3 DAYS

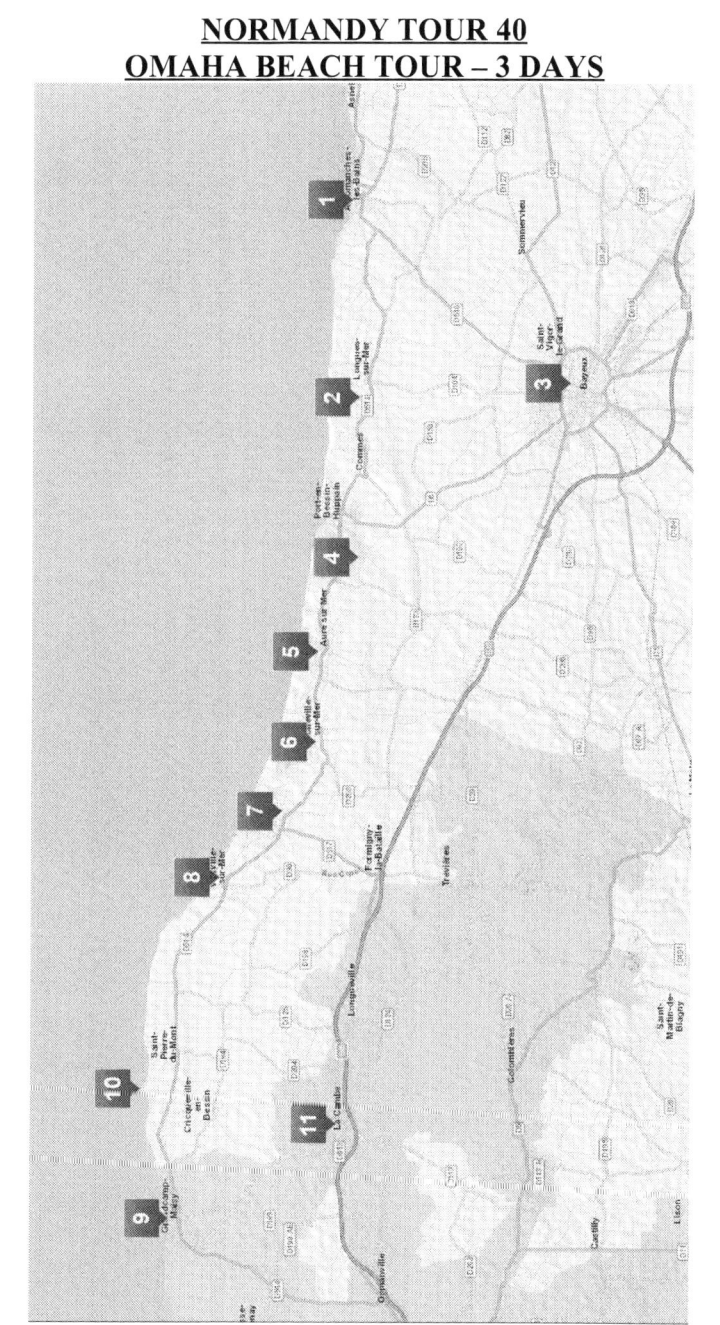

KEY: 1) Arromanche les Bains 2) Longues sur Mer 3) Bayeux
4) Port en Bessin 5) Ste Honorine des Pertes 6) Colleville sur Mer
7) Saint Laurent-sur-Mer 8) Vierville-sur-Mer 9) Grandcamp Maisy
10) La Pointe du Hoc 11) La Cambe

The famous "Bloody Omaha" Beach was the scene of a terrible battle at dawn on D-Day when the assault waves of the US 1st Infantry Division came up against stout resistance from the defending German troops. Centred on the American offensive, this 3-Day Tour takes you from the Mulberry harbour at Arromanches via Bayeux along 'Omaha' beach and continuing on to Pointe du Hoc and the Battery at Grandcamp Maisy, visiting the military cemeteries at Colleville-sur-Mer and La Cambe before ending the tour at the start of Utah Beach.

DAY 1
Arromanche les Bains

STAY AT: *the Municipal aire at* **Rue Francois Carpentier**, *in* **Arromanche les Bains**. *This aire is well located next to the campsite, by the town sports centre and tennis courts, with shops only 200m distant. Parking is in a medium sized tarmac car park overlooking the sea, with well-marked spaces bordered by the Sports Centre and its car park, there is a playground nearby and the beach is 250m away. Euro-Relais borne and drainage grid. This is a pleasant little seaside town with reasonable facilities and a nice beach/promenade.*

Facilities: *Water•Grey Drain•Black Drain•Toilets*
No. of spaces: *13*
Parking: *Free*
Services: *2€ Water*
Opening times: *All year*
GPS Coordinates: *N49.33833   W00.62556*
Alternative: *Camping Municipal, Ave de Verdun, 14117 Arromanche Open: 01/04 – 01/11*

Arromanches les Bains: This beach resort was a strategically vital site in the Landings and the artificial harbour, nicknamed "Port Winston", was assembled here in a matter of weeks and was to play a crucial role in enabling 500,000 tonnes of equipment to be brought ashore between June and the end of August. The 360 Cinema shows the 18 minute long film "The Price of Freedom" displayed on 9 curved screens - a mixture of pictures of the D-Day Landings in 1944 and of Normandy as it is today. Open 1/02 to 31/12.

The Musee du Debarquement is located right in front of the actual remains of the artificial "Mulberry B" harbour. Using models, photographs and a video show, this museum is devoted to the incredible feat of technology achieved by the British in building and setting up the artificial harbour. Open 1/02 to 30/12.

CONTINUE 5KM WEST ON D514 TO:
Longues-sur-Mer: This German artillery battery, covering Omaha and Gold beaches, gave the Allied ships a pounding on the morning of D-Day. It is the only coastal battery to have kept its guns, giving an impressive picture of what an Atlantic Wall long-range gun emplacement was really like. Open all year.
TAKE D104 10KM SOUTH TO:
Bayeux : The Battle of Normandy Museum is located in the first town in France to be liberated. Covering 2,300 sq m, this museum displays equipment, artefacts and a film to present a better understanding of the Landings in the context of the liberation of Western Europe. The museum can also provide all the background information you might want prior to a visit to the beaches. Open 15/02 to 24/12.
TAKE D6 9KM NORTH TO:
Port-en-Bessin: The Museum has some of the impressive remains, documents and personal items, found in the vessels sunk on or around D-Day that twenty-five years of underwater operations have brought up from the seabed. Through unique film and photo material the visitor gets a good impression of the underwater explorations. Open 1/06 to 30/09
CONTINUE WEST ON D514 4KM TO:
Ste Honorine des Pertes
<u>STAY AT:</u> *the Private aire in* **Route Omaha Beach** *in* **Ste Honorine des Pertes**. *This aire is owned by the village petrol station (Elan) and is quietly situated behind the garage, next to the campsite, in a large grass parking area, bordered on either side by farmland but offering little shade. The garage is ½ km West of the village centre, on the D514 road, but the village itself has few facilities. The spaces each have an electric hook up (included in tariff) and a Euro-Relais service point with double drainage platform. The garage owner is very friendly and the aire is well positioned on the coast road for visiting the various WWII sites, with it also being possible to walk to the coast from here (about 1km).*
Facilities: *Water•Grey Drain•Black Drain•Electric*
No. of spaces: *20*
Parking: *10€/ 24Hrs*
Services: *Incl*
Opening times: *All year*
GPS Coordinates: *N49.34833   W00.81722*

Alternative: Camping Municipal, Bvd Eindhoven, 14400 Bayeux
Open: 01/04 – 05/11

DAY 2

TAKE D514 WEST TO:

Colleville-sur-Mer: The American Cemetery, overlooking Omaha Beach, contains 9,387 perfectly aligned white crosses on a 170-acre plot conducive to meditation and remembrance. A chapel and a memorial add the finishing touch to this moving scene.

CONTINUE ON D514 WEST TO:

Saint Laurent-sur-Mer: The Omaha Beach Museum, actually located on Omaha Beach itself, covers 1200 m2 and presents a fine collection of uniforms, arms, vehicles and personal effects. Through several displays, maps and photographs, together with a film of witness accounts from American veterans, visitors will gain a clearer understanding of the landings at Omaha Beach and the raid on Pointe du Hoc. Military hardware also on display includes a landing craft, a Sherman Tank, and a 155mm Long Tom gun, the only one in Normandy. Open from 15/02 to 15/11.

CONTINUE ON D514 WEST TO:

Vierville-sur-Mer: The D-Day Museum presents fascinating material used during the Normandy landings, within rooms that are located near to the remaining elements of Omaha Beach's artificial port. The items show the technological advances made throughout that time and their impact on daily life, including the "Higgins Boat" barges, an armoured turret, and a collection of rare objects such as the tank "Goliath", the para-motorcycle, and the Enigma machine. Open from 1/03 to 15/11.

CONTINUE ON D514 WEST TO:

La Pointe du Hoc: Symbolising the courage of the young American soldiers involved in its storming, the famous Pointe du Hoc was one of the strongholds of the German fortifications taken by force by Colonel Rudder and his 225 Rangers (of whom only 90 survived). The site has spectacular scenery and remains as it was on that day; with its impressive appearance bearing witness to the intensity of the battles that took place here.

CONTINUE ON D514 WEST TO:

Grandcamp Maisy

STAY AT: the Municipal aire at **Rue du Moulin Odo** *in* **Grandcamp Maisy***. The aire is located on the south-eastern edge of the village, next to the fire station, close to open countryside but only a short walk*

to the village centre and its good range of shops/ bars/ restaurants. There are 34 individual level spaces with hook ups, on gravel hard standings separated by hedges, a picnic table and an AireServices borne with drainage grid. Despite being a little distance from the port one can still appreciate a pleasant view of the sea from any of its spaces.
Facilities: *Water•Grey Drain•Black Drain•Electric*
No. of spaces: *34*
Parking: *9€/ 24 Hrs*
Services: *Incl.*
Opening times: *All year*
GPS Coordinates: *N49.38614   W01.03777*
Alternative: *Camping Joncal, Le Port, 14450 Grandcamp Maisy Open: 01/04 – 01/10*

DAY 3

Grandcamp Maisy: The Rangers Museum tells the story of a crack American Rangers unit specially trained for a special D-Day assignment, namely the assault and capture of the Pointe du Hoc. The small museum has an 18-minute video, with models, photos and exhibits. Open 15/02 to 31/10.

The Maisy Battery, a large WWII German Headquarters and complex, defended the coast behind the Omaha Sector on D-Day. It is an open-air museum with an extensive display of WWII cannons, howitzers, a Landing Craft and other items. All of the buildings can be explored and there are over 2 miles of restored trenches and bunkers. Open 01/04 – 31/10

TAKE D113 SOUTH TO:
La Cambe: The German Military Cemetery, an impressive necropolis covering over 7 acres, is where the bodies of the 21,300 German soldiers who fell during the fighting throughout Normandy in 1944 are buried. There is a Memorial chapel at the entrance and a Peace garden with 1,220 maple trees.

TAKE N13 WEST and D913 NORTH TO:
Ste Marie du Mont: The Utah Beach Museum, built on the beach where the first American troops landed on June 6, 1944, recounts the story of D-Day in 10 sequences, from the preparation of the landing to the final outcome and success. This comprehensive chronological journey immerses visitors in the history of the landing through a rich collection of objects, vehicles, materials, oral histories and the award

winning film "Victory in the Sand". There is also an original B26 bomber, one of only six remaining examples still in existence worldwide, together with landing craft and other WWII militaria. Open 02/01 to 25/12.

STAY AT: *The Municipal aire at* **Rue du Moulin Odo** *in* **Grandcamp Maisy** *or Camping Joncal, Le Port, 14450 Grandcamp Maisy*

Above: La Pointe du Hoc   Below: Port en Bessin (both by Myrabella)

Above: Longues sur Mer by Lingureanu

Below: Aire at Grandcamp Maisy

NORMANDY TOUR 41
UTAH BEACH TO CHERBOURG – 3 DAYS

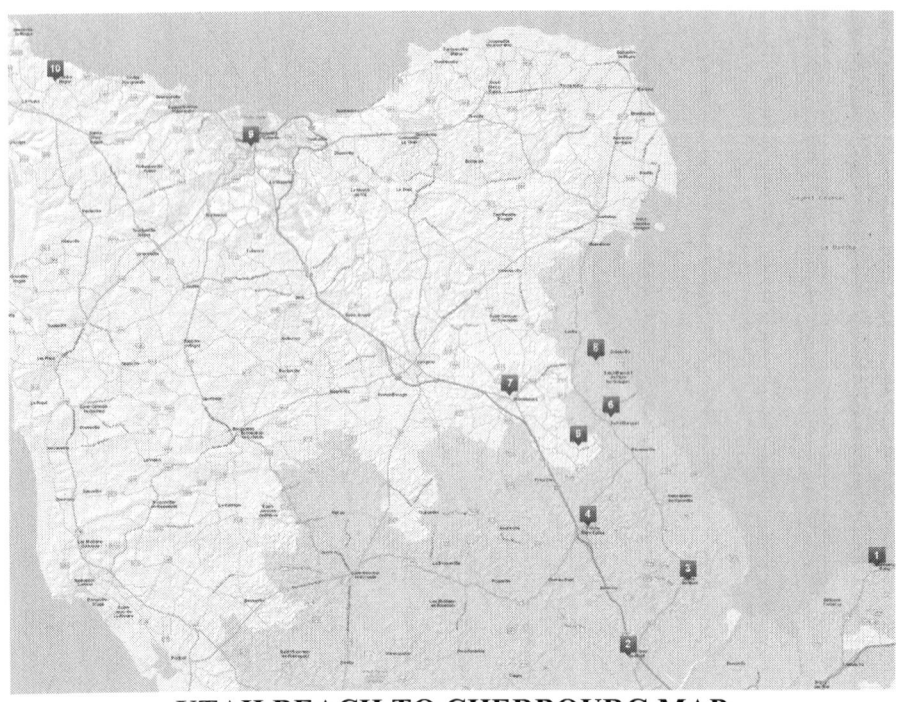

UTAH BEACH TO CHERBOURG MAP

KEY:

1) Grandcamp Maisy
2) St Come-du-Mont
3) Ste Marie-du-Mont
4) Ste Mere Eglise
5) Azeville
6) Saint-Marcouf
7) Montebourg
8) Quineville
9) Cherbourg-Octeville
10) Greville-Hague

From Carentan to Cherbourg, this 3-Day Tour follows the parachute drop of US 82nd and 101st Airborne Divisions around Sainte-Mère-Eglise, and the Landing on Utah Beach at Sainte-Marie-du-Mont. It then follows the route taken by the Allies in order to cut off the Cotentin Peninsula, isolate the German troops and capture the port of Cherbourg. After a hard fought assault, Cherbourg was liberated by three American divisions, who found the port completely destroyed. The Allies then set about reconstructing it and barely one month after its liberation, the first locomotives and other heavy equipment landed at makeshift wharves, quickly making Cherbourg the world's biggest ever port used for military purposes.

DAY 1
Grandcamp Maisy

STAY AT: *the Municipal aire at* **Rue du Moulin Odo** *in* **Grandcamp Maisy**. *The aire is located on the south-eastern edge of the village, next to the fire station. It's close to open countryside but only a short walk to the village centre and its good range of shops/ bars/ restaurants. There are 34 individual level spaces with hook ups, on gravel hard standings separated by hedges, picnic tables and an AireServices borne with drainage grid. Despite being a little distance from the port one can still appreciate a pleasant view of the sea from any of its spaces.*

Facilities: Water•Grey Drain•Black Drain•Electric
No. of spaces: 34
Parking: 9€/ 24 Hrs
Services: Incl.
Opening times: All year
GPS Coordinates: N49.38614   W01.03777
Alternative: Camping Joncal, Le Port, 14450 Grandcamp Maisy
Open: 01/04 – 01/10

TAKE D514/ N13 EAST and D913 NORTH 8KM TO:
St Come-du-Mont: The Dead Mans Corner Museum was the German paratroopers headquarters and the point where the men of the 101st Airborne Division encountered the German "Green Devils" for the first time. You can get an insight into the 3-day battle for Carentan on the site that has remained largely untouched. Open 02/01 to 23/12

TAKE D913 EAST 6KM TO:
Ste Marie du Mont: The Utah Beach Museum, built on the beach where the first American troops landed on June 6th 1944, recounts the story of D-Day in 10 sequences, from the preparation of the landing to the final outcome and success. This comprehensive chronological journey immerses visitors in the history of the landing through a rich collection of objects, vehicles, materials, oral histories and the award winning film "Victory in the Sand". There is also an original B26 bomber, one of only six remaining examples still in existence worldwide, together with landing craft and other WWII militaria. Open 02/01 to 25/12.

TAKE D14 NORTH and D13 WEST TO:
Sainte-Mere-Eglise: The Airborne Museum tells the true story of the "Longest Day" in pictures and mementos of the operations carried out

by the American 82nd and 101st Airborne Divisions. Open 01/02 to 30/11. Bornes de la Voie de la Liberte are the "milestones of liberty" - starting in Sainte-Mere, these markers can be seen stretching from Utah Beach and dotted along the path of the liberating US Army all the way to Bastogne in Belgium.

STAY AT: the **Parking behind the Museum in Rue de la Liberte in Ste Mere**. *The parking is located about 200m south of the small town centre in a large parking area next to the cemetery. This is a fairly quiet spot with picnic tables, a bbq and adjacent street lighting, but little shade and spaces are on grass accessed by a gravel track. There are no services here but a Euro-Relais service point is available at the Super U in town. The town has a small selection of shops and a Supermarket.*

Facilities: Toilets•Rubbish
No. of spaces: 40
Parking: 8€/ 24 Hrs
Services: None but service point at Super U
Opening times: All year
GPS Coordinates: N49.40735   W01.31265
Alternative: Camping Normandie, Rue 505th Airborne, 50480 Ste Mere   Open: 01/04 – 30/09

DAY 2
TAKE D15 EAST and D115 NORTH TO:
Azeville: The Battery d'Azeville was one of the first parts of the German coastal defenses to be constructed. There are over 350m of underground tunnels, 4 bunkers for 105mm guns and a number of adjoining buildings bearing the marks of the ferocious battle that took place over this section of the "Atlantic Wall". Open 01/04 to 14/12.

TAKE D269 and D69 EAST TO:
Saint-Marcouf: The Crisbecq Battery was the German's largest coastal artillery battery. Located on Utah Beach, with 21 blockhouses linked by more than 1km of trenches on a 4ha site, you can grasp some idea of life in the battery by visiting the recreation rooms, the hospital and kitchens, all of which have been restored. Open 01/04 to 15/11.

TAKE D14 NORTH and D71 WEST TO:
Montebourg
STAY AT: *The Municipal aire next to the Football Stade,* **off the D974 in Montebourg**. *The aire is located about 300m south of the town in a gravel parking area next to the town football pitch, with*

good views over the town. The aire is in a fairly quiet spot with picnic tables and bbq, but with little shade and no lighting. Artisanal service point with drainage grid. This is a small town with a reasonable selection of shops.
Facilities: *Water●Grey Drain●Black Drain●Electric*
No. of spaces: *10*
Parking: *Free*
Services: *Free*
Opening times: *All year*
GPS Coordinates: *N49.48488   W01.37465*
Alternative: *Camping Municipal, Rue de Port Sinope, 50310 Quineville   Open: 01/04 – 23/09*

DAY 3
TAKE D42 EAST TO:
Quineville: The WWII Museum chronicles the period from the declaration of war to the capitulation as seen through the daily lives of French civilians under the occupation. Aspects covered include how they fed and clothed themselves, how they travelled, and the roles of women and children as well as those of the resistance. There is a reconstruction of a French street under occupation, as well as a cinema. Open daily from 01/04 to 04/11.
TAKE D42 WEST and N13 NORTH TO:
Cherbourg-Octeville: The La Batterie du Roule, standing at the top of the hill "Montagne du Roule," is a large fort with a view over Cherbourg harbour. Opened in 1954 and completely renovated, this was the first Liberation Museum to be opened with various reconstructions, including numerous audio-visual displays from the Nazi Occupation to the D-Day Landings. The visit includes a guided trip to the underground fortifications. Open all year.
TAKE D901/ D45 WEST ALONG COAST TO:
Greville-Hague
<u>**STAY AT:**</u> the Municipal aire next to the Church, **off D237 in Greville-Hague**. The aire is in the centre of this small village, opposite the church and next to the village tennis court. It is a medium size tarmac car park backing onto open farmland, having little shade but having lighting at night. The parking is bordered by hedges and provides an AireServices borne with drainage platform. Boulangerie/grocer and a Bar/Tabac/News can be found in this pleasant, quiet, little rural village located only 1.5kms from the coast.

Facilities: *Water•Grey Drain•Black Drain*
No. of spaces: *8*
Parking: *Free*
Services: *2€ Water*
Opening times: *All year*
GPS Coordinates: *N49.67513   W01.80115*
Alternative: *Camping de Collignon, Rue des Algues, 50110 Tourlaville   Open: 01/02 – 30/11*

Left:Ste Mere Eglise by Avi1111

Right: Azeville by DSMD

Left: St Come du Mont by JrPol

NORD-PAS-DE-CALAIS TOUR 42
FORTIFIED TOWNS AROUND CALAIS – 3 DAYS

As Louis XIV's Commissioner General of Fortifications, the great French military architect Vauban, made his mark on the region by building a double line of fortified towns to protect the lands won back from the former rulers of the Low Countries. This 3-Day Tour visits the fortified towns of Bergues, Fort Nieulay in Calais, Gravelines, St Omer, Boulogne, Ambleteuse and Montreuil, where remarkable remains of the fortifications still exist.

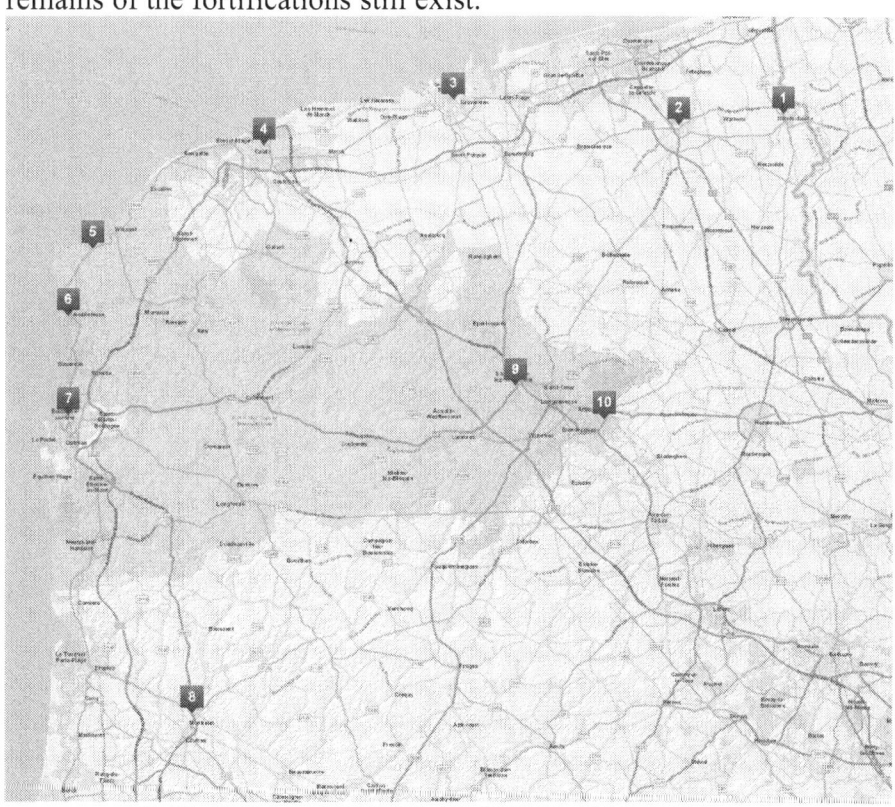

FORTIFIED TOWNS AROUND CALAIS MAP

KEY :
1) Hondschoote
2) Bergues
3) Gravelines
4) Calais
5) Tardinghen
6) Ambleteuse
7) Boulogne sur Mer
8) Montreuil sur Mer.
9) St Omer
10) Arques

DAY 1
Hondschoote

STAY AT: *the Municipal aire in the **Impasse off Rue de Bergues** in **Hondschoote**. Found next to the village sports field and one of the*

town's two windmills, this aire is bordered by tall hedges, on a long tarmac parking area in a cul-de-sac. Parking is 200m from the town centre and its shops, with a Raclet service point situated a short distance away from the parking.
Facilities: *Water•Grey Drain•Black Drain•Electric*
No. of spaces: *10*
Parking: *Free*
Services: *3€ Water or Electric*
Opening times: *All year*
GPS Coordinates: *N50.97642   E02.58034*
Alternative: *Camping Vauban, ave Vauban, 59380 Bergues   Open: 30/03 – 31/10*

Hondschoote is regarded as one of the finest towns in Flanders, having a distinctively Flemish atmosphere. A large number of the town's monuments survived the onslaught of the many battles fought in this area, and some are of impressive size, such as the town hall (built in 1556), the 16th C church of Saint Vaast and the 12th C Noordmeulen windmill.

TAKE D110 WEST 11KM TO:

Bergues: Vauban worked hard towards making this square shaped town invulnerable, but he was not the only one who gave the fortified town, with its ochre walls, a very particular appearance. With its fine yellow brick ramparts, this charming small town known as the 'Other Bruges' has been fortified by its inhabitants as far back as the 7th C, and was in fact reinforced up until the middle of the 19th C. Worth seeing in the area are the former pawnbroker's (now the town museum), the Grand Place, the Town Hall with its belfry, and the surviving remnants of the Abbey of Saint Winoc. There is also a range of shops and fine restaurants in the town.

TAKE D3 and D11 WEST 28KM TO:

Gravelines is a fortified and moated town extensively modified by Vauban, and a perfect place for walking. Still surrounded by ramparts (with guided tours all year round), the well-preserved fortifications offer a unique insight into 17th C town planning. The moat is ideal for boat trips, you can either rent your own electric boat to explore it, or join a guided tour and Gravelines also has a long-standing maritime tradition that is recounted in the town's small museums.

TAKE D119 23KM WEST TO:

Calais has retained an astonishing amount of its heritage. A 13th C watchtower with thick buttresses sits in the town centre, and nearby there is a tank, of almost 2 million litres capacity, covered by a vault as protection against mortar attacks, that collected rainwater from the nearby Notre Dame church. The massive Citadel was the home of the English kings during the English occupation from 1347 to 1558 and has retained a magnificent ammunition magazine, stables and bread oven. Fort Nieulay and Fort Risban sit at the port entrance, which was constructed on piles and controlled a lock that could flood the hinterland in the event of an invasion. Vauban considered it his masterpiece of defence, in the area around Calais.

CONTINUE WEST 22KM ON D940 TO TARDINGHEN and THEN EAST ONTO D249 TO:

Tardinghen

STAY AT: *the Private aire on* **La Ferme d'Horloge off the D249, West of Tardinghen***. This aire (Les Fleur des Champs) is privately owned by a local farm and is found close to Cap Gris Nez in an open grassy area with superb panoramic views. The pitches (on grass, off a gravel track) are quite remote, a bit exposed and without shade or lighting, but they are tranquil and do have glorious views to compensate. Separately, but nearby (a short walk away) the Artisanal service point can be found next to the barn at the 'Ferme de L'Horloge.' This is a very rural spot with plenty of birdsong and the farmer comes in the evening or early morning to collect fees, there is a Restaurant/Brasserie in Tardinghen and shops in Wissant (both a short dive away).*

Facilities: *Water•Grey Drain•Black Drain•Electric*
No. of spaces: *10*
Parking: *6€/ 24 Hrs*
Services: *4€ Water or 3€ Electric*
Opening times: *All year*
GPS Coordinates: *N50.86250   E01.64889 (Farm) N50.85658 E01.65136 (Parking)*
Alternative: *Camping Vauban, ave Vauban, 59380 Bergues   Open: 30/03 – 31/10*

DAY 2
RETURN ONTO D940 and FOLLOW IT WEST 8KM TO:
Ambleteuse, a small port in the Slack estuary, was occupied by the English in the middle of the 16th C. Henry VIII had the village

surrounded by ramparts with five bastions (in line with a new technique of sunken fortifications) and these very large structures on the south face are still visible today. At the end of the 17th C, when Louis XIV wanted to create a naval port, Vauban built a fort to protect the project but unfortunately it silted up soon after and this meant that work had to be abandoned. Napoleon, eager to invade England, later recommenced the work but had to abandon it for the same reasons. Today, the Vauban fort is classed as an historical monument and is the only remaining sea fort between Belgium and Cherbourg.

CONTINUE SOUTH ON D940 TO :

Boulogne-sur-Mer: A beachhead to England for both Caesar and Napoleon, Boulogne has one of the best-preserved fortified structures in France. The Romans built a rectangular enclosure here in the 2nd C, on the base of which Philippe Auguste's son built ramparts in the 13th C, as well as a strong, 5-sided chateau in one of the corners. This enclosure still separates the upper and lower parts of the town today and has become a pleasantly shady place for a stroll. Transformed in the 17th C, the chateau currently houses a museum with, amongst other things, a large collection of Eskimo masks. In the old town one can climb the Belfry, the former keep of a long-gone chateau, to admire the town and port, whilst the curious Notre-Dame basilica is an eclectic mix of architecture built in the 19th C. Audio-guides are available at the Château museum.

CONTINUE SOUTH 27KM ON D940 TO ETAPLES and D939 EAST TO:

Montreuil-sur-Mer

STAY AT: The Municipal aire in **Ave des Garennes** in **Montreuil sur Mer**. The aire is located in a medium sized gravel car park on the south side of this pleasant town. Offering several level spaces without shade but lit at night, this is a quiet position in a residential part of this charming walled town. The AireServices borne and drainage grid are next to a small toilet block. The town boasts beautiful old houses, churches, a citadel and imposing ramparts.

Facilities: Water•Grey Drain•Black Drain•Electric•Toilets
No. of spaces: 10
Parking: Free
Services: 2€ Water or Electric
Opening times: All year
GPS Coordinates: N50.45939   E01.75942

*Alternative: Camping la Pinedes, D940, 62630 Etaples sur Mer
Open: 15/03 – 20/11*

DAY 3

Montreuil-sur-Mer has seen every invasion and war that has ever troubled northern France. Its location -set on a spur overlooking three valleys, so as to control the sea and the road from Normandy to Flanders, ensured the town had great military importance. Its 3km long walls form one of the largest fortified structures in France and, being almost intact, make a superb walk whilst showing the evolution of military architecture over 700 years. Other highlights are the 16th C Citadel, the Saint-Saulve Abbey-church that houses one of the most curious religious treasures in France, 2 museums, a good selection of restaurants / bars and the picturesque cobbled streets with their 17th C houses, where Victor Hugo located part of his book "Les Misérables". Each summer the town presents a "Les Miserables" Sound and Light show.

TAKE D126 28KM EAST and D928 26KM NORTH TO :

Sant-Omer was founded in the 9th C, and by the 14th C it had become one of the largest and wealthiest towns in Europe. The expansion of the town eventually linked Saint-Bertin Abbey, whose remains can be seen today, with the collegiate church that has since become one of the most beautiful Gothic cathedrals North of Paris. Rebuilt during the Spanish period, the town's fortifications were reinforced by Vauban. The remains of the West face of the ramparts and the sloping ground at the front of the fortification have been incorporated into a landscaped park of 20 ha. A tour of the park reveals further evidence of the old fortifications, including a superb formal garden that has been constructed in a former trench. The old town has many fascinating features, including a library housing precious works printed before 1500, whilst the museum contains some very rich collections.

TAKE D211 3KM EAST TO:

Arques

STAY AT: *The Municipal aire in **Rue Michelet** in **Arques** is in a pleasant location, next to the large Beausejour lake and close to the 3* Municipal Campsite. In a large tarmac area with good security, the car park being locked at night 2100-0700, the parking is level, quiet, and has shade under trees. The Euro-Relais borne with a small raised drainage grid (hosepipe required) is next to the campsite. There are nice walks around the lakes and lots of birds and wildlife to see.*

Facilities: *Water•Grey Drain•Black Drain•Electric*
No. of spaces: *25*
Parking: *4€/ 24 Hrs*
Services: *2€ Water or Electric*
Opening times: *All year*
GPS Coordinates: *N50.74538   E02.30448*
Alternative: Camping Beausejour, Rue Michelet, 62510 Arques
Open: 01/04 – 30/10

Above Tardinghen aire   Below: Gravelines Photo by LimoWreck

Above: Bergues   Below: Ambleteuse (both by grassrootsgroundswell)

NORD-PAS-DE-CALAIS TOUR 43
FORTIFIED TOWNS AROUND LILLE – 4 DAYS

As Louis XIV's Commissioner General of Fortifications, the great French military architect Vauban, made his mark on the region by building a double line of fortified towns to protect the lands taken back from the former rulers of the Low Countries. This 4-Day Tour visits the fortified towns of Arras, Lille, Conde, le Quesnoy, Maubeuge, Avesnes, Bouchain and Cambrai, places where remarkable remains of the fortifications still exist.

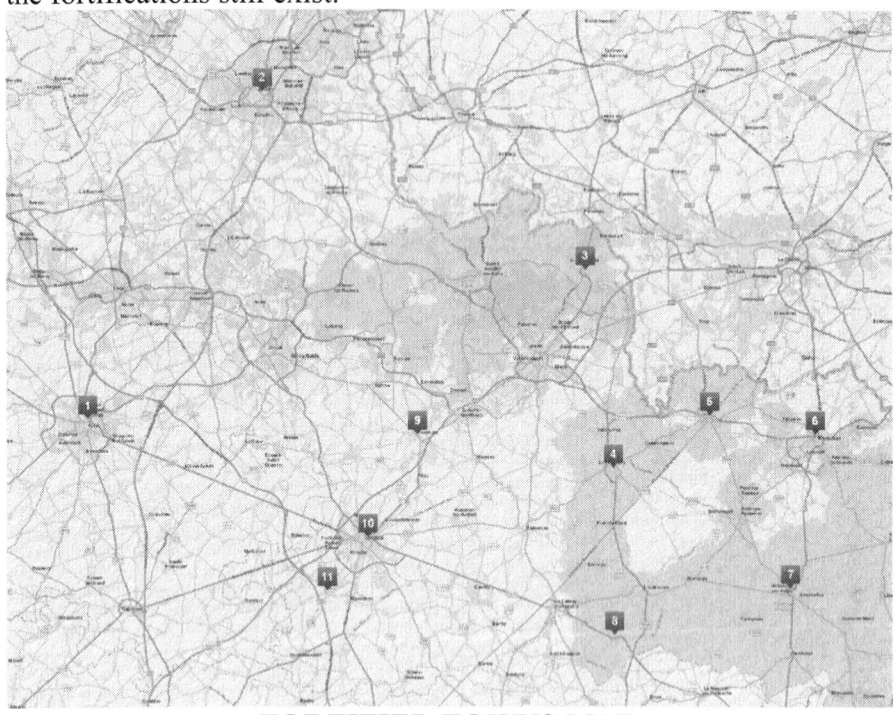

FORTIFIED TOWNS MAP

KEY TO MAP:
1) Arras	2) Lille	3) Conde-sur-l'Eacault	4) Le Quesnoy
5) Bavay	6) Maubeuge	7) Avesnes-sur-Helpe	8) Catillon
9) Bouchain	10) Cambrai	11) Marcoing	

DAY 1
Arras

STAY AT: *the Municipal aire in* ***Rue des Rosati in Arras****. Convenient and easy to find, this aire is situated on the northern side of Arras in a large tarmac parking area with 10 spaces reserved for camping cars (10 min walk into centre). Security is good, the car park being fenced* and lit at night, but there is no shade. The AireServices borne with a drainage platform is operated by jetons from the OT in the Town Hall. There is a good range of shops and places to visit in town, and a Carrefour supermarket within a short walk.

Facilities: Water •Grey Drain •Black Drain •Electric
No. of spaces: 10
Parking: Free
Services: 2€ Water or Electric
Opening times: All year
GPS Coordinates: N50.29461   E02.78788
Alternative: Camping Paille Haute, Rte de Sailly, 62156 Boirey Notre Dame   Open 30/03 – 31/10

Arras: Already a large town in Gallo-Roman times, and enjoying a Golden Age during the Spanish occupation, the town did not accept its defeat at the hands of the French King Louis XIII kindly. Consequently, the Citadel that was erected by Louis XIV was as much a restraint against the people of Arras as against the Spanish. The Citadel has retained a large part of its fortifications, with the surrounding area providing a superb wooded walk. Classified as a "Ville d'Art", Arras is also well known for its "Grand Place", comprising a unique collection of 155 houses in the same style, each one being uniquely decorated. Highlights of Arras are the underground tunnels in the "Petite Place," the ancient Saint-Vaast Abbey that houses a large museum, the remains of the ramparts, and the 18th C theatre.

TAKE A1 NORTH TO :
Lille: This veritable Fort, called the "Queen of Citadels" by Vauban, was built in three years and housed 3,600 men. It comprised five royal bastions linked by five, still almost intact, curtain walls that can be admired during a 2-km walk through the immense green areas around the Citadel. Other highlights are the remains of the Palais Rihour, erected in the 15th C at a time when Lille was the financial capital of Northern France, Paris Gate - a superb triumphal arch to the glory of Louis XIV, the Vieille Bourse (Old Stock Exchange) and the two gates of the Spanish enclosure, namely the Grand Gate and the Roubaix Gate.

TAKE A27 and EXIT @ JCN 29 ONTO N60/ D935 SOUTH TO:
Conde-sur-l'Eacault

STAY AT: *the Parking in* **Rue Henri Martrice** *in Conde-sur-l'Eacault. This large gravel parking area is situated 500m from the town centre, on the eastern side of Conde with ample spaces for camping cars. The parking is pleasantly sited next to a very large lake bordered by grass areas with some shade, a play area and picnic tables nearby. There are no services here, but there is a basic aire with service point next to the cemetery in Rue du Vivier in nearby Crespin.*
Facilities: *Rubbish bins*
No. of spaces: *10*
Parking: *Free*
Services: *None*
Opening times: *All year*
GPS Coordinates: *N50.44961   E03.60098*
Alternative: *Camping Mont des Bruyeres, Rue Basly, 59230 Mont des Bruyeres Open: 15/03 – 31/10*

DAY 2

Conde-sur-l'Eacault: At the confluence of the Escaut and Hayne Rivers, Condé became an essential fort as far back as Roman times. Reputed to be impregnable, it was nevertheless taken by Vauban and the French in six days, who then hastened to improve the medieval fortifications. He particularly reinforced the defensive flooding system, making it possible to flood 2,450 hectares around the town in 24 days. The fort was dismantled in 1923 but still has many remains, including part of the bastioned enclosure that constitutes a very pleasant walk. You can also visit the remains of the 12th C fort, known as the 'Arsenal', and the Jard canal, still guarded by its "Dames" - turrets that are impossible to walk round. Not to be missed are the Hôtel de Bailleul, built in the 15th C and reinforced at the corners by four turrets, and the 18th C Hôtel de Ville, built in the blue Tournai stone in a French style that stands out from the other buildings.

TAKE D935 14KM SOUTH ONTO D649 EAST and D934 7KM SOUTH TO:

Le Quesnoy lies near to the Mormal Forest, where oaks were planted in Roman times. In the 12th C, Baudin the Edifier built a chateau here that became the favourite residence of the most powerful princes in Europe. Fortified from the 16th to the 19th C, the town remains one of the best-preserved fortified towns in France. With the fortifications having been patiently restored since 1977, they now provide 100 ha of parkland, with 15kms of walks around the ramparts, enclosing the town nestled within. Highlights are the unique fortifications, the "Bastion Vert," fitted out as a siege hospital, and the 18th C Hôtel de Ville, whose grand staircase is classed as an historical monument.

TAKE D942 EAST 15KM TO :

Bavay: While the major part of the Roman remains lie beneath the modern town, visitors can still explore a site of 25,000m² containing the most important Gallo-Roman forum north of the Loire. It is also possible to see, beneath the Tourist Office, the hypercaust heating system for the Gallo-Romans baths.

STAY AT: *the Municipal aire in* **Chemin de Ronde** *in* **Bavay***. Parking here is in a large tarmac lay-by next to a minor road and opposite the town football pitch. It is also next to a spacious public park and is partly shaded by the large, adjacent trees. The aire has a basic artisanal service point with a platform drain. This is a pleasant, quiet location 250m from the centre of town, where the Gallo-Roman remains can be found.*

Facilities: *Water •Grey Drain •Black Drain*
No. of spaces: *10*
Parking: *Free*
Services: *Free*
Opening times: *All year*
GPS Coordinates: *N50.30002   E03.79554*
Alternative: *Camping Lac Vauban, Chemin de Ghissignies, 59530 Le Quesnoy Open: 30/03 – 31/10*

DAY 3
TAKE D649 EAST TO :

Maubeuge was captured and ransacked 16 times, from the 9th to 20th C, before again suffering severe damage in 1940. The five towers on the left bank of the Sambre River are remnants of the 56-ha fort built by Vauban, and there are many green areas that are ideal for a stroll, as well as an animal park that has been peacefully established in the western part. The monumental Mons Gate is a typical example of Mansart architecture and a Poncelet drawbridge has been rebuilt here, whilst further on, the fortifications still retain many outstanding features. The tourist office located in the Mons Gate can provide a walking guide leaflet around the fortress.

TAKE N2 21KM SOUTH TO :

Avesnes-sur-Helpe was created around 1080 on an escarpment overlooking the Helpe River and remained at the crossroads of the Netherlands, Burgundy and France for 1,000 years. Avesnes originally became a fort under Charles V and following this, its fortifications were continually improved. The town has a 60 m high tower that today is home to one of the most beautiful sets of bells in the North of France, whilst the spectacular Saint-Jean bastion, 22 m high, links the upper and lower parts of the town. Also of interest are; Vauban's Pont-des-Dames, a sluice bridge that controls the Helpe River, allowing the area north of the town to be flooded to prevent attack, Saint-Nicolas Collegiate church, dating back to the 12th C, and many beautiful mansions that show the influences of Art Nouveau.

TAKE D962/ D959 WEST and D934/ D643 SOUTH TO:
Catillon sur Sambre
*STAY AT: the Municipal aire off **Ave Groise (D643)** in **Catillon**. Pleasantly sited next to a canal are 4 spaces on tarmac reserved for motorhomes, with electric hook ups, an adjacent picnic table and a grassy area. There is no shade here, but there is lighting at night and it is only 300m to the centre of the village. A basic artisanal borne with a drainage grid. A large, free car park is also available on the other side of the canal – back along D643 and 100m on the right via a small access road – which is quiet and has plenty of room but offers no services.*
Facilities: *Water•Grey Drain•Black Drain•Electric*
No. of spaces: *4*
Parking: *5€ Electric incl.*
Services: *Free*
Opening times: *All year*
GPS Coordinates: *N50.07625 E03.64610*
Alternative: *Camping les 3 Clochers, Rue Jean Goude, 59400 Cambrai Open: 30/03 – 14/10*

DAY 4
TAKE D643 and D955 NORTH TO HASPRES, THEN D81 WEST TO :
Bouchain: Located at the confluence of the Escaut and Sensée Rivers, Bouchain was considered the key to the Netherlands during the 15th C due to its dams that enabled the valleys of these rivers to be completely flooded in less than a week. It was continually reinforced up to the 19th C and played a role again in 1940, when it blocked the

German army's advance for six days. The Ostrevant Tower is the most attractive remnant of this glorious past - a powerful, square building dating back to the 12th C that today houses a museum - whilst at the foot of the tower lies a large ammunitions magazine containing an enormous vaulted room. Of the fortifications built by Charles V in the 16th C, the Forge bastion still remains and is where you can see the start of a tunnel that went under the Sensée River; a technical exploit that shows the ingenuity of the engineers of the time. There is also a network of counter-mines (mine galleries that prevent any underground enemy attack using explosive mines) that lie beneath the upper town.

TAKE D630 15KM SOUTH TO:
Cambrai: With its 5 km of walls reinforced with bastions, its fifty towers and seven city gates, Cambrai must have looked impressive to the 16th C traveller. Today, despite the expansion of the town in the 19th C, which caused the removal of most of these fortifications, there are many remains to view. The most extraordinary of these is the network of underground counter-mines constructed under the Charles V Citadel, of which the gate, arsenal and barrack buildings remain. There is also the "Porte d'Eau," a water gate spanning the Escaut River, which defends the river access to the town using the three portcullises whose mechanism still exists today. Other highlights are the Château de Selles, a former prison where much of the prisoners' graffiti is still visible, the baroque style Notre-Dame Gate, Saint-Géry Church, housing a Rubens painting, and the Cathedral.

TAKE D644/ D56 7KM SOUTH TO :
Marcoing
STAY AT: *the Municipal aire in* **Rue de la Gare (off D15)** *in* **Marcoing***. Found next to the old railway station building and the canal, this aire is in a medium sized tarmac parking area bordered by trees and hedges, offering some shade, with lighting at night. The site is on the edge of town, 500m east of the town centre. The aire has an artisanal service point with drainage grid and 4 ehu's. It is a reasonable walk into the heart of this residential town, with only a small choice of shops, a bank and a bar/ cafe. The free services include electric, which comes on with the streetlights, and there are nice walks along the canal.*
Facilities: *Water •Grey Drain •Black Drain •Electric*
No. of spaces: *6*

Parking: *Free*
Services: *Free*
Opening times: *All year*
GPS Coordinates: *N50.12101   E03.18244*
Alternative: *Camping les 3 Clochers, Rue Jean Goude, 59400 Cambrai Open: 30/03 – 14/10*

Above: Arras by johanvanbetsbrugge   Below: Lille by Velvet

Le Quesnoy by Jolivet

Aire at Catillon sur Sambre

Page 302

PAYS DE LA LOIRE TOUR 44
NANTES TO ST NAZAIRE – 5 DAYS

This 5-Day Circuit starting in the city of Nantes heads north to the Chateaux of Clisson, Motte-Glain and Chateaubriant, before going west to the listed village of Kerhinet and the medieval walled town of Guerande. After visiting the seaside resort of La Baule, the tour stops in the port of Saint Nazaire and then South to Pornic before returning via the Safari park "Planete Sauvage" to Nantes.

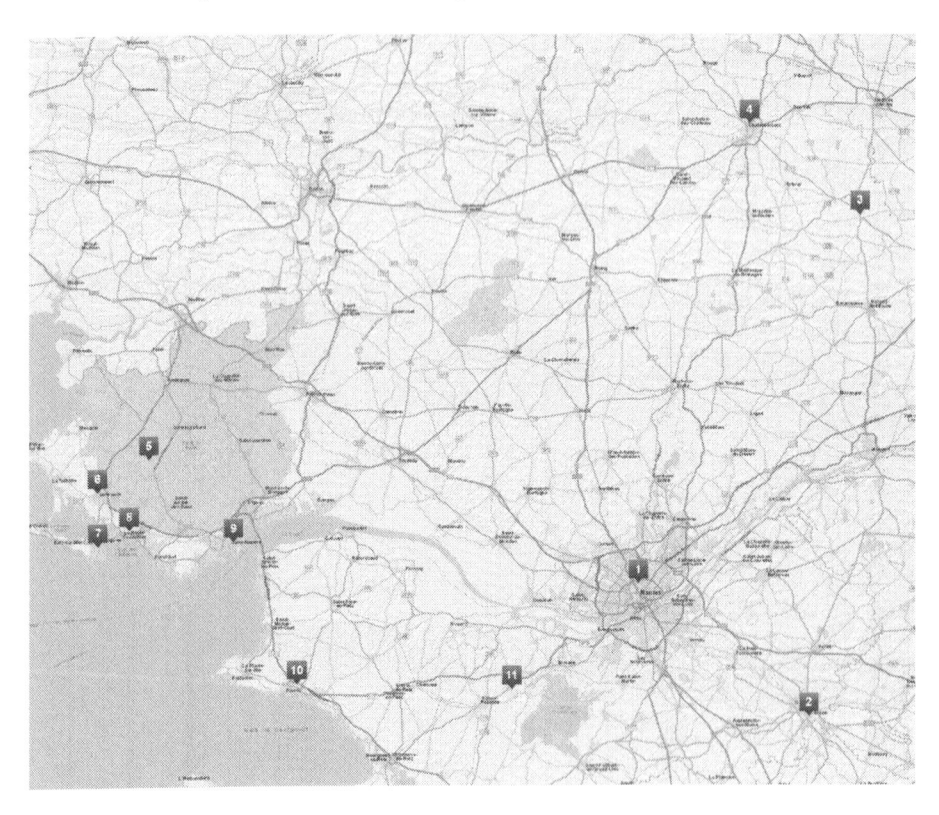

NANTES TO ST NAZAIRE MAP

KEY TO MAP:
1) Nantes
2) Clisson
3) La Chapelle-Glain
4) Chateaubriant
5) Kerhinet
6) Guerande
7) Le Pouliguen
8) La Baule
9) Ste Nazaire
10) Pornic
11) La Chevalerie

DAY 1
Nantes

STAY AT: *the private aire located on* **Boulevard Petit Port in Nantes**, *next to the campsite "Nantes Camping" where there are 15 spaces, shaded by trees and lit at night. This aire is managed by the CampingCarPark company and is in a medium sized parking area, with access via an automatic barrier operated by their CCP card, or by credit card via the machine at the entrance. The 15 large (50 sq m) spaces are on grass, separated by trees, and accessed by a tarmac track. Euro Relais service point with drainage platform is outside the aire and the pitches have access to 10A ehu's and wifi.*
Facilities: *Water •Grey Drain•Black Drain•Electric•Wifi*
No. of spaces: *15*
Parking: *12€/24Hrs*
Services: *Incl.*
Opening times: *All year*
GPS Coordinates: *N47.24333   W01.55673*
Alternative: *Nantes-Camping, 21 Bvd Petit Port, 44300 Nantes. Open all year*

Nantes: The architectural heritage of Nantes reflects the town's wealth and importance over the centuries. Medieval remnants of the town are still visible around the Gothic cathedral and in the tiny streets of Bouffay - a pedestrian area with half-timbered houses, creperies and bars, near to the moated Chateau des Ducs de Bretagne (where the famous Duchess Anne, twice Queen of France, was born). A 50-ton mechanical giant called the Grand Elephant carries passengers along the quayside from the Galerie des Machines, a museum that displays brilliant mechanical creations, on the site of an old shipyard. Nearby, the Museum of Nantes, spread over 32 rooms, explores the town's history, news and projects.

STAY AT: *The private aire located on* **Boulevard Petit Port** *in* **Nantes** *or Nantes-Camping, 21 Bvd Petit Port, 44300 Nantes*

DAY 2
TAKE D59 SOUTH-EAST TO:

Clisson: The 12th C Clisson Chateau, consisting of a 5-sided enclosure surrounded by round towers, has a double moat and fortified walls that made it so impregnable that the attacking English nicknamed it "the Butcher". Composed of buildings, fortifications and towers of different eras, with many various defensive elements and architectural styles, the Chateau is unique. Medieval displays take place in the summer. Open Feb – Dec.

TAKE D763 NORTH TO ANCENIS and D923/D876 NORTH TO:
La Chapelle-Glain: One of the first chateaux in the Loire-Atlantique, the Château de la Motte-Glain is a 12th C fortification modified in the 15th C. There are living areas and a chapel to visit, with an exhibition devoted to African hunting trophies and naturalized waterfowl birds, as well as furniture dating from the 17th C. Open 15/06 – 15/09.

TAKE D163 NORTH 16KM TO:
Châteaubriant: Chateau Chateaubriant was responsible for defending the English lands in France against the French. The chateau is composed of two main styles; a medieval part, around the keep with the residential complex and chapel, and a renaissance part, which includes the Palace with staircase, gallery and columns. An exhibition is held in the guardroom. Open all year.

STAY AT: *The Municipal aire is located on* **Rue de Tugny,** *in* **Chateaubriant***, next to the campsite "Les Briotais Camping" on the south side of the town. The aire is in a tarmac surface parking area with 6 marked spaces, lit at night, about 1 km from the town centre and its shops but there is a Leclerc Hypermarket within 400m. An artisanal service point with a large platform drain.*
Facilities: *Water•Grey Drain•Black Drain•Electric*
No. of spaces: *6*
Parking: *Free*
Services: *Free*
Opening times: *All year*
GPS Coordinates: *N47.70310   W01.37778*
Alternative: *Camping Les Briotais, Rue de Tugny, 44110 Chateaubriant   Open: 02/05 – 30/09*

DAY 3
TAKE D771/ N171 SOUTH-WEST TO ST NAZAIRE and D47 NORTH TO:
Kerhinet: This ancient listed village of farmers and weavers, in the Briere Regional Park, has been fully restored and pedestrianized. A guided trail through this traditional Breton village, with its thatched roofs, visits an inn, a workshop and the Thatch Museum. The museum has a Briere cottage interior dating back to 1900, displaying the habits and customs of the past.

TAKE D51 SOUTH-WEST TO:

Guerande: A medieval walled town, with fine ramparts, four fortified gateways and a good selection of shops and eating-places. The town is famous for its sea salt production, and the Salt Marsh Museum tells the history of Guérande salt and the people of the marshes. The nearby salt marshes are interesting for their fauna and flora, and the Océarium in Croisic has more than 4,000 specimens, including Australian sharks and tropical fish.

TAKE D774/ D45 SOUTH-WEST TO:
Le Pouliguen.

STAY AT: *The Municipal aire, located on* **Rue de l'Ocean in Le Pouliguen**, *is within 200m of the town centre and 250m from the beach. Located at the entrance to the town campsite, "Le Clein," the aire offers 26 level spaces on grass (accessed by a tarmac track) and is shaded by small trees. Access is via an automatic barrier controlled by a credit card machine that issues a code. AireServices service point with drainage platform, ehu's and toilet block. This is a well-maintained and well-located aire in a quiet spot with access to the campsite's toilets/ showers and wifi, as well as a laundrette and a play area. The price includes services, but there are only 12 hook-up points (16A) for 26 spaces. A good selection of shops/restaurants can be found within a short walk.*

Facilities: *Water •Grey Drain •Black Drain •Electric •Toilets •Wifi*
No. of spaces: *26*
Parking: *12€/ 24 Hrs*
Services: *Incl*
Opening times: *All year*
GPS Coordinates: *N47.27198 W02.43295*
Alternative: *Camping Municipal, Ave Kerdun, 44510 Le Pouliguen Open: 14/04 – 17/09*

DAY 4
HEAD EAST 1KM TO:
La Baule is best known for its beach and bay, where sand yachting, windsurfing, kite surfing, jetski and yachting are all popular, whilst the area of La Baule-les-Pins is pleasant for walking. Just North of La Baule is the Chateau de Careil, a 14th C fortified house with displays of furniture and costumes, candle lit night time tours are also held here. Open June - Aug

TAKE D213 EAST TO:

Saint-Nazaire: The major stages of the history of Saint-Nazaire are explained in its Ecomuseum. Bombed during the Second World War and rebuilt in the 1950s, Saint-Nazaire has since established itself as a legendary shipbuilding port. 2kms from the city centre, on a former bank of the estuary, sits the 6,000-year-old tumulus of Dissignac, one of the most remarkable sites of the region. Built around 4000 BC, it contains two megalithic tombs, each composed of a room preceded by a long narrow access corridor and one of the rooms has a cover slab engraved with symbols. The dolmen, with its 2m high pillars and cover table weighing 7 tons, is dominated by a 4m high Menhir. Free access in July and August.

The Sous-Marin Base, in the port, is the WWII German fortress that served as their submarine base for attacking the Atlantic Allied convoys and there is an actual submarine, the Espadion, moored nearby that can be explored.

TAKE D213 SOUTH TO:

Pornic
*STAY AT: This Municipal aire is located on **Le Val St Martin in Pornic**, next to the town's AquaCentre swimming pool, 400m from the centre of town. In a medium sized tarmac car park on the East side of the town, the aire offers 7 level spaces, is lit at night but has little shade and there are no facilities near to the aire. Flot Bleu service point with a drainage platform. This is a fairly pleasant spot, being quiet at night, near to a large lake with farmland to the north. Spaces are quite short though, under 7m.*

Facilities: *Water•Grey Drain•Black Drain*
No. of spaces: *7*
Parking: *Free*
Services: *2€ Water*
Opening times: *All year*
GPS Coordinates: *N47.12071 W02.09155*
Alternative: *Camping Les Bleuets, D213, Ste Marie sur Mer, 44210 Pornic   Open: 01/04 – 30/09*

DAY 5
Pornic is a picturesque fishing port, the surrounding cliffs revealing numerous coves blessed with beaches of golden sand and nearby is Noëveillard, a great picnic spot with beautiful views of Pornic. The town has several gardens and Neolithic monuments in the surrounding

area, and provides a nice spot for eating out in some fine seafood restaurants.

TAKE D13 15KM SOUTH and THEN EAST ON D758 18KM TO:

La Chevalerie: Planete Sauvage is a wildlife and marine park with a drive-thru section and various themed animal enclosures that you can walk through as well as a restaurant and picnic area. Open 04/03 – 26/11

TAKE D758/ D752 EAST TO:

Nantes

STAY AT:*The private aire located on* **Boulevard Petit Port** *in* **Nantes** *or Nantes-Camping, 21 Bvd Petit Port, 44300 Nantes.*

Above: Clisson Chateau by Cyril5555   Below: Guerande by Reichelt

Top: Pornic by Elodieda   Middle: Nantes   Below: Aire at Nantes

Page 309

PAYS DE LA LOIRE TOUR 45
THE MOST BEAUTIFUL TOWNS and VILLAGES – 5 DAYS

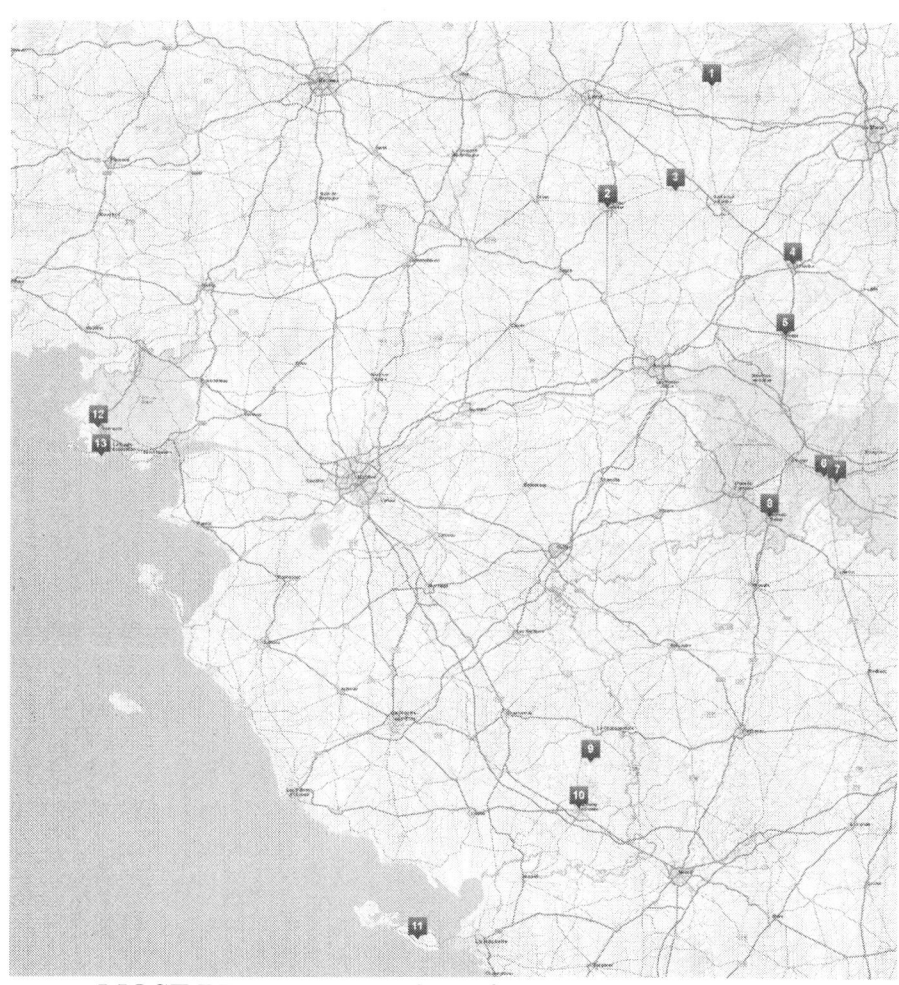

MOST BEAUTIFUL TOWNS and VILLAGES MAP

KEY TO MAP:

1) Ste Suzanne et Chammes
2) Chateau Gontier
3) Bouere
4) La Fleche
5) Bauge en Anjou
6) Turquant
7) Montsoreau and Candes St Martin
8) Montreuil-Bellay
9) Vouvant
10) Fontenay-le-Comte
11) Ile de Re
12) Guerande
13) Le Pouliguen

The Pays de la Loire region has several villages classed as the 'Most Beautiful Villages in France' as well as some towns that are classed as a 'Petit Cite de Caractere.' This 5-Day Tour starts at the village of Sainte Suzanne and visits several of these villages and towns before finishing at the medieval walled town of Guerande.

DAY 1
Ste Suzanne et Chammes

STAY AT: *the Private aire located on* **Rue Camp des Anglais in Ste Suzanne***, in a semi-rural location bordered by farmland. The aire, run by the CampingCarParks company, is located next to the cemetery on the north side of Ste Suzanne, offering parking on tarmac, with lighting at night but little shade. The aire has 21 spaces, with 6A ehu's and wifi, and is convenient for the village, being only 150m from the centre and 400m from the chateau. The aire is bordered by grassy areas and has a Euro-Relais service point with a drainage platform. Access is via an automatic barrier operated by the CampingCarPark membership card: if you do not possess one it is possible to obtain access via the machine at the entrance, payment by credit card only.*

Facilities: Water•Grey Drain•Black Drain•Electric•Rubbish•Wifi
No. of spaces: *21*
Parking: *12€/ 24 Hrs*
Services: *Incl.*
Opening times: *All year*
GPS Coordinates: *N48.09933 W00.35054*
Alternative: *Camping Croixe Couverte, D7, 53270 Ste Suzanne*
Open: *01/05 – 30/09*

Ste Suzanne et Chammes is a very interesting village, one of the "Most Beautiful Villages in France", still having its ramparts, chateau, picturesque narrow streets, old buildings and a museum. There is a small range of shops and eating-places, with walks around the village. Dominating the Erve valley, the village's 14th C ramparts provide impressive views of the Coëvron Hills and the Charnie Forest. The ramparts, the drawbridge and the Renaissance Château built by Fouquet de la Varenne, one of Henry IV's ministers, have now been returned to their former glory by restoration work carried out over a period of several years. The château is open all year round and a variety of themed visits are organised inside the fortress; there is also a water mill and a nearby Dolmen to visit, whilst the little back streets and many trails are ideal for walkers.

TAKE D7/ D24/ D79 SOUTH and D28 WEST TO:
Chateau Gontier is a listed town, boasting narrow cobbled streets, old halls, a convent and the half-timbered houses of the old quarter. Guided tours are available from the tourist office, whilst a street theatre festival is a major attraction in the summer. Near to the town is the Refuge de L'Arche, a unique site in Europe that is sanctuary to 1,500 wild animals. Next to l'Arche you can find the artisanal chocolate factory, of Roland Réauté, with its museum; and the Liberty factory, making high quality cutlery, where you can see all the stages of cutlery manufacture.
TAKE D28 17 KMS EAST TO:
Bouere
STAY AT: *the Municipal aire located on* **Rue de Sencies in Bouere**. *This very pleasant aire is located on the site of the old municipal campsite, on the eastern side of the village and about 150m from the village shops. The pitches are well laid out in pairs on grass, are separated by high hedges and some have shade under mature trees. There is a Euro-Relais service point with drainage platform. The aire is only 100m from a large 1.5ha fishing lake, and there are good walks nearby. Shops in the village include a boulangerie, grocer and a café/tabac/news, and there is also a 12th C church, a listed cemetery and some old industrial workings.*
Facilities: *Water•Grey Drain•Black Drain•Electric•Toilets•Wifi*
No. of spaces: *15*
Parking: *Free*
Services: *2€ Water or Electric (Jetons from shops/ Mairie)*
Opening times: *All year*
GPS Coordinates: *N47.86333   W00.47611*
Alternative: *Camping du Parc, Rte de Laval, 53200 Chateau Gontier Open all year*
DAY 2
TAKE D28 EAST and D306 33KMS SOUTH TO:
La Fleche is classified as a "Town of Art and History" with various buildings dating from the 16th, 17th and 18th C. Buildings of note are the Presbytery, several mansions, hotels and the sub-prefecture building, there is also a large private zoo on the town outskirts.
TAKE D938 18KMS SOUTH TO:
Bauge en Anjou: Its pre-Renaissance style chateau, with its arched Plantagenet staircase, was built in the 15th C on the ruins of an 11th C.

fortress. The 17th C Hotel Dieu hospital houses one of the most beautiful apothecaries in France, with a collection of more than 650 pots, the medicines and the pharmacopoeia of the 17th C. An exhibition traces the life of the hospital in the 17th C, visiting the chapel, the chapter room, the refectory and the garden. A "Blue" route in this charming Balzac town follows the quiet streets past the houses of the king's councillors, the many homes of the 16th and 17th C, the court of the second empire, the bandstand and the cross of Anjou that became the cross of Lorraine.

TAKE D938 19KMS SOUTH and D347 16KMS SOUTH TO SAUMUR, THEN D947 13KMS EAST TO:
Turquant
STAY AT: *the Municipal aire located on* **Rue Ducs d'Anjou** *in* **Turquant**. *The aire here is behind the church in this small village, close to the Loire River, in a nice medium sized parking area with trees giving some shade. There are some small shops in the village (boulangerie, epicerie, tabac and newsagent), about 50m distant. An artisanal service point with drainage platform, and rubbish bins. There is a small play area/park adjacent, plenty of walks around this Troglodyte village and cycle rides through the vineyards, the museum of 'Pomme Tapee' is nearby.*
Facilities: *Water•Grey Drain•Black Drain•Rubbish*
No. of spaces: *10*
Parking: *Free*
Services: *2.5€ Water (Jetons from shops/ Mairie)*
Opening times: *All year*
GPS Coordinates: *N47.22386   E0.02914*
Alternative: *Camping l'Isle Verte, D947, 49730 Montsoreau   Open: 01/04 – 30/09*

DAY 3
CONTINUE ON D947 2KMS EAST TO:
Montsoreau is another of the "Most Beautiful Villages in France." Benefitting from its lovely setting on the River Loire, the 15th C chateau (made famous by Alexandre Dumas' novel "La Dame de Montsoreau") is reflected in the waters of this legendary river. The village has flower-decked streets, with slate-roofed, white stone houses, green pathways lead out to the Saumur vineyards, and there is also the historic church and a heritage trail.
TAKE D751 1KM EAST TO:

Candes St Martin: A former fishing and river port that sprang up where the Rivers Vienne and Loire meet, Candes-Saint-Martin displays a contrasting picture with its black slate roofs and its white stone walls that adorn the houses and the Collegiate Church of Saint-Martin. This village is also classified as one of "Most Beautiful Villages in France".

RETURN TO SAUMUR and TAKE D347 16KMS SOUTH TO:

Montreuil-Bellay: Located in the Anjou Natural Regional Park, this medieval town has retained much of its history with the ramparts, chateau and fortified gates still visible and the town is easily explored on foot by following the marked trail. The furnished rooms of the chateau can be visited, as well as the local workshops in the town.

Montreuil-Bellay

STAY AT: *the Municipal aire located on* ***Rue Georges Girouy in Montreuil-Bellay****. Found next to the town Municipal Campsite, this aire is in a large gravel car park, shaded by trees, lit at night and close to the Chateau, Park and River. Shops and the town centre are approx 400m away. There is a Euro-Relais borne with grey drain, but bollards make access difficult. This is a very picturesque setting beneath the Chateau and next to a lovely riverside park, and you can climb up the steep steps to the excellent Chateau and through to the Old Town. Parking is very quiet at night, but not allowed here between 1000 – 1900 hours in high season. Jetons are available from the shops or the OT in town (not from the campsite).*

Facilities: *Water•Grey Drain•Black Drain•Toilets*
No. of spaces: *30*
Parking: *Free*
Services: *2€ Water (Jetons from shops/ OT)*
Opening times: *All year*
GPS Coordinates: *N47.13260   W0.15825*
Alternative: *Camping les Nobis, Rue Georges Girouy, 49260 Montreuil Bellay Open: 01/04 – 06/10*

DAY 4

Loudun is 18kms to the east of Montreuil, a town with white walls made from tufa stone and roofs variegated with Roman tiles and slates. Loudun is a town with very rich 17th C architecture notably the Renaudot Museum, the Collegiate Church of Ste Croix, St Hilaire Gothic Church, the Martray Gate and the Square Tower.

TAKE D938 SOUTH TO THOUARS, BRESSUIRE, LA CHATAIGNERAIE and D31 TO:
Vouvant is encircled by a loop of the River Mère and stands behind a wonderfully well-preserved fortified wall. The keep called, "Mélusine Tower," is all that remains of the chateau that watches over the whitewashed houses and the magnificent 11th C Romanesque church.
TAKE D938 SOUTH TO:
Fontenay-le-Comte: A "City of Art and History", Fontenay has been endowed with an original and diverse heritage – the medieval arcades of the Place Belliard, half-timbered houses, the famous Hôtel de la Sénéchaussée, the Fountain of the Four Tias and the chateau built in 1580 by a companion of King Henry IV. The old town centre has been completely restored, and with its network of streets being unchanged since the medieval era, the town is one of the most beautiful in the Vendee.
TAKE D938 / D137 /N11 and N237SOUTH TO LA ROCHELLE and D735 ONTO:
Ile de Re
CONTINUE WEST ON D735 TO:
St Martin de Re
STAY AT: the Municipal aire located on **Rue du Rempart** in **St Martin**. *The aire here is outside the town campsite, on the south side of town, next to the ramparts. It is a medium sized tarmac parking area with level parking and is accessed by an automatic barrier. The aire is fairly convenient for the town, there is some shade, and it is lit at night by street lighting. Raclet services with a drainage platform. This is a quiet spot, with only a short walk to the shops/ supermarket/ OT (300m) and about 600m to the harbour and beaches, the adjacent campsite has toilets and wifi access. Check to make sure that there is an empty space in the aire before paying to enter, and do not leave after having paid, as re-entry is not allowed and there are no refunds. The campsite is open 13/02 – 13/11 with a snack bar, small shop, toilets/showers, laundry and cycle hire. This nice old 17th C fortified town built by Vauban has plenty of eating-places.*
Facilities: *Water•Grey Drain•Black Drain•Electric*
No. of spaces: *17*
Parking: *11€/ 25 Hrs*
Services: *2€ Water or Electric*
Opening times: *All year*

GPS Coordinates: N46.19935   W01.36544
Alternative: Camping Municipal, Rue du Rempart, 17410 St Martin
Open: 13/02 – 13/11

DAY 5
CONTINUE WEST ON D735 TO:
Ars en Re lies at the westernmost tip of the island and can be easily spotted thanks to its church steeple, whose 40-m high, black and white spire still serves as a landmark for sailors. The village grew up around the salt marshes in the 11th C and 60 salt workers still farm the Fier d'Ars salt marshes today, it is also possible to visit an oyster farm nearby.

RETURN EAST ON D735 TO:
La Flotte: A pretty little fishing and yachting port with a rounded, 200m-long jetty built in 1840, and peaceful, flower-decked streets of low-roofed houses with white walls and traditional green or blue shutters. Nearby are the remains of a Cistercian Abbey, the Fort de la Pree and a museum of Island Life.

TAKE D735 EAST TO LA ROCHELLE and D137 NORTH ONTO A83 @ JCN 7.
CONTINUE ON A83 TO NANTES and THEN N165/ N171/ D213 WEST TO:
Guerande: This medieval walled town, with fine ramparts and four fortified gateways, has a good selection of shops and eating-places. The town is famous for its sea salt and the Salt Marsh Museum tells the history of Guérande salt and its people, whilst the salt marshes are also interesting for their fauna and flora. The Océarium in nearby Croisic has more than 4,000 specimens, including Australian sharks and tropical fish.

TAKE D774/ D45 SOUTH-WEST TO:
Le Pouliguen
STAY AT: *the Municipal aire located on* **Rue de l'Ocean** *in* **Le Pouliguen***. This aire is located at the entrance to the town campsite "Le Clein" and offers 26 level spaces on grass accessed by a tarmac track and shaded by small trees. The aire is within 200m of the town centre, where there is a good selection of shops/ restaurants, and 250m from the beach. Access is via an automatic barrier controlled by a credit card machine that issues a code. AireServices service point with drainage platform, ehu's and toilet block. This well maintained and well-located aire sits in a quiet spot that has access to the 3**

campsite for toilets/showers plus wifi, whilst there is also a laundrette and play area in the campsite too. Price includes services, but there are only 12 hook-up points (16A) for 26 spaces.
Facilities: *Water •Grey Drain •Black Drain •Electric •Toilets •Wifi*
No. of spaces: *26*
Parking: *12€/ 24 Hrs*
Services: *Incl.*
Opening times: *All year*
GPS Coordinates: *N47.27198   W02.43295*
Alternative: *Camping Municipal, Ave Kerdun, 44510 Le Pouliguen Open: 14/04 – 17/09*

Top Left: Maillezais by Maillezais Bottom Left: La Roche sur Yon by Guillamot
Above: L'Ile d'Yeu by Orikrin1998   Below: Foussais Payre aire

PAYS DE LA LOIRE TOUR 46
THE VENDEE COAST and L'ILE D'YEU – 4 DAYS

This 4-Day Tour begins in the medieval village of Foussais-Payre, then heads north-west to a former mining village before visiting the two ruined abbeys at Maillezais, in the marshes of the Marais Poitevin. Travelling west, the tour visits the historic towns of Saint-Michel-en-l'Herm and La Roche-sur-Yon and then continues on to the seaside resorts of Les Sables-d'Olonne, Saint Hilaire de Riez and Saint Jean de Monts. On the fourth day the tour stops at the port of Fromentine, where you can catch the ferry for a 30 minute crossing to the fascinating L'Ile d'Yeu.

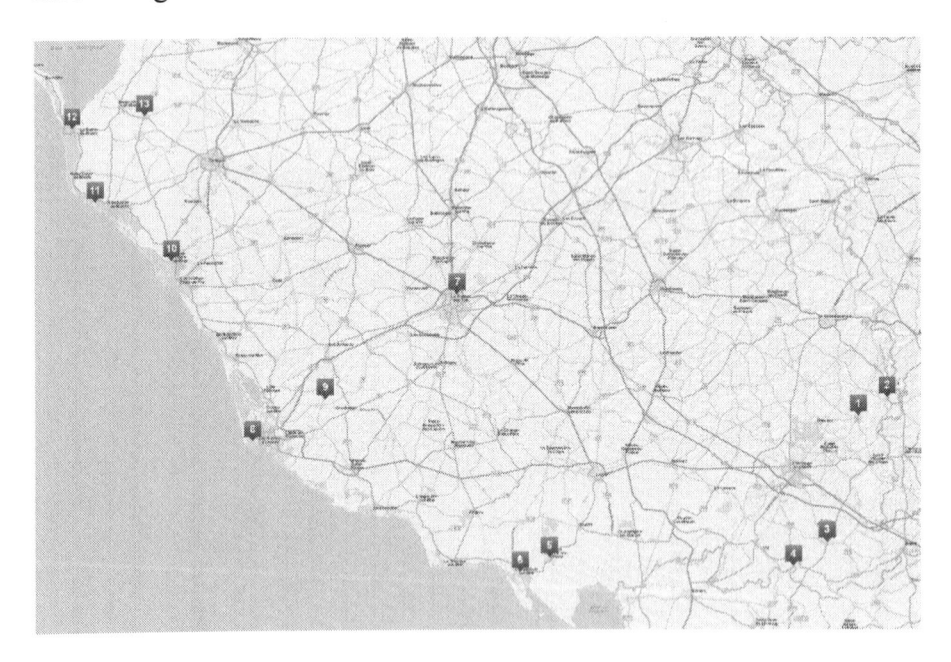

THE VENDEE COAST and L'ILE D'YEU MAP

KEY TO MAP:
1) Foussais-Payre
2) Fayemoreau
3) Maillezais
4) Maille
5) Saint-Michel-en-l'Herm
6) L'Aiguillon
7) La Roche sur Yon
8) Les Sables-d'Olonne
9) Ste Foy
10) Ste Hilaire de Riez
11) Saint Jean de Monts
12) Fromentine
13) St Gervais

DAY 1
Foussais-Payre
STAY AT: *the Municipal aire, located on* **Rue Francois Laurent** *in* **Foussais-Payre***, which is in a large gravel car park with plenty of parking space backing onto open countryside. It is bordered by trees providing shade, and has an adjacent grass area with picnic tables. The parking is within 100m of the village centre, where there are a couple of shops, with WC's about 50m distant. This is a quiet position 50m from the Mairie, with an artisanal borne and a large platform drain, in a rural spot on the edge of this nice little village. There are well signposted country walks and bike rides starting from the village, and a small playground for children.*
Facilities: *Water•Grey Drain•Black Drain*
No. of spaces: *20*
Parking: *Free*
Services: *Free*
Opening times: *All year*
GPS Coordinates: *N46.52980   W0.68237*
Alternative: *Camping Joletiere, La Joletiere, 85200 Mervent   Open: 01/04 – 30/10*
Foussais-Payre: Located on the border of the Mervent-Vouvant forest, this small village bears witness to two golden ages of architecture. Erected between 1050 and 1100, its Romanesque church is one of the most remarkable in Lower Poitou, whilst the Renaissance era graced the village with prestigious buildings such as the Halles, constructed in the 16th C.
TAKE D49 NORTH and D67 WEST TO:
Faymoreau is a small, former mining village, having miner's houses, workshops, the chapel and a modern museum with displays informing the visitor about the mine and the life of the miners. Open February – November.
TAKE D3/ D15 20KMS SOUTH TO:
Maillezais: On a former limestone island of the Gulf of Pictons, Maillezais and its region are located in the Marais Poitevin Regional Park, also known as "Green Venice" because of the covering of green duckweed on its waterways. The Marais Poitevin is a landscape of marshlands covering 1,000 sq km; a maze of islets criss-crossed by picturesque canals now used for boating or canoeing, as well as numerous paths for bikes or on foot. Traditional "barques" (a boat like

a punt) can be hired by the day in Maillezais, and for walkers there are 90 km of signposted hiking trails, 6 signposted mountain bike trails, and an 80 km cycle path. The town has a ruined 10th C Abbey with remains of a cathedral, dormitory, kitchen and ramparts, and 6km to the north is the Abbey of Nieuil sur l'Autise. Founded in 1068, this abbey benefited from the protection of the Dukes of Aquitaine and was granted the status of Royal Abbey in 1141 by Eleanor of Aquitaine, the Queen of France. The Abbey is one of the few remaining almost intact Poitevin monastic buildings, with its church, convent buildings and the only complete Romanesque cloister still in existence.

TAKE D15/ D25 SOUTH TO:
Maille
<u>*STAY AT:*</u> *The Municipal aire located on* **Rue Petite Cabane, in Maille,** *outside the municipal campsite. Located 300m from the centre of this small rural village, in a gravel parking area next to the canal, this is a pleasant position on the western side of the village. There is a toilet block in the campsite, with showers, picnic tables, washing up sinks and ehu's available. Artisanal service point with drainage platform. This is a quiet location next to the Canal de Bourneau, shaded by mature trees but without lighting, offering good walks along the canal towpath and level cycle routes. There are few facilities in the village, just a bar and boulangerie. The fee is payable at the Canal office, the price including 2 people, electric, showers and wifi.*
Facilities: *Water•Grey Drain•Black Drain•Electric•Toilets•Wifi*
No. of spaces: *8*
Parking: *8€/ 24 Hrs*
Services: *Incl.*
Opening times: *All year*
GPS Coordinates: *N46.34040   W00.79602*
Alternative: *Camping Municipal, Rue de Trigalle, 85420 Maillezais*
Open: 02/04 – 30/09

DAY 2
TAKE D25/ D746 WEST TO:
Saint-Michel-en-l'Herm is a former island of the Gulf of Pictons, now surrounded by rich farming land reclaimed from the sea over the centuries. It has a sunshine quota comparable to that of the Riviera, whilst being only 6 kms from the Vendée beaches. The town has a remarkable historical past; a Royal Abbey of which you can see the

marble altar in the current church, the Abbey gardens, chapter house and the refectory can all be visited.

TAKE D747 NORTH TO:

La Roche-sur-Yon is a Napoleonic town with several ornamental gardens and a magnificent 450-seat Italian style theatre - listed as an historical monument for its facade, roof, auditorium and interior decor. The town has an historic centre, a large Art and History museum, an exhibition of mechanical animals and a Chocolate museum. South of the town, located on the edge of the Yon River in Nesmy, is the Mill of Rambourg, where the miller explains the secrets of flour milling as well as the operation of the mill wheel and its mechanism.

TAKE D160 SOUTH and D87/ D109 EAST TO:

Sainte Foy

STAY AT: *the Municipal aire located on* **Allee de la Mairie in Sainte Foy**. *The aire is in a tarmac parking area with just 3 spaces bordered by grass areas, is lit at night but offers little shade and sits next to a large car park about 100 m north of the village centre. There is an artisanal borne with a platform drain and 2 electric sockets. Although only having 3 spaces, this is a nice little aire with free services – the adjacent large car park has ample level spaces - and there is a park next to the aire with a play area and picnic tables. It's a short walk to the few shops; boulangerie, mini-mart, bar/tabac and restaurant and there is a fishing lake with a golf course just outside the village.*

Facilities: *Water•Grey Drain•Black Drain•Electric*

No. of spaces: *3*

Parking: *Free*

Services: *Free*

Opening times: *All year*

GPS Coordinates: *N46.54658   W01.67225*

Alternative: *Camping La Bergerie, L'Yvonniere, 85150 La Chapelle d'Achard   Open: 14/04 – 15/10*

DAY 3

TAKE D80 SOUTH TO:

Les Sables-d'Olonne: is a seaside resort on the Côte de Lumière. The port, founded in 1218 and developed in the 15th C under the patronage of Louis XI, became France's leading fishing port by the end of the 17th C, with fishing activity still being important in the town today. The town has several museums, a Zoological park, fine beaches, an old quarter and four harbours to explore, in addition to exhibitions, guided tours and concerts. To the north of the port the Foret d'Olonne, with its 5 km of wild coastline and its fine sand beach, offers a pleasant location to spend the day.

TAKE D38 NORTH TO:
Saint Hilaire de Riez is a pleasant seaside town with good beaches, and older buildings as well as modern holiday accommodation. There is a children's amusement park, a water park, an outdoor museum, numerous restaurants and a reasonable selection of shops and services.

*STAY AT: the Municipal aire located on **Chemin des Vallees in Saint Hilaire de Riez**, about 2km east from the centre of town (with its shops and restaurants). The aire is in a large tarmac parking area next to the town campsite and a large leisure lake, and has marked spaces facing onto a grassed area, with some shade on one side under mature trees and lighting at night. An UrbaFlux service point with drainage platform. This is a pleasant and quiet spot overlooking a lake, but is a bit remote from the town and any facilities; a cycle track is adjacent and there are walks around the lake. There is also a second aire in St Hilaire at Avenue des Becs, north of the town but closer to the beach.*

Facilities: *Water•Grey Drain•Black Drain•Toilets*
No. of spaces: *10*
Parking: *Free*
Services: *3€ Water*
Opening times: *All year*
GPS Coordinates: *N46.73162   W01.91128*
Alternative: *Camping des Vallees, Chemin des Vallees, 85270 Saint Hilaire de Riez Open: 14/04 – 15/10*

DAY 4
TAKE D38 NORTH TO:
Saint Jean de Monts is a seaside resort bordered by 8 kms of beautiful fine sand beaches, with bathing water of excellent quality. This resort, like the entire Vendée coastline, enjoys a privileged climate; the sunshine is comparable to that of the Mediterranean, giving the beaches the name "Coast of Light".

TAKE D38 NORTH TO:
Fromentine: Take a 30 min high speed catamaran ferry to the Ile d'Yeu, an island that has been inhabited from around 5000 BC. Covering an area of 23 sq km it has a great diversity of landscapes: long beaches, coastal dunes bordered by woods, sandy coves with high cliffs, footpaths criss-crossing the valleys and,

alongside the cliffs, houses with tiled roofs and coloured shutters. The Ile d'Yeu was the first tuna port on the Atlantic coast and is still an active fishing port today - landing on its quays monkfish, hake, sole, turbot, sea bream, crabs and other crustaceans. An island of 5000 inhabitants, 25% of whom are less than 25 years old, the Ile d'Yeu is a lively and friendly location for a day trip.

NOTE: See page 324 for the "Walking Tour of the Island".
TAKE D22 and D948 EAST TO:
Saint Gervais
STAY AT: *the Municipal aire located on* **Rue des Primeveres** *in* **Saint Gervais***. The aire is in a medium sized tarmac car park reserved for motorhomes, with little shade but with lighting at night. A small grass area borders the 10 level spaces, with farmland to the south. The aire is about 10km from the beach and 200m to the village centre, having an AireServices service point with a large platform drain. This modern, quiet aire is on the south side of this small village, has a small park adjacent, and is only a short walk away from the village's few shops, restaurant and bar.*

Facilities: *Water•Grey Drain•Black Drain•Electric*
No. of spaces: *10*
Parking: *Free*
Services: *3€ Water or Electric*
Opening times: *All year*
GPS Coordinates: *N46.89995   W02.00146*
Alternative:
Camping Corsive, Rte de la Corsive, 85550 Fromentine
Open: 01/04 – 31/10

Chateau Gontier by Bréget

A CIRCULAR WALKING TOUR OF L'ILE D'YEU

Departing from St-Sauveur:
Dominating the village of St-Sauveur is the 11th C Church: from the church follow Rue du Général Leclerc, then take the 2nd left - Rue de Beauregard. Here is found La Maison Seigneuriale, built in the 17th C. by the Lord of the Island of Yeu to house his tax collector. Continue straight on to Rue Ker Guérin, cross into Rue Ker Viroux - one of the highest points of the island - then straight on to Route Croix Blanche. At the end of the path turn right and continue straight ahead to the Y-junction, take the left branch and then take the small path immediately to the left. Shortly after this, on the left, are the 'Dog-and-Horse' cup-shaped stones. At the intersection, turn left on the path to La Meule village with its small white houses. Continue to the end of Rue de la Meule (D22A) and below the village is the Port de la Meule; this small harbour is the only accessible port on the south coast of the island, whilst on the heights stands a Chapel dating from the 11th C. Retrace your steps and take the first turning on the right, Rue Ker Rabaud, and follow the path for 1 km before turning right towards La Pierre Tremblante (a huge block of stone 7m long that 'trembles' on its base). Continue along the coast to the Fontaines Beach, then further on take the path on the left and you will be able to see the Semaphore station, still occupied by the Navy. At the crossroads, turn right and walk 400m before reaching the Stones of Pain et Beurre, which resemble bread and butter, then follow the Menhir des Soux or "Pierre du Tonnerre", remains of an old destroyed dolmen, whose slab would have been one of the pillars. Continue straight along the Chemin des Vieilles and turn right onto the Gargourite cul-de-sac, which leads to the small port of Les Vieilles. Retrace your steps to enjoy a panoramic view of the Vieilles beach and the entire coast to the Pointe des Corbeaux lighthouse. Continue to the village of La Croix and follow Rue de la Croix east, then turn left on to the path of the Roche a Robion, which crosses the Ilias Marsh (this track may be a bit overgrown). After a while you reach the Conches Wood composed of maritime pines and oaks; we are now on the eastern part of the island - a coast of fine sand beaches and coniferous wooded dunes. Continue north along the coast to the beach of the Marais Mottou, then turn left onto Chemin Marais Mottou and after 800m, at the junction, turn left to Les Nates. In the village turn right onto Chemin Chiron Chat

Moreau, which leads onto Chemin Ker Pierre l'Ane, and finally left onto Chemin Petit Clou, which ends in the village of Martinières. Turn right onto the tarmac road (D22B) to return to St Sauveur.

Above: Montsoreau by Heyde

Middle: Loudun by Papay79

Below: Aire at Sainte Suzanne

PICARDY TOUR 47
THE "CHEMIN DES DAMES" TOUR – 1 DAY

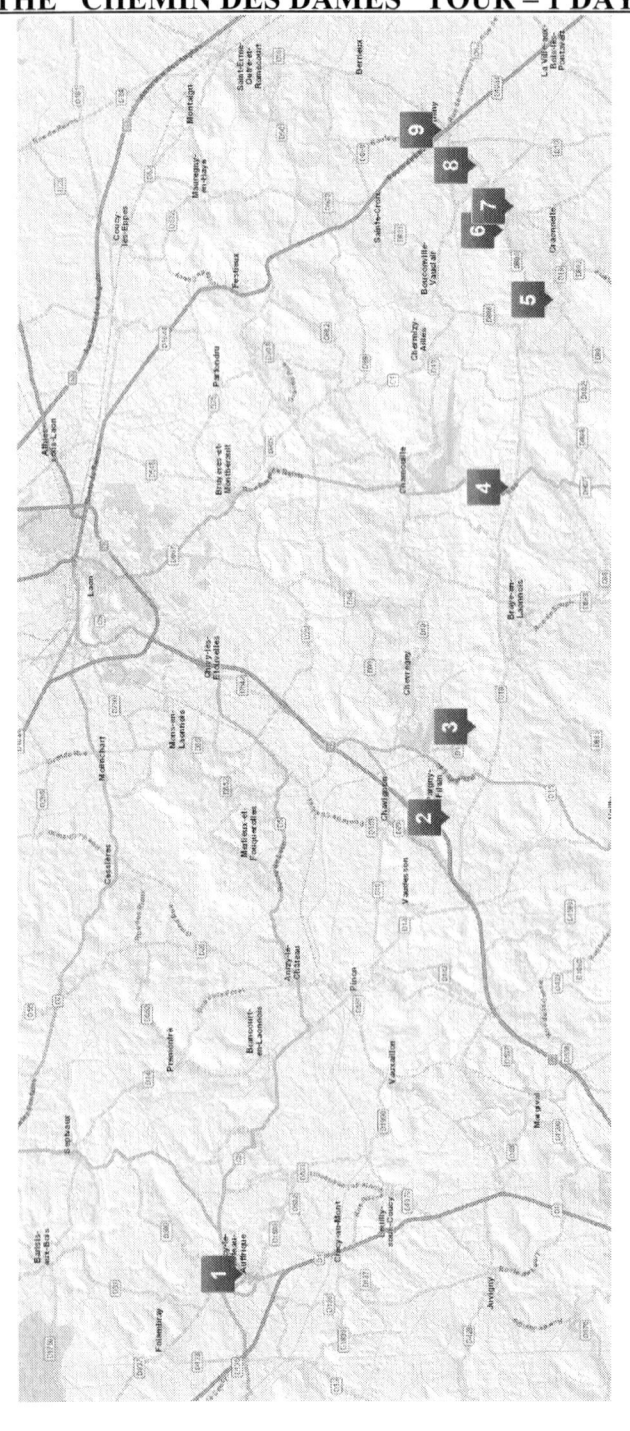

THE "CHEMIN DES DAMES" MAP (Opposite):

Key:
1) Coucy le Chateau Auffrique
2) Fort de la Malmaison
3) Panorama of La Royère
4) Cerny-en-Laonnois
5) Oulches-la-Vallee-Foulon
6) Plateau de Californie
7) Craonne
8) National Tank Monument
9) Corbeny

The 1-Day "Chemin des Dames" Tour follows the ridge road running between the Route Nationale N2 and the village of Corbeny, high above the valleys of the Aisne and the Ailette - a historical site, and one affording fine views over the surrounding countryside. It was regularly used by the daughters of king Louis XV, hence its name, but is most famous as the scene of terrible fighting in the First World War, particularly that of the failed Nivelle offensive in 1917 which led to the first mutinies of the war. The "Chemin des Dames" runs alongside the D18 road for about 35 km, and along its route is a history trail of eight major sites connected with great offensives of the First World War, each with illustrated information boards for visitors.

DAY 1

Coucy-le-Chateau-Auffrique: The medieval chateau of Coucy, perched on a promontory overlooking the valley of l'Ailette, was once the largest feudal castle in the whole of Christendom. The impressive remains cover an area of more than 4 ha on top of a rocky spur that towers over a broad panorama.

STAY AT: *the Municipal aire in* **Coucy le Chateau Auffrique,** *in* **Chemin du Val Serain (off D937).** *This aire is located in a designated parking area on the western side of the village, offering parking on tarmac in marked spaces, it is lit at night with little shade, and has a picnic table adjacent. The spaces are separated by low hedges and bordered by grass verges, each having a hook up point. Urba Flux service point with platform drain and a small toilet block adjacent. This is a well laid out aire with level spaces, reserved for motorhomes, situated in a quiet spot about ½ km from the centre of this small rural village. The fee, payable by credit card at a machine, includes water and 24 hrs of electricity (each space has a power point) – the machine issues a code allowing use of services as well as access to the toilets. A short walk takes you to a leisure lake and the aire is 300m from the Chateau and the museum. A grocery shop, boulangerie, pharmacy and eating-places can be found in the village.*

Facilities: *Water •Grey Drain•Black Drain•Electric •Toilets*

No. of spaces: 12
Parking: 5€/24 Hrs
Services: Incl
Opening times: All year
GPS Coordinates: N49.52004   E03.31396
Alternative: Camping du Lac, Le Moulinet, 02000 Monampteuil
Open 01/04 – 30/09

TAKE D5/ D14 16KM SOUTH-EAST ONTO THE D18 EAST:
Fort de la Malmaison are the ruins of a Séré de Rivières fort, just north of the D18. Built in 1878, its strategic position made it the scene of fierce fighting throughout WWI and it was occupied by both sides at some time. There is a WWII German cemetery nearby, where almost 12,000 soldiers are buried.

CONTINUE EAST ALONG D18 TO:
Panorama of La Royère offers fine views of the Ailette valley, where violent battles took place, and is associated with the Malmaison offensive (of October 1917) and the part played by French colonial troops in the war. Reconstructions of the trenches give an insight into the fighting.

CONTINUE EAST ALONG D18 TO:
Cerny-en-Laonnois: Shared by two war cemeteries, one German and the other French, this little chapel is the official remembrance site for the "Chemin des Dames". The cemeteries contain 12,676 bodies, of which over 6,000 are contained in two ossuaries.

CONTINUE EAST ALONG D18 TO:
Oulches-la-Vallee-Foulon: Caverne du Dragon is an old quarry that was used as an underground barracks by the Germans, it is now a "living museum" with sniper positions, hospital, dormitory, a chapel and first aid post, recreating the daily lives of the German soldiers at the front. Using modern animation techniques, artefacts, sound recordings, picture archive material and video footage, the Caverne du Dragon is one of the most important historical and educational sites linked to the First World War. There are guided tours in English and views over the Aisne valley to enjoy.

CONTINUE EAST ALONG D18 TO:
Monument to the Basques: A monument in memory of the French 36th Infantry Division, most of whose troops came from south-west France.

CONTINUE EAST ALONG D18 TO:

Plateau de Californie: This was the scene of the offensive launched on 16th April 1917 by General Nivelle, which was a terrible failure and led to mutinies amongst the soldiers. There is a marked trail (with information boards and picnic tables) where remains of the trenches and shell craters can still be seen, along with wonderful views over the Aisne valley.

CONTINUE EAST ALONG D18 TO:

Craonne: When wars come to an end, towns and villages must be rebuilt. The completely destroyed village of Craonne was rebuilt however in another position, thanks to the generosity of Sweden. On the site of the old village is an arboretum of Remembrance, and the churned up ground still shows signs of the fierce fighting that took place there. An observation tower, 20m high, allows a fine view of the "Chemin," as well as the plain of Champagne

CONTINUE EAST ALONG D18 TO:

The National Tank Monument is at the foot of the "Chemin des Dames", where in 1917, French tanks were used for the first time in battle when an attack was launched towards Juvincourt. Despite the use of 128 13-ton, 6 man Schneider tanks in the offensive against the German positions, the attack was a complete failure because of the slope of the hill and the weight of the tanks. Tanks on display date from the 1950s.

CONTINUE EAST ALONG D18 TO:

Corbeny

<u>**STAY AT:**</u> *the Municipal aire in Corbeny, in Rue Marc Lavetti (D18). This aire is located in a designated parking area on the Northern side of the village, with parking on gravel in 3 marked spaces but having little shade. The spaces, separated by low hedges and bordered by grass verges, overlook a large lake. This is a well laid out aire with level spaces, reserved for motorhomes, situated in a quiet spot about 200m from the centre of this large rural village, but has no service point. There are a few shops and eating places in the village.*

Facilities: *Rubbish bins*
No. of spaces: *3*
Parking: *Free*
Services: *None*
Opening times: *All year*
GPS Coordinates: *N49.46461   E03.82736*

Alternative: *Camping du Moulin, Rue du Moulin, 02820 Aizelles*
Open: 01/04 – 15/10

Above: Coucy le Chateau by Farwell   Below: Chemin des Dames by Poudou99

Above: Plateau du Californie by Poudou99   Below: Coucy le Chateau aire

PICARDY TOUR 48
LAON TO SOISSONS – 4 DAYS

Starting from the hilltop medieval city of Laon, with its 80 listed historical buildings, this 4-Day circuit visits the beautiful Vauclair Abbey before following the WWI "Chemin des Dames" trail. The medieval chateau at Coucy follows, and then the cathedral town of Soissons, before the tour enters the Forest of St Gobain with its ruined abbeys and charming forest walks, finally returning to Laon.

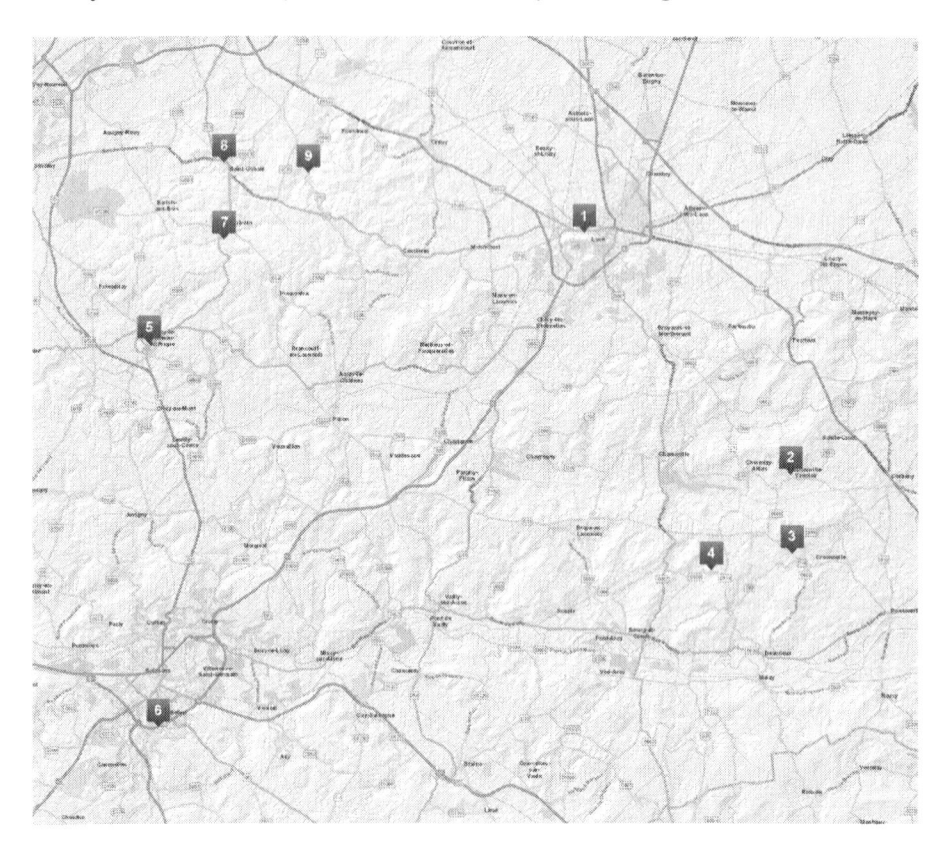

LAON TO SOISSONS MAP

KEY TO MAP:
- 1) Laon
- 2) Bouconville-Vauclair
- 3) Oulches-la-Vallee-Foulon
- 4) Paissy
- 5) Coucy-le-Chateau-Auffrique
- 6) Soissons
- 7) Septvaux
- 8) St Gobain
- 9) Saint-Nicolas-aux-Bois

DAY 1
Laon
STAY AT: *the Municipal aire in* **Promenade de la Couloire (off D54)** *in* **Laon**. *This aire is in a lay-by beneath the town ramparts, where there are 6 spaces for motorhomes, bordered by grass areas and lit at night but with little shade. Parking is 200m from the town centre and its shops, but there is no service point here.*
Facilities: *Rubbish bins*
No. of spaces: *6*
Parking: *Free*
Services: *None*
Opening times: *All year*
GPS Coordinates: *N49.56215   E03.62594*
Alternative: *Camping la Chenaie, Allee la Chenaie, 02000 Laon Open: 30/03 – 30/09*

Laon is a hilltop medieval city, with 80 listed historical buildings, medieval streets around the cathedral and walks around the ramparts. The 12th C Cathedral is a fine example of the Gothic age, famous for its towers and rose windows. The Museum of Art and Archaeology has a collection of Greek vases and pottery; remarkable 18th C earthenware; Gallo-Roman, Merovingian and medieval objects; and archaeological artifacts. Souterrains de la Citadelle, a trail that follows tunnels under the old citadel, offers guided tours throughout the year, making it possible to explore the history of the city by visiting the underground passages and learning about their history from the Middle Ages until their use in various wars from the 16th to 20th C.

TAKE D1044 SOUTH and D881 TO:
Bouconville-Vauclair: Vauclair Abbey, the ruins of an important Cistercian monastery, has a medicinal herb garden and orchard of rare fruit trees. The walking trail "Saint-Victor," an 11 km circular walk (blue markings) starting at the Vauclair car park, passes through the forest and areas still showing signs of damage from the First World War.

STAY AT: *the* **Car Park (off D886)** *at* **Vauclair Abbey**. *This is a large tarmac car park in the midst of the forest, surrounded by grass areas, and has shade in places but no lighting. Parking is 300m from the abbey and very tranquil, but there is no service point here.*
Facilities: *None*
No. of spaces: *20*

Parking: *Free*
Services: *None*
Opening times: *All year*
GPS Coordinates: *N49.45151   E03.74294*
Alternative: *Camping du Moulin, Rue du Moulin, 02820 Aizelles Open: 01/04 – 15/10*

DAY 2
FOLLOW D886 SOUTH TO:

Oulches-la-Vallee-Foulon: Caverne du Dragon, an old quarry that was used as an underground barracks by the Germans, with sniper positions, a hospital, dormitory, chapel and first aid post, is now a "living museum" recreating the daily lives of the German soldiers at the front. Using modern animation techniques, artefacts, sound recordings, picture archive material and video footage, the Caverne du Dragon is one of the most important historical and educational sites linked to the First World War. There are guided tours in English and views over the Aisne valley.

CONTINUE WEST ON D8/ D102 FOR 3KM TO:

Paissy, a village that was carved out of a hillside, has a number of troglodyte caves that were used for medieval habitation.

RETURN NORTH BACK ONTO D18:

The **"Chemin des Dames"** is a ridge road running along the D18 between the Route Nationale N2 and the village of Corbeny, high above the valleys of the Aisne and the Ailette - a historical site affording fine views over the surrounding countryside. It was used by the daughters of King Louis XV, hence its name, but is most famous as the scene of terrible fighting in the First World War, particularly that of the failed Nivelle offensive in 1917 which led to the first WWI mutinies. The "Chemin des Dames" runs alongside the D18 road for about 35 km, having along its route a history trail of eight major sites connected with great offensives of the First World War, each with illustrated information boards for visitors.

NOTE: See Tour 47, the "Chemin des Dames" Tour, for more detailed information.

CONTINUE ON THE D18 EAST and TAKE D14/D5 NORTH WEST TO:

Coucy-le-Chateau-Auffrique

<u>**STAY AT:**</u> *the Municipal aire in* **Coucy le Chateau Auffrique,** *in Chemin du Val Serain (off D937). This aire is located in a designated*

parking area on the western side of the village, offering parking on tarmac in marked spaces, it is lit at night with little shade, and has a picnic table adjacent. The spaces are separated by low hedges and bordered by grass verges, each having a hook up point. Urba Flux service point with platform drain and a small toilet block adjacent. This is a well laid out aire with level spaces, reserved for motorhomes, situated in a quiet spot about ½ km from the centre of this small rural village. The fee, payable by credit card at a machine, includes water and 24 hrs of electricity (each space has a power point) – the machine issues a code allowing use of services as well as access to the toilets. A short walk takes you to a leisure lake and the aire is 300m from the Chateau and the museum. A grocery shop, boulangerie, pharmacy and eating-places can be found in the village.

Facilities: *Water•Grey Drain•Black Drain•Electric •Toilets*
No. of spaces: *12*
Parking: *5€/ 24 Hrs*
Services: *Incl.*
Opening times: *All year*
GPS Coordinates: *N49.52004   E03.31396*
Alternative: *Camping du Lac, Le Moulinet, 02000 Monampteuil Open: 01/04 – 30/09*

Coucy-le-Chateau-Auffrique: The medieval chateau of Coucy, perched on a promontory overlooking the valley of l'Ailette, was once the largest feudal castle in the whole of Christendom. The impressive remains cover an area of more than 4ha on top of a rocky spur that towers over a broad panorama.

DAY 3
RETURN TO N2 and TAKE N2 SOUTH TO:
Soissons: Abbey St Jean des Vignes, with its 75m high twin towers, was founded in the 11th C and it was one of the richest of the Middle-Ages. As well as the beautiful frontage there is an impressive cloister, the outbuildings and the monk's refectory to visit. The Gothic Cathedral was badly damaged during WWI and although it has been totally restored, signs of the conflict are still visible on its walls. Soissons Museum, situated in the ancient St Leger Abbey, displays paintings and many historical items from the town.
RETURN TO:

Coucy le Chateau Auffrique
STAY AT: *the Municipal aire in* **Coucy le Chateau Auffrique**, *in* **Chemin du Val Serain (off D937)** *or Camping du Lac, Le Moulinet, 02000 Monampteuil*

DAY 4
TAKE D5/ D13 NORTH 8KM TO:
Septvaux: This tiny village, in an attractive forest location, has an interesting church and an ancient washhouse, as well as a café/brasserie. Prémontré Abbey, 2kms south of Septvaux (on the D14), was founded in the 12th C and has three superb buildings that are now home to a hospital centre. Parts of the Abbey are open to the public, who can visit its gardens, chapel and monumental staircase.

TAKE D13 NORTH TO;
St Gobain: 9,000 ha of forest surround this small town, which as well as having enjoyable walks along its pleasant roads lined with architectural features, this is also the birthplace of the Royal Glassworks, founded by Colbert. Shops, services and a supermarket can be found in town.

TAKE D7 7KMS EAST TO:
Saint-Nicolas-aux-Bois where there are remains of the old Benedictine Abbey of St Nicolas and the fortified Priory of Le Tortoir, dating from the 14th C. These buildings are not open to the public but can be viewed from outside. Nearby (on the D730) are the "Roches de l'Ermitage", an unusual pile of rocks marking the departure point for 3 different walks in the forest; a short walk around the rocks (2 km - circular, white markings); or the "Sentier de l'étang" (lakeside path) round trip (5 km - circular blue markings); or the "Abbeys" round trip (15 km - circular, red markings).

CONTINUE NORTH ONTO D1044 and FOLLOW IT EAST TO:
Laon
STAY AT: *The Municipal aire in* **Promenade de la Couloire (off D54) in Laon**, *or Camping la Chenaie, Allee la Chenaie, 02000 Laon.*

Above: Laon by Uoaeil

Middle: Soissons by Pline

Below: Oulches Photo by Poudou99

Above & Middle:
Aire at Laon

Below: Aire at Coucy Le Chateau

PICARDY TOUR 49
FORTIFIED CHURCHES TOUR - 2 DAYS

A 2-day Tour of the Fortified Churches of the Thiérache area of Picardy, a region that in the 16th and 17th centuries was the scene of endless frontier conflicts due to its position between France and the Spanish empire of Charles V. Unpaid soldiers would regularly plunder the region and there were many highwaymen ready to rob the local populace. In an effort to combat this turmoil, the village people got together and agreed to fortify the one strong building in their village - the church. And so the fortified church was born: with their keeps, watchtowers and arrow slits, they played an important part in protecting the people and property of the Thiérache.

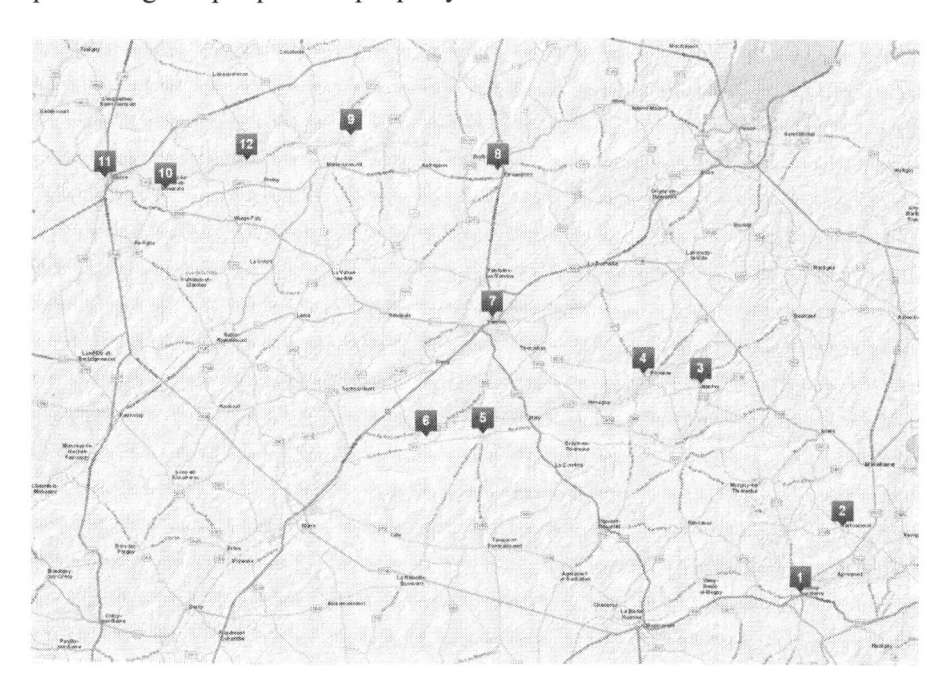

FORTIFIED CHURCHES MAP

KEY TO MAP:

1) Rozoy sur Serre
2) Parfondeval
3) Jeantes
4) Plomion
5) Burelles
6) Prisces
7) Vervins
8) Etréaupont
9) Englancourt
10) Beaurain
11) Guise
12) Malzy

DAY 1
Rozoy sur Serre

STAY AT: *the Municipal aire in* **Rozoy sur Serre**, *in* **Rue de la Praille (off D977)**. *The aire is located to the North side of Rozoy in a small tarmac parking area, next to a minor road – there is little shade here but it is lit at night and has a picnic table. The 5 individual places reserved for motorhomes are separated by low hedges and bordered by grass verges. An Urba Flux service point with drainage platform. This is a small, modern, rural aire, in a quiet location on the outskirts of the village - a 400m level walk to the centre of the village. There is a small selection of shops here including a superette, a boulangerie and a restaurant, whilst the nearby former railway line is good for walks/cycling.*

Facilities: *Water •Grey Drain •Black Drain*
No. of spaces: *5*
Parking: *Free*
Services: *2€ Water*
Opening times: *All year*
GPS Coordinates: *N49.71358   E04.12188*
Alternative: *Camping Municipal, 08290 Rumigny   Open: 01/04 – 30/09*

TAKE D977 NORTH-EAST TO:

Parfondeval: This village, belonging to the association of the "Plus Beaux Villages de France", is a small, neat collection of red brick houses with grey slate roofs, narrow streets and a village duck pond - a typical Thiérache village. There is the fortified church of St Medard built in the reign of Louis XIII, where the guardroom-refuge can be visited as well as a nearby wash-house and a Tool museum.

TAKE D29 and D748 NORTH-WEST TO:

Jeantes: The church here is nothing remarkable on the outside, but it has a fascinating interior featuring a truly amazing contemporary décor of over 400 sq.m. of frescos painted by Charles Eyck, a Dutch master glassmaker and creator of beautiful stained glass windows.

CONTINUE WEST ON D747 FOR 4 KM TO:

Plomion: With its wooden market hall and impressively large fortified church, Plomion is a typical Thiérache village. The church has two broad towers framing the porch, a watchtower, 60 arrow slots and many signs and symbols (diamonds, hearts, etc.) carved onto the walls of the building, as well as a spiral staircase leading to the guardroom inside one of the towers. In its day, the church was permanently garrisoned.

CONTINUE WEST ON D37 TO:
Burelles is a typical fortified church illustrating the various defensive systems used; it has corbelled turrets with 50 or so arrow slots covering every possible angle of attack, from long distance to close range. There is also an upper hall within the church where all the villagers sheltered until their attackers had left; it held enough supplies for four days of siege.

and THEN D61 TO:
Prisces: Local white stone was used to build the church nave and the choir in the 12th C, and then in the 16th C the church was fortified with a red brick keep, which at 25 m is the tallest keep in the Thiérache.

TAKE N2 NORTH TO:
Vervins: A little town in the centre of Thiérache that has beautifully restored ramparts and towers, plus a fine group of buildings around the town hall. The town museum is spread through three halls, displaying items of geology, archaeology and art/history.

TAKE N2 8KMS NORTH TO:
Etréaupont: Between here and Guise the main road often runs parallel to the "Green Lane", a long, grassy footpath that is a paradise for walkers. This Thiérache "Axe Vert" was created from a disused railway line and is open to all types of "hikers" (those on foot, horseback or mountain bike), with the old stations converted into stop-over "gîtes". It extends for nearly 40 km, from Guise to Hirson, and runs along the leafy banks of the river Oise.

TAKE D31 WEST and D774 TO:
Englancourt

STAY AT: *the **Parking in Rue de l'Eglise, in Englancourt**. This is located to the north side of this hamlet in a small tarmac parking area, next to the church – there is little shade here but it is quiet, lit at night and has views over the countryside. There are several places available, bordered by grass verges. No service point or shops in the village.*

Facilities: *None*
No. of spaces: *6*
Parking: *Free*
Services: *None*
Opening times: *All year*

GPS Coordinates: *N49.91698   E03.79988*
Alternative: *Camping Val d'Oise, rue Mont d'Origny, 02580 Etreaupont   Open: 01/04 – 30/10*

DAY 2

Englancourt: With its keep and two turrets, towering over the surrounding countryside and the Oise valley, this fortified church is an imposing defensive structure and offers a fine panoramic viewpoint. The church also has a statue of the Virgin that has widely been reported to "blink" at certain times.

CONTINUE WEST ON D31 TO:

Beaurain: A massive fortified church can be found in the village with a large square keep-like bell tower with arrow slits, built of brick on a stone base.

CONTINUE WEST ON D960 TO:

Guise: The impressive ruins of the chateau of the Dukes of Guise with its massive keep, cover more than 17 ha, having many restored galleries, an underground dungeon and vaulted halls. Also in the town is the "Familistère", a large building housing many families, designed in the 19th C by the industrialist Monsieur Godin. Striving to improve the living conditions of his workforce, Godin built them accommodation with modern conveniences and offered them a range of other services and activities, such as a nursery, swimming pool, theatre, grocery shop and a laundry.

TAKE D462 EAST TO:

Malzy

<u>**STAY AT:**</u> the Private aire in **Malzy**, in **Rue des Marichoux (off D462)**. This aire is located in the grounds of a fishing lake business "L'Etang des Sources" on the western side of the small village. Parking is on grass and has a little shade but no lighting, the aire, adjacent to the lakes with just 4 spaces available, is closed Tues, Wed and Thursdays unless you make a reservation in advance. AireServices service point and toilets nearby. This is a pleasant, quiet, rural spot overlooking the lakes, but it will probably appeal more to anglers because of the large trout and carp lakes. Snacks and drinks are available, as well as picnic tables and wifi. Fishing in the lakes is only allowed between 12/03 till 06/11, there is a cycle track nearby and bikes are available to hire. A short walk will take you into the village, but there are no facilities there. Parking is in a secure spot, near to the house, and gates are closed 19.00 till 07.30.

Tel: 03 23 60 28 34, Mob; 06 83 87 88 76
Facilities: *Water •Grey Drain•Black Drain•Electric•Toilets*
No. of spaces: *4*
Parking: *5€/ 24 Hrs*
Services: *2€ Water or Electric*
Opening times: *All year*
GPS Coordinates: *N49.90598   E03.72162*
Alternative: *Camping Vallee d'Oise, Rue du Camping, 02120 Guise*
Open: 01/04 – 30/09

Above: Parfondeval by Anabase4   Below: Plomion by Havang(nl)

Above: Englancourt by Clenet   Below: Rozoy sur Serre aire

PICARDY TOUR 50
THE SOMME REMEMBRANCE TOUR - 2 DAYS

The signposted 2-Day Somme Remembrance Tour takes you on the 40-mile route of the Battle of the Somme, from Albert to Peronne, with information boards along the way. The only aire in the area is at Doullens, but Camping du Port de Plaisance, in Peronne, or Camping Velodrome, in Albert, also make good bases for doing this tour.

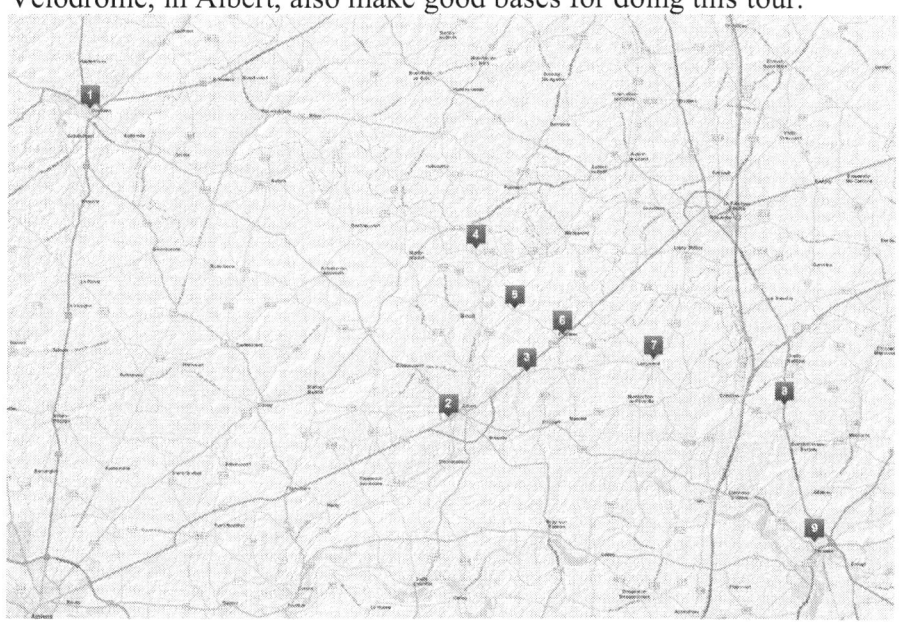

SOMME REMEMBRANCE MAP
KEY TO MAP:
- 1) Doullens
- 2) Albert
- 3) La Boisselle
- 4) Beaumont-Hamel
- 5) Thiepval
- 6) Pozieres
- 7) Longueval
- 8) Rancourt
- 9) Peronne

DAY 1
Doullens

STAY AT: *the Municipal aire in* **Doullens, in Rue Pont l'Avoine (off N25).** *The aire, in a small tarmac parking area with 4 large spaces reserved for motorhomes and shaded by trees, is close to the centre of town (200m) and next to the gardens of a small museum. There are numerous shops and eating-places within walking distance. AireServices borne with platform drain.*

Facilities: Water •Grey Drain •Black Drain •Electric •Rubbish
No. of spaces: *4*
Parking: *Free*
Services: *2€ Water or Electric*
Opening times: *All year*
GPS Coordinates: *N50.15395   E02.34251*
Alternative: *Camping Velodrome, Rue Henri Dunant, 80300 Albert Open: 01/04 – 15/10*

TAKE D938 EAST 31KM TO:

Albert: Evacuated in the autumn of 1914, Albert was almost completely destroyed under constant bombardment. The famous 'leaning Virgin' was the gilded statue on top of the basilica: hit by an artillery shell, it leaned out horizontally for over three years – a legend grew up among Allied soldiers that its fall would signal the end of the war. British soldiers occupied the town from July 1915 onwards, using it as a vital military centre, particularly during the Somme offensive in 1916. Staff headquarters, depots for equipment and supplies of all kinds, hospitals, the scene for constant lines of troops and vehicles going to and from the front line – it was a crucial hub of activity and became a symbol of endurance for the British Army. The Somme 1916 Museum occupies what was originally the crypt beneath the basilica, which was used as aircraft shelters in WWII. Alcoves depict scenes of trench life, realistically displayed and set up with original uniforms and equipment, while display cases contain quantities of weaponry and other war material rescued from the surrounding fields and old trenches after the war. Open 22/01 – 15/12

TAKE D929 NORTH 4KM TO:

La Boisselle: Lochnagar Crater, just 500m east of the village, is a vast and impressive crater left in open farmland by a tremendous explosion in the opening moments of the Battle of the Somme. British miners secretly dug tunnels for hundreds of metres beneath the fields and under a German fortification - the final chamber was then packed with explosives and detonated just ahead of the battle's initial attack, on 1st July, 1916. The resulting hole is 30m deep and 100m in diameter.

HEAD WEST ON D20 3KM TO AVELUY and TAKE D50 NORTH TO:

Beaumont-Hamel: Newfoundland Memorial. The well-preserved trench system, the only survival of its kind in the Somme, gives a vivid impression of the events of the opening day of battle. Commemorating the disaster that befell the Newfoundland Regiment, this site preserves both the Allied front and Reserve lines and the German front line across a grassy slope. It has three battlefield cemeteries, with monuments to the Highland Division (a fine statue of a Highlander) and the 29th Division. Visitors can walk the duck-board lined trenches and climb up to the viewing-point, the caribou statue (emblem of Newfoundland), on top of a mound with arrows pointing to battle sites all around… and to Newfoundland, 3,000 miles away to the west. An Interpretative Centre shows the kind of Newfoundland household that these soldiers came from, and explains the tragic sequence of events that took place here on the morning of 1 July 1916.

TAKE D73 SOUTH 4KM TO:

Thiepval: The small village of Thiepval is all that remains of a substantial village and château, destroyed in the fighting in 1916. Fighting was intense here throughout the summer of 1916, and many writers have left descriptions of the conditions suffered in the struggle to seize the heights. German strongholds such as the Schwaben Redoubt, close to Thiepval, made the ridge almost impregnable. Also sited here is the great, Memorial to the Missing, giving the names of men who died in the fighting in this area and whose bodies have never been identified. The vast memorial, with its arched pillars designed by Sir Edwin Lutyens and inaugurated by the Prince of Wales in July 1932, stands on the highest point of the ridge above the River Ancre and is visible from many miles around. Visitors from all over the world lay wreaths or private tributes here, and a ceremony is held on 1 July each year to commemorate the opening of the Battle of the Somme. The memorial to the missing of the Somme is a focal point for most British visitors to the battlefields, particularly educational groups. There is a visitor centre sunk into the ground, approached down sloping walkways, that offers visitors historical information on Thiepval set in the context of the Great War, as well as having a small shop with drinks and the usual facilities. There is also a museum here with a gallery dedicated to the Battle of the Somme, a replica 1916 fighter plane and multimedia displays. Open 01/03 – 31/10

*<u>STAY AT:</u> the **Parking in Thiepval, off Rue du Chateau (D151)**. This is in a medium sized tarmac parking area with several spaces bordered by grass, next to the small museum, close to the Memorial and surrounded by open farmland. There is no shade or lighting here, and no service point.*

Facilities: None
No. of spaces: 6
Parking: Free
Services: None
Opening times: All year
GPS Coordinates: N50.05263   E02.68788
Alternative: Camping Velodrome, Rue Henri Dunant, 80300 Albert
Open: 01/04 – 15/10

DAY 2
TAKE D73 SOUTH 4KM TO:
Pozières: Lying astride the main Albert-Bapaume road, Pozières was a designated target for the first day's advance in the Battle of the Somme, but did not fall until the end of the month. The remains of a German blockhouse, known as 'Gibraltar,' still recalls the bitter fighting of the summer of 1916. Two memorials commemorate the Australian troops' first attacking engagement, and the Tank Corps Memorial has four small-scale tanks at its corner.

TAKE D147 SOUTH and D20 EAST 7KM TO:
Longueval: The National Memorial and South African Museum, cemetery and Visitor Centre, commemorate the intense action of the South African troops in the adjacent Delville Wood, known to the British Army as 'Devil's Wood'. The Memorial stands on the edge of the wood in which the South African troops were committed to in the Battle of the Somme in July 1916. It was a tragic but triumphant first experience of the war for the South Africans; commanded to capture the German-held wood, they endured an intense and ferocious struggle – of the 3,200 men who entered the wood to take it from the occupying troops, only 143 men were unharmed when they emerged five days later. Despite these efforts, the wood was never completely captured by the South African forces. It was not until another month of fierce fighting had passed, on 25 August, that the 14th (Light) Division finally took the wood and overcame German resistance.

CONTINUE SOUTH-EAST 9KM ON D20 TO:
Rancourt : La Chapelle du Souvenir Français is next to a vast military cemetery, with British and German cemeteries close by, Rancourt being the only French memorial site in the Somme.

TAKE D1017 SOUTH TO:
Péronne: was occupied by German troops until early in 1917, and again during the great German advance in 1918. Almost completely

ruined by the end of the war (it changed hands several times, with French and German troops struggling to seize it from each other), it was rebuilt during the 1920's and is now a busy and attractive town with ancient ramparts and broad lagoons by the River Somme. Mont St Quentin, a hill on the edge of the town, was recaptured by Australian troops in 1918: the fine memorial showing a 'Digger' (slang name for the Australian soldiers) is the replacement of an earlier statue, more militaristic in attitude, which was destroyed by occupying forces during the Second World War.

The Historial de la Grande Guerre Museum is housed in a striking modern building inserted into an ancient fortress. An international museum, it has four large open rooms displaying social history in the combatant nations (mourning wear, children's games, commemorative objects, letters, propaganda, trench art, newspapers) as well as war equipment, uniforms and a continually running film of war topics and artists' work showing their response to war conditions. One of the rare complete sets of the German artist Otto Dix's series of prints of the war is displayed as an introduction to the main exhibit rooms. There is also a bookshop, cafeteria and a small cinema (with a film on the Battle of the Somme showing in English, French or German). Open all year.

STAY AT: *the **Parking in Place Andre Audinot, Peronne,** in a medium sized tarmac parking area with level shaded spaces, next to the Historial Museum. There is a pleasant wooded and grassy area adjacent, with a lake outside the museum that is housed in the old chateau. There are numerous shops and eating-places within walking distance, as well as a good café in the museum. There is no service point here.*

Facilities: *None*
No. of spaces: *6*
Parking: *Free*
Services: *None*
Opening times: *All year*
GPS Coordinates: *N49.92915   E02.93261*
Alternative: *Camping Port de Plaisance, Rte de Paris, 80200 Peronne Open: 01/03 – 31/10*

Page 350

Top Left: Albert by © Raimond Spekking

Middle Left & Bottom Right: Parking at Peronne

Bottom Left: Aire at Doullens

Above Right: Thiepval by Hartford

ABOUT THE AUTHOR

A keen motorhomer for many years and with numerous motorhoming holidays enjoyed in France, Alan Russell and his wife Sue eventually decided to relocate to that beautiful country. Drawn to the magnificent Auvergne region, they bought a property amongst the extinct volcanoes of the Cantal department in 2008, where they now currently run gites. Alan is also the creator and owner of the website www.motorhomingfrance.co.uk that has been online since 2006.